The Legend of the Anti-Christ

The Legend of the Anti-Christ

A History

STEPHEN J. VICCHIO

WIPF & STOCK · Eugene, Oregon

THE LEGEND OF THE ANTI-CHRIST
A History

Copyright © 2009 Stephen Vicchio. All rights reserved. Except for brief quotations in critical publications or reviews, no part of this book may be reproduced in any manner without prior written permission from the publisher. Write: Permissions, Wipf and Stock Publishers, 199 W. 8th Ave., Suite 3, Eugene, OR 97401.

Wipf & Stock
A division of Wipf and Stock Publishers
199 W. 8th Ave., Suite 3
Eugene, OR 97401

www.wipfandstock.com

ISBN 13: 978-1-55635-680-3

Cataloging-in-Publication data:

Vicchio, Stephen J.

The legend of the Anti-Christ : a history / Stephen J. Vicchio.

ix + 384 p. ; 23 cm. Includes bibliographical references.

ISBN 13: 978-1-55635-680-3

1. Antichrist—History of doctrines. 2. Antichrist—Biblical teaching. 3. Antichrist in art. 4. Antichrist—Islam. 5. Newman, John Henry, 1801–1890. 6. Nietzsche, Friedrich Wilhelm, 1844–1900. I. Title.

BT985 V53 2009

Manufactured in the U.S.A.

Contents

Preface / ix

1. Precursors to the Anti-Christ Idea / 1
2. The Idea of the Anti-Christ in the New Testament / 39
3. The Anti-Christ in the Early Church Fathers / 76
4. The Anti-Christ in Islamic Thought / 114
5. The Anti-Christ in the High Middle Ages / 156
6. The Anti-Christ in the Reformation / 192
7. Anti-Christ in Christian Art / 232
8. Frederick Nietzsche and the Anti-Christ / 268
9. The Anti-Christ and John Henry Newman / 304
10. The Anti-Christ in Contemporary Life / 341

Afterword: Why So Much Emphasis on the Anti-Christ and Demonic in the Contemporary World? / 379

*For Tryn and Kathleen D,
two women who have added much support
to this project.*

Preface

I

IN THE FALL OF 2005, I was reading 2 John chapter 2 in the library of Saint Mary's Seminary and University in Baltimore. I became curious about the few references to the Anti-Christ in that letter, so I consulted my friend and New Testament scholar Mike Gorman about how many good scholarly treatments of the history of the Anti-Christ there have been in the Christian tradition. Dr. Gorman said he did not know, but he told me about Bernard McGinn's *Anti-Christ*, a two thousand year history on the idea of the Anti-Christ.

I immediately found McGinn's book, and was favorably impressed. Indeed, Professor McGinn seems already to have written the book I contemplated writing. Nevertheless, I continued with my plan to write a book about the Anti-Christ. For the next two years, I collected my research, and then began the writing of the book. Along the way, I found a number of other scholars who had completed scholarly books on the Anti-Christ. Among these scholars are: Wilhelm Bousset, R. H. Charles, Kenneth Emmerson, Paul Misner, Walter Kaufmann, Rosemary Muir Wright, the Rev. P. Huchede, Robert C. Fuller, Bonita Rhoads, and Julia Reinhard Lupton.

II

This study begins with an analysis of precursors to the Christian Anti-Christ Legend, including materials from Babylonia, Persia, the Canaanites, and the Hebrew Bible, particularly the Book of Daniel, the best example of ancient Hebrew apocalyptic literature. In this chapter, we make a number of parallels from these sources that may have influenced the New Testament idea of the Anti-Christ.

Preface

In the second chapter of the work, we examine and discuss various New Testament passages on the Anti-Christ. As we shall see, some of these are specifically and implicitly about the Anti-Christ, while others are not. More specifically, we examine texts in 2 John, 2 Thessalonians, and Revelation. Among this material, we show a number of images that have been interpreted in the history of Christianity as pertaining to the Anti-Christ. Among these are the identity of the Man of Sin, the nature and meaning of the beasts in Daniel and Revelation, and the identity of the Temple that Thessalonians suggests the Anti-Christ will preach from.

"The Anti-Christ in the Early Church Fathers," chapter three of this work, is an analysis of the interpretations of the Anti-Christ theme in the first ten centuries of Christianity. In this period, several new claims are made about the Last Enemy, including the notions that the Anti-Christ will be a Jew, from the tribe of Dan, and that his initial followers shall also be Jews.

The fourth chapter of this study is a treatment of the idea of the Anti-Christ in Islam. Among Islamic scholars, a host of literature on the figure of the Djaal (the Arabic word for Anti-Christ) has developed, principally from the seventh to the fourteenth centuries. Among the Islamic perspectives on the Anti-Christ are the beliefs that he will have only one eye. He will appear at the end of time and be defeated by Isa (Jesus); and his armies will be the people of Gog and Magog from Ezekiel 38 and 39.

"The Anti-Christ in the High Middle Ages," the fifth chapter of this study, deals with late Medieval treatments of the Anti-Christ theme. The chapter begins with works by three tenth-century scholars, Adso of Montier-en-der, Arnulf of Rheims, and Lambert of Saint Omer. The remainder of the chapter is how Christian thinkers in the eleventh to fifteenth centuries have interpreted the works of Adso, Arnulf, and Lambert.

Chapter six deals with the Anti-Christ in the Reformation. The principal idea in this chapter is the development of the Papal Anti-Christ theory, as well as Counter-Reformation responses to that theory. The Iconography of the Anti-Christ is explored in chapter seven of this study, where we discuss several dozens images of the Final Enemy. Chapter eight is a treatment of German philosopher Frederich Nietzsche and his essay, *Der Anti-Christ*, written in 1888 and published in 1895. Among the more important observations that Nietzsche makes in this essay is that he believed that he was the Anti-Christ.

Preface

In chapter nine of this study we describe and discuss the Anglo-Catholic John Henry Newman and his perspectives on the Anti-Christ. In the first half of Newman's life he was a firm believer in the Papal Anti-Christ Theory, while in the second half, he gave up the theory. In the closing chapter of this study, chapter ten, we explore and discuss various uses of the Anti-Christ image in contemporary culture, including the image in literature, film, and modern scholarship.

III

Over the course of constructing this study, I have incurred a number of debts to students, colleagues, friends and family members. Among my students I am grateful to Martin Shuster, Jennifer Boyd, and Tryn Lashley. Ms. Lashley has helped in the preparation of the manuscript, as well as a number of editorial decisions. I also wish to thank some colleagues at the College of Notre Dame, including president, Mary Pat Seurkamp, Dr. Deborah Frankilin, Sister Sharon Kanis, Catriona McLeod, Sister Marie Michelle Walsh, and Margaret Steinhagen.

Among my colleagues at Saint Mary's Seminary, I wish to thank Fr. Tom Hurst, Michael Gorman, Zenaida Bench, and the staff of their fine library, Thomas Raszewski, Anita Prien, Patricia Brown, and Susi Ridenour. I would also like to thank K. C. Hanson and his editorial staff at Wipf and Stock Publishers. And finally, to my lovely wife Sandra and my two sons, Reed and Jack, I am indebted for putting up with me in the onerous project of another book. My wife is my best friend, confidant, and partner in life. She plays all those roles to near perfections. It is to her this book is dedicated.

SJV
Independence Day, 2007
Baltimore

1

Precursors to the Anti-Christ Idea

> The figurative language of the prophets is taken from the analogy between the world natural and the empire or kingdom considered as a world politic . . . Setting of the sun, moon, and stars; darkening the sun, turning the moon to blood, and falling stars from the heavens are acts of the kingdom of God.
>
> —Isaac Newton, *Observations on Prophecies*

> To determine our Lord's attitude toward the subject of apocalyptic literature is one of the really urgent tasks confronting New Testament scholars.
>
> —George Eldon Ladd, *Journal of Biblical Literature*

> The New Testament canon excluded as apocryphal a number of books, some on the grounds that the message was Gnostic, and did not accord with the community's idea of Christ's life and mission, some because of their claims to legitimacy was vitiated by fiction.
>
> —Jeffrey Burton Russel, *A History of Heaven*

INTRODUCTION

IT IS LIKELY THAT the roots of the idea of an Anti-Christ stretch back to Ancient Near-Eastern ideas of God doing battle with mythological or evil forces at the end of the world. This idea appears to have existed in Ancient Persian eschatology, where Ahura Maszda (the Good God) will do battle with Angra Mainya (an Evil God) at the end of time.

It is more likely that the idea of the Anti-Christ was even more widespread. The idea of a battle of God with the Devil was closely interwoven with related mythological ideas of God involved in a battle with a

Dragon-like monster. Traces of these related ideas can be seen in the Old Testament and in ancient Babylonian and Canaanite mythology as well.

In this initial chapter we will look carefully at these ancient near-eastern myths, in the hope of making some general observations of the relationship of these myths to the Old Testament, and ultimately, to the idea of the Anti-Christ in the New Testament. The best place to begin our analysis of a battle between God and the forces of Evil, or a Dragon-like beast is the Babylonian battle of the God Marduk with Tiamat. We will turn to this tradition in the next section of this chapter.

In addition to this Babylonian material, we will also explore sources from the Canaanites, the Persians, from Old Testament Jewish Apocalyptic thought, and from the Dead Sea Scrolls, as precursors to the Christian idea of the Anti-Christ. We also will explore some traces of the Babylonian and Canaanite creation stories in the Old Testament.

MARDUK SLAYS TIAMAT

Wilhelm Bousset, in his introduction to the English version of his *Anti-Christ Legend*, leaves little doubt about his view of the origins of the Anti-Christ legend when he tells us:

> It may be safely affirmed that no popular myth can compare with that of the Anti-Christ legend in general interest, widespread diffusion, and persistence, from a hoar of antiquity down to the present time. In the present work, which deals mainly with the early Christian and medieval aspects of the subject, no attempt is made to trace the origin of the saga much father back than about the dawn of the new era. But the author leaves no doubt on the mind of the reader that he regards it not merely as a pre-Christian tradition quite independent from the New Testament writings, but as prior even to the oldest of Old Testament records themselves.[1]

Bousset, and his predecessors Gunkel and Pinches, believe that the origins of the Anti-Christ legend are to be found in ancient Babylon and surrounding areas. It is in Theophilus G. Pinches' *Religious Ideas of the Babylonians*,[2] and in Hermann Gunkel's *Creation and Chaos*[3] that Bousset believes we are to find the origins of the Anti-Christ legend.

Wilhelm Bousset quotes Thomas Pinches' *Religious Ideas of the Babylonians*, concerning this Dragon of Chaos myth. Bousset tells us: "In Mr. Th. G. Pinches' *Religious Ideas of the Babylonians*, we plainly see how the myth of Tiamat, "the Dragon of Chaos," prevalent among the Akkadian founders of Babylonian and by them transmitted to the later Assyrian Semites, is the very first and oldest element in the current mythologies of these ancient peoples."[4]

At the same time, Bousset goes on to talk about the relationship of the Tiamat myth with the dragons in Revelation: "At the same time this primeval dragon of Revelation, as well as of the independent Anti-Christ legend, that the descent of one from the other can scarcely any longer be denied."[5]

The most prevalent mythology in pre-Israelite times was the Baal mythology of Canaan. The Baal myth is complex, varying in details and emphasis between peoples. The basic features, however, are fairly simple. The Baal religion centered on the cycles of nature necessary for survival in the ancient world, like growing crops and raising livestock. In a desert culture, these things played an important role, and water played a major part in the Baal myth and images.

All cultures of the Ancient Middle East who had a mythology like the Baal myths believed in a cosmic struggle at the beginning of time. The cosmic struggle between the gods often symbolizes or personifies the struggle for life in these desert peoples.

Among many cosmologies of the ancient world there is a story of a struggle between God and Demonic Forces of some sort. Often it is in context of a sexual battle, where an older generation of gods, sometimes involving a female agent of Chaos, is vanquished by a male hero of Order. One of the oldest versions of this tale is to be found in the *Enuma Elish*, the Babylonian creation story, which comes from a period of 2000 to 1700 BCE.

The *Enuma Elish* suggests that before the time of the gods, the world was nothing but a chaotic watery waste. The first tablet of the *Enuma Elish* begins this way for the Babylonians:

> When in the height heaven was not named,
> And the Earth beneath did not yet bear a name,
> And the primeval Apsu, who begat them,
> And Chaos, Tiamat, the mother of them both
> Their waters were mingled together,
> And no field was formed, no marsh was to be seen.[6]

The universe was ruled by Apsu (god of fresh water) and Tiamat (the god of salt water), a dragon-like creature. Tiamat and Apsu produced Mummu, the god of the waves. Tiamat and Apsu also gave birth to a pair of huge serpents, Lakmu and Lahamu. In turn, these serpents produced Anshar, the god of the heavens, and Kishar, the god of the earth and the underworld. The first tablet tells us:

> Then there were created the gods in the midst of heaven,
> Lahmu and Lahamu were called into being...
> Ages increased...
> Then Ansar and Kisar were created, and over them...
> Long were the days, then there came forth...
> Anu, their son...[7]

These new gods were noisy, or so the story goes. This upset Apsu and Tiamat, for they could not sleep with the noise. They discussed the possibility of killing the new gods, but Ea, the all knowing god, knows of their plan and captured Apsu and Mummu. This made Tiamat furious, and he created a large army to fight against Ea:

> Tiamat made weighty her handiwork,
> Evil she wrought against the gods of her children.
> To avenge Apsu, Tiamat planned evil.
> But how she collected her forces, the god unto Ea divulged.[8]

Ashar, the father of Ea, told him to send Anu to fight Tiamat, but Anu and Ea were frightened by Tiamat's army, so they sent forth Marduk. Marduk promised to slay Tiamat, but only if he was given the highest authority over all the gods.

> To set out against Tiamat his heard prompted him.
> He opened his mouth and spoke, "If I, you avenger
> Conquer Tiamat and give you life,
> Appoint an assembly and make my fate preeminent and proclaim it."[9]

The gods accorded Marduk this honor, and held a great feast for Marduk to celebrate his new post:

> The great gods, all or them, who decree fate,
> They entered in before Ansar, they filled...
> They kissed one another in the assembly...
> They made ready for the feast, at the banquet they sat;
> They ate bread, they mixed sesame wine.
> The sweet drink, the mead, confusing their...

They were drunk with drinking, their bodies were filled.
They were wholly at ease, their spirits were exalted.
Then for Marduk, their avenger, did they decree the fate.[10]

Marduk, with bows and arrows, lightning, wind, a hurricane, and a special net, went forth to meet Tiamat in his chariot. When they met, Marduk caught Tiamat in his net. Tiamat opened her mouth to swallow the net, but Marduk unleashed the hurricane, which filled Tiamat's belly. Marduk shot an arrow into Tiamat's belly, speared her with a lightning bold, and split her in two. Marduk raised half of Tiamat's body to become the sky, while the other half became the earth. Tiamat's army fled in the confusion, but Marduk captured them with his net, and cast them into the underworld. The fourth tablet of the *Enuma Elish* describes the battle:

> As Tiamat opened her mouth to its full extent,
> He drove in the evil wind, while she had not yet shut her lips.
> The terrible winds filled her belly.
> And her courage was taken from her,
> And her mouth she opened wide.
> He seized the spear and burst her belly,
> He severed her inward parts, he pierced her heart.
> He overcame her, and cut off her life
> He cast down her body and stood upon it.[11]

This Babylonian story of a male deity slaying a female dragon or serpent, in an attempt to tame Chaos, is a classic example of a God doing battle with the demonic. Traces of the Babylonian Epic can be found throughout the Old Testament. We shall take a close look at these traces in the next section of these chapter.

Another ancient near-eastern text from an archeological dig at Ras Shamra describes a dragon with seven heads. Ugarit was the capital of the Ugarit kingdom. It was discovered as an ancient city lying in a large mound ten kilometers north of present day Latakia, on the Mediterranean coast of northern Syria.

Many texts were discovered at Ugarit, including the "Legend of Keret," the "Aghat Legend," the "Myth of Baal-Aliyah," and the "Death of Baal." These texts revealed a Canaanite mythology. One tablet reveals the Canaanite pantheon, with Babylonian equivalents EL, Asherah, and Baal as the principal deities.[12]

These texts also reveal the Canaanites had a version of the male deity slaying the female serpent of the sea. They also reveal that the serpent

(Lotan) had seven heads, and was defeated by Baal with a great sword. Like the Babylonians, the Canaanite Lotan was a multi-headed dragon of the sea; and like *Enuma Elish*, the dragon is defeated with a sword by a god of order.

This notion that the idea of the Anti-Christ grew out of the mythology of the ancient near-east was first suggested by German scholar Wilhelm Bousset in his book, *The Anti-Christ Legend*. Bousset claims that this dragon myth was associated with the Babylonians, and "Not merely of the later Assyrians, but also of their far more Akkadian and Sumerian precursors."[13]

The same theory has also been suggested by Hermann Gunkel. Gunkel advanced the hypothesis of an esoteric oral tradition, and attempts to support his view with passage from the *Apocalypse of Ezra*.[14] Gunkel also makes a connection between the Babylonian myth and the chapters 12 and 13 of the Book of Revelation. Wilhelm Bousset, himself speaks of the contributions of Gunkel:

> Gunkel's work may be regarded accordingly as the starting point of the new method of interpretation of Revelation. To the study of contemporary history and of textual criticism is superadded that of traditional history, by which both are controlled but not superseded, as might appear from occasional passages in Gunkel's work.[15]

These two thinkers Wilhelm Bousset and Hermann Gunkel provide us with the place to begin our study: an ancient mythology that tells of a chaos monster that is defeated by a god of order. We see this belief among the Babylonians, with the Canaanites, and also with the ancient Jews.

OTHER COSMIC BEASTS IN ANCIENT MYTHOLOGY

The Sumerians told the tale of a sea monster named Asag, who was defeated by Ninurta, one of the sons of Enlil, and the separator of the heavens and the earth. In this tale, Ninurta restrains the flood to form the Tigris River. Then Ninurta appoints his mother Ki as a sort of Mother Earth. At this point Ninurta is elevated to the high God position.

In one version of the tale, Ninurta battles a sea monster named Imdugud (Akkadian Anzu). In this version, Anzu steals the Tablets of Destiny, which Enlil required to continue his rule. Ninurta slays a series of monsters that are called "Slain Heroes," and are represented by a dragon, a gypsum, the Palm Tree King, Lord Saman-ana, a bison, a scorpion, and a seven-headed serpent. The last of these monsters is clearly a version of the cosmic drama between a god and a sea monster. After Anzu is killed, Ninurta delivers the tablets to his father, Enlil.

The cult of Ninurta can be traced back to the oldest times of Sumerian culture. In an inscription found at Lagah, an ancient Sumerian city, he appears under the name Ningirsu, that is "the Lord of Girsu," Girsu being the name of ¼ within Lagash.[16]

This myth of Ninurta remained popular under the Assyrians. Two of the kings of Assyria bore the name Tukulti-Ninurta. The Assyrian king Ashurnasirpl II (who reigned 883 to 859 BCE), built a temple to Ninurta in the capital city of Calah (now Nimrud). Ninurta was also associated with the planet Saturn.

Ancient Indian mythology also has a version of this cosmic struggle. The monster is called Vritra, who is also depicted as a sea serpent. Vritra is defeated, like many of these other cosmic myths, by a good God. In this case it is Indra, who is also responsible for separating the heavens and the earth.

In this Indian tale, Vritra is pregnant with cosmic waters. When Indra breaks her back, the pregnant waters are released. Indra is also responsible for separating *sat*, that which exists, from *asat*, that which does not exist. In ancient Indian mythology, Indra is among a group of gods called *Adityas*.[17]

BABYLONIAN PARALLELS TO THE OLD TESTAMENT

There are a number of parallels to these Babylonian and Canaanite myths to be found in the Old Testament. Psalm 74:14 refers to the crushing of the heads of Leviathan, the Hebrew name for the serpent:

> Thou didst crush the heads of Leviathan,
> Thou didst give him as food for the creatures of the wilderness.[18]

Some modern Biblical scholars see Psalm 74:12–17 and the monster there as a representation of some Gentile ruler. These same scholars often see Jeremiah the same way:

> Nebuchadnezzar the king of Babylon has devoured me, he has crushed me; he has made me an empty vessel; he has swallowed me like a monster; he has filled his belly with alluring foods, he has rinsed me out.[19]

This passage also uses the same Hebrew verb, *hamam*, where elsewhere Yahweh is said to have "crushed the heads of Leviathan." It is likely that this line from Jeremiah is also related to the cosmic struggle between Yahweh and the sea monster. It also uses the noun, *chodesh*, the most common word for monster in the Hebrew Bible.

Psalm 104:26 refers to Leviathan frolicking in the sea, and Isaiah 27:1 tells us that Leviathan will be punished by God with a great sword. This passage in Isaiah also describes Leviathan as a twisting serpent, a dragon that is to be slain in the sea.

In the Old Testament, Yahweh does battle with the Chaos monster, but Leviathan is only one of the names for the monster. The names Rahab, Yam, Tannim, and Tehom are also given to the cosmic beast. Job 3:8 suggests that Leviathan continues to lurk in the cosmic ocean, seeking occasions to destroy the created order.

The name Rahab is use in several places in the Hebrew Bible to discuss a mythological monster of the deep. The motif of the slaying of a dragon appears at Job 9:13 and Psalm 89:10. Similarly in Isaiah 51:9, the Lord also defeats Rahab and cuts him to pieces with a sword. This poetic symbolism has much in common with the Ras Shamra literature, and is probably the prototype to later Christian legends like Saint George and the Dragon.

In the celebration of the New Year's Festival in ancient Judaism, Yahweh annually subdues the monster and then ascends to the divine throne as ruler of the cosmos. By this victory, God sustains creation and preserves the structures of creation against the threat of destruction. Indeed, one way to interpret chapter 41 of the book of Job about Leviathan is in these mythological terms.

Some exegetes have suggested that the story of Jonah and his being swallowed by a great fish may also bear remnant of the cosmic battle between Yahweh and the Leviathan. The first is called a *da'ig*, the same term used to describe Leviathan in chapter 41 of the Book of Job.

Chapter 41 of the book of Job presents a description of the beast, Leviathan. After describing his body and great strength, the text tells us that Leviathan "sneezes forth flashes of light."[20] Out of his mouth go "flashes of light, sparks of fire leap forward..."[21] Out of his nostrils "comes forth smoke, as from a boiling pot."[22] These allusions to fire and smoke most likely relate to the fact that Tiamat, Lotan, and Leviathan were all thought to be fire-eating dragons.

Not all references to Leviathan in the Hebrew Bible concern the myth of the Creation Battle. Psalm 104:26, for example, refers to the monster frolicking in the sea. This may be to give the impression that Leviathan is the greatest of sea creatures, but it is also important to point out that the book of Job tells us that only God can control Leviathan by pulling him out of the sea with a hook (41:2).

In Ugaritic myths, Lotan is a seven-headed serpent or dragon. He is either a pet of the god Yaw, or he is Yaw himself. Yaw is also known as Yam, the god of the sea, or Nahar, the god of the River. Among the Canaanites, Lotan was also called Yam. The Prince of the Sea, the Crooked Serpent, and the Tyrant with Seven Heads.

In Canaanite mythology, the name of the seven-headed monster is Lotan, who contends with Baal, for control over rule of the earth. It is likely that Leviathan and Lotan come from the same Semitic root. *LTN*.

The name Lotan or Lawtan was also a name for an Egyptian god, who is also known as a Retanu. Among the Hittites, this god was called Hahunu or Illuyanka and is also symbolized by a great snake. In Greek culture, he appears as Ladon, a serpent that guarded the golden apples of Hesperides.

The images of the mythological battle between God and the Chaos monster was also used as a metaphor in the Old Testament for conflicts between Israel and her enemies in the Old Testament. Ezekiel 29:1–16, 32:2–8, and Habakkuk 3:1–19 are good examples. The first of these passages is an account of the overthrow of the rule of Pharaoh and his armies. The second passage, from chapter 32 of Ezekiel, is also an account of the overthrow of the Egyptians that is placed in the context of a cosmic battle.

The passage from the third chapter of Habakkuk is also a description of a cosmic battle, where Yahweh "crushes the head of the wicked house," and "trampled the sea with his horses, churning the mighty waters."

Traces of this cosmic battle between Yahweh and a monster of the deep can also be seen in Psalm 89:9–10, Job 9:13, Job 26:12, and Isaiah 51:9. These passages use the name Rahab as the cosmic beast. Psalm 89 tells us:

> Thou dost rule the raging of the sea.
> When its waves rise, you still them.
> Though didst crush Rahab like a carcass.
> Thou didst scatter thy enemies with a mighty arm.[23]

Job 9:13 and 26:12 make similar allusions:

> God will not turn back his anger;
> Beneath him bowed the helpers of Rahab. (Job 9:13)[24]

> By the power he stilled the Sea;
> By his understanding, he smote Rahab. (Job 26:23)[25]

The prophet Amos also alludes to the cosmic battle between God and the sea serpent:

> And though they hide from me at the bottom of the sea
> There I will command the serpent, and it shall bite them.[26]

Isaiah leaves little doubt that he has adopted the cosmic myth of destroying Leviathan/Rahab. He tells us:

> Awake, awake, put on strength
> O arm of the Lord.
> Awake, as in days of long ago.
> Was it not Thou that cut Rahab to pieces,
> That did pierce the dragon? (Isaiah 51:9)[27]

Isaiah makes a similar reference in the opening of chapter twenty-seven:

> In the day the Lord with his hard and great and
> Strong sword will punish Leviathan, the fleeing serpent
> Leviathan, the twisting serpent, and He will slay the dragon
> That is in the sea. (Isaiah 27:1)[28]

Some scholars suggest that in Psalm 2 the Emperor Pompey is depicted as the dragon of chaos, and thus his figure is exalted into myth. Without this kind of infusion of Hebraic myth, the legend of the Anti-Christ could not have developed in Hellenistic and Roman times.

Echoes of the cosmic battle between God and Leviathan/Rahab can also be seen in the Jewish Apocrypha. In 2 Ezdras, for example, the text tells us:

> But unto Leviathan you gave the seventh part, namely, the moist.
> And you have kept him to be devoured when you wish and by whom.[29]

Another apocryphal text, *2 Baruch*, makes unmistakable reference to the defeat of Leviathan and Behemoth by God at the end of time:

> And Behemoth shall be revealed from his place
> And Leviathan shall ascend from the sea, these
> Two great monsters which I have created on the fifth
> Day of creation.[30]

It should be clear from the discussion given above that, like the Babylonians and Canaanites who came before them, the ancient Jews had a version of a cosmic myth, whereby God defeats a multi-headed sea dragon on the fifth day of creation. It is also clear, by looking at the passages from 2 Ezdras 6:52 and 2 Baruch 29:3–8 that some factions of ancient Judaism believe that God will again defeat the great sea beast at the end of time.

In addition to these parallels mentioned above, there are also a number of references in the Hebrew Bible that seem to allude to the Babylonian idea that creation was preceded by a watery waste. The opening line of Genesis seems to recall that tradition:

> In the beginning God created the heavens and the earth. The earth was without form and void, and darkness was upon the face of the deep; and the Spirit of God moved across the face of the waters.[31]

Among the other parallels between *Enuma Elish* and the first few chapters of Genesis are the following: in both Divine Spirit and cosmic matter are coexistent and coeternal; the Divine Spirit exists independently of cosmic matter in both tales. In the Babylonian story, Primeval Chaos, Tiamat is enveloped in darkness, while the ancient Jews used the cognate Tehom, which is enveloped in darkness.

In both stories, light emanates from the gods; both stories mention the creation of a firmament or bowl over the earth; both tales create the land dry, and both mention the making of the stars, the sun and the moon; both tales contain similar stories about the creation of human beings; and in both narratives the gods rest and celebrate when creation is complete. Thus, the ancient Jewish doctrine of creation seems not to be unique among peoples of the Ancient Near-East.[32]

As early as the *Sibylline Oracles* in the first century, as well as in the Book of Revelation, Christianity adopted the dragon imagery in the Book of Daniel. The *Sibylline Oracles* VIII. 88 tells us:

> The fiery-eyed Dragon when he comes on the waves
> With full belly, and shall oppress the children of thee,
> Famine also pending and fratricidal strife,

Then is nigh the end of the world and the last day.³³

Several lines later, at VIII.154, the text adds:

> From the Asian land he shall come mounted on the Trojan chariot,
> With the python's fury; but when the isthmus he shall cross,
> Changing from sea to sea in eager search of all,
> Then shall he encounter the great beast of black blood.³⁴

Sibylline Oracles V.28 also speaks of a demon "who has fifty horns received, Lord shall he be a dire serpent begetting heavy war."³⁵

PERSIAN INFLUENCES ON THE IDEA OF THE ANTI-CHRIST

In addition to the Babylonian and Canaanite sources mentioned above, a third major precursor to the legend of the Anti-Christ can be seen in the ancient Persian religion, Zoroastrianism. In the Persian myth of cosmic eschatology, we find two agents which are both male entering into a cosmic competition in the classic male warrior tradition. These two cosmic principals, Ahura Mazda and Angra Mainya, are also part of a moral testing in the afterlife, in which the righteous went to heaven and the wicked, or more particularly the ignorant or confused, were subject to trial by fire as disembodied spirits.

John Bowker writes of the affinities between ancient Persia and ancient Israel. Bowker writes:

> It might be thought that it is not particularly surprising "common ground," because the extreme form of duality namely dualism, is not particularly credible, and has not, in any case, ever been seriously stated or worked out. The former statement may be true (though it would have to be qualified on grounds of experience, as will be seen below), the latter statement is certainly not true. Dualism has been worked out in at least two great and widely influential systems of thought, Zoroastrianism and Manicheanism. To discuss Zoroastrianism as though it were a single entity is in fact misleading, because it changed considerably in the course of history.³⁶

Despite these misgivings of Bowker, what we do know about Zoroastrianism in its original form are the following things. First, the movement was founded by Zoroaster, a Persian who most likely lived in the seventh and sixth centuries BCE. Second, the name of the sacred text for Zoroastrians is the *Avesta*. And finally, the Zoroastrians had a number of theological ideas that may have been an influence on later Judaism and Christianity.

Scholar R. C. Zaehner summarizes Zoroaster's major doctrines:

1. There is a supreme Wise God (Ahura Mazda)
2. The world is divided between forces of Truth and forces of the lie, represented by Angra Mainya.
3. Human beings are endowed with free will, so they might choose between Ahura Mazda and Angra Mainya.
4. Because human beings are free, they are responsible for their own fate, which will be determined in a Final Judgment Day.[37]

In Zoroastrian eschatology, at the end of time, God will perform some cosmic renovations, in which the dead will be purged of all evil. This ordeal, in Zoroastrianism, will involve rivers of molten metal. The formative role of purgation in the Judgment Day is described by Cohn: "That requital which thou wilt assign to the two parties, O Mazda, by the bright blazing fire of molten metal, is a sign to be given by all living beings, to destroy the wicked man, and to save the just."[38]

In the Zoroastrian point of view there is a belief in two cosmic gods, one good and one evil. These gods are spoken of in the *Avesta*, a sacred text for the ancient Persians: "I will speak out concerning the two spirits of whom, at the beginning of existence, the Holier spoke to him who is Evil: "Neither our thoughts, nor our teachings, nor our wills, nor our choices, nor our words, nor our deeds, nor our convictions, nor yet our souls agree."[39]

In Zoroastrianism, Ahura Mazda and Angra Mainya are twins, equal in power and intelligence:

> In the beginning the two spirits who are well endowed twins were known as the one good and the other evil in thought, word, and deed. Between them the wise choose the good, not so the fools. And when these spirits met they established in the beginning life and death that in the end the evil shall meet with the worst existence, but the just with the best mind. Of these two spirits, he who was of the lie chose to do worst things; but the Most Holy Spirit, clothed in rugged heaven chose Righteousness, as did all those who sought with zeal to do the pleasure of the Wise Lord by doing good works.[40]

This description in Zoroastrianism is different from the classic combat myth in Babylon and Canaan in that there is no direct fighting between Ahura Mazda and Angra Mainya. But the war in Zoroastrianism is a spiritual one, where the two powers vie for the souls of humans. In Zoroastrianism, the images of Light and Dark are associated with the two gods.

Another ancient Persian tradition posits the belief in Zervan Arkarana, or "Boundless Time," as a supreme deity above and beyond Ahura Mazda and Angra Mainya. In this tradition, when the soul leaves the body it must cross a bridge of Chinvat (also called Kinvad). This word *kinvad*, means something like "the bridge of the Accountant," where judgment will take place. For three days good and evil spirits contend for the possession of the soul, after which the reckoning takes place. Some western scholars have argued that this tradition may also have had some influence on Jewish and Christian eschatology.

It should be clear that several developments from the ancient Persians may have been borrowed by the ancient Jews. First, the cosmic struggle between good and evil. Second, belief in immortality of the soul, as well as resurrection of the body, with a reckoning at the end of time in a Final Judgment. Third, the notion that cosmic struggle are symbolized by Light and Darkness. And finally, that the good god (Ahura Mazda) and the evil god (Angra Mainya) both have angelic helpers in their quests. Mazda's minions were called *spentas*, while Angra Mainya's angels were called *daevas*. These ideas from Zoroastrianism are directly related, as we shall see later, to the heart of ideas in the New Testament about the development of the Anti-Christ legend. Two other major precursors of the Anti-Christ legend are the Old Testament and Jewish Apocalyptic thought which we shall turn to in the next sections of this chapter.

Not all scholars who write about the Anti-Christ agree that the idea may have had Persian beginnings. Writing for the *Reformed Theological Review*, George Knight says:

> Most Bible dictionaries and encyclopedias take for granted that the greater part of the images in Jewish apocalyptic are traceable back to Persian origins. This at once, I believe, is highly questionable. The Persian way of thinking was dualistic. It divides into two. There was Light and there was Darkness. This dualistic thinking is, of course, a great advance upon polytheism. No more in Persia do we find a plethora or gods, all of whom are nothing but hu-

Precursors to the Anti-Christ Idea

man apotheoses of human foibles and failings. Persian dualism is a noble deification of the basic reality of human experience, viz., that there is Light and that there is Darkness, and that there is Good and there is Evil, and that these two realities are quite evidently at war with each other, not only in the natural world, but also within the human heart and human society.[41]

Knight goes on to quote Second Isaiah chapter 45, which says "I am the Lord Thy God, and there is no other." Indeed, Knight goes on to say that Isaiah tells us:

> I form light (*asah*) and create darkness (*bara*).
> I make good (*shalom*) and create woe (*ra*).
> I am the Lord who dos all these things.[42]

Knight points out that the Old Testament writers argue against Persian dualism. In their view, both light and darkness were made by the god of Israel, the all-powerful Yahweh.

Soderblom and others object to the Persian influences on Jewish and Christian eschatologies, on the grounds of extraordinary differences between Jewish and Persian eschatology.[43] But as Bousset has forcibly protested, it is one-sided proceeding to emphasize all the differences, while passing over the striking similarities.[44] Indeed, Bousset points out that Jewish and Persian views of eschatology may share a common much older source than either of them.[45]

APOCALYPTIC IN HELLENISTIC TIMES

Gradually, the last enemy of the kingdom of God came in Hellenistic times to be thought of as the antitype of the messiah. Many Jewish writings from the Hellenistic times, including the Book of Daniel, began to develop this anti-messiah type. A passage in Numbers 24:7 may serve as a representative example. The text speaks of a figure where

> Water shall flow from his buckets
> And his seed shall have
> Abundant water.
> His king shall be higher than Aga,
> And his kingdom shall be exalted.[46]

This, and many other Old Testament passages, began in the Hellenistic period to be explained in apocalyptic terms, often referring to the end of the world, and the coming of a false messiah. The *Third Sibyllines* also in the late first century began to be interpreted in a similar fashion.

In the older portions of the *Book of Enoch*, the appearance of the Messiah is spoken of as taking place at the end of all struggles and judgments (90:37). In the pseudo-Solomonic Psalms (17:27–39) of the time of Pompey, and in the fourth book of Ezra, of the times of the Flavian emperors, the anti-messiah is a godless power of heathen nations who are overpowered by the Messiah and his forces.

In the nearly contemporary *Apocalypse of Baruch* (40:1–2), a passage describes the destruction of the last impious king by the Messiah and his forces. This conception is not yet influenced by Christianity, and thus the expectation of a personal opponent to the Messiah is found in pre-Christian Judaism.

Other pre-Christian apocalyptic passages from the Hellenistic period also are extant. Robert H. Mounce sums up these passages: "A major role of the apocalypse was to explain why the righteous suffered and why the kingdom of God was delayed. Prophecy had dealt primarily with the nation's ethical obligations at the time when the prophets wrote. Apocalyptic focused on a period of time yet future when God would intervene to judge the world and establish righteousness."[47]

This Hellenistic apocalyptic literature is often dualistic (like Zoroastrianism), in that two opposing supernatural powers do battle. Hellenistic apocalyptic writers often suggest that Satan or evil powers now control the earth, but they will be defeated in an age to come by the direct intervention of God, who will create a perfect new world in which the good will prevail.

The writers of Hellenistic apocalypses looked upon their times as the worst of days, filled with suffering and pain for God's people. Thus, apocalypses from the period usually included a promise that God would intervene in human history, destroy evil, and bring the troubles of his people to an end. This hope centered on the swift return of the Messiah, who would usher in the end of the age and bring about his kingdom. Hellenistic apocalypses often suggest the end is near, and God is going to judge the world and reward his faithful and suffering people.

G. B. Caird gives a clear summary of these Hellenistic apocalypses:

> They encourage Jewish resistance to the encroachments of paganism, by showing that the national suffering was foreseen and

provided for in the cosmic purpose of God and would issue in ultimate vindication. It is characteristic of these writings that they portray the present crisis against the background of world history. The present struggle is seen as part of an age long struggle between the kingdom of Light and the Kingdom of Darkness, and victory over the immediate enemy as the embodiment of the final victory of God. It is also characteristic of them that they are written in symbolic language.[48]

Most people living in the Hellenistic period were familiar with the apocalyptic literary form. The Book of Daniel reflects both the content and form of these Hellenistic apocalypses. The Book of Revelation also was written with the apocalyptic form and content in mind, as we shall see in the next chapter.

APOCALYPTIC MATERIALS IN THE OLD TESTAMENT

Apocalyptic literature is a type of Jewish and Christian writings that developed between the testaments and had its roots in Old Testament prophecy. After the days of the post-exilic prophets, God no longer spoke to Israel through the living voice of inspired prophecy. The prophetic forecasts of the coming of God's kingdom and the salvation of Israel had not been fulfilled. Instead of the kingdom of God, a succession of evil enemies rules over ancient Israel: Persia, Greece, and Rome.

The hope of the kingdom of God grew dim. God seemed to offer no longer words of comfort and salvation to his chosen people. Apocalyptic literature, both Jewish and Christian, arose to meet these needs. Following the pattern of canonical Daniel, various unknown authors wrote alleged revelations of God's plan in relationship to current evils.

Certain characteristics mark the genre of apocalyptic literature. First, they claim to be revelations from God. Second, they tend to be imitative, often of other biblical materials. Third, they are usually anonymous, often claiming that they were written by some religious luminary from the past. Fourth, apocalyptic literature is often quite symbolic, full of images and visions of the End Times. And finally, apocalyptic literature tends to be pseudo-predictive. The authors take their stand in the distant past and rewrite history under the guise of prophecy.

Many, perhaps most, scholars (R. H. Charles, H. H. Rowley, and D. S. Russell, for example) have argued that apocalyptic literature is the child of traditional Hebrew prophecy. Post-exilic eschatological prophecies in the Old Testament seem to provide a natural link between the classic, pre-exilic prophets and apocalyptic literature. The above scholars point to Ezekiel 38 and 39; Isaiah 24–27; 34–35, and 56–66; Joel; and Zechariah 9–14, as the seed bed for apocalyptic thinking.[49]

Not all scholars, however, agree with this view. An alternative was proposed by Gerhard von Rad, who argued that the essence of apocalyptic was its deterministic view of history, a view unaffected by prophecy. Still other scholars, Wilhelm Bousset, for example, points to the foreign influences of Zoroastrianism and others. T. Francis Glasson and Franz Boll thought the origins of apocalyptic were to be found in ancient Greece. And a minority report from Rudolf Otto thought pre-Hindu Indo-Aryan thinking may have been an influence.[50]

The book of Daniel provides an archetype for later apocalypses to imitate. In the book of Daniel, we find a number of apocalyptic traditions that are to appear in later apocalypses. Among these categories or expressions are several worth mentioning: the idea of the Son of Man, the War of Gog and Magog; and the idea of the Abomination of Desolation, to name a few.

The word "abomination" appears infrequently in the Old Testament. The idea is most often expressed in the verb, "to detest," and the adjective "detestable." Two main Hebrew words are used to express these ideas. The first *shiqqutz* is usually employed in relation to idols. It is used to describe anything that is contrary to the Lord and his work. The related noun, *sheqqetz* is used to describe anything that brings defilement.

Isaiah also employs the term at 66:3 and 66:17. Jeremiah uses it at 32:34. It also can be found at Proverbs 26:25. The passages from Isaiah suggest that those who eat the flesh of a pig are abomination. Jeremiah refers to nonbelievers who erected a house of abomination in his name; and the passage from Proverbs reminds us not to trust those who speak graciously, for they may have seven abominations in their heart.

The expression, "Abomination of Desolation," is used a number of times in the book of Daniel. Daniel 9:27; 11:31 and 12:11 are good examples. Daniel 9:27 refers to "an abomination that desolates." Daniel 11:31 describes how the traditional burnt offerings will be abandoned in the end times and replaced by an "abomination that makes desolate." Daniel 12:11 also mentions the "burnt offerings being taken away and replaced by an abomination that desolates."[51]

Precursors to the Anti-Christ Idea

Various candidates exist for the identity of the abomination that desolates. Some though it refers to Syrian king Antiochus IV Epiphanes setting up an altar in the Temple, and then sacrificing a pig on it. Others suggest it was the destruction of the Temple in 70 CE, and still others, that the abomination that desolates will come in the end times. Whatever interpretation we give to the phrase, it clearly is used in New Testament apocalyptic literature, as well as two places in the gospels (Matthew 24:15 and Mark 13:14).

A second Old Testament apocalyptic expression that influences the idea of the Anti-Christ in the New Testament is "the Son of Man." The Hebrew expression, *ben Adam* is used by God when he addressed Daniel at 8:17, and over 80 times when addressing Ezekiel. The writer of Daniel also uses the phrase to describe a figure he saw in a night vision at Daniel 7:13–14. He also used it at 8:16–18 in reference to the End Times. Some say this figure is connected to the "saints of the most high" mentioned in 7:22, to whom dominion is given. Whatever interpretation is given to the figure, it is borrowed in the extra-canonical *Similitudes of Enoch*, in Acts, and in Revelation.

Jesus calls himself the Son of Man eighty-two times in the gospels. The phrase is also used at Acts 7:56, Revelation 1:13 and 14:14. Many of Jesus' uses of the phrase are in the third person. Presumably, he borrowed the phrase from the book of Daniel, and it is likely the Jews of Jesus' day were familiar with the term.

Jesus used the term in a variety of ways. (1) As a substitute for the personal pronoun "I," for example at Matthew 11:19, 16:13 and Luke 9:58. (2) Jesus also uses the term when making important proclamations, as in Matthew 20:28, Mark 10:45, and Luke 9:56. (3) On one occasion, John 5:27, the phrase is employed without the definite article "the." There it is used with an "a" preceding the phrase. (4) Jesus also used Son of Man when referring to his resurrection, or resurrection in general. Matthew 19:28, 24:30, and Mark 13:26 are good examples of this use.

The phrase Son of Man is also employed in the New Testament when Jesus refers to his role in judgment, as in Matthew 13:41 and Luke 21:36. And finally, the phrase is used when Jesus refers to his passion and death. The phrase has this context at Matthew 17:12; Mark 9:12; and Luke 9:44.

All these references to the Son of Man in the New Testament clearly are related to the prophecies using the phrase at Daniel 7:13 and 8:17. Jesus certainly thought of himself as a fulfillment of those prophecies.

The expression "the Day of Yahweh's vengeance" or "The Day of the Lord" are other common apocalyptic expressions in the Old Testament. Isaiah 34:7–8 provides an illustrative example:

> Wild oxen shall fall with them,
> And young steers with the
> Mighty bulls.
> Their blood shall be soaked with blood
> And their soil made rich with fat.
> For the Lord has a day of vengeance,
> A year of vindication by Zion's cause.[52]

The vengeance of God or the Day of Vengeance is spoken of at Isaiah 35:4; 47:3; 59:17; 61:2; Jeremiah 46:10; 50:15, and four dozen other Old Testament verses. What they all have in common is the belief that God's wrath or vengeance will come at the end of time, when a reckoning will come and the kingdom of God shall be established.

The Book of Daniel also uses the expression, "The Man of Sin" in several places, including 7:8, 11, 20, and 21, where the prophet also describes the "little horn," two further images later employed by the New Testament.

Chapter nine of the Book of Daniel contains a vision on the course of history, describing its length as being seventy weeks. This image had led many interpreters to apply this figure, in various ways, to the coming of the Anti-Christ. Most scholars identify the tyrant in chapter seven, the little horn in chapter eight and the reference to the seventy weeks in chapter nine of Daniel to be mentions of the Anti-Christ.

One final image in the Book of Daniel that may be important in this study is the identity of the "little horn." Most scholars connect the tyrant of chapter seven with the vision in chapter eight. Throughout Christian history, as we shall see in this study, many thinkers have identified the tyrant in chapter seven of Daniel, as well as the "little horn" in chapter 8, with the idea of the Anti-Christ.

As we shall see, we will return to all of these images from the Book of Daniel many times in this study; and when we do, exegetes in the Christian traditions often identify these passages with the Final Enemy.

The sixth-century BCE book of Zechariah is a post-exilic view of the end of the world, after the fall of Jerusalem in 586 BCE. Chapters nine to fourteen of Zechariah consist of two oracles on the End Times. The first oracles (chapters 9–11) gives an outline of God's providential deals with his people down to the time of the Advent. The second oracle of Zechariah (chapters 12–14) points out the glories that await Israel in "the latter days." These chapters also give a description of the final conflict and the triumph of God's kingdom.

The book of Zechariah uses may of the traditional Jewish apocalyptic categories mentioned above, including the phrase, "in that day," and "at that day," which are used sixteen times. It is also clear that the writer of Zechariah believes that the final confrontation will occur in Jerusalem, which occurs 23 times in chapters 12 to 14.

One final apocalyptic expression that had a later influence on New Testament Apocalyptic can be found in chapters 38 and 39 of Ezekiel. In this chapter, we find a figure Gog who will be the leader of a great army that attacks Israel in the end times. Ezekiel argues that this force will be defeated by God himself on the mountains of Israel. The slaughter will be so great, it will take seven months to bury all the dead. (Ezekiel 39:12) We mention the defeat of Gog and Magog in this chapter because the image will be taken up in the book of Revelation.

These three expressions are not the only influences the Old Testament has on apocalyptic literature in the New Testament, but, as we shall see, they are three of the most important ones in discussing the origins of the legend of the Anti-Christ in the New Testament.

In addition to the themes mentioned above, a number of other Jewish apocalyptic themes can be found in intertestamental literature. Among these are the "Son of Sin," and the notion of the "Son of Perdition." More will be said about these themes in the following chapter on the Anti-Christ in the New Testament.

The expression Son of Perdition is found in 2 Thessalonians 2:3 and John 17:12. It is a name commonly associated with the Anti-Christ. It is a term used by the Eastern Orthodox Church that identifies the Son of Perdition with the *Katechon*, the one who restrains. The term is also in popular use among the Church of Jesus Christ of the Latter Day Saints (the Mormons). It is used to refer to people who will not take a role in the glory of God in the afterlife. In the Mormon *Doctrines of the Covenants*, the Sons of Perdition are described as "inhabiting a kingdom which is not a kingdom of glory."[53]

Other Old Testament apocalyptic passages can be seen as early as the prophet Amos, who most likely wrote in the early eighth century BCE. At

Amos 5:20; 8:8–9; and 9:1–6, the prophet uses apocalyptic categories like the Day of the Lord, on that day, and the bite of a Sea Serpent.

Some Christian thinkers have pointed to Psalm 2:2 as a reference to the Anti-Christ. The Hebrew of this verse says:

> The kings of the earth set themselves,
> And the rulers take counsel together,
> Against the Lord and His anointed one,
> Saying, "Let us burst their bonds asunder,
> And cast their cords from us."[54]

The word translated as "anointed" in this passage is *Mashiyach*, or Messiah. Since Christ is the Messiah in the Christian churches, then this figure is seen by some as an Anti-Christ.

ISAIAH AND EZEKIEL AND THE APOCALYPTIC

Isaiah 24–27 are another good example of Old Testament apocalyptic literature. These chapters begin with a description of the end of the world:

> Behold the Lord will lay waste the earth and make it desolate, and he will twist its surface and scatter its inhabitants. And it shall be, as with the people, so with the priest; as with the slave so with the mater, as with the maid, so with the mistress, as with the buyer, so with the seller, as with the lender, so with the borrower; as with the creditor, so with the debtor. The earth shall be utterly laid waste and utterly despoiled; for the Lord has spoken these words.[55]

The text gives a picture of unrelieved, world-wide desolation in which all on earth will be involved. None will escape. Yahweh finally will deal with the world and its sin. Isaiah 24 continues with a description of the desolation until verses 15–23, where it tells us that Yahweh will triumph with his people in the End Times.

Chapter 25 of Isaiah continues with the exultation at the triumph of Yahweh. The chapter describes how Jerusalem will become a heap, a ruin, a "no city." In contrast, God's people will be catered to with an abundance of good things, and for them death will be removed forever. Believers will enjoy the final triumph, while those who like Moab who rejected the opportunity of joining with the people of God, will be trodden down into the dung pit.

Chapter 26 of Isaiah begins with a son of deliverance and a description of the Heavenly City that awaits believers: "In that day this song will be sung in the land of Judah: 'We have a strong city; he sets up salvation and walls the bulwarks. Open the gates, that the righteous nation will keep the faith and may enter it.'"[56]

Chapter 26 continues with a description of the way of righteousness and judgment on the unrighteous. Verses 11–15 give an account of what Yahweh has done for his people and the end of their enemies. Isaiah 26:19 tells us, "The dead shall live, their bodies shall arise. Oh dweller in the dust, awake and sing for joy."[57] The end of chapter 26 of Isaiah also describes the coming indignation: "For behold the Lord is coming forth out of his place to punish the inhabitants of the earth for their iniquity, and the earth will disclose the blood shed upon her, and will no more cover her slain."[58]

The opening of chapter 27 of Isaiah conveys the destruction of a Great Serpent Monster, not unlike the Babylonian myth discussed earlier in this chapter: "In that day the Lord with his hard and great and strong sword will punish Leviathan the twisting serpent, and He will slay the dragon that is in the sea."[59]

Chapter 27 continually uses the expression "in that day," and "in the days to come," like 27:6: "In the days to come, Jacob will take root. Israel shall blossom and put forth shoots, and fill the whole world with fruit."[60]

Chapter 27 of Isaiah concludes with another mention of the End Times: "In that day from the river Euphrates to the Brook of Egypt, the Lord will thresh out the grain, and you will be gathered one by one, of people of Israel. And in that day, a great trumpet will be blown, and those who were lost in the land of Assyria and those who were driven out of the land of Egypt will come and worship the Lord on the holy mountain of Jerusalem."[61]

In these chapters, the writer of Isaiah continually uses apocalyptic categories, like "in that day," the notion that the End Time will come at the sound of a trumpet, and that Yahweh's final victory will come at the top of a mountain in the city of Jerusalem. Indeed, throughout these chapters, Isaiah gives us a detailed account of the ends of the world and what will happen to the earth's inhabitants.

The book of Ezekiel was written in response to the invasion and capture of Jerusalem by the Babylonian King Nebuchadnezzar, and the subsequent exile of the Jews to Babylonian. The Book of Ezekiel foretells a return of the Jews to their homeland, and the violent destruction of their future enemies. The book ends with God's admonition to the Jews, reminding them of their suffering and exile as a result of their lack of faith. Ezekiel tells us that after their return to their homeland, proper worship will resume, and God will no longer turn away from them.

Ezekiel 8 and 39 contain a description that subsequently will be used by the Anti-Christ traditions in Christianity and in Islam. This story in Ezekiel 38 and 39 is about Gog and Magog, and the parts they play in the End Times.

JEWISH APOCALYPTIC AS A SOURCE OF THE ANTI-CHRIST LEGEND

Apocalyptic literature was a genre of prophetic writing in Judaism that developed after the Exile and was popular in the last few centuries BCE. The word Apocalypse comes from the Greek for "revealing" or "uncovering." Among the books of Jewish Apocalyptic literature that may have had an influence on the Anti-Christ legend in the New Testament are *The Assumption of Moses, The Psalms of Solomon, The Books of Enoch, the Sibylline Oracles,* and *The Apocalypses of Esdras.*

George Caird sums up the nature of Jewish Apocalyptic:

> The first readers were almost certainly well versed in the sort of symbolic language and imagery in which these books were written. Wherever there had formerly been Jews or pagans, they would read the language of myth as fluently as any modern reader of the daily papers reads the conventional symbols of a political cartoon. Much of this language we can construct ourselves from the Old Testament and Jewish apocalyptic writings on the one hand, and from Greek and Roman literature, inscriptions and coinage on the other.[62]

Jewish Apocalypses are literary reports of a fearful, often violent, visions that reveal truths about the past, present, and most especially, the future in highly symbolic and poetic terms. In these visions, the writer often supposes himself as transported into another realm beyond ordinary space and time. Often they are accompanied by angelic messengers, or are revealed pictures of the end of the world.

The affinity of ideas between Zoroastrianism and ancient Judaism began to manifest themselves in the relationship of Cyrus the Great to Jewish culture and the rebuilding of the Temple. The Zoroastrian vision of Judgment Day became woven into the Jewish prophetic tradition in the ensuing centuries.

The ancient Jews adopted a Light/Dark images in their apocalyptic times. They also adopted the idea of a Judgment Day at the end of time, as well as the idea of a resurrection at the end of time. These ideas are expressed quite well in Daniel 12, written during the reign of Antiochus IV: "At that time shall arise Michael, the great prince who has charge of your people. And there shall be a time of trouble, since has never been since there was a nation until that time; but at that time, your people shall be delivered. And many of those who sleep in the dust of earth shall awake, some to everlasting life, and some to everlasting shame and contempt."[63]

James J. L. Ratton begins his discussion with apocalyptic materials in the Book of Daniel this way:

> That part of Daniel's prophecy with which we are concerned related to the events bound up with history of the fourth or Roman Empire. These events may be divided into three groups. First, the coming of Christ, the His rejection and earth; second the destruction of the city and Temple of the Jews by a king, or the little horn, of the Roman Empire; and third, the transfer of the Kingdom from the Romans to the "Saint of God."[64]

This comment of Ratton's refers to the mention of a "little horn" in the eighth chapter of Daniel. The same figure is referred to at Daniel 7:25 that tells us: "He shall speak words against the Most High, and shall wear out the Saints of the Most High. And shall think to change the times and the law."[65]

Ratton tells us that the Ancient Jews "took themselves to be the saints of God." They looked upon this prophecy as promising the restoration of the kingdom, which the Babylonians had taken from them. Ratton continues:

> They watched the rise and fall of the kingdoms foretold by Daniel. They calculated the time of the advent of the Messiah from the data furnished by Daniel, and they expected the coming of the Messiah when He came. But they expected Him to come with power and majesty, to establish his kingdom upon earth. They expected also the little horn, "with eyes like a man, and a mount speaking great things."[66]

In Ratton's view, Daniel 7 and 8 had an important role in the development of the Anti-Christ legend in the New Testament.

The book of Daniel also contains many of the features of the Chaos monster, and the war of Order against Chaos, we have seen in many of the sources in this chapter. Many scholars have suggested that the idea of the Anti-Christ can be traced back to the second century BCE. Indeed, Syrian Antiochus IV Epiphanes, the persecutor of the Jews, may appear in the book of Daniel as a kind of Anti-Christ at Daniel 7:8, 19–25; 8:9–12; and 11:21–45. In these passages, the Anti-Christ the king of the north (Daniel 11:40) will appear as a mighty king with great armies, and that he will destroy three kings (the three horns of 7:8 and 25). The Edomites, Moabites, and Ammonites are to be spared by the king (Daniel 11:41). The Libyans and Cushites will follow in his train (Daniel 11:43). The Anti-Christ will persecute the saints (Daniel 7:25), and he will reign for 3 ½ years (Daniel 7:25). And finally, he will set up in the Temple "the abomination of desolation" (Daniel 8:13, 9:27, and 12:11).

The prophet Daniel records a number of other visions that later will be seen as precursors to the Christian idea of the Anti-Christ. Chapter seven of Daniel speaks of a vision of four beasts, and uses the apocalyptic image of the Son of Man. Chapter eight of the Book of Daniel introduces the idea of a fierce king "whose power shall be mighty, but not his own power." Chapter nine of Daniel includes a vision connected to Jeremiah 25:11 and 29:10 that prophesized a Babylonian Captivity of 70 years. The author of Daniel extended the time of the Captivity to "seventy weeks of years." Chapter nine of Daniel also speaks of a covenant that will be made in one week: "In half the week, He shall abolish sacrifice and oblation. And on the Temple wing shall be the horrible abomination, until the ruin that is decreed is poured out upon the horror."[67]

Daniel 9:26 speaks of a "prince who is to come." Daniel 9:27 tells us this prince will broker a seven year peace treaty between Israel and other nations; however, three and a half years into that treaty, the prince will break the agreement. These verses are often seen by many interpreters to refer to the Anti-Christ.

Another passage at Daniel 11:37 is used by many exegetes as a precursor to the Christian idea of the Anti-Christ. Speaking of a king that is to come, Daniel tells us, "He shall have no regard for the gods of his ancestors or for the one in whom women delight; for no god shall he have regard, for he shall make himself greater than all."[68]

Precursors to the Anti-Christ Idea

Many of these passages from the Book of Daniel are thought by Biblical scholars to be related to the rule of Antiochus IV Epiphanes, who was the eighth of twenty-six kings over the period of Syria in Alexander's empire. Some scholars say Antiochus is the "little horn" in Daniel 8:9. Other passages in Daniel that are thought to be related to Antiochus IV are 8:9–14; 8:23–24, and 11:21–35. The later passage outlines a number of prophecies that relate the conquering of Egypt by a Syrian king. The same king shall abolish burnt offerings in the Temple, and shall consider himself greater than any god. And "he shall prosper until the period of wrath is over."[69] And he shall deal with the strongest fortresses by the help of a foreign God."[70]

In Daniel 8:23–24, refers to a king who shall arise "skilled in intrigue." He shall: "Grow strong in power and shall cause fearful destruction and shall succeed in what he does. He shall destroy the powerful and the people of his holy ones. By his cunning, he shall make deceit prosper under his hand, and in his own mind he shall be great."[71]

In the second century BCE, these passages were thought to refer to Antiochus IV. And in early Christianity, these same passages were believed to refer to the Anti-Christ, The Final Enemy.

One final passage in Daniel that many exegetes have suggested in connection to the Anti-Christ in 9:26–27, which describes a "prince who is to come." The Hebrew text looks like this:

> After the sixty-two weeks, an anointed one shall be cut off and shall have nothing, and the troops of the prince who is to be come shall destroy the city and the sanctuary. Its end shall come with a flood, and to the end there shall be war. Desolations are decreed. He shall make a strong covenant with many for one week, and for half of the week he shall make sacrifices and offerings cease; and in their place shall be an abomination that desolations, until the decreed end is poured out upon the desolators.[72]

It is likely that the prince mentioned in this passage is Antiochus IV. The passage also contains many elements that will become incorporated into early Christian views on the Anti-Christ, such as the Final Enemy having an army, as well as the end times involving an abomination that desolates.

These images in the Book of Daniel, and Jeremiah, as well as apocalyptic images in the prophet Ezekiel, are frequently quoted by early

Christian writers in regard to the Anti-Christ, as well as in subsequent exegetical traditions in the history of Christianity.

From the second century BCE on, these predictions of Daniel's were passed on from generation to generation, and out of them came one of the major sources of the Christian Anti-Christ legend. Eventually, the figure of the Anti-Christ was no longer associated with Antiochus IV, and became the type of God-opposing tyrant who was discovered now in this and now in that historical personage.

To the author of the *Psalms of Solomon*, it is Pompey, the captor of Jerusalem, blasphemer of the sanctuary of God, that is the divine adversary, the dragon of the "last times." The dragon's destruction is celebrated as a great act by God in chapter two of this text.[73] In another apocryphal work, *The Assumption of Moses*, the picture of a cruel tyrant is outlined who seems to combine features of Antiochus IV and Herod the Great.[74]

In the small apocalypse in the *Ascension of Isaiah*, in chapters 3 and 4, we see the idea that a king of this world, that is called Beliar (or Belial) will descend from the heavens in the form of a man, who is depicted as the matricidal tyrant, Nero. Indeed, a number of stories about Emperor Nero as the Anti-Christ arose in very early Christianity. We will discuss some of these tales in a later section of this chapter.[75]

In *First Enoch*, which was written when the Jews were under the rule of the Greek Empire, we begin to see a shift from the ancient prophetic tradition to a new apocalyptic tradition. The "Book of the Watchers," which is part of *First Enoch*, gives us the example of the judgment of the dead in the Jewish tradition. The Book of Daniel, written during the Maccabean Revolt against the Syro-Greek dynasty, the Seleucids, is another early example of Jewish apocalyptic.

FALSE PROPHETS IN THE OLD TESTAMENT

In the history of the Old Testament exegeses, many commentaries often relate comments about false prophets in the Old Testament back to refer to passages about the Anti-Christ in the New Testament. The two most important of these passages are found in Deuteronomy. The first of these is Deuteronomy 13:1–5. The Hebrew text looks something like this:

> If a prophet arises among you, or a dreamer of dreams, and gives you a sign or wonder, and the sign or wonder comes to pass, and if he says, "Let us go after other gods, which you have not known,"

Precursors to the Anti-Christ Idea

and "Let us serve them," you shall not listen to the words of that prophet or to that dreamer of dreams; for the Lord your God is testing you, to know whether you love the Lord your God with all your heart and all your soul. You shall walk after the Lord your God and fear him, and keep his commandments, and obey his voice, and you shall serve Him and cleave to Him.[76]

Another Old Testament passage about false prophets that is often pointed to in regards to the Anti-Christ is Deuteronomy 18:20–22. The text tells us:

But the prophet who presumes to preach a word in my name which I have not commanded him to speak, or who speaks in the name of other gods, that same prophet shall die. And if you say in your heart, "How can we know the word which the Lord has not spoken?" When a prophet speaks in the name of the Lord, if the word does not come to pass, or come true, that is a word which the Lord has not spoken; the prophet has spoken it presumptuously, you need not be afraid of him.[77]

The pronouncement that a prophet preaching other gods shall die in this passage is often pointed to in discussions of the fate of the Anti-Christ in the Christian tradition. At times, the New Testament writers sometimes take up the criterion for a valid Divine revelation in this passage—that something comes from God if it comes true, or comes to pass.

Another passage in the Old Testament records a story where Yahweh is seen to be requesting from his heavenly counsel as to what he should do with a court of false prophets. This exchange is recorded in 1 Kings 22:19–23. In this passage, false prophets are used as a test by Yahweh to see if the faithful hold true to the Lord's ideas. This idea of using false prophets as a tool is also employed by Saint Paul at Romans 9:14–23.

ANTI-CHRIST INFLUENCES IN ROMAN TIMES

In the Roman period, the character of the Emperor Caligula (37–41 CE) influenced the history of the Anti-Christ legend. The fearful time Caligula gave an order to governor Petronius to erect a statue of Caligula in the Temple of Jerusalem. With this act, many Jews were reminded of the predictions in the Book of Daniel, which seemed to have reached their fulfillment.

Later, the expectations of the Anti-Christ were carried over in relationship to the Emperor Nero. Not long after the death of Nero, rumors began to arise in the Christian tradition that he was not really dead, but that he was alive and well and would reappear.

The most complete treatment of the Emperor Nero as the Anti-Christ can be found in James J. L. Ratton's *Anti-Christ: An Historical Review*. Ratton begins chapter 8 this way: "The connection between Nero and the "Destroyer" of Daniel, in the Book of Revelation, merits a more detailed notice than can be given to it in the commentary on the text."[78]

Ratton identifies the Destroyer of Daniel with Beliar. He then goes on to describe the superstition regarding Nero: that he should die a violent death, and reappear some time afterward as a conqueror and reestablish his kingdom. Suetonius points out that Nero had been formerly told by astrologers that it would be his fortune to at last be deserted by the world. Many early Christians began to interpret Nero's return as the coming of the Anti-Christ, and an ushering in of the last days.[79]

Daniels' fourth beast and his "little horn" were regularly identified with Emperor Nero. And in the end, he will "make war against the saints, and overcome them." (Daniel 17:21) Nero was also identified with the Anti-Christ because Nero's domination happened in three and a half years, the time predicted by Daniel 7:25.[80]

Since Nero was in good relations with the Parthians, the story goes, he had gone into exile with them. The report circulated, we are told by Suetonius, that Nero will return with a Parthian army to recover Rome. As late as the year 100 CE, the belief that Nero was still alive was held by many. This belief can be found in *The Ascension of Isaiah*, and was adopted by many Jewish apocalyptic writers.

The author of the 4th *Jewish Sibylline*, written around 79 CE, suggests the theory about Nero as Anti-Christ. In the fifth *Jewish Sibylline*, written by a Jew at the end of the first century CE, the subject of Nero as the Anti-Christ is mentioned three times. The figure of Nero is distorted into a ghostly demon. He will return on the last days to wage war against the Roman authorities.[81]

In both Jewish and Christian thought this view of Nero was adopted, and on this soil the Anti-Christ legend of early Christianity would arise. This story of the living Nero was also adopted by the final redactor of the Book of Revelation, who used this material to construct chapters 13 and 17 of the Apocalypse. There Nero is the beast that arises out of the abyss

(Revelation 17:8) and Nero is the head "as it had been slain" (Revelation 13:3 and 14). In early Christian times, Nero was identified with the tyrant who receives worship over the entire earth (Revelation 13:4 and 8), and the terrible opponent of the Lamb in the last great decisive battle (Revelation 17:14 and 19:19ff).

Another figure sometimes associated with the Anti-Christ in early Christian times is the Emperor Caligula, who ruled from 37 to 41 CE. Caligula gave the order, never carried out, to erect his statue in the Temple at Jerusalem. This was seen by early Christians who were Jews as an abomination.

Without doubt, early Christians thought the "number of the beast" (Revelation 13:18) refers to the Anti-Christ. In the majority of ancient manuscripts that number is 666, though other traditions have 616.

ESCHATOLOGY OF THE ESSENES AS INFLUENCE OF ANTI-CHRIST LEGEND

The Essenes were followers of a Jewish way of life that flourished from the second century BCE to the first century CE. They are mentioned in Josephus in a number of places. The discovery of their library at Qumran, usually called the Dead Sea Scrolls, was one of the great archeological discoveries in the twentieth century.[82]

The Essenes are important for our purposes because many eschatological ideas can be found in texts found at Qumran. Among these are the *Books of Jubilees* and *First Enoch*. Cohn describes the importance of these texts. "More clearly than any passage in the Hebrew Bible, *Jubilees* and *First Enoch* tell of a Last Judgment, which is to come at the end of time."

In the early chapters of *First Enoch*, which many scholars date from the third century BCE, a sage sees a vision in which God, at the end of time, will come down from heaven, accompanied by 10,000 angels, takes his stand on Mount Sinai and pronounces Judgment Day.

The Essenes called themselves the "Sons of Light," in opposition to the Jewish majority, or, the "Sons of Darkness." In the *War Scroll* among the Dead Sea Scrolls, the Essenes recast the history of the Jews in terms of a cosmic war between forces of good and evil. The Essenes looked forward to the Day of Judgment, when they expected God to send an army to defeat their enemies. The Essenes show us that early Christianity was but one of Jewish sects animated by apocalyptic beliefs.

The *Book of Jubilees* also contains a good bit of Christian eschatological imagery. In *Jubilees*, Mastema or Belial is the leader of a host of demons which seems to suggest are the angels that seduce the daughters of men in Genesis 6:1–4. The author of *Jubilees* is persuaded (like the Zoroastrians were) that ever since the flood, peoples' health and security have been deteriorating, generation by generation.[83]

Jubilees also uses the expressions the "Sons of Light," and the "Sons of Darkness." The children of righteousness are ruled by the Prince of Light, and walk in the ways of light, but the children of falsehood are ruled by the Angel of Darkness, and walk in the ways of darkness. For the Essenes, the sons of Light were members of their sect, while the sons of Darkness often were ordinary Jews lying outside the sect.

The writer of *Jubilees* is a firm believer in the Messiah, and the coming of a Messianic Age, as is the writer of *First Enoch*. *Jubilees* makes only one direct reference to the Messiah at 31:18. He seems to identify the Messiah with the Maccabean family, and suggests the Messianic Age will be a temporary kingdom. *Jubilees* suggest that the Messianic Kingdom will be brought about gradually by the progressive spiritual development of the human race, and a corresponding transformation of the natural world.

The members of the Messianic Age were to have 1,000 years of peace and happiness. During this period, the powers of evil were to be restrained (Jubilees 23:29). The Final Judgment is to take place at the end of the Messianic Age (Jubilees 23:30), a view that might have derived from Zoroastrianism.

One text discovered at Qumran designated as 1QpHab is a commentary on Habakkuk, one of the sixth century BCE minor prophets. This text refers to an opponent of the "Teacher of Righteousness," a leader of the Qumran community. This opponent is called a "Liar," "a Spouter of lies," "a false prophet," and a "traitor at the end."[84] This text may well have been one of the antecedents of early Christian views of the Anti-Christ.

The Essenes retold the entire story of Israel in the *Book of Jubilees*, in terms of a cosmic war, not all that different from the traditions found in this chapter. The Final Judgment is to take place at the close of the Messianic Kingdom (Jubilees 23:30). It embraces both the human and superhuman worlds (*Jubilees* 23:10 and 14). At the Final Judgment, there will be no respect of persons, but all will be judged according to their opportunities and abilities (*Jubilees* 23:15).[85]

Precursors to the Anti-Christ Idea

It should be clear that Christianity took over many of these ideas, and we meet numerous traces of them in the New Testament, the topic we take up in the next chapter, "The Anti-Christ in the New Testament."

CONCLUSIONS

In this chapter we have looked at a number of sources and materials that may have been influences on the New Testament ideas of the Anti-Christ. In the beginning of the chapter, we examined tales in Babylonian and Canaanite mythology that may have been related to the Anti-Christ legend. Specifically, we looked at the Babylonian and Canaanite tales of the slaying of a female god by a male warrior. In the ancient-near-east, the female god is frequently understood as the god of Chaos and symbolized by a sea serpent or dragon.

As we have seen, various names for this god of chaos existed in the Middle East, including Tiamat, Rahab, Lotan, and Leviathan. Indeed, we have explored the uses of these terms in the Old Testament in this chapter.

We have also explored some influences that the ancient Persian religion, Zoroastrianism, may have had in the development of the Anti-Christ story in the New Testament. Whatever the influence of ancient Persia on Israel, it is clear the two cultures shared a number of theological ideas, including belief in a cosmic figure of evil, belief in a Judgment Day, and a battle between the Forces of Light and the Forces of Evil.

In addition to this material, we have also explored in this chapter some precursors to the Anti-Christ theme in Jewish apocalyptic literature. As we have shown, the book of Daniel, the Dead Sea Scrolls, the *Ascension of Isaiah*, the *Psalms of Solomon*, and the *Sibbyline Oracles*, all contain materials that might have been incorporated into the New Testament idea of the Anti-Christ. It is to the New Testament that we wish to turn in the next chapter.

NOTES

1. Wilhelm Bousset, *The Anti-Christ Legend* (London: Hutchinson, 1896) xi–xii.
2. Hermann Gunkel, *Creation and Chaos* (Grand Rapids: Eerdmans, 2006 [orig. German 1895]).
3. Theophilus G. Pinches, *Religious Ideas of the Babylonians.* (London: Constable, 1906; reprinted, IndyPublishers, 2002).

4. Bousset, *The Anti-Christ Legend*.
5. Ibid.
6. The *Enuma Elish: The Seven Tablets of Creation* (London: 1902). Tablet I, lines 1–6. The editions of Babylonian and Canaanite texts I have used in this chapter are those of James B. Pritchard, *Ancient Near Eastern Texts Relating to the Old Testament*, 3rd ed. (Princeton: Princeton University Press, 1969). For more on the Babylonian creation myth, see Hermann Gunkel, *Creation and Chaos*; *The Standard Babylonian Creation Myth: Enuma Elis* (Damascus: State Archives of Assyria Cuneiform Texts, 2005) and Alexander Heidel, *The Babylonian Genesis* (Chicago: University of Chicago Press, 1963).
7. Ibid., lines 9–14.
8. Ibid., Table II, lines 1–4.
9. Ibid., Tablet III, lines 57–60.
10. Ibid., Tablet III, lines 131–39.
11. Ibid., Tablet IV, lines 99–107.
12. R. P. Carroll, *From Chaos to Covenant* (London, 1981). Also see: W. F. Albright, "The Role of the Canaanites in the History of Civilization," (Baltimore: Johns Hopkins University Press, 1942); J. C. L. Gibson, *Canaanite Myths and Legends* (Edinburgh, T. & T. Clark, 1978).
13. Bousset, *The Anti-Christ Legend*, 8.
14. Hermann Gunkel, *Schopfung und Chaos* (Göttingn: Vandenhoeck and Ruprecht, 1895).
15. Bousset, *The Anti-Christ Legend*, 9.
16. Henri Frankfurt, *The Art and Architecture of the Ancient Orient* (New Haven: Yale University Press, 1996) 29–45.
17. *Hindu Myths: A Sourcebook Translated From the Sanskrit* (New York: Penguin Classics, 2004) 63–72.
18. Author's translation, Psalm 74:14.
19. Jeremiah 51:34. (Author's translation).
20. Job 41:18 (Author's translation).
21. Job 41:19 (Author's translation).
22. Job 41:20 (Author's translation).
23. Ibid., Psalm 89:9–10.
24. Ibid., Job 9:13.
25. Ibid., Job 26:12.
26. Ibid., Amos 9:3.
27. Ibid., Isaiah 51:9.
28. Ibid., Isaiah 27:1.

Precursors to the Anti-Christ Idea

29. 2 Esdras 6:52.
30. *2 Baruch* 29:3–8. For more on Leviathan and its relationship to other ancient near-eastern myths, see F. M. Cross, *Canaanite Myth and Hebrew Epic: Essays in the History of the Religion of Israel* (Cambridge: Harvard University Press, 1972); F. M. Cross, *From Epic to Canon: History and Literature in Ancient Israel* (Baltimore: Johns Hopkins University Press, 1998); and Y.Kaufmann, *The Religion of Israel from its Beginnings to the Babylonian Exile* (Chicago: University of Chicago Press, 1960).
31. Genesis 1:1 (author's translation).
32. For more on these parallels, see *Gilgamesh* edited by John Gardner and John Maier. (New York: Vintage, 1984); Nahum M. Sarna, *Understanding Genesis: The Heritage of Biblical Israel* (New York: Schocken, 1972) 1–35; and W. F. Albright, "The Babylonian Matter in the Pre-deuteronomic Primeval History in Genesis 1–11," *Journal of Biblical Literature* 58 (1939) 91–103.
33. Ibid.
34. Ibid.
35. Ibid.
36. John Bowker, *Problems of Suffering in the Religions of the World* (Cambridge: Cambridge University Press, 1970) 270–71.
37. R. C. Zaehner, *The Dawn and Twilight of Zoroastrianism* (New York: Putnam, 1961) 60–61.
38. Norman Cohn, *Cosmos, Chaos, and the World to Come* (New Haven: Yale University Press, 1933).
39. The version of the *Avesta* I have used for this analysis is Yasmine Jhabvala's *Vers Ahura Mazda* (Berlin: Lang, 1992). I have also consulted: James Darmesteter, *Avesta Khorda Avesta: Book of Common Prayer*; Prods O. Skjrv, *Gathas of Zarathustra* (London, 1991); and Henry Bleeck, *Avesta: The Religious Beliefs of the Parsees Four Vols.* (London: Adamant Media Corporation, 2001).
40. Quoted in Bowker, *Problems of Suffering*, 271. For more on Zoroastrianism, see J. H. Moulton, *Treasure of the Magi* (London: Kessinger, 1997); C. F. Horn, *Ancient Persia* (London: Kessinger, 1942); Frances Power Cobbe, *The Sacred Books of the Ancient Persians* (London: Kessinger, 2005).
41. George A. K. Knight, "Anti-Christ," *The Reformed Theological Review* (January-April 1873) 1.
42. Ibid., 2.
43. Nathan Soderblom, *La vie future, d'apres le mazdeime* (Stockholme, 1901) 301.
44. Bousset, *The Anti-Christ Legend*, 509.
45. Ibid.

46. Numbers 24:7. (RSV translation).
47. Robert H. Mounce, *The Book of Revelation*, New International Commentary on the New Testament (Grand Rapids: Eerdmans, 1997) 119.
48. G. B. Caird, *A Commentary on the Revelation of St. John the Divine*, 2nd ed., Black's New Testament Commentaries (London: Hendrickson, 2006) 9
49. R. H. Charles, *Apocrypha and Pseudepigrapha of the Old Testament*, 2 vols. (Oxford: Clarendon, 1913); H. H. Rowley, *The Relevance of Apocalyptic: A Study of Jewish and Christian Apocalypses From Daniel to Revelation*; D. S. Russell, *The Method and Message of Apocalyptic*.
50. Gerhard von Rad, *Old Testament Theology*, 2 vols. (New York: Harper & Row, 1965), particularly 301ff and 407ff.; Bousset, *The Anti-Christ Legend*; T. Francis Glasson, *The Second Advent* (1947); T. Francis Glasson, *His Appearing & His Kingdom* (1953); Franz Boll, *Sphaera* (Berlin, 1903); Rudolf Otto, *The Kingdom of God and the Son of Man* (Boston, 1943).

    Further views on the origins of apocalyptic literature can be found in John J. Collins, "Apocalyptic Literature," in Robert A. Kraft and George W. E. Nickelsburg, *Early Judaism and its Modern Interpreters* (Philadelphia: Fortress, 1949); Paul D. Hanson, *The Dawn of Apocalyptic* (Philadelphia: Fortress, 1975); David Hellholm, *Apocalypticism in the Mediterranean World and Near East* (Tübingen: Mohr/Siebeck, 1983); Christopher Rowland, *The Open Heaven: A Study of Apocalyptic In Judaism and Early Christianity* (New York: Crossroad, 1982).
51. Daniel 9:27; 11:31; and 12:11.
52. Isaiah 34:7-8 (RSV).
53. *Book of Doctrines and Covenants* (Salt Lake City: Herald, 1978). Second 76:13.
54. Psalm 2:2. (Author's translation).
55. Isaiah 24:1-3 (author's trans.).
56. Isaiah 26:1-2 (author's trans.).
57. Isaiah 26:19 (author's trans.).
58. Isaiah 26:21 (author's trans.).
59. Isaiah 27:1 (author's trans.).
60. Isaiah 27:6 (author's trans.).
61. Isaiah 27:12-13 (author's trans.).
62. Caird, *Revelation*, 6.
63. Daniel 12:1-3 (author's trans.).
64. James J. L. Ratton, *Anti-Christ: An Historical Review* (London: Burns & Oates, 1897) 21.
65. Daniel 7:25 (RSV).

Precursors to the Anti-Christ Idea

66. Ratton, *Anti-Christ*, 21.
67. Daniel 9:27 (author's trans.).
68. Daniel 11:37 (author's trans.).
69. Daniel 11:21–35 (RSV).
70. Ibid.
71. Daniel 8:23–24 (RSV).
72. Daniel 9:26–27 (author's trans.).
73. *Psalms of Solomon,* chapter 2. The versions of the Apocrypha and Pseudigrapha I have used in this chapter is James H. Charlesworth, *The New Testament Apocrypha and Pseudepigrapha: A Guide to Publications, With Excursus on Apocalypses* (New York: Cambridge University Press, 1987); and Charlesworth, *The Old Testament Apocrypha and Pseudepigrapha: Prolegomena for the Study of Christian Origins* (New York: Cambridge University Press, 1985).
74. *The Assumption of Moses.* I have used the Schmidt and Merx edition, *De Assumptio Mosis* (Berlin, 1868). I have also consulted the R. H. Charles, *The Assumption of Moses* (London, 1897); and Ceriani's Latin text, *Monumenta Sacra et Profana* (Berlin, 1861).
75. *The Ascension of Isaiah.* I have used both the 1877 Dillman edition, *Ascensio Isaiae Aethiopice et Latine*, published in Leipzig, as well as R. H. Charles, *Ascension of Isaiah* (London, 1900).
76. Deuteronomy 13:1–5 (author's trans.).
77. Deuteronomy 18:20–22 (author's trans.).
78. Ratton, *Anti-Christ*, 92.
79. Ibid., 95.
80. Ibid., 96–97.
81. *The Sibylline Oracles.* I have consulted Geffcken's *Komposition und Entstehungszeit der Oracula Sibyllina* (Leipzig, 1902). For more on the Sibylline oracles, see Milton S. Terry, *The Sibylline Oracles: Translated from the Greek into Blank Verse* (London: 1918); and the edition by H. N. Bate (London, 1918).
82. *The Book of Jubilees.* I have used R. H. Charles, *The Book of Jubilees* (London, 1913). I have consulted reference to Jubilees in Martin Abegg, *The Dead Sea Scrolls Bible.* (San Francisco: HarperCollins, 1999).
83. Ibid.
84. L. J. Lietaert Peerbolte, *The Antecedents of Anti-Christ* (Leiden: Brill, 1996) 277–79.
85. In preparing my remarks on the Dead Sea Scrolls, I have consulted the following: Millar Burrows, *The Dead Sea Scrolls* (New York: Viking, 1956); *The Scrolls and the New Testament* edited by Krister Stendahl (New York: Harper Brothers, 1957); William Sanford LaSor, *The Dead Sea Scrolls and the New*

Testament (Grand Rapids: Eerdmans, 1972); John M.Allegro, *The People of the Dead Sea Scrolls in Text and Pictures* (Garden City, NY: Doubleday, 1958); John Trevor, *The Untold Story at Qumran* (Westwood, NJ: Revell, 1965); and J. T. Milik, *Ten Years of Discovery in the Wilderness of Judea* (London: SCM, 1959).

2

The Idea of the Anti-Christ in the New Testament

> Then I saw a Beast emerge from the sea; it had seven heads and ten horns,
> And each of its heads was marked with blasphemous titles.
>
> —Revelation 13:1

> The circumstances surrounding Nero's suicide by sword blow in 68 CE—let alone the more bizarre aspects of his reign—were so mysterious that they gave rise to a host of stories and legends.
>
> —Bernard McGinn, *Anti-Christ*

> There will be three signs of the coming of the Lord. First, a sign spread out in heaven (Matthew 24:30). Second, the sign of the sound of the trumpet (Matthew 24:31a). And third, the resurrection of the dead (Matthew 24:31b).
>
> —*The Didache* early second-century document.

INTRODUCTION

As WILHELM BOUSSET HAS so convincingly shown, a tradition was evidently current in Jewish thought around the time of Jesus about the Anti-Christ. This tradition underlay the teachings of both John the Divine and Paul concerning the Anti-Christ.[1] This tradition appears to have contained the following elements. The coming of the Anti-Christ was prevented by the Roman Empire. When the Empire should fail, the Anti-Christ, not of foreign birth but a Jewish false Messiah, would establish himself in the Temple at Jerusalem and require men to worship him.

His reign would last for three and a half years; and through miraculous powers he will convert people to his cause.

Later, the Anti-Christ's real character will be exposed, the believing Jews fled into the wilderness would be pursued by him, followed by being slain by the coming of the true Messiah, who will defeat the Anti-Christ with the breath of his mouth. This tradition was in part followed and in part contradicted by the Apocalypse and Paul; but in its background was the Book of Daniel, with its fierce foreign oppressor, the Apocalyptic Belial, a supernatural spirit who would antagonize God at the end of time.

The term *Anti-Christos* occurs five times in the New Testament. Most of these appear in 1 John (2:18, 2:22, and 4:3), and one in 2 John 7. In all these references, they refer to a figure who brings a different perspective on Jesus, particularly one that says He was "never in the flesh." In none of these references does the term refer to a celestial embodiment of evil, nor as an equivalent of Satan, nor as a son of Satan. In much contemporary literature, the idea of the Anti-Christ has become a synonym with the demonic, or as an off-spring of the devil; but, as we shall see, the materials from the New Testament of the Anti-Christ make none of these claims.

Christianity adopted many of the themes we have seen in the first chapter. In this second chapter, we principally explore many of early Christianity's applications of these ideas. Ideas about the Anti-Christ in the New Testament chiefly can be found in a number of texts. In some portions of the New Testament we find small apocalypses related to the Anti-Christ. Two examples of these small apocalypses can be found in Mark 13 and Matthew 24.

A second place in the New Testament where we can find views of the Anti-Christ is in the letters of Paul, specifically, in 2 Thessalonians 2:3–12 and 2 Corinthians 6:15. A third place, are the epistles of John (1 John 2:18–22; 4:3; and 2 John 7). And finally, some observations related to the Anti-Christ can be found in the book of Revelation, particularly Revelation 11:4–13; 13:1–18; chapter 17; and 19: 11–21. Analyses of these passages, and their relationship with the early Christian development of the idea of the Anti-Christ, are our principal tasks in this chapter.

APOCALYPTIC LITERATURE IN THE NEW TESTAMENT

Although apocalyptic literature constitutes its own independent genre, as we have seen in chapter one, it still plays an important role in the New

Testament. In each of the four canonical gospels, a central story is given involving Jesus describing a coming apocalypse in a manner that is consistent with traditional apocalyptic literature.

Apocalyptic literature is a genre that developed specifically in Jewish and Christian contexts, with most of the material being produced between 200 BCE and 200 CE. Biblical apocalypses are closely related to prophetic literature as we have seen in the materials from Daniel, Isaiah, and Ezekiel in the first chapter of this work.

But the genres of prophetic literature and apocalyptic literature are not identical. There are at least two important differences between the two. The first difference is that the prophets saw themselves as acting in the here and now, offering advice and guidance from God, while writers of apocalypses offered "secret" teachings that are most relevant for the End Times.

A second important different between apocalyptic and prophetic literature is that the prophets, by and large, saw the will of God unfolding within historical events and through activities of the Jewish people, while apocalyptic writers saw God's will as only being manifested in a realm that exists beyond the historical process. For the apocalyptic tradition, historical events are seen as symbols of what is going on in a level of reality that goes beyond history.

The apocalyptic teachings attributed to Jesus share a number of basic features with the standard format of the apocalyptic genre. On a literary level, the method of presentation involves visions that are heavily laden with symbolic imagery. There is also an inkling that in Jesus' pronouncements about apocalyptic matters, some things remain hidden. Jesus' speeches about the End Times also share a view with other apocalyptic literature that history unfolds in a predetermined fashion, and that nothing will happen that is not associated with the will of God.

The nature of coming disasters is another theme that the teachings of Jesus share with other apocalyptic literature. Wars, earthquakes, famines, stars falling from the sky, eclipses, and other strange events are often depicted by apocalyptic writers. These descriptions of the End Times, like descriptions in the Book of Daniel and Isaiah 24–27, are always seen as being far worse than anything human beings have previously experienced.

Often these descriptions, whether in Jesus' pronouncements on the End Times or in Old Testament apocalypses, typically involve a cosmic battle between good and evil, God and Satan, or Christ and the Anti-

Christ. Most often, these cosmic battles are fought on earth between humans allied with Satan or the Anti-Christ and those allied with God and His Son.

Although apocalypses constitute only a small portion of the gospels, its core feature is central to the entire gospel message. The "good news" of Christianity is typically conceived as a message of love and peace, but the promise of this cosmic battle at the end of time, where Satan and the Anti-Christ will be defeated is not seen as inconsistent with this central message.

Many of these features of the New Testament apocalyptic can be seen in what are sometimes called the "Little Apocalypse," Mark 13, Luke 21, and Matthew 24, which will be discussed at some length in the next section of this chapter.[2]

THE ANTI-CHRIST AND SMALL APOCALYPSES IN MARK 13, LUKE 21, AND MATTHEW 24

Mark 13 contains Jesus's predictions of the destruction of the Temple in Jerusalem, as well as the coming of a disaster for Judea, and a discourse on eschatological matters. After the teachings in the Temple in Mark 12, Jesus lingers for another day teaching in the Temple in chapter 13. After teaching for the day, Jesus leaves the Temple, and an unnamed disciple remarks how great the building is.

The Temple was an enormous building by standards in the ancient world. Some scholars estimate it reached a height of 150 feet, and was adorned with gold, silver, and other precious metals. Jesus responds to the disciple by saying, "Do you see all these tall buildings? Not one stone here will be left on another, every one will be thrown down."[3]

Jesus suggests here that the Temple will be destroyed, although he offers no details about when or how. These are the last words of Jesus he will utter in the Temple. Later Jesus travels back to the Mount of Olives and privately sits opposite the Temple with Peter, James, John, and Andrew. They ask him when the Temple will be destroyed, and will they be given a sign that it is about to happen? Jesus replies:

> Beware that no one leads you astray. Many will come in my name and say, "I am He!" And they will lead many astray. When you hear wars and rumors of wars, do not be alarmed; This must take place, but the end is still to come. For nation will rise against

nation, and kingdom against kingdom; there will be earthquakes in various places; there will be famines. This is but the beginning of the birth pangs.[4]

Jesus seems to suggest a number of things that will usher in the Last Days. He predicts they will be harassed by various governments, that they should say whatever comes to mind, as it will be God speaking through them, and that Jesus's message is to be given to all nations. Families will be torn apart, and "All men will hate you because of me, but he who stands firm to the end will be saved."[5]

> When you see the desolating sacrilege set up where it ought not to be (let the reader understand) then those in Judea must flee to the mountains; the one on the housetop must not go down or enter the house to take anything away; the one in the field must not turn back to get a coat. Woe to those who are pregnant, and to those who are nursing infants in those days. Pray that it may not be in winter. For in those days, there will be suffering, such as has not been from the beginning of creation until now, no, and never will be.
>
> And if the Lord had not cut short those days, no one would be saved; but for the sake of the elect, whom he chose, he has cut short those days. And if anyone says to you at that time, "Look, here is the messiah," or "Look, there He is." Do not believe it. False messiahs and false prophets will appear and produce signs and omens, to lead astray, if possible, the elect. But be alert, I have already told you everything.[6]

Jesus's comment about the "desolating sacrilege" is most likely a reference to Daniel's abomination that desolates. It may refer to Antiochus IV, to Caligula, or to the destruction of the Temple by the Romans in 70 CE. Whatever the reference, Jesus foretells other things as well in this small apocalypse.

In addition to the predictions of the destruction of the Temple, and the event in Judea, Jesus also foretells a universe shaking event, followed by his triumph. Jesus says:

> But in those days, after the tribulation, the sun shall be darkened, and the moon shall not give her light, and the stars in the heavens shall fall, and the powers that are in the heavens shall be shaken. And then shall they see the Son of Man coming in the clouds with great power and glory. And then shall he send his angels, and shall gather together his elect from the four winds, from the uppermost

part of the earth to the uttermost part of heaven. Now learn a parable of a fig tree; when her branch is yet tender, and puts forth leaves, you know that summer is near. So you in like manner, when you shall see these things come to pass, know that it is near, even at the doors. I say to you, this generation shall not pass, until all these things be done. Heaven and Earth shall pass away, but my words shall not pass away.[7]

Jesus concludes these discourses by saying that no one but the Father knows when these things will happen, not even the Son. He then tells a parable of a man going on a long journey.[8] We begin this chapter with a description of Mark 13 because it becomes clear that Jesus sees himself as part of the Jewish apocalyptic tradition. In addition to various predictions, Jesus also uses some apocalyptic language and categories, like his use of the Son of Man image.

Jesus also foretells the destruction of the Temple in Jerusalem in Matthew 24. In verses 1–3, he speaks of the destruction and the troubles before it. This is followed by a long discourse on other signs and misery that will presage the end of the world (verses 29–41). The chapter concludes with an exhortation to watchfulness in verses 42–51. Matthew 24 speaks of "The Day of the Lord," "the Son of Man," and a "Time of Tribulation," other apocalyptic categories at the time of Jesus. Matthew 24:4 and 10 also speak of "false prophets," another possible source for the idea of the arrival of the Anti-Christ. In both Mark 13 and Matthew 24 we see that Jesus was familiar with the Jewish apocalyptic tradition, and its tendency to depict events related to the end of the world. Although there are no explicit mentions of the Anti-Christ in these chapters, it is clear that Jesus saw his ministry as part of the apocalyptic tradition.

In Matthew 24:15, Jesus quotes the Book of Daniel; but the messianic Son of Man here is not opposed, as in Daniel, by a ruler who at the same time destroys the religious and national side of the theocracy, but by a great number of pseudo-prophets and pseudo-messiahs (Matthew 24:5) who are thought of as fanatical representatives of a Jewish natural Messianic idea.

A third small apocalypse among the gospels is found at Luke 21, where Jesus again predicts the destruction of the Temple in Jerusalem. Again, he tells us "Not one stone shall be left upon another." And again, Jesus' disciples ask when these things will occur. Jesus responds by telling them not to follow the teachings of deceivers (verse 8.), and that his followers should not be frightened by catastrophes generally associated with the End Times (verses 9–11).

These small apocalypses predict that the church throughout its history will witness many Anti-Christs. Mark 13:6, 21–22 and Luke 21:8 speak specifically of false teachers. In Mark 13:6, Jesus mentions that "Many will come in my name and say 'I am he.' And they will lead many astray."[9] A few verses later in the same chapter, Jesus comments, "And if anyone says to you at that time, 'Look, here is the Messiah,' or 'Look, there he is'—do not believe it. False prophets and false messiahs will appear and produce signs and omens to lead astray, if possible, the elect. But be alert. I already have told you everything."[10]

In Luke 21:8, Jesus makes a similar claim: "And he said, 'Beware that you are not led astray, for many will come in my name and say, 'I am He' and 'The time is near!' Do not go after them.'"[11]

In these small apocalypses, Jesus, through eschatological discourses to his disciples, fueled expectations of an imminent end, as well as cautioning against predicting the date of the End Times.

THE ANTI-CHRIST IN THE JOHANNINE EPISTLES

Among the Catholic epistles in the New Testaments, if Hebrews is the Epistle of Priesthood, James, the Epistle of Practice, and First Peter, the Epistle of Hope, then the First Epistle of John, is the Letter of Life, or "Eternal Life." To have eternal life for the letters of John is to have the gospel equivalent of being in the "Kingdom of God," or Paul's "being in Christ."

The epistles of John are anonymous, but the author was clearly some venerable father of the first-century Church. The apocalyptic categories of light and darkness, good and evil, and love and hate pervade the Johannine epistles. These epistles have a dual focus: an emphasis on the Incarnation, and an emphasis on the love of God. The core of the doctrine of the Incarnation for John is that God was in Christ, that is, in Jesus, who was "born of the Virgin Mary, and suffered under Pontius Pilate." God stooped low for humanity and our salvation.

One can imagine the author of John's epistles to be a venerable bishop who, hearing of the spread of false doctrines in his city, writes a pastoral letter about these false teachings and teachers. Second John in a very real way is a reiteration of some themes in the first letter. 2 John is like a miniature version of 1 John, with hardly a phrase in the second letter not found in the first. The author of both letters is a "John, the Elder." Many scholars suggest this is the same man as John the Elder of Ephesus.

The other glory in the Johannine epistles is its magnificent insistence on the primacy of love in the Christian life. John uses the word love 52 times. The author of John's epistles would agree with Thomas Carlyle that "there is nothing inexorable but love." On the writer of John's letters, Browning wrote:

> Like Dante, he loved well, because he hated—
> Hated wickedness, and all that hinders loving.

John never tires of saying things like, "Little children love one another," but he also blazes indignantly at pseudo versions of Christianity, which, feigning love for God, looks with loveless eyes upon its Christian brethren. It is in the context of these railings against false prophets that mentions of the Anti-Christ arise in the Johannine epistles.

The word *Anti-Christos* (Anti-Christ) appears only in John's epistles, though there are parallels to those passages in Revelation, and the letters of Paul. The term *Anti*-Christos appears five times in First and Second John—once in the plural form and four times in the singular form. The writer of John's epistles seems to suppose his readers are acquainted with the idea of the Anti-Christ. In 1 John 2:18, the writer tells us, "Children, it is the last hour! As you have heard, the Anti-Christ is coming . . ."[12] First John 4:3 also suggests these early Christian already had an idea of the Anti-Christ: "And every spirit that does not confess Jesus is not from God. And this is the spirit of the Anti-Christ, of which you have heard that it is coming . . ."[13]

The writer of John's epistles also supplies some observations of the character and workings of the Anti-Christ: "Who is the liar but the one who denies that Jesus is the Christ. This is the Anti-Christ, the one who denies the Father and Son."[14]

In 2 John 7, we get another description of the character of the Anti-Christ: "Many deceivers have gone out into the world, those who do not confess that Jesus Christ has come in the flesh; any such person is a deceiver and the Anti-Christ."[15]

Thus, John suggests that false teachings and deception are signs that the Anti-Christ is at work in the world. First John 2:18 also tells us that the time of the Anti-Christ is the "last hour," in accordance with Jewish apocalyptic beliefs about the end of the world. In the Johannine epistles, the Anti-Christ seems to describe any false teacher, false prophet, or corrupter of the Christian faith. John's letters also sometimes seem to indicate that the Anti-Christ is a particular person or spirit of deception that speaks false teachings, and whose presence is a sign of the end times.

One peculiar element about 2 John 7 is that the tense changes from the past "has come" [*elluthota*] in the flesh (1 John 4:2) to the present participle "as come [*erchomenon*] in the flesh." This makes it possible that this is a reference to Jesus' Second Coming: he is coming (i.e., will come) in the flesh. (Compare 1 John 2:28 and 3:2.) Some exegetes translate the participle *erchomenon* in the past tense, as if its meaning were identical to 1 John 4:2.

First John 4:3 suggests that the Anti-Christ is "in the world already." 1 John also posits the idea that the Anti-Christ is among a class of Anti-Christs: "As you have heard, the Anti-Christ is coming, so many Anti-Christs have come. From this we know that is the last hour."[16]

The writer of John's letters speak of "many Anti-Christs," who typify the "spirit of the Anti-Christ, that was both present in the first century ("is in the world already"), and continues to exist down to this day. As the writer concludes, such an anti-Christ (or opponent of Christ) is anyone who "denies that Jesus is the Christ," "denies the Father and Son," "does not confess Jesus," and does not "confess the coming of Jesus."

1 John 2:26–27 suggests that John the Divine wrote to the recipients of his epistle for the purpose of directly warning them of a "spirit of error," a false Messiah, so that they will not be deceived. The text tells us: "I write these things to you concerning those who would deceive you, as for you the anointing that you received from him abides in you, and so do not need anyone to teach you. But as his anointing teaches you about all things, and is true and not a lie, just as it has taught you, abide in him."[17]

From John's epistles, then, we get several marks of the Anti-Christ:

1. He will come at the last hour.
2. He is a liar and deceiver.
3. He will deny the Father and Son.
4. He is associated with any false teacher, false prophet, or corrupter of the Christian faith.

5. He is one among many Anti-Christs that are yet to come and are already here.

Paul tells us that the End Times will come completely without warning, "like a thief in the night." (1 Thess 5:2, 4.) He tells us that when one hears the cry of command, the archangel's call, and the sound of God's trumpet (4:16), it will already be too late. Paul's metaphor of a thief in the night precludes any possibility that we will know the End Times with signs or warnings before hand.

Paul goes on in 2 Thessalonians to deny that the *parousia*, or the Day of the Lord, is already here because

> that day will not come unless the rebellion comes first and the lawless one is revealed, the one destined for destruction. He opposed and exalts himself above every so-called God or object or worship, so that he takes his seat in the temple, declaring himself to be God ...And you know what is now restraining him, so that he may be revealed when his time comes...whom the Lord Jesus will destroy with the breath of his mouth, annihilating him by the manifestation of his coming. The coming of the lawless one is apparent in the working of Satan, who uses all signs, lying wonders, and every kind of wicked deception for those who are perishing, because they refused to love the truth and be saved.[18]

Crossan and Reed comment on these passages:

> On the one hand, that is like saying that the night thief will not come unless there is first the sound of breaking windows and smashing doors. One is therefore safe until after that happens, so that the metaphor of unpredictability breaks down. On the other, those absolutely enigmatic events seem to indicate a continuation, intensification, and specification of the persecution mentioned in 1 Thessalonians.[19]

THE ANTI-CHRIST IN THE BOOK OF REVELATION

When we move from the other books of the New Testament to the Revelation of Saint John the Divine, we feel that we have crossed over from familiar territory to an alien world. Revelation, to the modern reader, is a weird and fantastic book full of angels and trumpets, and earthquakes, of beasts, dragons, and demons. We should not be surprised to learn that the early Church had some doubts about the canonical status of Revelation.

The Idea of the Anti-Christ in the New Testament

The Christian Bible ends with the Book of Revelation. The book was canonized due to three related things: (1) its authorship; (2) its tendency to inspire millennial thinking and fervor; and (3) the question of how this strange book fits with the remainder of the canon. For our purposes, the second item is of the most importance, in that Revelation offers a series of images and visions that have taken on apocalyptic significance in the history of the Church.

John the Divine's Apocalypse gives us the opportunity to save the kingdom of God. He uses Daniel's references to Gog and Magog, which are to march against the Messiah at the end of time (Rev 20:8). He also personifies the Roman Empire as the Final Enemy (Rev 17:11); and he puts forth the Emperor Nero, as well as a multitude of other false prophets who mislead the cult of a world kingdom and its rule (Rev 13:11–17; 16:13; 19:20; and 20:10).

Like other apocalypses, the Book of Revelation shows a dependence on various other religious works, borrowing 245 times from the Old Testament, many from Daniel, nine from the New Testament, and several suggestive references from non-canonical literature. The book is written mostly in prose; 37 of 394 verses of Revelation are poetry. The book's language is clouded with mystery, symbolism, myth, and numerology. The number seven, for example, is used 54 times, applying to churches, seals, heads, trumpets, angels, bowls, and plagues. Multiples of 12 and 1,000 are also used throughout the book. In the history of the Christian tradition, many scholars have tied some of these images to their views of the Anti-Christ.

Revelation is the finest example of early Christian apocalyptic literature. The Bible contains only one other book of the same genre, Daniel; but, as we have shown in the first chapter, between 200 BCE and 100 CE, Judaism produced many such books. For the most part, these books fell into disrepute and were gradually forgotten, so that it is only in recent times we have rediscovered many of them. We now possess, in whole or in part, about 30 early apocalypses, and a study of them has enormously increased our knowledge and understanding of Revelation.

Contrary to popular belief, and to the surprise of many Christians, the words "Anti-Christ" or "Anti-Christs," do not appear in the Book of Revelation. It does speak of the Tribulation, the beast, the dragon, the Whore of Babylon, and of false prophets, but nowhere does it use the word Anti-Christ.

The Legend of the Anti-Christ

Nearly all New Testament scholars agree that the Anti-Christ is to be found in *Revelation*, but they disagree about where he is to be found. Some say the Anti-Christ is to be identified with the "beast" of Revelation 11:7, others with the "Red Dragon" of chapter 12. Other scholars, with the description of an animal having "seven heads and ten horns" in chapter 13, while many claim the Anti-Christ is identified with a beast with "two horns like a lamb," and spoke "like a dragon," in Revelation 13:11.

Still other scholars suggest the "the scarlet colored beast" with "seven heads and ten horns," is the Anti-Christ, or finally, Satan "loosed out of his prison," and "seducing all nations" of chapter 20 is the best description of the Anti-Christ in the New Testament.

Although the Book of Revelation does not use the term Anti-Christ, it does warn against a false Christ image that becomes a living icon and an object of worship:

> Then I saw another beast that rose out of the Earth; it had two horns like a lamb, and it spoke like a dragon. It uses all the authority of the first beast, whose mortal wound had been healed. It performs great signs, even making fire come down from heaven to Earth in the sight of all; and by the signs it is allowed to perform on the part of the beast, it deceives the inhabitants of Earth, telling them to make an image for the beast that had been wounded by the sword, and yet lived.[20]

Bernard McGinn begins his discussion of the Anti-Christ in the Book of Revelation this way: "The mythological frame work of heavenly opposition between the forces of good and evil that sets the stage for the coming of the Anti-Christ is described in chapter 12, the famous vision of the pregnant Queen of Heaven who is attacked by a 'huge Red Dragon, which has seven heads and ten horns.'"[21] McGinn goes on to point out: "This Dragon, identified with the Devil in verse 13, does not prevail over the Woman and her male child, the Messiah. He is cast down to earth "to make war on the rest of her children, that is, all who obey God's commandments and bear witness for Jesus."[22]

THE DRAGON IN REVELATION

Revelation 12 and 13 introduce us to a tradition in the New Testament that is highly symbolic and perhaps related to the mythic cosmic struggle between Yahweh and Leviathan. The identity of the dragon is suggested in Revelation 12:9: "And the great dragon was cast out, that old serpent, called the Devil, and Satan, which deceives the whole world: he was cast out into the earth, and his angels were cast out with him."[23]

John the Divine associates the beast with the demonic, and that a principal characteristic of the great dragon is the ability to deceive "the whole world." The appearance of the great dragon in chapter 12 of Revelation, with its heads and horns, is likely related to chapter 13:1–4, as well as in chapter seventeen.

Revelation 12 presents the Red Dragon as having seven heads and twelve horns, while Revelation 13 depicts the beast as a mirror image with ten horns and seven heads. The crowned heads of the Red Dragon likely refer to seven provincial Roman rulers and the ten horns to ten Roman Emperors. In reverse, the crowned horns refer to seven Roman Emperors, and the heads to ten provincial rulers.

We know from Suetonius and Josephus that the early Romans counted Julius Caesar, and not Augustus, as the first Roman Emperor. Thus, by this reckoning, although there were scores of Roman Emperors, only ten ruled from the beginning of the Roman Empire to the time of the Jewish Revolt in the first century CE. This Revolt lasted seven years, though sacrifices were halted and the Temple was destroyed only after three and a half years in 70 CE.

It is also likely that the seven heads represent the Herodian Dynasty, a provincial power that was sometimes known as the Red Dragon. The color of red reflects Herod's Idumean ancestry, that is Edom, where the soil was red. Indeed, the word *edom* in ancient Hebrew means "red."

There may be many reasons this provincial power is given so much play in Revelation chapter twelve, but probably the most significant one is related to Herod's attempt to kill Jesus as an infant. This may be reflected in Revelation 12:3–6, which tells us:

> Then another portent appeared in heaven: a great red dragon with seven heads and ten horns, and seven crowns on his head. The tail swept down a third of the stars of heaven and threw them to the earth. Then the dragon stood before the woman who was about to bear a child, who is to rule all the nations with a rod of iron. But her child was snatched away and taken to God and His throne, and the woman fled into the wilderness, where she had a place prepared by God, so that there she could be nourished for one thousands two hundred and sixty days.[24]

Another way to judge historical understandings of the End Times, then, is to look carefully as what particular thinkers believe about these images: the Red Dragon, the Whore of Babylon, and the woman with child in Revelation 12. As we shall see, in this history there are many different understandings of these images, some connected to the Anti-Christ, and some unconnected to the Final Enemy.

Chapter 12 of Revelation provides the best New Testament depiction of the ancient combat myth we have seen in Babylonia and the land of Canaan: "Then another portend appeared in heaven: a great red dragon with seven heads and ten horns, and seven diadems on his head. His tail swept down a third of the stars of heaven and threw them to the earth" (Revelation 12:3–6).[25]

A few verses later, Revelation describes a war in heaven, quite like that found in early Jewish apocalyptic writings, between the angel Michael and the Dragon:

> And war broke out in heaven; Michael and his angels fought against the Dragon. The Dragon and his angels fought back, but they were defeated, and there was no longer a place for them in heaven. The Great Dragon was thrown down, that ancient serpent, who is called the Devil and Satan, the deceiver of the whole world—he was thrown down to the earth and his angels were thrown with him. (Revelation 12:7–9)[26]

Chapter 13 of Revelation speaks more about the nature of this heavenly battle, and it introduces two more mythological beasts. This chapter has as one of its antecedent's chapter 7 of Daniel, where four beasts are introduced:

> I Daniel saw in my vision by night the four winds of heaven stirring the great sea, and four great beasts came up out of the sea, different from one another. The first was like a lion and had eagle's wings. Then, as I watched its wings were plucked off, and it was lifted up from the ground and made to stand on two feet like a human being; and a mind was given to it. Another beast appeared, a second one that looked like a bear. It was raised up on one side, had three tusks in its mouth among its teeth and was told, "Arise! Devour many bodies!" After this, as I watched, another appeared like a leopard. The beast had four wings of a bird on its back and four heads, and dominion was given to it. After this, I saw in the visions of the night a fourth beast, terrifying and dreadful and exceedingly strong. It had great iron teeth and was devouring,

breaking into pieces, and stamping what was left with its feet. It was different than all the beasts that came before it, and it had ten horns. I was considering the horns, when another horn appeared, a little one coming up among them; to make room for it, three of the earlier horns were plucked by the roots. There were eyes like human eyes in this horn, and a mouth speaking arrogantly. (Daniel 7:2–8)[27]

These four beasts of Daniel have long been identified with the Babylonian Empire, the Median Empire, the Persian Empire, and the Empire of Alexander the Great. While Daniel saw four beasts arising from the sea, John the Divine saw one beast that has the features of all four:

Then I saw a Beast emerge from the sea: it had seven heads and ten horns, and each of its heads was marked with blasphemous titles. I saw that the beast was like a leopard, with paws like a bear and a mouth like a lion; the Dragon had handed over to it his own power and his own throne and his world-wide authority. I saw that one of its heads seemed to have a fatal wound, but that this deadly injury was healed, and, after that, the whole world had marveled and followed the beast. (Revelation 13:1–3)[28]

Most scholars agree that if Daniel's four beasts were four great kingdoms of the ancient world, John's single beast was a kingdom Christianity was dealing with at the end of the first century, the Roman Empire.

G. K. Beale points out a connection between Revelation 13:7–8 and Daniel 7:14, which speaks of "one like a son of man" who received his authority from God. Beale points out that three different elements are present in both Daniel 7:14 and Revelation 13:7–8. Beale writes: "... the contexts of Daniel 7 has served as the controlling pattern of John's thoughts so far in vv. 1–7a and part of this pattern continues to be reflected in vv. 7b-8: (1) granting of sovereign authority (Daniel 7:14a), (2) over everyone on earth who will offer worship (Daniel 7:14b), (3) all of which is directly associated with a cosmic 'book' (Daniel 7:10b)."[29]

Beale seems to suggest that the author of Revelation has applied the wording of Daniel 7:14 to the beast in order to show that the beast's efforts to conquer may be an ironic parody of the son of man's final triumph.[30]

After this description of the Beast in Revelation 13:1–10, John the Divine offers a description of a Second Beast in Revelation 13:11–18

Then I saw another beast that arose out of the earth; it had two horns like a lamb, and it spoke like a dragon. It exercises all the authority of the first beast on its behalf, and it makes the Earth and its inhabitants worship the first beast whose mortal wound has been healed. It performs great signs, even making fire come down from heaven to Earth in the sight of all; and by the signs it is allowed to perform on behalf of the beast, it deceives the inhabitants of Earth, telling them to make an image for the beast that had been wounded by the sword and yet lived; and it was allowed to give breath to the image of the beast could even speak and cause those who do not worship the image of the beast to be killed.

Also, it causes all, both small and great, both rich and poor, both free and slave, to be marked on the right hand or the forehead, so that no one could buy or sell who does not have the mark, that is, the name of the beast, or the number of its name. This calls for wisdom: let anyone with understanding calculate the number of the beast, for it is the number of a person. Its number of 666.[31]

This second beast is also mentioned in Revelation 16:13, where it is called a "false prophet." What to make of this second beast has long been a question of Christian theology. We can begin our discussion of the second beast by making four conclusions we know about it. First, the second beast is called a false prophet. Second, the purpose of the second beast is to make people worship the first beast. Third, the second beast will have a powerful economic and social influence on earth. And finally, the number of the beast is 666.

The number 666 appears in three places in the Old Testament. The first appears in 2 Chronicles 9:13. "Now the weight of the gold that came to Solomon in one year was 666 talents of gold." This passage has a parallel in 1 Kings 19:14: "Now the weight of gold that came to Solomon in one year was 666 talents of gold."[32]

The number 666 also appears in a genealogy in Ezra 2:13, where it mentions "the son of Adonikam, 666."[33] It does not appear that these Old Testament passages will help us unravel the number 666 in Revelation.

The earliest record of Revelation 13:18 is a fragment of an early manuscript of the Apocalypse from the Oxyrhynchus site. It gives the number of the beast as 616. Many of the early Church Fathers, like Irenaeus for example, regarded the 616 as a scribal error. Many believed the 666 refers to Emperor Nero whose name written in Aramaic was valued as 666 in Jewish gematria.

The best explanation for the number 666 is to be found in ancient Hebraic gematria, where each of the Hebrew letters is assigned a numerical value. Thus, aleph, the first letter is 1; bet, is 2; gimel, 3 etc. Using this technique, the name Nero Caesar, or Neron Qaisar in Hebrew, we get the following values:

N	R	W	N	Q	S	R
50	200	6	50	100	60	200

Vowels were not written in ancient Hebrew, but if we add up the values of the consonants we get 666, the number of the beast in Revelation 13:18. We must remember that Revelation is most likely a Christian document at the end of the first century, and that Nero was identified as the Anti-Christ by many early Christians. Thus, the best explanation of the number 666, is the view that the Emperor Nero, who ruled the Roman Empire from 54–68, and who was one of the first great persecutors of Christianity, is the best understanding of what the number 666 means.

There is a second lengthy description of the Beast in chapter 17 of Revelation. In this passage, John depicts the prostitute Babylon (Rome) riding on the beast. An angel in Revelation 17 tells us:

> The beast you have seen once was and now is not; he is yet to come up from the Abyss, but only to go to other destruction. And the people of the world…will think it miraculous where they see how the beast once was and now is not and is still to come. Here there is need for cleverness, for a shrewd mind; the seven heads are the seven hills, and the woman is sitting on them. The seven heads are also seven emperors. Five of them have already gone, one is here now, and one is to come again. When he comes again, he will be here a short while. The Beast who once was and now is not, is at the same time the eight and one of the seven, and he is going to his destruction.[34]

The Whore of Babylon is another image from Revelation that sometimes is associated with the Anti-Christ. She appears in chapter 17 of the Apocalypse, where John the Divine describes her: "The Great Whore that sits upon the waters, with whom the kings of the earth have committed fornication, and the inhabitants of the earth have been made drunk with the win of her fornication" (Revelation 17:1–2).

She has the titles "Mystery Babylon the Great," "The Mother of the Harlots," and "Abomination of the Earth." She is described as being "drunk with the blood of the saints, and the martyrs of Jesus." (Revelation 17:5–6)

Her apocalyptic downfall is predicted to come at the hands of the kingdom with seven heads and ten horns.

Revelation 17:4-5 gives us this further description of the Whore of Babylon: "The woman was clothed in purple and scarlet, and adorned with gold and jewels and pearls, and in her hand is a cup full of abominations and the impurities of her fornications. And on her forehead was written a name, a mystery: Babylon the Great, mother of whores and of earth's abominations."[35]

Revelation 17:12 tells us: "And the ten horns that you saw are ten kings who have not yet received a kingdom, but they are to receive authority as kings for an hour, together with the beast."[36]

Revelation 17:18 clearly identifies the great city that will or does rule the earth as Rome: "The woman that you saw is the great city that rules over the kings of earth."[37]

Other descriptions of the Whore of Babylon can be seen at Revelation 17:9-11 and verses 15-17. The Whore of Babylon is an important theme in Christian iconography, as we shall see in chapter seven of this work.

Many biblical scholars have identified the Whore of Babylon with Rome, and subsequently with any other power to subjugate Christians. The figure is treated by most of the primary Christians exegetes, including Calvin, Luther, and other prominent theologians. The image of the Whore of Babylon is important for our purposes because it is frequently tied, as we shall see, to various views about the Anti-Christ in the history of Christianity.

In our analysis, the seven hills are the seven hills of Rome. The head that has been and will come again is Nero. When he returns, it will only be for a short while, the ushering in of the last things. Early Christians believed that Nero was the Anti-Christ. He did not really die in 68 CE, and will return with an army at the end of time. The emperor Nero was the first of Christian Anti-Christs, and his number was 666.

A number of the mythological elements we saw in the first chapter of this study clearly have been adopted by the writer of Revelation. The cosmic battle between good and evil, the lopping off the head of the dragon with a sword, and the identification of the serpent of Genesis three are all mythological elements employed by Saint John the Divine. The mythological references to two beasts may be connected to the long traditions of Behemoth and Leviathan, the two beasts described in chapters 40 and

The Idea of the Anti-Christ in the New Testament

41 of the book of Job. Like the two creatures of Revelation, one is from the sea, and the other the land.

The identification of the second beast as a false prophet may be connected to the false prophet mentioned in the little Apocalypses of Mark 13:22 and Matthew 24:11. The author of Revelation also adopts and refines a good bit of material in the book of Daniel, particularly its apocalyptic visions of chapters seven through twelve.

Several other Old Testament apocalyptic themes appear in Revelation. Two in particular should be mentioned here. First, the writer of Revelation incorporates the images of Gog and Magog introduced in chapters 38 and 39 of Ezekiel. In Revelation 20:7–8, we get this description of Gog and Magog in the End Times:

> And when the thousand years have expired, Satan shall be loosed out of his prison. And he shall go out to deceive the nations which are in the four corners of the Earth, Gog and Magog, to gather them together to battle: the number of whom is as the sand of the sea. And they went up on the breadth of the earth, and compassed the camp of the saints about, and the beloved city: and fire came down from God out of heaven, and devoured them.[38]

Here, Gog and Magog are identified as the nations of the four corners of the Earth, and their attack is represented as an eschatological battle much like that found in Ezekiel. This passage in Revelation is clearly an echo of Ezekiel 38 and 39, where Gog is portrayed as a leader of a confederacy uniting Israel's enemies of the north (Europe) the east (Persia), and the south (Cush and part of Africa). At some future time when Israel will be reunited in its land and experience peace and prosperity, these forces will strike against the defenseless Jews.

In Revelation 20:8, Gog and Magog are mentioned as two representatives of the world's rebellious nations. They are to be deceived by Satan following his release from prison. As in Ezekiel, Gog and Magog are destined in Revelation for destruction.

Revelation 20:7–8 tells us: "When the thousand years are ended, Satan will be released from his prison and will come out to deceive the nations at the corners of the earth. Gog and Magog, in order to gather them for battle, they are as numerous as the sands of the sea."[39] The text continues: "They marched up over the breadth of the earth and surrounded the camp of the saints and the beloved city. And fire came down from heaven and consumed them. And the Devil who had deceived them was thrown into a lake of fire and sulfur, where the beast and the false prophet were. And they will be tormented day and night forever and ever."[40]

Like in the Book of Daniel, the peoples of Gog and Magog will be warriors in the End Times. They will surround the city and the "camp of saints." Eventually, they will be defeated and cast into fire and torment.

In British legend, Gog and Magog were two mythological beasts captured and employed as porters at the gate of the royal palace of London's Guide Hall. The effigies of Gog and Magog have been replaced twice since they were erected during the reign of Henry V.

Revelation also adopted the idea of the "Son of Man." John the Divine uses the phrase several times in his text. Among these is Revelation 1:13: "And in the midst of the lamp stands I saw one like the Son of Man, clothed with a long robe, and with a golden sash across his chest."[41]

This reference in Revelation, and others at 1:7 and 14:14, are clearly related to Daniel 7:13, which tells us: "As I watched in the night visions, I saw one like a human being coming with the clouds of heaven. And he came to the Ancient One, and was present before him."[42]

The expression, "Son of Man" is also used by Saint Paul in 1 Thessalonians, where Paul tells us: "When they say, 'There is peace and security,' then sudden destruction will come upon them, as labor pains come upon a pregnant woman, and there will be no escape. But you beloved, are not in darkness for that day to surprise you like a thief."[43]

Here Paul seems to suggest that the End Times will come without warning, and that believers will be in better condition than those who do not believe.

The Old Testament uses the phrase "Son of Man" to refer to a particular human being (Ezekiel 2). The figure of the Son of Man appears in the pseudepigraphal *First Enoch*, and in chapters 37–71 of the *Similitudes of Enoch* where the phrase Son of Man is found sixteen times. In this text, the son of man is a preexistent divine being (48:2 and 62:7). He is chosen by the lord of spirits (46:3), and appears "on that day" to deliver the elect from persecution (62:7ff). On that day, he will remove rulers of the earth who have persecuted the people of the Lord (46:4–8). The rulers will suffer when they see the Son of Man sitting on his glory throne (62:2–5). Thus in the *Similitudes* the Son of Man is a heavenly figure who will come to save the righteous and to judge the evil world.

The phrase, "Son of Man" took on Messianic significance in early Christianity, primarily due to Jewish eschatology found in the book of Daniel in a vision "like a Son of Man," coming in the clouds. The title "Ancient One" or "Ancient of Days" are used three times in chapter seven of Revelation to refer to God. The expression "ancient of days" is used at Daniel 7:9, 7:13, and 7:22. In all three cases, the expression appears to refer to God, but at 7:13 the phrase is associated with the Son of Man: "I saw in the night visions, and behold with the clouds of heaven there came one like a son of man and he came to the Ancient of Days, and was presented before him."[44]

In Hebrew the expression "Son of Man" generally refers to an individual man from the genus man (Numbers 23:19 and Psalm 8:4–5, for example). In Psalm 80:17 the King of Israel is called the Son of Man whom God has raised up for Himself. Daniel uses the phrase to describe a personage he saw in a night vision. In the Old Testament, the term appears to refer to a messianic figure predictive of the Messiah.

The phrase is continued in the *Similitudes of Enoch*, which is the second part of *First Enoch*. The dominant themes throughout the work are eschatological ones. The central parable has caught the attention of scholars because of the Son of Man materials found there. The text reaches its peak in the third parable, where the author reveals the angels who guard the flood waters are about to release the water to the earth. Those who are sinners will meet their doom because they have "denied the name of the Lord of the Spirits."[45]

The seventh chapter of Daniel also gives us a vision of a great kingdom, the fourth kingdom on earth, which seems to begin shortly after Daniel's time (second century BCE.) It seems to be referring to the Roman Empire. It will come into existence and dominate the world in the first century CE. Daniel seems to imply that this fourth beast shall be the last world kingdom to appear on earth.

In Daniel's view, a "little horn" shall arise on the fourth beast, and it will exercise tremendous political power. In the Christian tradition this little horn of the fourth beast is often identified as the Anti-Christ. Chapter eleven of Daniel introduces another figure called the Willful King, who will exalt himself against God, will take himself the title of God. Thus, many also identify the Willful King with the Anti-Christ.

ANTI-CHRIST AND THESSALONIANS

One final passage related to the New Testament view of the Anti-Christ is found in 2 Thessalonians 2:3–12. Unlike many of the other books of the New Testament, Paul's letters to the Thessalonians can be dated with some precision. The famous Delphi inscription enables us to know that Gallio of Acts 18:12 became Roman proconsul of Achaia, whose capital was Corinth, in the summer of 51 CE. By that time, Paul had been in Corinth for 18 months (Acts 18:11). He must have arrived early in 50 CE. No time seems to have separated Paul's time in Corinth and Thessalonica. Therefore, we can date the two letters to the Thessalonians to late 50 CE.

In the modern period, the interpretation of 2 Thessalonians has proved to be much more controversial than I Thessalonians, chiefly because of three related problems. First, the letter's relationship to 1 Thessalonians has been the subject of considerable debate. Secondly, many scholars consistently have denied the Pauline authorship of 2 Thessalonians. And finally, the precise nature of the context of the letter has proven to be elusive among New Testament scholars. For our purposes, we shall assume the letter was written by Paul to a first century group of Christians. We will also assume that Paul was the author of 1 Thessalonians.

The elusive nature of the apocalyptic discourse of 2 Thessalonians 2:1–12 had made it fertile ground for exegetical speculation from the early Church Fathers on. Since the early Church saw this passage as prophetic, exegetes frequently tied the passage to historical circumstances of their own time. In addition to these historical circumstances exegetes have also attempted to identify various elements of the pericope. Chief among these elements are: (1) the identity of the "man of Lawlessness in 2:3; (2) the mention of the rebuilding of a Temple at 2:4; (3) the nature of the restraining force in 2:6; and (4) the discussion of non-believers in verses 7 to 12 of chapter two.

Paul's second letter to the Thessalonians, which seems to have been written very soon after the first, was written to clear up some difficulties concerning Paul's comments about the Second Coming in the first letter. If the readers were under the impression that Jesus' return is imminent, they must know that certain things have to happen first.

Paul begins the second letter to the Thessalonians by giving thanks for the converts' steadfastness in the face of persecution. They will be rewarded when Christ comes in glory, as their persecutors will be punished.

In the second chapter, Paul reveals that Jesus will not return until the Man of Sin is revealed. This phrase, "the Man of Sin," is a kind of Devil's messiah who, in the last days was expected to war on God and his saints. 2 Thess 2:6–7 mentions someone or something that is presently restraining him. This is most likely the Roman Empire.[46]

The apostle Paul when he declares the appearance of the Man of Sin, the opponent who rises against everything which contains good and God's service, will precede the coming of Christ (2 Thess 2:3–4) no doubt also thought in the first place of a pseudo-Messiah in personal recollection of the bitter opposition to the Gospel by Judaism filled with political Messianic thought (1 Thess 2:15).

For his picture of the Anti-Christ Paul no doubt took some traits from the description of Antiochus Epiphanes in the Book of Daniel, and from the Emperor Caligula in his own day, who had his image in the form of Jupiter erected in the Temple of Jerusalem. Paul's high conception of the superhuman virtues of Jesus is also reflected in his description of the Anti-Christ.

Some scholars make a number of connections among the "little horn" of chapters 7 and 8 of Daniel, Paul's "Man of Sin," and the beast of the book of Revelation. These three images are often seen as synonyms for the Anti-Christ, and that may be what Paul has in mind in his description in 2 Thessalonians.

Most scholars see a connection between the Man of Sin of 2 Thessalonians 2 and the "little horn" of chapter seven of Daniel. They also see a connection between one or more of the beasts in Revelation 13, and the "Great Harlot" and "Babylon" in Revelation 17 and 18. Although most scholars see connections among these elements, they often disagree on how they are related.

The Pauline "Day of the Lord," will be preceded by a "revolt" and the revelation of "the Man of Sin." The latter will sit in the Temple of God, showing himself as if he were God. He will work signs and wonders by the power of Satan. He will seduce those who do not receive the love of truth, so that they might be saved. But the Lord God will kill him with the breath of his mouth, and the brightness of his coming.

In Paul's view, then, the "Day of the Lord" will be preceded by "the Man of Sin," known in the Johannine epistles as the Anti-Christ. The "Man of Sin" is preceded by a "revolt." The major impediment to the Second Coming is the Roman Empire that now restrains the "Man of Sin."

In Paul's view of the Anti-Christ he merely follows a Jewish tradition that began in the imagery of the prophets Ezekiel and Daniel. But unlike the images in John's epistles and Revelation, where the Emperor Nero was thought to be the Anti-Christ, in Paul, the Anti-Christ has no apparent political significance.

The gospel of John, like the Epistles of John, Revelation, and Matthew and Luke, sees the coming of false prophets as a sign of the end times. John 5:43 tells us: "I have come in my Father's name, and you do not accept me. If another comes in his own name, you will accept him."[47]

From all this we are able to understand how, in the Epistles of John, the Anti-Christ is connected to false teachings (1 John 2:18, 22; 4:3; 2 John 7), and in the appearance of false teachings in general, are one of the crowning points of the end of the world and the second coming.

This notion of false prophets and deceivers is also found in 2 John 7, where John writes, "For many deceivers are entered into the world, who confess not that Jesus Christ has come in the flesh. This is a deceiver and an Anti-Christ."[48] Many years earlier Jesus had warned John and the other disciples to "Take heed that no man deceive you. For many shall come in my name saying, 'I am Christ' [pretending to preach or act by Christ's authority] and shall deceive many—including true Christians."[49]

The apostle Paul also warns of "false apostles" and deceitful workers" (2 Corinthians 11:13–15), disguised as "ministers of righteousness," who went about deceiving Christians into believing "another gospel." (Galatians 1:6–9 and Acts 20:28–31.) These false teachers and false brethren—anti-Christs—were "tares among wheat," (Matthew 13:24–30, and verses 36–42). They sounded sincere and godly, but were far from real Christians. These false Christians were hard to discern from the real thing, which made it easy for them to rise to leadership positions. From there, they infected the Church with false doctrines, deceiving many. As we shall see, these New Testament images of "false prophets," false Messiahs," and "false brethren" who are really Anti-Christs, play a key role in subsequent Christian scholarship on the Anti-Christ legend.

THE ANTI-CHRIST AND 2 CORINTHIANS

Of all of Paul's letters, the second letter to the Corinthians is as close as Paul comes to an autobiography. Paul's life is offered with none of the jagged edges filled in. The letter is an authentic, uncensored, and sometimes bewildering account of Paul's life. Anyone who reads 2 Corinthians will notice an abrupt change that comes over the letter after the ninth chapter. Until then, Paul's tone has been one of thankfulness and reconciliation. But in chapter ten this attitude suddenly changes to a fierce defense of Paul's work, and a denouncing "false apostles," who Paul believed were forces of the Devil.

On the other hand, 2 Corinthians is a subtle text full of language that is an exegetical nightmare. Paul uses a variety of literary and rhetorical strategies, in his attempt to establish the foundations of his faith. From 2 Corinthians, we derive the idea of the "old" and "new" covenants; and Saint Augustine devoted an entire book to 2 Corinthians 12:1–9. Chief concerns for our purposes in 2 Corinthians are what we might call "Paul the Visionary," specifically his revelation in 2 Corinthians 12. Also of interest for our purposes is 2 Corinthians 6:15, and its use of the Beliar figure.

In 2 Corinthians 12:1–12, Paul refers to the "signs of a true apostle," and apologizes to the Corinthians for not making these signs more clearly. Again, Paul seems to be worrying about "false apostles" that may try to deceive the faithful.

One other passage in Saint Paul is sometimes used in connection to discussions of the Anti-Christ is 2 Corinthians 6:15. The Revised Standard Version translates the verse this way: "What agreement does Christ have with Beliar? What does a believer share with an unbeliever?"[50]

The Hebrew word Belial or Beliar is the name of a Devil in many apocryphal Jewish documents. In the "War of the Sons of Light and Sons of Darkness," a text found among the Dead Sea Scrolls, Belial is the leader of the Sons of Darkness: "But for the corruption that have made Belial, an angel of hostility. All his dominions are in darkness, and his purpose is to bring about wickedness and guilt. All the spirits associated with him are angels of destruction."[51]

Some exegetes suggest that the name Beliar comes from Psalm 18:4–5: "The cords of death encompass me, the torrents of perdition assailed me. The cords of Sheol entangle me, the snares of death confronted me."[52]

The rivers of Belial are spoken of throughout apocryphal literature. The figure appears to have been a god of the underworld, and later becomes a name that plays a role in the Anti-Christ tradition. In the *Ascension of Moses*, we get a description of the beginning of the End Times (10:1), where "then will God's rule be made manifest over all his creatures, and then will the Devil have an end."[53]

Belial, it should be clear, is connected to the fallen angel's story, and was thought to be the chief of the bad angels against Michael and his minions. The figure also appears in the apocryphal "Testament of the Twelve Patriarchs," where humans must choose between God and the forces of Belial. In this text, we get the notion that when the Messiah comes, he will do battle with Belial and his angels. In some early circles of Jewish Apocalyptic and early Christianity, Belial was claimed to be the Messiah. This led some first century Christians to label him the Anti-Christ.

In other early Christian association Belial was used as a synonym for Satan or Lucifer. Throughout Christian history, the name has been used for both purposes, as a synonym for the Devil, and as a name for the Anti-Christ.

Belial played a heavy role in the Christian apocrypha and pseudepigraphia. He appears in *Jubilees*, where uncircumcised heathens are called "sons of Belial," and in a number of other texts as well. Belial is mentioned in the fragments of a Zadokite work, *The Damascus Document*, which says that at the time of the Anti-Christ, "Belial shall be let loose against Israel, as God has spoken through the prophet Isaiah" (6:9).[54] The fragment also speaks of the "three nets of Belial," which stand for wealth, fornication, pollution of the sanctuary (6:10–11).[55]

In the Damascus Document, Belial is sometimes presented as a leader of the fallen angels, a rebel, much like Mastema, and sometimes as an agent of Divine punishment. The fragments also say that anyone who is ruled by Belial, and who speaks of rebellion, should be condemned as wizards and fortune-tellers, another element frequently identified with the Anti-Christ in early Christianity.

In another non-canonical work, *the Martyrdom of Isaiah*, Belial is depicted as an angel of lawlessness, and the ruler of the world (2:4). Belial also has a significant role in the *Ascension of Isaiah*. *The Ascension of Isaiah* is a composite work which falls into two parts. Chapters 1–5 are known as *The Martyrdom of Isaiah*, with chapters six through eleven a vision by the prophet. Chapter 3:13 to 4:22 is sometimes called the "Testament of

The Idea of the Anti-Christ in the New Testament

Hezekiah." Apart from these three main parts, there have been a number of additions and insertions that can be attributed to a final redactor.[56] The image of Belial appears in all three sources. He is the leader of the fallen angels, and a deceiver in the ways of the Lord.

In the history of the West, Belial is sometimes associated with the Anti-Christ in particular and the demonic in general. In early Christianity, the name Belial is sometimes associated with Emperor Nero who would return as the Anti-Christ. Belial is mentioned in Walter Scott's *Ivanhoe*, in Victor Hugo's *The Infernal Ambassador to Turkey*, in Aldous Huxley's *Ape and Essence*, in Dumas Alexandre's *The Three Musketeers*, and in Book II of Milton's *Paradise Lost*. In Milton's account, Belial realizes the war against heaven has been lost, and now hopes that God will forgive him, and allow him to return to heaven.

It appears that Paul was familiar with early Christian beliefs about the Anti-Christ. It is just as clear that Paul's initial readers were also familiar with the idea. He may or may not have identified the Anti-Christ with Belial, and he suggests that the coming of the Anti-Christ will be preceded by particular events. Paul gives three stages of the development of his doctrine of Last Things—the leaven of inequity, a great apostasy, and the arrival of the Man of Sin.

PAUL'S USE OF THE WORD *APOCALYPSIS*

Saint Paul uses the words *apocalypsis* and *apocalypto* nineteen times in the seven generally recognized authentic letters of Paul. In each of eight of these references, Paul makes the claim that he has received a revelation directly from God the Spirit, or from Jesus Christ. In the other eleven examples, while these words may refer to revelations, Paul sometimes says it will occur in the future, as in Romans 8:18; sometimes Paul seems to suggest it is already happening in a metaphorical sense in the here and now, as in Romans 1:17–18. On other occasions, Paul seems to use these terms purely hypothetically. Consider 1 Corinthians 14–6 and 26, for example: "Now brothers and sisters, if I come to you speaking in tongues, how will I benefit you unless I speak to you in some revelation or knowledge, or prophecy, or teaching?"[57] "What should be done then, my friends? When you come together each one has a hymn, a lesson, a revelation, a tongue, or an interpretation. Let all things be done for building up."[58]

The eight instances where Paul refers to his own experiences or revelation are at Galatians 1:12; 1:16; 2:21; 3:23; 1 Corinthians 21:1; 2 Corinthians 12:7; and Romans 16:25. Of the four from Galatians, in one (1:12) he claims it came to him directly through revelation. In two (1:16 and 2:23), Paul uses different language to convey his vision. ("His son" and "faith.") In the fourth one (2:2), Paul claims his trip to Jerusalem was taken by "revelation."

In the three citations from Corinthians, they speak in general terms about the revelations and visions that Paul has had. In the citation from the final chapter of Romans (16:25), Paul's experience is a bit more mysterious. But if we compare 16:25 to 1:5, it is clear that the revelation referred to is Paul's call to "bring about the obedience of faith in all the Gentiles." Thus, we might conclude that when Paul uses the words *apocalypsis* and *apocalypto*, when speaking of his own experience, have nothing to do with eschatology.

THE ANTI-CHRIST AND FALSE PROPHETS

A number of passages in the New Testament have been used over the centuries to show a connection between the Anti-Christ and false prophets. This material is as old as Deuteronomy 18:20–21 that tells us: "But the prophet who presumes to speak a word in my name which I have not commanded him to speak, or who speaks in the name of other gods, that same prophet shall die."[59]

Second Peter 2:1 speaks of "false teachers among you who will secretly introduce destructive heresies," even denying the sovereignty of God, "will have swift destruction brought on them."[60] Romans 16:17 urges us to: "Brothers and sisters, to keep an eye on those who cause dissensions and offenses, in opposition to the teaching that you have learned; avoid them."[61]

These passages and many others have been used in the history of Christian exegeses as evidence for the coming of the Anti-Christ, as well as the Final Enemy being a deceiver and a false teacher. Matthew 7:15 has been used for similar purposes. The text tells us that both good and bad people are known by their deeds.[62]

In the Gospel of John 5:43, Jesus tells us: "I have come in my Father's name, and you do not accept me; If another comes in his own name, you will accept him."[63]

These and many other pericopes are often tied to I John 2, where 2:22 talks of "men who will lead you astray,"[64] and II John 4:1–3 that tells us to: "Do you believe in every spirit but test the spirits to see whether they are from God, because many false prophets have gone out into the world."[65]

In Acts of the Apostles 20:29–30, Paul tells us: "I know that after I have gone, savage wolves will come among you, not sparing the flock. Some will even come from your own group distorting the truth in order to entice disciples to follow them."[66]

False prophets are also spoken of in a number of other passages in the New Testament. And many of those passages have often been linked to the Anti-Christ in the history of Christian interpretation.

In the gospel of Luke, Jesus refers to the idea of false prophets in the Old Testament: "Woe to you when all men speak well of you, for that is how their fathers treated the false prophets."[67]

In Acts, Paul and Barnabus encounter a false prophet named Elymas Bar-Jesus, on the island of Cyprus. Acts 13:6–12 tells us:

> They traveled through the whole island until they came to Pasphos. There they met a Jewish sorcerer and false prophet named Bar-Jesus, who was an attendant of the proconsul, Sergius Paulus. The proconsul, an intelligent man, sent for Barnabus and Saul because he wanted to hear the word of God. But Elymas the sorcerer (for that is what his name means) opposed them and tried to turn the proconsul from the faith. Then Saul, who was called Paul, filled with the Holy Spirit, looking straight at Elymas and said, "You are a child of the Devil and an enemy of all that is right. You are full of all kinds of deceit and trickery. Will you never stop perverting the right ways of the Lord? Now the hand of the Lord is against you. You are going to be blind, and for a time you will be unable to see the light of the sun."
>
> Immediately mist and darkness came over him, and he groped about, seeking someone to lead him by the hand. When the proconsul saw what had happened, he believed, for he was amazed at the teaching about the Lord.[68]

ANTI-CHRIST AND THE TRIBE OF DAN

One early Christian tradition about the Anti-Christ suggests that the Final Enemy will be from the tribe of Dan, and that his followers will be Jews. This claim in the early Church was supported by two Biblical passages. The first of these is Genesis 49:17, that refers to Dan "shall be a serpent, a viper that bites the horse's heels."[69] This passage may refer to the fact that the tribe of Dan was historically believed to be one that fell into idolatry during Biblical times, leading members of the other eleven tribes into idolatry as well.

In Revelation 7:1–8 we get a description of eleven of the tribes of Israel. The tribe that is missing is Dan. It seems to suggest that none of the 144,000 Jewish evangelists shall come from the tribe of Dan. There are, however, other lists of the tribes of Israel where some of the twelve are missing, so that may be what is the case in chapter seven of Revelation as well.

The notion that the Anti-Christ and his followers will be of Jewish descent is often based in the early Church on Daniel 11:37. This verse in the Hebrew Old Testament looks this way: "He shall pay no respect to the gods of his ancestors, or to the one beloved by women; he shall pay no respect to any other god, for he shall consider himself greater than all."[70] The following verse tells us: "He shall honor the god of fortresses instead of these, a god whom his ancestors did not know, he shall honor with gold and silver, with precious stones and costly gifts."[71]

In the early Church these verses in Daniel were taken to mean that the Anti-Christ will not worship the God of Israel, and that he will use bribery to persuade believers to follow him. Some exegetes in the early Church also tie these verses to John 5:43 that seem to suggest that the Anti-Christ may be accepted as the long-awaited Jewish Messiah.

Both Irenaeus' *Against Heresies* and Hippolytus' "On Christ and Anti-Christ," held of tradition that Anti-Christ will be a Jew, and that he will come from the tribe of Dan. Irenaeus bases his judgment on Jeremiah 8:16, the Hebrew of which goes like this: "The snorting of their horses is heard from Dan; at the sound of the neighing of their stallions the whole land quakes."[72]

Irenaeus remarks that Dan is, in view of this tradition, not in the Apocalypse (Rev 7:5–7) among the 144,000 saved ones of the twelve tribes.[73] For Irenaeus, Dan became a symbol of wrong-doing. He [Dan] was placed in the north (Num 2:25) because, as Irenaeus says, "This is a region of darkness and evil."[74] As Irenaeus puts it:

> And Jeremiah does not merely point out his [Anti-Christ] sudden coming, but he even indicates the tribe from which he will come where he says, "We shall hear the voices of this swift horses from Dan; the whole earth shall be moved by the voice of the neighing of his galloping horses; he shall also come and devour the earth, and the fullness thereof, the city also, and they will dwell therein." This too is the reason that this tribe is not reckoned in the Apocalypse along with those which are saved.[75]

Bousset also speaks on the idea of the Anti-Christ coming from the tribe of Dan. He tells us: "Nevertheless the opinion that the Anti-Christ is to come from Dan occurs also in the Testament of the Twelve Patriarchs, a document probably of Jewish origin. Unfortunately the text is here so corrupt that no definite conclusion can be arrived at."[76]

Bousset suggests that the belief that the Anti-Christ shall come from the tribe of Dan is of Jewish origins. It may well have been a common Jewish belief around the time of the writing of the Book of Daniel.

THE ANTI-CHRIST IN THE POST-GOSPELS PERIOD

James J. L. Ratton describes the mood of second century Christianity toward the Anti-Christ: "At the beginning of the second century the Churches of the chief cities of Hellenized Asia exercised a great influence on the Christianity of the East."[77] Ratton goes on to identify the "Greek word *Anti-Christos* with the Beliar tradition of the Jews." This "emphasized the antagonism of the Destroyer against Christ to the exclusion of his predicted function as the Destroyer of the city and the Holy Place."[78] Ratton goes on to mention Polycarp and Irenaeus as the first post-biblical writers to treat the Anti-Christ.

A brief remark should be made about a number of second century sources that mention the word *Anti-Christos*. The chief one of these is a mentioning of the term in Polycarp's *Letters to the Philippians*. The reference comes at 7:1 of the letter, which is generally dated around 135 CE. Chapter seven of this letter contains three condemnations of heretics that are called "Anti-Christ," "from the devil," and the "first-born of Satan." This tradition may in fact be the source of the later Christian view that the Anti-Christ shall be a son of Satan.

Whether or not this is true, it is clear the Polycarp quotes 1 John 4:2–3 directly, when he speaks of "anyone, then, who does not confess that Jesus Christ has come in the flesh, is an Anti-Christ."[79]

It is also clear from Polycarp's letter shared with First John that the Anti-Christ is to make an eschatological appearance as a metaphysical being, and that this being was expected to be an opponent of Christ that precedes that parousia. This tradition may well be a Christianization of the Jewish tradition of the eschatological coming of Beliar (or Belial).

The author(s) of First and Second John use(s) it is to describe and legitimize the situation of the Johannine community. By interpreting the conflict this way, as a splitting of the community in the coming of the Anti-Christ, the author(s) represent(s) this conflict as being planned by God, and as proof for the nearness of the End Times.

At any rate, it is clear that Polycarp shares a number of characteristics and elements of the Anti-Christ with judgments about the Final Enemy that are made in materials from the New Testament. The next mention of the word *Anti-Christos* appearing in the Christian tradition comes with Irenaeus, the second/third century bishop of Lyons. We explore Irenaeus' view, as well as a number of other Church Fathers, in the next chapter of this study.

Ratton goes on to describe the contribution of Irenaeus to the Anti-Christ tradition in the Roman Church: "The third mention of Anti-Christ is in the book of Saint Irenaeus, *Against Heresies*. But the exposition of the teaching of Irenaeus regarding Anti-Christ requires a chapter to itself. Whether directly or indirectly all writers on Anti-Christ have drawn their inspiration from St. Irenaeus. All their arguments are found in his writings."[80] Ratton's estimation of Irenaeus' contribution is right on the money. As we shall see in the next chapter, he is the most important early patristic thinker on the Christian idea of the Anti-Christ.

CONCLUSIONS

In this second chapter, we have attempted to accomplish several things. First, we talked about the apocalyptic language of Mark 13, Luke 21, and Matthew 24, and the influence the book of Daniel may have had on these texts. Second, we have described and discussed the various places in the New Testament texts where the Anti-Christ is explicitly mentioned. Chief among these are 1 John 2:18 and 22, 1 John 4:3, and 2 John 7. We also have discussed a number of other New Testament passages that may be connected to the early Christian idea of the Anti-Christ. Among these texts are various passages in the book of Revelation, as well as a discussion by Paul in 2 Thessalonians, and possibly a mention in 2 Corinthians 6:15.

What we have learned from these passages are at least five things. First, the writer of John's epistles had an early view of the nature and activities of the Anti-Christ. Second, the same can be said for Saint Paul, as well as his initial readers of 2 Thessalonians. Third, New Testament writers on apocalyptic materials borrowed heavily from the book of Daniel as well as from chapters 38 and 39 of Ezekiel. Fourth, many of the earliest writers on the idea of the Anti-Christ identified him with the Emperor Nero. And finally, many of the New Testament writers identified the figure of the Anti-Christ with terms that appear in the Old Testament, like Son of Man, and Desolation of Abomination, as well as Man of Perdition, Gog and Magog, and the idea of various false prophets.

Along the way, we have made a number of other observations in this chapter about the meaning of the two beasts in Revelation and the significance of the number 666. We also have made some mythological connections between the Babylonian and Canaanite myths, and early Jewish apocalypses discussed in chapter one, and traces of these texts to be found in the New Testament. In chapter three, we take up the image of the Anti-Christ as it developed in the first several centuries of Christianity. As we shall see, there are some new elements to the Anti-Christ legend to go along with what we have seen so far in the first two chapters of this work.

In this chapter, we have shown that the prophecies of the Book of Daniel, the Babylonian dragon myth, elements from Zoroastrianism, and a man to come full of Satanic might, combined to provide for the early Church two solutions to vexing theological issues—the origins and overthrow of evil and the problem of theodicy.

NOTES

1. Wilhelm Bousset, *Der Anti-Christ* (Göttingen: Vandenhoeck & Rup-recht, 1895.)
2. For more on New Testament apocalyptic literature, see Paul D. Hanson, *The Dawn of Apocalyptic: The Historical and Sociological Roots of Jewish Apocalyptic Eschatology* (Philadelphia: Fortress, 1975) revised edition in 1979; I have also consulted the following in completing this section of chapter two of this work: "Gospels (Apocryphal)" in *Dictionary of Jesus and the Gospels*, edited by J. B. Green and S. McNight (Downers Grove, IL: InterVarsity, 1992)

286–91; "Apocryphal Pauline Literature," in *Dictionary of Paul and His Letters*, edited by G. F. Hawthorne and R. P. Martin (Downers Grove, IL: InterVarsity, 1993) 35–37; and "Apocryphal and Pseudepigraphal Literature," in *Dictionary of the Later New Testament and its Development* edited by R. P. Martin and P. H. Davis. (Downers Grove, IL: InterVarsity, 1997) 68–73.

3. Mark 13:1–2 (RSV). In addition to these two small apocalypses, there is a third in the New Testament at Luke 21. This chapter also foretells the destruction of the Temple (verses 5 and 6), saying about the End Times (verses 7 to 11), foretelling of the prosecution of the disciples (verses 12 to 19), the desolation of Jerusalem (verses 20–24), and the coming of the Son of Man (verses 25–28). In the construction of this chapter, I have used the following sources: Wayne Gruden, *The Gift of Prophecy in the New Testament and Today* (London: Crossway, 2000.); Robert L. Thomas, *The Mater's Perspective on Biblical Prophecy* (Grand Rapids: Kregel, 2002.); David Hunt, *A Cup of Trembling: Jerusalem and Bible Prophecy* (Eugene, OR: Harvest, 1995); Mark Hitchcock, *The Complete Book of Bible Prophecy* (Wheaton, IL: Tyndale); and Michael Hoggard, *By Divine Order: Scripture, Numerics, and Bible Prophecy* (Oklahoma City: Hearthstone, 2000.)
4. Mark 12:5–8.
5. Mark 12:13.
6. Mark 12:14–23.
7. Mark 12:24–27.
8. Mark 12:34–37.
9. Mark 13:6 (RSV).
10. Mark 13:21–22 (RSV).
11. Luke 21:8 (RSV).
12. 1 John 2:18.
13. 1 John 4:3.
14. 1 John 2:22.
15. 2 John 7.
16. 1 John 4:3.
17. 1 John 2:26–27. (RSV).
18. 2 Thessalonians 2: 3–10 (author's trans.).
19. John Dominic Crossan and Jonathan L. Reed, *In Search of Paul* (San Francisco: HarperCollins, 2004) 171–72.
20. Revelation.
21. Bernard McGinn, *Anti-Christ: Two Thousand Years of the Human Fascination with Evil* (New York: Harper, 1994) 51.
22. Ibid.

23. Revelation 12:9 (RSV).
24. Revelation 12:3–6 (RSV).
25. Revelation 12:3–6.
26. Revelation 12:7–9.
27. Daniel 7:2–8.
28. Revelation 13:1–3.
29. Quoted in L. J. L. Peerbolte, *The Antecedents of Anti-Christ*, 144.
30. Ibid.
31. Revelation 13:11–18.
32. 1 Kings 19:14.
33. Ezra 2:13.
34. Revelation 17.
35. Revelation 17:4–5 (RSV).
36. Revelation 17:12 (RSV).
37. Revelation 17:18 (RSV).
38. Revelation 20:7–8.
39. Revelation 20:7–8 (RSV).
40. Ibid., 20:9–10.
41. Revelation 1:13.
42. Daniel 7:13.
43. 1 Thessalonians 5:3–5 (RSV).
44. Daniel 7:13 (author's trans.).
45. Larry R. Helyer, *Exploring Jewish Literature of the Second Temple Period* (Downers Grove, IL: InterVarsity, 2002) 384.
46. In addition to the translation "Man of Sin," he is also described by some translators as "Man of Lawlessness." 2 Thessalonians 2:3 uses the Greek *harmartia*, which is the New Testament's most common word for "sin." The Greek at 2 Thessalonians 2:7 is *anomea*, which primarily refers to a violation of the law. The Greek of 2 Thessalonians 2:8 refers to the *anomas*, those who are not subject to God's laws. Thus, there are many variations on how to translate 2 Thessalonians 2.
47. John 5:43.
48. 2 John 7.
49. Matthew 24:4–5.
50. 2 Corinthians 6:15.
51. "War of the Sons of Light and Sons of Darkness," in R. H. Charles, *The Apocrypha and Pseudepigraphia of the Old Testament* (Oxford: Clarendon

Press, 1913). This text, which was discovered with the Dead Sea Scrolls, is also known as the "War Rule,: "The Rule of War," and "The War Scroll." It was found in Cave IV, and is known as 4Q 491.

52. Psalm 18:4-5 (author's translation).
53. A. F. Ide, *Moses: The Making of Myth and Law*. (London: Monument Press, 1992) p. 9.
54. "The Damascus Document," was also found among the Dead Sea Scrolls. It is designated as 4Q266-273.
55. Ibid. The Damascus Document is a collection of rules and instructions reflecting the practices of a sectarian Jewish community. In 1896, Talmud scholar, Solomon Schechter, found some fragments of a document which later were seen as part of the "Damascus Document." For more on this manuscript, see the *Damascus Document Reconsidered* Edited by M. Broshi (Jerusalem, 1992.) Also see C. Rabin, *The Zadokite Documents* (Oxford: Oxford University Press, 1958).
56. "Martyrdom of Isaiah," 2:4; R. H. Charles, *The Apocrypha and Pseud-epigraphia of the Old Testament* (Oxford: Clarendon, 1913). The "Ascension of Isaiah," is an pseudepigraphical Old Testament book. It is usually dated in the latter half of the second century CE.
57. 1 Corinthians 14:6 (RSV).
58. 1 Corinthians 14:26 (RSV).
59. Deuteronomy 18:20-21 (author's trans.).
60. 2 Peter 2:1 (RSV).
61. Romans 16:17 (RSV).
62. Matthew 7:15 (RSV).
63. John 5:43 (RSV).
64. 2 John 2:22 (RSV).
65. 2 John 4:1-3 (RSV).
66. Acts 20:29-30 (RSV).
67. Luke 6:26 (NIV).
68. Acts 13:6-12 (NIV).
69. Genesis 49:17 (author's trans.).
70. Daniel 11:37 (RSV).
71. Daniel 11:38. (RSV).
72. Jeremiah 8:16 (author's translation).
73. Irenaeus, *Against Heresies*, Book V, chapter 30.
74. Ibid.
75. Ibid.

76. Wilhelm Bousset, *The Anti-Christ Legend*. (London: Hutchinson and Company, 1896) p. 158.
77. James J. L. Ratton, *Anti-Christ: An Historical Review*, p. 107.
78. Ibid.
79. L. J. Lietaert Peerbolte, *The Antecedents of Anti-Christ*. (Leiden: Brill, 1996) 112.
80. James J. L Ratton, *Anti-Christ: An Historical Review*, 114.

3

The Anti-Christ in the Early Church Fathers

> The fathers spoke of the Anti-Christ primarily as the eschatological end-time figure who would immediately precede Christ's return. That is, patristic literature presents a composite and complex figure of the Anti-Christ.
>
> —William Weinrich, "Anti-Christ in the Early Church"

> And each person ought to question his own conscience, whether he is the Anti-Christ. For in Latin, an Anti-Christ is [a person who is] contrary to Christ.
>
> —Saint Augustine, *Tractates on the Epistles of John*

> We find it written regarding Anti-Christ . . . that Dan is a lion's whelp, and he shall leap from Bashan.
>
> —Hippolytus "The Anti-Christ"

INTRODUCTION

Among figures in the early church, a number of references to the Anti-Christ can be found in the record of the first five centuries of Christianity. In this chapter, we take a close look at two apocryphal works, the *Epistle of Barbabus* and the *Apocalypse of Peter*, which mention the idea of the Anti-Christ. In a second section of this third chapter, we look at Polycarp's "Epistle to the Phillipians" and Justin Martyr's *Dialogue With Trypho*, which also provide some insights on the early Christian doctrine of the Anti-Christ.

In the main section of this chapter, we explore the works of Irenaeus (second and third centuries CE), Hippolytus (second and third centuries CE), Cyril of Jerusalem (fourth century CE), Jerome, and Augustine that deal with the Anti-Christ. As we shall see, of these figures, Irenaeus has the fullest treatment of the Anti-Christ legend.

We also deal in this chapter with other Christian thinkers from the first to the fifth centuries who have written on or discussed the Anti-Christ in the first five centuries of the Church. Among these thinkers are Cyril of Jerusalem, Cyprian, and Jerome.

In a final section of this chapter, we shall explore the comments of a number of thinkers from the Dark Ages on the idea of the Anti-Christ. Among these thinkers are Gregory the Great and John of Damascus.

THE ANTI-CHRIST IN APOCRYPHAL LITERATURE

The earliest post-biblical account of the Anti-Christ can be found in the *Didache*, also known as the *Doctrine of the Twelve Apostles*. It is most likely a first-century work, and may have been completed in Rome. The *Didache* is mentioned by Eusebius, and is divided into three parts. The first part gives a description of the proper "Way of Life," along with a list of vices to be avoided. The second part deals mostly with the sacraments of Baptism and the Eucharist. The third part speaks of teachers or doctors (*didaskaloi*). At the end of part three, the *Didache* speaks of "false prophets" and the Anti-Christ. Part three of the *Didache* has a number of similarities with the little apocalypses of Mark 13 and Matthew 24. Chapter 16:3–4 of the *Didache* suggests that "In the last days, the false prophets and corrupters will be multiplied,... and then shall appear the Deceiver of the World as the son of man."[1] Like Matthew 24, the *Didache* offers three signs of the coming of the end times. (Matthew 24:30–31)

Chapter 16 of the *Didache,* also describes the coming of the end of the world:

> Then shall appear the world deceiver as the Son of God, and shall do signs and wonders, and the earth shall be delivered into his hands ... but those who endure in their faith shall be saved from under the curse itself. And then shall appear the signs of the truth; first, the sign of the outspreading in heaven; then, the sound of the trumpet; and third, the resurrection of the dead; yet not of all, but as it is said: The Lord shall come and all His saints with Him. Then shall the world see the Lord coming upon the clouds of heaven.[2]

The beginning of chapter 16 of the *Didache* also refers to the Anti-Christ:

> The whole time of your faith will not profit you unless you are made complete in the last times. For in the last days false prophets and corrupters shall be multiplied, and sheep shall be turned into wolves... and then shall the deceiver of the world appear, pretending to be the Son of God. And He shall do signs and wonders, and the earth shall be delivered into his hands.[3]

The final chapter of the *Didache* is entirely about end-time teaching. Like John and Paul, and many who will follow them, the author of the *Didache* tells us:

> For in the last days false prophets and seducers shall be multiplied, and the sheep shall be turned into wolves, and love shall be turned to hate; and because iniquity abounds, they shall hate each other, and persecute each other, and deliver each other up; and then shall the Deceiver of the world appear as the Son of God, and shall do signs and wonders, and the earth shall be delivered into his hands.[4]

The author of this first-century document is most likely referring to the Anti-Christ, as well as to the often held beliefs in the first few centuries of Christianity that the Anti-Christ may be mistaken for Christ, and that he will perform miracles like those of Christ. This document also refers to the common view that the Anti-Christ will practice deception.

A second early Christian work that mentions the Anti-Christ is the *Epistle of Barnabus*, a Greek document from the mid-second century CE. The *Epistle of Barnabus* employs a deeply allegorical method of interpretation, suggesting an Alexandrian author. Indeed, the letter is mentioned by both Clement and Origin around the year 200 CE. Speaking of the *Epistle of Barnabus*, McGinn writes, "this product of Alexandrian Christian also mentions Anti-Christ beliefs."[5]

The *Epistle of Barnabus* also speaks of the fourth beast in the Book of Daniel and suggests that it may be connected to the Anti-Christ. It speaks of a time when the Anti-Christ will rise up.

The *Apocalypse of Peter*, another second-century Christian work, describes a vision that Peter has in heaven. In the course of his narrative, Peter describes an angel: "And he showed me in his right hand the souls of all men. And on the palm of his right hand the image of that which shall be accomplished at the last day."[6]

This mark described by Peter may be the mark of the beast described in Revelation (13:18; 16:2; and 19:20). *The Apocalypse* also supplies a vision of Hell, where blasphemers are hung by their tongues, women who wear make-up are hung by their hair over a bubbling fire, and women who have had abortions are set in a lake formed from the blood and gore of the sins of the unworthy.

The *Apocalypse of Elijah* is another anonymous apocryphal work. It offers a revelation given by an angel of God. Most scholars date this text around the year 200. It has five parts. Part III tells of the arrival of the son of lawlessness, the Anti-Christ. It describes the Anti-Christ in great detail. The Anti-Christ is skinny legged, his eye brows reach down to his ears, and he is bald with a tuft of grey hair at the front. Part V of the *Apocalypse of Elijah* gives a description of the end of the world, including the destruction of the man of lawlessness/Anti-Christ.

A mid-second-century text, *The Shepard of Hermas* also makes a number of references to the end of the world. In the Fourth Vision, chapter one, the shepard walks down a road and encounters a horrifying beast that later thinkers have identified with the Anti-Christ. In chapter two of the *Shepard of Hermas*, after passing the beast, the shepard meets a woman who explains what has just occurred. She links the experience with the encountering of the Anti-Christ.[7]

First Maccabees is a deutero-canonical book of the Book of Maccabees, written by a Jewish writer around 100 BCE, after the restoration of an independent Jewish state. The book is included in the Roman Catholic and Eastern Orthodox canons. Some Protestant churches regard it as historically useful, though not canonical.

First Maccabees 14:14 alludes to a group of renegade Jews who were supporters of the Seleucid Empire. The text tells us: "He gave help to all the humble among his people: he sought out the law and did away with all the renegades and outlaws."[8]

In the history of the early Church this verse was sometimes used as an apocryphal passage that refers to the Anti-Christ.

THE ANTI-CHRIST IN FIRST AND SECOND CENTURIES OF CHRISTIANITY

Something related to the Christian Anti-Christ legend can also be seen in an apocryphal text known as the *Tiburtine Sibyl*. The text was written around 380 BCE. The text purports to prophesy, after the fact, the arrival of a Christian Emperor. The text tells us: "Then will arise a king of the Greeks whose name is Constans. He will be a king of the Romans and the Greeks. He will be tall of stature, of handsome appearance with shining face, and well put together in all parts of his body."[9]

This document also suggests that "At the time the Prince of Inequity who will be called Anti-Christ will arise from the tribe of Dan."[10] Some early Christians derived the notion that the Anti-Christ shall be a Jew from a verse in the Book of Daniel: "He shall honor the God of fortresses instead of these; a god whom his fathers did not know, he shall honor with gold and silver, with precious stones and costly gifts."[11]

Some Medieval Christians believed that this passage from the *Tiburtine Sibyl* indicates that the Anti-Christ may be a Moslem. The name Constans could refer to the Emperor Constantine or to the city of Constantinople, and thus the Anti-Christ may refer to a Turkish leader.

Two passages in the *Sibylline Oracles* present Beliar as an eschatological opponent who will appear in the last day. One of these passages not only describes Beliar, but it also speaks of an eschatological appearance of false prophets. The text tells us this:

> But whenever this sign appears throughout the world, Children born with grey temples from birth, afflictions of men, famines, pestilence, and wars, change of times, lamentations, many tears alas, how many people's children in the countries will feed on their parents with piteous lamentations. They will place their flesh in cloaks and bury them in the ground, mother of peoples, defiled with blood and dust. O very wretched dread evildoers of the last generation, infantile, who do not understand that when the species of females does not give birth, the harvest of articulate men has come. The gathering together is near when some deceivers in place of prophets, approach, speaking on earth. Beliar will also come and do many signs for men. Then indeed there will be confusion of holy chosen and faithful men, and there will be a plundering of these and of the Hebrews. A terrible wrath will come upon them when a people of ten tribes will come from the east to seek the people which the shoot of Assyria destroyed, of their fellow Hebrews. Nations will perish after these things.[12]

Beliar also features prominently in another passage:

> Then Beliar will come from the Sebastenoi and he will raise up the height of the mountains, he will raise up the sea the great fiery sun and shining moon, and he will raise up the dead, and perform many signs for me. But they will not be effective in him. But he

will, indeed, also lead men astray, and he will lead astray many faithful, chosen Hebrews and also other lawless men who have not yet listened to the word of God. But whenever the threat of the great God draws nigh and a burning power comes through the sea to land, it will also burn Beliar and all overbearing men, as many as put faith in him.[13]

Beliar is depicted as a deceiver, who will lead astray many of the faithful Jews. He will raise up mountains, as well as the dead. It is clear in these passages, and others as well in the *Sibylline Oracles* that Beliar will appear at the end of time as an Anti-Christ like figure.

Other early Christians, because of John 5:42–43 believed that the Anti-Christ will be accepted as the Jewish Messiah, and even set himself up in a Third Temple of Jerusalem.

John 5:42–43 looks this way in the RSV: "But I know that you do not have the love of God in you. I have come in my Father's name, and you do not accept me; if another comes in his own name, you will accept him."[14] Like many of the other New Testament passages we have seen above, the "other that comes in his own name" has been thought by some New Testament scholars, both ancient and modern, to be a reference to the Anti-Christ.

Polycarp was a first- and second-century celebrated figure of the early Church. Tradition has it that Polycarp was a direct pupil of the apostle John, and lived between 70 and 155 CE. Tradition also suggests that Polycarp was martyred in February of 155. His *Epistle to the Phillipians* was written around 135. In this letter, Polycarp briefly mentions the Anti-Christ. His point of view was depended on the perspective in the Johannine letters.

Polycarp of Smyrna was a well-known bishop of Asia Minor who was prominent not long after time of the Book of Revelation. In his *Letter to the Philippians*, Polycarp quotes 1 John 4:3: "For everyone who does not confess that Jesus Christ has come in the flesh is an Anti-Christ and a Devil."[15] This leads us to the belief that in the second century, the term *AntiChristos* referred to human adversaries who bring heretical doctrines. We also learn that in Polycarp's time, the Anti-Christ is also linked to the Devil. Polycarp's most important and long-lasting observation about the Anti-Christ is that the final enemy is to be identified with various heretics of his day, and chief among these were the Gnostics.

Justin Martyr (c. 100–165) was a Platonic philosopher who converted to Christianity. He lectured on the relationship of Greek philosophy to Christianity and was martyred sometime between 163 and 167. In his *Dialogue with Trypho*, Justin makes three references to the Anti-Christ, in chapters 32, 51, and 110. In chapter 32, Justin argues there will be two comings in the end times. Justin writes: "and he whom Daniel foretells would have dominion for a time, and times and an half, is even already at the door, about to speak blasphemous and daring things against the Most High."

In chapter 51, Justin makes a reference to "false prophets," quite like that of Mark 13:22, where the text speaks of "False messiahs and false prophets who will appear and produce signs and omens, to lead astray, if possible, the elect."[16] In chapter 110 of the *Dialogue with Trypho*, Justin uses the language of 2 Thessalonians that Christ will only return after the appearance of the "man of apostasy."

Justin Martyr clearly identifies the "man of apostasy" as "he who can only be the Anti-Christ who will do powerful deeds on the earth against us Christians."[17] Justin Martyr (ca. 100–165) in his *Dialogue with Trypho* makes a distinction between two different Advents in the End Times. One of these is to be connected with the Anti-Christ who "will have dominion for a time," and the other refers to the Second Coming of Christ.[18]

Tertullian, (155–222), the first of the great Latin fathers, in his *Against Marcion* identifies the Anti-Christ with heretics of his day, including second-century Gnostic, Marcion. Tertullian also thought that the man of lawlessness was synonymous with the Roman Empire. In a commentary on Daniel 7 he expresses belief in the *Nero redivivus*, and that the Anti-Christ was identified with the Empire in his own day.

In this passage, Tertullian identifies the Anti-Christ with the Roman Empire:

> For the mystery of inequity is already at work; only he who now hinders must hinder, until he be taken away. What obstacle is there but the Roman state, the falling away of which, by being scattered into ten kingdoms, shall introduce the Anti-Christ upon its own ruins? And then shall be revealed the wicked one, whom the Lord shall consume with the spirit of His mouth, and shall destroy with the brightness of his coming; even him whose coming is after the working of Satan, with all power and signs, and lying wonders, and with all deception of unrighteousness in them that perish.[19]

Indeed, throughout *Against Marcion*, Tertullian makes a number of comments about the Anti-Christ, like this passage from section V: "The Man of Sin, the son of perdition, who must first be revealed before the Lord comes, who opposes and exalts himself above all that is called God or that is worshipped; and who is to sit in the temple of God and boast himself as being God ... According indeed our view, he is Anti-Christ, as it is taught to us by both the ancient and the new prophecies, and by the apostle John."[20]

ANTI-CHRIST IN THIRD AND FOURTH CENTURIES

Cyril of Jerusalem, a fourth-century doctor of the church, was bishop of Jerusalem. Most of what we know of his life comes from his contemporaries Epiphanius, Jerome, and Rufinus. Cyril's *Catechetical Lectures*, written around 350 CE, contains materials on the Anti-Christ. The lecture, which is principally about Christology, contains an analysis of the exegesis of Daniel 7:13–27. In this section, Cyril warns against being led astray "by that false Anti-Christ." He calls the Anti-Christ "a highly skilled magician that deals in deceit, evil art, and enchantment."[21]

This notion of the Anti-Christ being a magician, as we have seen earlier, is as old as first-century Christianity, where Simon Magnus was believed by many early Christians to have been the Anti-Christ.

Again, commenting on Daniel 7:9–14, Cyril tells us: "But this aforementioned Anti-Christ is to come when the times of the Roman Empire shall have been fulfilled, and the end of the world is now drawing near. There shall rise up ten kings of the Romans, reigning in different parts, perhaps, but all about the same time, and after these, an eleventh, the Anti-Christ who by magical craft shall seize upon Roman power."[22]

In the same passage, Cyril suggests that: "Signs and wonders of his magical deceit as having beguiled the Jews, as though he were the expected Christ. He shall afterwards be characterized by all kinds of crimes of inhumanity and lawlessness, so as to undo all unrighteous and ungodly men ... against us Christians.[23]

Again, Cyril speaks of the Anti-Christ beguiling his people, the Jews:

> Having beguiled the Jews by lying signs and wonders of his magical deceit, until they believe he is the expected Christ, he will afterwards be characterized by all manner of wicked deeds of in-

humanity and lawlessness, as if to outdo all the unjust and pious men who have gone before him. He shall display against all men, and especially against us Christians, a spirit that is murderous and most cruel, merciless and wily. For three years and six months only shall he be the perpetrator of such things; and then shall he be destroyed by the glorious second coming from heaven of the only-begotten Son of God, our Lord and Savior Jesus, the true Christ, who shall destroy him with the breath of his mouth, and deliver him over to the fire of Gehenna.[24]

Cyril argues that the Anti-Christ will attain power over the kingdoms of the earth through force and fraud. The Anti-Christ, Cyril maintains, will be accepted as the Messiah by Jews. He also argues that the Anti-Christ will rebuild the Temple at Jerusalem, and enthrone himself there as God.[25]

In Cyril's fifteenth lecture, he speaks of the Second Coming and the Anti-Christ when he writes: "But since it was needful for us to know the signs of the end, and since we are looking for Christ, therefore, that we may not die deceived and be led astray by the false Anti-Christ."[26] A little later in the same lecture, he warns his readers to: "Make safe thy soul. The Church now charges thee before the Living God; she declares to thee the things concerning the Anti-Christ before they arrive."[27]

In lecture 15, Cyril tells us that the Anti-Christ's malice "will surpass the combined wickedness of all the evil doers gone before him,"[28] and that he will be "like an ocean in which all human and diabolical wickedness shall meet."[29] It is clear that Cyril believed that Christians could be deceived by the Anti-Christ, and that there will be a number of activities that are to precede the coming of the Anti-Christ. Cyril also hints that the Anti-Christ will involve persecutions that may or may not occur at the end of time.

Cyril believes that the end of the world was at hand; that the apostasy of Paul speaks about in 2 Thessalonians 2:3 applies to heretics of his day, particularly the Arians and Sabellians. Indeed, he calls these groups "forerunners of the Anti-Christ." Cyril also identifies the "many who say they come in my name" in Matthew 24:5 as Simon Magus and Meander. Cyril of Jerusalem, who lived from 315–387, also suggests that the Anti-Christ will be a Jew, and will be worshipped by them.

Cyril also gives a description of the actions of the man of lawlessness and a description of the coming Anti-Christ, as well:

> At first he will feign mildness and will appear to be learned and an understanding man, with pretended prudence and kindness ...And afterwards, his character will be written large in evil deeds of humanities and lawlessness of every kind, so as to outdo all wicked and godless men that were before him. He will display a murderous, most absolute, pitiless and unstable temper toward all men, but especially toward Christians.[30]

Cyril closes his analysis of the Anti-Christ with a plea to his followers:

> So be warned, my friend, I have given you the signs of the Anti-Christ. Don't just store them in your memory. Pass them on to anyone who does not know them. If you have a child of the flesh, teach him right away. If you are a godparent, teach your godchild immediately, lest he should take the false Christ for the true one. For the "mystery of iniquity" already does work.[31]

Of all the church fathers, the fullest treatment of the legend of the Anti-Christ is to be found in Books IV and V of Irenaeus' *Against Heresies*. Irenaeus, who lived from 130 to 202 CE, was born in Asia Minor and became bishop of Lugdunum in Gaul. His writings were formative in the early developments of Christian theology. Irenaeus was a student of Polycarp's, who in turn was a disciple of John the evangelist.

The purpose of Irenaeus' *Against Heresies* was to refute various teachings of a number of heresies in the first few centuries of the church. Chief among these heresies was Gnosticism. Until the discovery of the Library at Nag Hammadi in 1945, *Against Heresies* was the fullest extent description of Gnosticism.

Saint Irenaeus describes the Anti-Christ this way:

> By the things which shall be under Anti-Christ it is shown that the Devil, being a rebel and a thief, desires to be adored as God; and being a slave, wants himself to be proclaimed a king. For he, taking to himself all the might of the Devil, will come, not as a just king, nor as one in God's obedience, sanctioned by law, but being impious, unjust, and lawless, as a rebel and unrighteous, and a murderer, as a thief summing up the rebellion of the Devil and himself.[32]

Irenaeus continues: "And while he sits aside idols, to persuade men that he, himself, is God, he will exalt himself, the one idol, containing in himself the various errors of all other idols, that those who by many abominations adore the Devil, may be this one idol, be slaves to him."[33]

Irenaeus goes on to quote Saint Paul: "Of whom the Apostle, in the Second Epistle to the Thessalonians thus speaks, "For except there has come a departure first, and the man of sin shall have been revealed." The Apostle, you see, plainly declares his apostasy, and that he is exalted above all that is called God, or that is worshipped."[34]

Saint Irenaeus uses a number of the themes concerning Anti-Christ already present in the second century, including the notions that the Final Enemy shall be a deceiver, that he shall claim to be God, and that he will be associated with the Devil who is also a deceiver.

Irenaeus gives an account of the workings of the Anti-Christ in Book V of *Against Heresies*:

> And not only by these things, but also by the things in the days of Anti-Christ. It is shown that he (Satan), though an apostate and thief, desires to be worshipped as God; and though he is a slave, yet he desires to be proclaimed as king. For he (Anti-Christ) shall come, taking up all the power of the devil, not as a just or God-fearing king, but impious, lawless, and unjust, as a traitor, murderer, and thief, gathering up in him the apostasy of the devil, removing idols, indeed, in order to persuade men that he is God.[35]

Again in Book V of *Against Heresies*, Irenaeus speaks of the time of the Anti-Christ: "By means of the events which shall occur in the time of the Anti-Christ it is shown that he, being an apostate and robber, is anxious to be adored as God, and although a mere slave, he wishes to be proclaimed a king. For he being educated with all the powers of the Devil, shall not come as a righteous king ... but as an impious, unjust, and lawless one."[36]

A little later in Book V, Irenaeus again discusses the Anti-Christ. After quoting Isaiah three times, Irenaeus wrote: "All these indisputably refer to the resurrection of the just, which takes place after the advent of the Anti-Christ, and the destruction of all the nations under him, when the just shall reign on the earth, growing in the vision of the Lord, and through Him will become used to contain the glory of God the Father; and with the holy angels shall have converse, and fellowship and spiritual union in the kingdom."[37]

Also in Book V, Irenaeus concludes his comments on the Anti-Christ: "But when this Anti-Christ has devastated all things in this world, he will reign for three years and six months, and will sit in the temple of Jerusalem, and then the Lord will come from the heavens in the clouds, in the glory of the Father, sending this man and those who will follow him into the lake of fire."[38]

Irenaeus also suggests that the end of the world will be associated with the end of the Roman Empire: "John and Daniel have predicted the dissolution and desolation of the Roman Empire, which shall precede the end of the world and the Eternal Kingdom of Christ. The Gnostics are refuted, those tools of Satan, who invent another Father different from the Creator."[39]

In this one small paragraph, Irenaeus ties the End Times to the end of the Roman Empire, while identifying false prophets with the Gnostics. In another paragraph from the same chapter, Irenaeus writes: "In a still clear light has John, in the Apocalypse, indicate to the Lord's disciples what shall happen in the last times, and concerning the ten kings which shall then arise, among whom the empire which now rules the earth shall be partitioned. He teaches us what the ten horns shall be which were seen by Daniel."[40]

A few chapters later, Irenaeus again discusses the Anti-Christ: "Moreover, another danger, by no means trifling, shall overtake those who falsely presume that they know the name of Anti-Christ. For if these men assume one number, when this Anti-Christ shall come having another, they will be easily led away by him, as supposing him not to be the expected one, who must be guarded against."[41]

In these few short paragraphs, Irenaeus reiterates many of the ideas in early Christianity about the Anti-Christ: that the end of the world will be associated with the Fall of the Roman Empire; that the Anti-Christ will be associated with deception; and that the Anti-Christ is to be associated with false teachings, particularly the Gnostics.

In addition to these fairly conventional observations about the Anti-Christ, Irenaeus also offers some new elements about the idea. In a long discussion of the number 666, he suggests that it "shows the recapitulation of that entire apostasy which happened in the beginning, and in the intervening times, and which will happen in the end."[42]

Irenaeus argues that the Anti-Christ must recapitulate all evil in the same way that Jesus must recapitulate all good. In the same way that God must become man to atone for the sins of men, the Anti-Christ, Irenaeus argues, will come as a man, and becomes a figure that embodies all evil, separating the just from the unworthy.

Along the way, Irenaeus also reveals that the Anti-Christ will be born a Jew, from the tribe of Dan. He also points out that the tribe of Dan is conspicuously absent from the number of the saved in chapter 7 of Revelation. Indeed, Irenaeus goes on to point out that in Jewish apocalyptic the tribe of Dan was to be the origin of the last messiah.

Irenaeus uses John 5:43, as other patristics do, to describe the Anti-Christ. He is called *allos* (other) because he is alienated from the Lord. (Against Heresies 5.24.4) He also concurs with the early Church view that the Anti-Christ will come from the tribe of Dan, and bases this view on his interpretation of Jeremiah 8:16. Irenaeus also applies the story of the unjust judge in Luke 18 to refer to the Anti-Christ.

Because of the persecution of Christians during Irenaeus' time, the Bishop of Lyons was one of the first Christians theologians to identify the Anti-Christ with the Roman Empire. Thus, Irenaeus adhered to many of the traditional early perspectives on the Anti-Christ, including the notion that he will be a Jew, from the tribe of Dan, and that the final enemy was associated with the Roman Empire.

Hippolytus, who lived from 160 to the mid 230s, was a disciple of Irenaeus. His principal work is called *Refutations of all the Heresies*, which is also known by its first part, the *Philosophoumena*.[43] Hippolytus also wrote a commentary on the book of Daniel, written in the beginning of the third century. In the fourth book of the commentary on Daniel, Hippolytus wrote a great deal about the Anti-Christ. Like many before him, Hippolytus believed that the Anti-Christ would be a Jew from the tribe of Dan. Commenting on Revelation 12:2, Hippolytus says that the Anti-Christ will adroitly conceal his sins, and will pass for the most virtuous of men.[44]

Hippolytus also tells us a number of other things about the Final Enemy. In section six of his essay on the Anti-Christ, Hippolytus sums up his view of the Anti-Christ:

> Now as the Lord Jesus Christ, who is also God, was prophesied under the figure of a lion, on account of his royalty and glory, in the same way have the scriptures beforehand spoken of Anti-Christ as a lion, on account of his tyranny and violence. For the deceiver seeks to liken himself to all things to the Son of God. Christ is a lion, so Anti-Christ is a lion. Christ is a king, so Anti-Christ is a

king. The Savior was manifested as a lamb, so he too in like manner will appear as a lamb without, while within a wolf. The Savior came into the world circumcised, and he will come in the same way. The Savior raised up and showed his holy flesh like a temple, and he will raise a temple of stone in Jerusalem.[45]

Like many other Christian thinkers of his time, Hippolytus identifies the beast of Revelation with the Romans. Indeed, he goes on to give a description of the beast: "Then he says, 'A fourth beast, dreadful and terrible, it has iron teeth and claws of brass.' And who are these but the Romans? Which kingdom is meant by the iron—the kingdom which is now established; for the legs of that image were of iron. And after this, what remains, beloved, but the toes of the feet of the image, in which part is iron and part clay, mixed together."[46]

Hippolytus goes on to identify those ten toes with the ten kings predicted in Daniel: "As these things, then, are in the future, and as the ten toes of the image are equivalent to so many democracies, and the ten horns of the fourth beast are distributed over ten kingdoms..."[47]

Commenting on Romans 11:30, Hippolytus suggests that the Anti-Christ will be defeated by certain people of western nations. But he will soon recover from those battles, and have control over all the nations of the Earth. Hippolytus also, along with St. Ambrose, believed in a view that John the evangelist did not die, but rather disappeared and shut himself up in a tomb.[48] Hippolytus argues that John will return to disclose the artifices of the Anti-Christ, since he foretold for centuries before hand the man of sin.[49]

Hippolytus uses Jeremiah 8:16, Genesis 49, and Deuteronomy 33 to prove that the Anti-Christ will come from the tribe of Dan, and he thought the raising up of the Temple in 2 Thess 2:4 refers to the Temple in Jerusalem. He refers to "raising a Temple of stone by the Anti-Christ."

Hippolytus also makes the identification that the followers of the Final Enemy shall be Jews:

> And under this was signified none other than Anti-Christ, who is also himself to raise the kingdom of the Jews. He says that three horns are plucked out by the root by him, that is, the kings of Egypt, and Libya, and Ethiopia, whom he cuts off in the array of the battle. And he after gaining terrible power over all, being nevertheless a tyrant, shall stir up tribulation and persecution against men, exalting himself against them. For Daniel says: "I considered

the horn, and behold that horn made war with the saints, and prevailed against them, until the beast is slain and perished, and its body given to the burning of fire.⁵⁰

Hippolytus, who was martyred in 236, was the author of a work called *The Dogmatic Treatise on Christ and Anti-Christ* around the year 200. In the beginning of chapter 61 of this work, Hippolytus speaks of a Dragon who "persecuted the woman which brought forth the man-child." Later he refers to a "tyrant that is to reign and persecute the Church." It is likely that Hippolytus' references are to the Anti-Christ.⁵¹

Hippolytus, in his work on the consummation of time, does not hesitate to affirm that Anti-Christ will heal lepers, make the lame walk, cast out demons, and raise the dead to life. Hippolytus tells us, Anti-Christ will know the most secret and hidden things. He will move mountains, walk on the waves of the sea, turn day into night, and vice versa. He will direct the course of the sun at will, and finally, he will appear as being the master of the elements.⁵²

Theodoret, who lived from 393 to 457 and was heavily involved in the Nestorian controversy, identified the man of lawlessness of 2 Thessalonians 2:7 with various contemporary heretics of his day. He also believed, as many of the patristics did, that the Anti-Christ will arrive from the tribe of Dan. Other thinkers who believed the Anti-Christ will come from the tribe of Dan include: Prosper of Aquitaine, Ambrose, and Gregory the Great.

Other opinions from the same period, like those of Jerome, Tertullian, and St. Augustine, maintained that St. John was as dead as the other apostles. Hippolytus also believed, as Tertullian, Ambrose and Gregory did, that the events recorded in the book of Daniel and Revelation were not allegories, but rather narrations of historical fact.⁵³

Hippolytus was of the opinion that Paul wrote the second letter to the Thessalonians, for the purpose of dissuading people from believing that the Second Coming was at hand.⁵⁴ Other thinkers, like Hilary (fourth century) and Cyprian (third century), however, were convinced the end times were soon to come. Cyprian, in book IV of his *Testimonies*, tells us: "The day of tribulation begins to dawn upon us; the world is near its end; the time of the Anti-Christ is close at hand; let us prepare for the combat."⁵⁵

Cyprian also tells us in his *Epistle to the People of Thibaris* that Christians are "nearing the time of the Anti-Christ, and thus they must be prepared for martyrdom." "For you ought to know and to believe, and to hold it for certain that the day of affliction has begun to hang over their heads, and that the end of the world and the time of the Anti-Christ is to draw near, so that we must all stand for the battle."[56]

Finally, Hippolytus thought that at the end of time, the Anti-Christ, like Jesus, will heal lepers, make the lame walk, cast out demons, and raise the dead to life. He will know the most secret and hidden things. He will move mountains, walk on the waves of the sea, and turn day into night, and vice versa. Hippolytus says that the Anti-Christ will direct the course of the sun at will, and he will appear as the master of the elements. Hippolytus thought that the Anti-Christ will appear to perform miracles similar to those wrought by Christ, in order to eclipse his glory. He will also, in Hippolytus' view, take on a number of honors afforded to the true messiah.

David Dunbar, writing about the views of the end times of Irenaeus and Hippolytus says, "[From them] we get a kind of mainline eschatology, which may have been quite widespread during the closing decades of the second century."[57]

Fourth-century thinker, Lactantius, in his *Divine Institutes*, sums up the Christian view of the Anti-Christ in the early fourth century:

> A king shall arise out of Syria, born from an evil spirit, the overthrower and destroyer of the human race, who shall destroy that which is led by the former evil, together with himself ... But that king will not only be most disgraceful in himself, he will also be a prophet of lies, and he will constitute and call himself God, and will order himself to be worshipped as the son of God; and power will be given to him to do signs and wonders, by the sight of which he may entice men to adore him. He will command fire to come down from Heaven and the sun to stand and leave its course and an image to speak, and these things shall be done at his word ... Then he will attempt to destroy the temple of God and persecute the righteous people.[58]

Lactantius also identifies the last things to occur after the fall of Rome:

> These are the things which are spoken of by the prophets as about to happen hereafter ... The subject itself declares that the fall and

ruin of the world will shortly take place; except that while the city of Rome remains it appears that nothing of this kind is to be feared. But when that capital of the world has fallen, and shall begun to be a street, which the Sibyls say shall come to pass, who can doubt that the end has now arrived to the affairs of men and the whole world?[59]

Lactanius was also among the church fathers who believes, as Irenaeus and Saint Hilary, and Saint Justin do, that the world will last only 6,000 years, because according to 2 Peter 3:8, the world was created in six days and each day represents 1,000 years. Cyprian holds the same view and Augustine regards it as probable. Saint Ambrose, on the other hand, says this view has no credence.[60]

Lactantius, Italian born apologist and educated in North Africa by Arnobius, mentions a number of the key elements of the early Christian view of the Anti-Christ, including the judgment that he will be a prophet of lies; he will call himself God; and he will have the power to do signs and wonders.

One final thinker from the fourth century is Athanasius of Alexandria. This Christian bishop and Patriarch of Alexandria lived from approximately 298 to 373. Athanasius is important for our purposes because he was one of the early church fathers to identify the Anti-Christ with heresies of his day. For Athanasius, the Anti-Christ is to be seen as Ariuis (256–336) and his followers.

During the Council of Carthage in the mid-third century, one of the questions for debate was whether heretics should be rebaptized. There were a number of opinions expressed in the *Protocols of the Council of Carthage*. Among those was Bishop Secundinus of Carpis who said, "Those who do not rebaptize heretics are Anti-Christs."[61]

ANTI-CHRIST IN THE FIFTH CENTURY

The two most important Christian thinkers on the Anti-Christ in the fifth century are Jerome and Augustine, Jerome's most important remarks on the Anti-Christ are to be found in his *Commentary on the Book of Daniel*, as well as a number of his letters. Augustine speaks of the Anti-Christ in a number of places, including several references in the *City of God*.

Among Jerome's letters are several mentions of the end things and the Anti-Christ. In a letter to Pope Damascus, written from the desert of

Chalcis, Jerome speaks of the division of the Christian Church into East and West. In the letter he also repeats the Johannine phrase, "He who is not of Christ is of the Anti-Christ." In another letter written to Damascus, which is a commentary on Luke 15:11–32, the prodigal son, Damascus mentions the idea of the Anti-Christ sacrificing a kid to himself, a sort of reverse first fruits ritual.[62] In a third letter to Eustochium on virginity, Jerome also mentions the Anti-Christ. Jerome comments:

> But such virgins as there are said to be among the various heretical sects and with the most foul Manichean are to be considered harlots, not virgins. For the author of their body is the devil, how can they honor what has been framed by his foes. But because they know that the word "virgin" is glorious, they shelter wolves in sheep's clothing. Anti-Christ pretends to be Christ, and they falsely clothe shamefulness of life by the honor of that name.[63]

In his commentary on the Book of Daniel, Saint Jerome discusses typological readings of the book. Jerome writes: "Therefore, as the Saviour has both Solomon and other saints as types of his coming, so Anti-Christ is to be understood to have as a type of himself the most wicked king Antiochus, who persecuted the saints and violated the Temple."[64]

These same types of typologies continue throughout the Middle Ages. Thomas Aquinas, for example, claims that all evil characters who come before Anti-Christ are, nevertheless, symbols of the Anti-Christ.[65]

In Jerome's commentary on Daniel, he tells us that the Anti-Christ will be born in Babylon, apparently connecting the Anti-Christ to impiety in general. Jerome also tells us that the Anti-Christ will have incomparable eloquence, and he will represent Jesus as an imposter, attacking his teachings and doctrines. Jerome also says that at the end of the world, after the destruction of the Roman Empire, ten kings will divide the remnants among them. Then an eleventh king will enter the scene and will conquer three of their number: the kings of Egypt, Ethiopia, and Africa. After their deaths, the remaining seven kings will lay their scepters at the feet of the Anti-Christ.[66]

Saint Jerome believes the Anti-Christ will be defeated by certain nations from the West, who will give the Anti-Christ a great naval battle. But the Anti-Christ will recover from this defeat, and eventually will go on to rule the Earth.[67] Jerome thinks that the images of Gog and Magog symbolize the Anti-Christ's battle against the Church. Gog will be the

Anti-Christ himself, and Magog will be his army. As a result of this battle, the holy sacrifice of the mass shall no longer be offered in public on altars. The Church shall be devastated, their sacred vessels desecrated, their priests scattered and separated from their flocks.[68]

Jerome claims that the restraining force of 2 Thessalonians 2:6 is the Roman Empire, that the Anti-Christ is the Devil himself, and that the enthroning of the Anti-Christ is to be understood as a leader of the Church, and not a reference to the Temple at Jerusalem. Jerome also notes the discrepancy between 1290 and 1335 days assigned to the Anti-Christ in Daniel 12, and concludes there must be a surplus of 45 days of peace after the death of the Anti-Christ.[69]

Jerome was vehemently against any ideas that the end of the world was at hand. he was also against any form of millenarianism. Indeed, he edited Victorinus' *Commentary on Revelation* to remove any hints of a thousand year earthly reign.[70] Jerome also rejected, as Augustine did, the Nero *redivivus* theory. Other thinkers of the period, however, endorse the theory, including John Chrysostom, Commodian, and Ambrosiaster. Saint Martin of Tours, a fourth-century German doctor of the Church,[71] thought that the Emperor Nero will arise along with the Anti-Christ. Nero will control the Western half of the Christian Empire, and the Anti-Christ the Eastern half. Victorinus of Pettau, who died at the beginning of the fourth century, combined the *Nero redivivus* theory with the belief that the Anti-Christ will come from the tribe of Dan. Victorinus says the Anti-Christ will erect a temple in his image, and will force all to circumcision.

Saint Jerome also identifies the second beast of Revelation 13 with the Anti-Christ.[72] Jerome believes that the "time" mentioned in Daniel 12:14 is generally employed in scripture to signify a year. In discussing Daniel 12:45, Jerome says that the Anti-Christ will ascend from the top of a mountain into the air, like a magician. God will overwhelm him, however, by his glory, and shall precipitate the Anti-Christ to the earth by a single puff of his breath.[73]

This reference to magicians is most likely related to the fact that in Roman times Simon Magus, also called Simon the Sorcerer and Simon of Gitta, was thought by some in the early Church to be the Anti-Christ. He is mentioned in Justin Martyr's *Apologies* and in Irenaeus' *Against Heresies*. The apocryphal *Acts of Peter* gives a legendary account of Simon Magus' death. While performing magic for Emperor Claudius in the forum, in order to prove he was God, he is said to have levitated. While suspended in the air, the apostles Peter and Paul pray to God to stop the flying, and Simon Magus falls to his death.[74]

Saint Jerome also mentions the coming of the Anti-Christ in a number of his letters. In a letter written to Ageruchia in 409, for example, Jerome reiterates a number of the early Christian judgments on the Anti-Christ, when he writes: "But what am I dong? While I talk about the cargo, the vessel itself founders. He that letteth is taken out of the way, and yet we do not realize that Anti-Christ is near. Yes, Anti-Christ is near whom the Lord Jesus Christ 'shall consume with the spirit of his mouth.' 'Woe unto them,' he cries, 'that are with child, and to them that give suck in those days ...'"[75]

Saint Jerome, as well as Ambrose and Thomas Aquinas, believe, on the evidence of Daniel 11:45 that the mountain on which the Anti-Christ will be defeated at the end of time is the Mount of Olives. All three thinkers say that Anti-Christ will ascend from the top of this mountain into the air, as did Simon Magnus at Rome. But God shall overwhelm him by the splendor of his glory, and shall precipitate him to the north by a simple puff of his breath, according to 2 Thessalonians 2:8.[76]

Saint Augustine wrote in several places on the Anti-Christ. The three principal sources for comments on the Anti-Christ are the *City of God*, his commentary on 1 John, and in letter number 199.

Emmerson points out that in Book XX of *The City of God*, Saint Augustine includes many of the standard features regarding the Anti-Christ: "Anti-Christ is Satan's agent, the great false prophet of the beast (the godless city), the leader of the devil's final persecution of the faithful. In his sermons on the Johannine epistles, on the other hand, Augustine develops the second expectation of multiple Anti-Christs already living."[77]

Like many of his predecessors, as well as those who come after him, Augustine identified the Anti-Christ with many heresies of his day and before. Augustine ties this idea to the notion of John's epistles that there are already many Anti-Christs at work.

In Book XVIII of the *City of God*, Augustine refers to the defeat of Anti-Christ by Jesus, which the bishop of Hippo says is foreordained in 2 Thessalonians 1:9. Augustine comments, "Truly Jesus Himself shall extinguish by His presence the last persecution which is to be made by the Anti-Christ." Following Paul, he refers to Jesus defeating the Anti-Christ by the breath of his mouth.[78]

In Book XX, chapter 13, Augustine discusses whether the three and a half year reign of the Anti-Christ is to be included in the thousand year reign of the Devil. Augustine comments: "The last persecution of the Anti-Christ shall last for three years and six months, as we have already said, and as is affirmed both in the book of Revelation and by Daniel the prophet. Though this time is brief, yet not without reason is it questioned whether it is comprehended in the thousand years in which the devil is bound and the saints' reign with Christ, or whether this little season shall be added over and above to these years."[79]

In the same book of the *City of God*, Augustine speaks of the prophecies of Daniel and how they are related to the Anti-Christ. Augustine tells us: "Daniel prophecies of the last judgment in such a way as to indicate that Anti-Christ shall first come and carry on his destruction to the eternal reign of the saints. For when in prophetic vision he had seen four beasts, signifying four kingdoms, and the fourth conquered by a certain king, who is recognized as Anti-Christ, and after this the eternal kingdom of the Son of Man, that is to say, of Christ."[80]

Augustine goes on to say he does not know the answers to these questions, but he surmises that the three and a half years are not part of the thousand year reign of Satan. At Book XX, chapter 19, of the *City of God* Augustine again discusses the Anti-Christ in relation to what Paul has to say in 2 Thessalonians. Augustine reiterates that the Second Coming will not occur until there is first the coming of the Anti-Christ.[81] Augustine refers to the last times as the Day of the Lord. He also comments that it is uncertain whether the Temple on which the Anti-Christ shall sit is "the ruins of the Temple built by Solomon, or is the Church."[82]

In chapter 23 of Book XX of the *City of God*, Augustine comments on Daniel's predictions about the Anti-Christ and judgment in such a way as to indicate that the Anti-Christ shall first come, and to carry on his description to the eternal reign of the saints."[83] Augustine agrees with earlier Christian exegetes that three of the four beasts in Daniel 7:15–28 are the kings of Assyria, Persia, and Greece. The fourth beast, for Augustine, is the kingdom of the Anti-Christ, which "fiercely, though for a short time, will assail the Church before the last judgment of God and shall introduce the eternal reign of the saints."[84]

Again, in a separate passage in chapter 23 of Book XX of the *City of God*, Augustine refers to a passage in the twelfth chapter of Daniel. Augustine tells us: "But he who reads this passage [Daniel 12] even half asleep, cannot fail to see that the kingdom of the Anti-Christ shall fiercely, though for a short time, assail the Church."[85]

For Augustine, the period of the Anti-Christ shall be short, and it will come prior to the eternal reign of the saints. Augustine seems to share many of the early church beliefs about the Anti-Christ, including the notion that he will be a deceiver, and that he will come prior to the end of the world.

In Book XX, chapter 23, Augustine also suggests, "The kingdom of Anti-Christ shall fiercely, though for a short time, assail the Church."[86] In chapter 19 of the same book, Augustine discusses 2 Thessalonians 2, where he tells us:

> For what does he [Paul] mean by "For the mystery of inequity doth already work; only he who now holdeth, let him hold until he be taken out of the way: and then shall the wicked be revealed." I frankly confess I do not know what he means . . . However, it is absurd to believe that these words of the apostle, "Only he who now holdeth, let him hold until he is taken out of the way," refer to the Roman Empire, as if it were said, "Only he who now reigneth, let him reign until he be taken out of the way." And then shall the wicked be revealed: no one doubts that this means Anti-Christ.[87]

In Book XX, 30 of the *City of God*, Augustine remarks that the events pertaining to the end of the world will happen in the manner they have been foretold, but as to the accidental circumstances, God alone knows the order in which they will happen.[88]

Augustine's most lengthy comments on the idea of the Anti-Christ come in his Homilies on 1 John. In his homilies, Augustine rejects the notion that the Anti-Christ will be an offspring of the Devil, as well as the idea that the Emperor Nero was the Anti-Christ. Augustine also has negative things to say, like his friend Jerome, of any form of millennialism.

The gist of Augustine's argument on the Anti-Christ can be seen in the following quotation:

> Now, then, brothers, if actions are to be asked about, we find not only that many anti-Christs have gone outside, but that many are not yet manifest who have not at all gone outside. For however many the Church holds [who are] perjurers, swindlers, sorcerers, users, slave dealers, and all the things that it is not possible for us to number—all these things are contrary to the teachings of Christ, are contrary to the word of God. But the word of God is Christ;

whatever is contrary to the word of God is in Anti-Christ. For the Anti-Christ is the one contrary Christ.[89]

A second quotation brings Augustine's central argument on the Anti-Christ in a clearer resolution: "But let us now be saddened. "They have gone out from us, but they were not of us. For if they had been of us, they would no doubt have remained with us. If then they have gone out from us, they are anti-christs. If they are anti-christs they are liars; if they are liars, then they deny that Jesus is the Christ."[90]

Augustine argues that anyone who leaves the Church were never really part of the Church, for if they were part of the Church, they would not have left. If they have left, then they are Anti-Christs. And if they are Anti-Christs, then they are liars.

It is likely that Augustine was speaking of heretics from his day. These heretics, if they have left the Church, were never really a part of the Church. Thus, in Augustine's view, anyone who has left the Church is an Anti-Christ and a liar.

In his comments on First John, Augustine also comments that "Whoever calls himself Universal Bishop, or even desires in his pride to be called such, is the forerunner of Anti-Christ."[91] Augustine also suggests in his commentary on First John that the Anti-Christ should be read as a warning against Christians whose faith is in vain.[92]

In another section of Augustine's tractates on the letters of John, the bishop of Hippo asks if there is any sign to show that someone is an Anti-Christ. He answers by saying, "Prick up the ears of the heart. We were anxiously struggling and were stating 'Who knows? Who discerns?'"[93] Augustine continues: "Every spirit that confesses that Jesus Christ has come in the flesh is of God. And every spirit that does not confess that Jesus Christ has come in the flesh is not God, and this is the Anti-Christ of whom you have that he is going to come, and he is not in this world. Our ears are pricked up for the discerning of spirits, and we have heard such a thing whereby we may not at all in the least discern."[94]

A few pages later, Augustine reaffirms these basic ideas about the Anti-Christ: "Therefore, you come against Christ, you are an Anti-Christ. Whether you are within or without, you are an Anti-Christ. But when you are within, you are hidden; when you are without, you are obvious. You dissolve Jesus and you deny that he has come in the flesh; you are not of God."[95]

Augustine seems to suggest that not only are there heretics who have left the Church and thus are Anti-Christs, there are also Anti-Christs that remain hidden within the Church. Those who are outside the Church are obvious, those who remain in the Church are difficult to detect.

In another tractate on John's epistles, Augustine again makes his central argument about the Anti-Christ. "For all who do not love God are strangers, are Anti-Christs."[96] Augustine agrees with many of his contemporaries that the Anti-Christ and his minions may come from heretics of the Church, but at the same time he rejects a number of traditional beliefs about the Anti-Christ. Among these are the notion that the end of the world will soon come, and that the Emperor Nero is to be identified as the Anti-Christ.

In the *City of God* (Book XX, chapter 30), Augustine tells us that the events pertaining to the end of the world will happen in the manner they have been foretold, but as to their accidental circumstances, God alone knows the order in which they will take place. He has revealed nothing explicitly on this point, and consequently, our knowledge of them is confined to mere conjecture, possessing a greater or lesser degree of probability. Experience alone, in Augustine's view, will not put us in possession of the desired information.[97]

Saint Augustine also rejects the idea that the Anti-Christ will appear as a son of the Devil, and that the Anti-Christ will be born of a virgin.[98] He also, along with Jerome, Tertullian, Isidore, and Epiphanius, rejects the notion that Saint John was not really dead.

Saint Augustine, by using 2 Peter 3:8, suggests that since God created the world in six days, and Second Peter tells us that for God each day will b a thousand years, it follows that the world will last 6,000 years. This position was also held by Irenaeus, Hilary, and Saint Ambrose. But Huchere tells us "Several other Fathers give it no credence."[99]

Saint Augustine also speaks briefly about the relationship between Satan and the Anti-Christ. The Bishop of Hippo takes the position that the Anti-Christ is a human agent of the demonic. As Emmerson remarks: "Usually, as in Augustine, Anti-Christ is merely described as the human agent of the devil. He will be a man of evil, born of Jewish parents, and then possessed by the devil."[100]

Julius Firmicus Maternus, another fourth-century Latin writer and astronomer, in his *De erroribus profanarum religionum*, "On the Errors of Profane Religions," discusses at some length the relationship between the

Devil and the Anti-Christ. Maternus concludes that they have a "father-son" relationship. This work of Maternus is preserved in a manuscript at the Vatican Library, which was printed at Strassburg in 1526. It has most recently been translated by Clarence A. Forbes, in an edition by the Newman Press.[101]

One other way that Saint Augustine contributed to subsequent Christian views of the End Times is his effort of taking the seven days of creation as a paradigm for what he believed were the seven ages of world history. The first day extends from Adam to the flood; the second from the deluge to Abraham. It is equal to the first not in length of days but in the number of generations, there being ten from Abraham to Jesus.[102]

From Abraham to the advent of Christ there are, as Matthew calculates, three periods: one from Abraham to David, a second from David to the captivity, and a third from the Babylonian Captivity to the birth of Christ. There are thus five ages in all, we are now living in the sixth age, in Augustine's view. It is not known how many generations it will last.[103]

In the seventh age God will rest, as in the seventh day of creation. The seventh age shall also be our Sabbath. It will also be the time, in Augustine's view, for the End Times, and the coming of the Anti-Christ. This view of history had deep influences on subsequent views of Christian history, both in the Dark Ages and beyond.[104]

Saint Augustine finishes the *City of God* which capped an on-going shift away from literal understandings of apocalypticism. Instead, Augustine approached the Millennial issues allegorically, as a spiritual state collectively entered by the Church at Pentecost, and as a matter of individuals, rather than all mankind.

Although Augustine preserves the concept of a communal last judgment in the distant future, he interprets the struggle depicted in Revelation as a metaphor for the struggles faced by the individual Christian here and now. Saint Augustine moved the Church out of the apocalyptic business, or at least away from literal readings of the text.

John Chrysostom (347–407) wrote a multitude of homilies on II Thessalonians. About 2:6–9, he writes: "When then is it that witholdeth, that is, hindereth him from being revealed? Some indeed say, the grace of the Spirit, but others the Roman Empire, to whom I most of all accede. Why? Because if he meant to say the Spirit, he would not have spoken obscurely, but plainly. But because he said this of the Roman Empire, he naturally glanced at it, and covertly and darkly. For he did not wish to bring upon himself superfluous enmities, and useless dangers . . ."[105]

A final fourth and fifth-century Christians thinker on the Anti-Christ was John Chrysostom, who lived from 347 to 407 CE. John was an Antioch native and became Patriarch of Constantinople in 398. His most important works were his brilliant homilies, including a series on the letters of John. Like many of his contemporaries, John Chrysostom believed that the Anti-Christ will be a Jew from the lost tribe of Dan; his principal followers will also be Jews; and the Anti-Christ is to come in the form of a resurrected Emperor Nero.

John Chrysostom also believed that the end of time would correspond with the end of the Roman Empire, and that Emperor Nero, and the Man of Lawlessness are one and the same. About 2 Thessalonians 2:6–9, John tells us: "He speaks here of Nero, as if he were a type of Anti-Christ. For he too wished to be thought of as a god. And he well said, 'the mystery'; that is, it works not openly, as the other, nor without shame. For if there was found a man before that time, he means he was not much behind Anti-Christ in wickedness."[106]

John goes on to say that the Man of Lawlessness shall be destroyed by the breath from the mouth of Lord Jesus, and, in the meantime, the Anti-Christ's work shall coincide with the working of Satan.[107]

ANTI-CHRIST IN THE DARK AGES

Of the period between the fall of Rome in the fifth century and the beginning of the High Middle Ages around 1000, several prominent thinkers wrote about the Anti-Christ. Among these thinkers are John of Damascus, a seventh- and eighth-century Syrian theologian, and Gregory the Great.

Gregory (540–604), Italian Churchman was pope from 590 to 604. Among his chief accomplishments were the centralization of the papal administration, sending missions to the British Isles, and a major reformation of the mass. He is credited with the origin of Gregorian chant, and coined the phrase, "the seven deadly sins."

Gregory speaks of the Anti-Christ in two places. His *Dialogues*, written around 590, and his commentary on Job, called the *Moralia in Job*, completed between 580 and 595. In the *Dialogues* Gregory proclaims that the end times are near. As he puts it, "I don't know what is happening in other parts of the world, but in this country where we live, the world no longer announces its ends but demonstrates it."[108]

In the *Moralia*, Gregory makes several comments on the Anti-Christ. He calls the Anti-Christ the "head of all hypocrites ... who feign holiness to lead to sinfulness."[109] Gregory identifies Behemoth and Leviathan from chapters 40 and 41 of the book of Job as symbols for Satan and the Anti-Christ. The tail of Behemoth in Job 40:11 is identified by Gregory as the Anti-Christ. The description of Leviathan's sneeze in Job 41:9 Gregory takes to be the Anti-Christ's final explosion.[110]

Like many thinkers before him, Gregory identifies the Anti-Christ as an embodiment of the Devil. Indeed, in the *Moralia*, Gregory tells us, "The Devil Himself in the last times will be called Anti-Christ when he has entered into that vessel of destruction."[111] Gregory primarily uses an allegorical method in interpreting scripture. Thus, many of the images he finds in the book of Job are tied to signs of the demonic and the Anti-Christ.

Gregory seems to suggest that the imminence of the coming of the Anti-Christ can be seen in the fall of the Roman Empire. He also implies that the work of Anti-Christ can "be seen daily among the wicked." The Roman Pope seems to argue that any action against the Church is, as McGinn points out, "nothing less more than an attack of the Final Enemy."[112]

At times, Gregory seems confused about how the Anti-Christ will be defeated. He quotes 2 Thessalonians 2:8 that the Anti-Christ will be defeated by the breath of God's mouth, but he also, using Daniel 12 and 20:12, alludes to the possibility that the angel Michael will defeat the Anti-Christ at the end of time.

Pope Gregory also makes the connection between the Anti-Christ and the Jews. Gregory suggests that since the Jews did not accept Christ, they are still looking for the coming of their Messiah. Gregory says that Anti-Christ will be a follower of the Old Law. He will be circumcised, and he will be from the lost tribe of Dan. Gregory suggests that the conversion of the Jews will mark a turning point in the reign of Anti-Christ. After establishing his political power, he will set to work converting the faithful.[113]

Gregory points out in the *Moralia* that those followers of Anti-Christ who refuse to obey him shall perish in the midst of the most excruciating torments. They shall be tortured by infernal engines of pain such as have never been thought of before. The persecutors will add to the terror of punishment.[114] About the prestige of Anti-Christ miracles, Gregory exclaims: "What a frightful temptation for the human heart! Behold a martyr who delivers over his body to torture, and his executioner performs miracles before his eyes! Where is the virtue that would not receive a profound shock in presence of such a scene? Woe, then, to the land and sea! Because the Devil is come down unto you having great wrath, knowing that he has but a good time."[115]

The notion that the Anti-Christ was to be identified with the papacy was also something for which Gregory was responsible. Many of the formulators of the Reformation, like Martin Luther, for example, suggest that it was Gregory who first made the papacy to be identified with the Anti-Christ. More is said about this in a later chapter on "The Anti-Christ in the Reformation."

This notion that Gregory the Great was the first Pope to be identified with the Anti-Christ was held by John Wycliffe, Martin Luther, and continues well into the present day. Harold O. J. Brown, in his book, *Protest of a Troubled Protestant*, is a good example of this view. The Rev. Brown writes:

> In every age there has been those who considered the claims of a single bishop to supreme authority to be a sure identification of the corruption of the church, and perhaps even to the work of the Anti-Christ. Pope Gregory I (AD 590–604) indignantly reproached Patriarch John the Faster of Constantinople for calling himself the universal bishop; Gregory did so to defend the rights of all the bishops, himself included, and not because he wanted the title for himself.[116]

Contemporary Anglican scholar J. N. D. Kelly, in the *Oxford Dictionary of the Popes*,[117] also makes the Gregory-Anti-Christ connection, as does Norman Geisler and Ralph MacKenzie, in their *Roman Catholics and Evangelicals*.[118]

The other thinker in the Dark Ages extensively to write on the Anti-Christ was John of Damascus. John was among the greatest of the Eastern Fathers. He was among the greatest defenders of orthodoxy in the East. His comments on the Anti-Christ can be found in his *De Fide orthodoxa*. There he comments on 2 John 2:18 and suggests "Everyone who does not confess that the Son of God is God come in the flesh, and that He who is perfect God also became perfect man, while remaining God, is the

Anti-Christ."[119] But John of Damascus rejects Gregory's idea that Satan is the Anti-Christ. He chooses instead to identify the Anti-Christ with various Christological heresies of his day, particularly the Nestorians and Monophysites.[120]

John of Damascus also held the view that the Anti-Christ will be an illegitimate offspring, and that he will come from the tribe of Dan. John also suggests, as Cyril and Jerome do, that the Anti-Christ will be of incomparable eloquence when he returns to the earth. The Anti-Christ will represent himself as an imposter of Christ who will attack the doctrines and institutions of the Church.

John of Damascus, like many of his predecessors, is of the opinion that the Anti-Christ will be of illegitimate birth, though he stops short of saying that he will be the son of Satan—a position that Augustine and others were adamantly against.

John of Damascus tells us that chapter 15 of *Apocalypse* suggests that at the end of the world the angel of darkness shall be loose for a while. During this time, he shall have full liberty to attack the Church, and use every possible artifice for its destruction. Anti-Christ shall be his most docile agent, wonderfully adapted to seduce the people.[121]

John of Damascus believes that the temple mentioned in chapter 12 of the *Apocalypse* is the Temple in Jerusalem, which the Anti-Christ shall have rebuilt and in which he shall have Divine honors paid to him. Damascus suggests that it is there, according to the prophet Daniel, that the abomination of desolation shall be in the Temple, seated in the holy place.[122]

Other thinkers in the Dark Ages who have dealt with the Anti-Christ include: Procopius, the court historian for Emperor Julian, Gregory of Tours, and Odo of Cluny. Bernard McGinn discusses these three thinkers at length in his monumental work, *The Anti-Christ: Two Thousand Years of the Human Fascination with Evil*.[123]

Gregory of Tours was a sixth-century French monk. He is best known for his *Historica Francorum*, "History of the Franks." In Book One, he speaks of the End Times: "But as to the end of the world beliefs which I learned from our forefathers, that Anti-Christ will come first. He will first propose circumcision asserting that he is Christ. Next he will place his statue in the Temple at Jerusalem to be worshipped, just as we read that the Lord said, 'You shall see the abomination desolate standing in the holy place.'"[124]

Gregory goes on to point out that the time of these things is unknown to men, but it is known "to the Father alone."[125] Gregory was clearly aware of the tradition that the Anti-Christ will be a Jew, and his first followers will be Jews—as well as the tradition that he will set himself up in the Temple at Jerusalem to be worshipped as a God.

Odo of Cluny (878–942) was the second abbot of the monastery at Cluny. Odo reformed a number of monasteries in Europe, particularly in France and Italy. Odo speaks of the Anti-Christ in his epic poem on the Redemption called "Occupatio," where he too reiterates a number of observations about the Anti-Christ found in earlier Christian traditions.[126]

Procopius was a sixth-century Christian scholar, who was a legal advisor to Roman Emperor Julian. He is the author of a *Secret History*, which contains a short history of the coming of the End Times.[127] Like Gregory of Tours and Odo of Cluny, Procopius reflects many of the early Christian understandings of the Final Enemy, such as he will be a Jew, and his initial followers will be Jews.

Both Isidore of Seville (560–635) and the Venerable Bede (673–735), two other Dark Ages thinkers, expected the Anti-Christ at the end of what they both called "the sixth age," the age of the Church.[128]

Another Dark Ages text in the Christian tradition is the *Apocalypse of Pseudo-Methodius*, a seventh-century apocalypse that contributed to the eschatological imagination of later Christendom.[129] The work is written in Syriac in the late seventh century. It was written as a reaction to the Moslem conquest of the Middle East, and is falsely attributed to the fourth-century bishop, Methodius of Olympus.

The text contains many familiar eschatological themes and images, including the rise and rule of the Anti-Christ, the invasion of the armies of Gog and Magog, and a great tribulation that will precede the end of the world. A new element in the *Apocalypse of Pseudo-Methodius*, most likely adopted from the Tiburtine Sibyls, is a Messiah-like Last Emperor.[130]

The text of the *Apocalypse of Pseudo-Methodius* was translated into Greek soon after its completion, and then into Latin by the eighth century, and Slavonic around the same time. Its precise date is difficult to ascertain. Dates proposed by recent historians have ranged from 644 to 691.[131]

Aelfric of Eynsham (ca. 955–1010), English abbot and homilist, is another early commentator on the Anti-Christ. In the preface to his *Catholic Homilies*, Aelfric discusses the great tribulation to come and the many false prophets who claim to be Christ. Aelfric also suggests, as other

Medieval exegetes do, that the Anti-Christ might be the embodiment of the Devil.[132]

Aelfric points to the prologue of the Book of Job, where Satan calls fire from above to destroy the patriarch's animals. For Aelfric, this is evidence that Anti-Christ shall have far beyond the normal capacities to control nature—one of the traditional characteristics of the final enemy.[133]

Aelfric also suggests that at the end of the world, with the appearance of the Anti-Christ will also come a period of false miracles and deceit. He gives a metaphor in which he suggests that false teachers and deceivers shall become the "limbs" of the Anti-Christ, presumably suggesting they will be the armies of the final enemy.[134]

TRADITIONAL CHRISTIAN IMAGES AND QUESTIONS ABOUT THE ANTI-CHRIST

One major point we have discovered in these first three chapters is that there are a number of questions and symbols from the Old and New Testaments related to the Anti-Christ. Among these in the Old Testament are: the role of Gog and Magog from chapters 38 and 39 of Ezekiel; the identity of the Son of Man in Daniel 7:13; the meaning of the Day of the Lord throughout the Old Testament; the meaning of the phrase, "the Abomination of Desolation" used in the book of Daniel; and the nature of the four great beasts of chapter seven of Daniel.

Among images, symbols, and questions related to the New Testament doctrine of the Anti-Christ are:

- the identity of the beast coming out of the sea in Revelation 13
- the identity of the Red Dragon in Revelation 12 and 13
- the identity of the two beasts in Revelation 13
- the meaning of the number 666
- the identity of the Son of Man in Revelation 1
- the identity of the man of lawlessness in 2 Thessalonians 2:7
- the nature of the apostasy at 2 Thessalonians 2:3
- the reference to the rebuilding of the Temple in 2 Thessalonians 2:4
- the identity of the restraining force at 2 Thessalonians 2 6

- the nature of the powers and wonders of lawlessness in 2 Thessalonians 2:9.

One way to tell a history of apocalyptic thought in the Christian tradition is to see how various thinkers have answered these questions, or made sense of these images, over the centuries. Over the centuries, the man of lawlessness, and the images of the beasts in Daniel and Revelation have been identified with many people, movements, and supernatural forces. The meaning of the Son of Man, the Day of the Lord, and the Abomination of Desolation have meant many things for many people. And how all these images are related to the Anti-Christ of John's epistles have occasioned an extraordinary number of opinions in the Christian tradition. This is just as true of the role in the End Times that Gog and Magog will play, as well as the meaning of the mark of the Anti-Christ, the number 666. All these images and questions are important ones in understanding the history of the Christian Apocalyptic tradition. In some ways, this book is little more than making a catalogue of responses to these images and questions.

CONCLUSIONS

As we have seen, Christian thinkers on the Anti-Christ from the first to the eighth century, were primarily concerned about a number of issues with regard to the Anti-Christ. Many of these issues are related to questions that arose from the New Testament's treatments of the Anti-Christ. Among these issues are: the identity of the restraining force in 2 Thessalonians 2:6; the identity of the man of lawlessness in 2 Thessalonians 2:7; the identity of the apostasy described in 2 Thessalonians 2:3; the reference to the Temple in 2 Thessalonians 2:4; and the nature of the powers and wonders of lawlessness in 2 Thessalonians 2:9.

In addition to various perspectives on these issues, the early Church Fathers were concerned with a number of other questions as well regarding the Anti-Christ. Will the Anti-Christ be a Jew, and will he come from the tribe of Dan? Is the Anti-Christ to be associated with Emperor Nero of Rome? Is the Anti-Christ to be identified with early Christian heresies? Is the Anti-Christ the same as Satan? Who will defeat the Anti-Christ? God with a single breath, or Michael the Archangel?

As we have seen, the answers to these questions are as numerous as the number of Church Fathers who have written about them. Some identify the man of lawlessness with the Anti-Christ, some don't. Some thinkers like Gregory the Great and Psuedo-Hippolytus, believe that the Anti-Christ and Satan are synonymous. Some of the early Church Fathers thought that Emperor Nero was the Anti-Christ. Other thinkers believe that the Anti-Christ should be identified as various early Christian heresies. At the same time the Church was dealing with these issues, the religion of Islam also was developing a tradition on the Anti-Christ. We will take up this tradition in the next chapter of this work.

NOTES

1. *The Didache* was discovered in an archeological dig in the late nineteenth century. The version I have used here is J. B. Lightfoot, *The Apostolic Fathers* (London: Kessinger, 2003).
2. *The Didache: Text, Translation, and Analysis*, edited by Aaron Milavec (New York: Glazier, 2004) chap. 16.
3. *Didache* 16:3–4.
4. Cyrcil C. Richardson, "Didache," in *Early Christian Fathers* (London: Touchstone, 1995). Also see the translation by Charles H. Hoole. In *Early Christian Writings* (London: Penguin, 1987).
5. Bernard McGinn, *The Anti-Christ: Two Thousand Years of Human Fascination with Evil* (New York: Harper, 1994) 57–58.
6. *Apocalypse of Peter*, quoted in ibid., 58.
7. Lightfoot, *The Apostolic Fathers*.
8. 1 Maccabees 14:14 (RSV).
9. "The Triburtine Sybil," in E. Maass, *De Sybllarum Incicibus* (Berlin, 1879) 146.
10. Ibid.
11. Daniel 11:38 (author's trans.).
12. L. J. Lietaert Peerbolte, *The Antecedents of Anti-Christ* (Leiden: Brill, 1996) 333–34.
13. Ibid., 334.
14. John 5:42–43 (RSV).
15. Polycarp *Letter to the Philippians* 7:1.
16. Mark 13:22 (RSV).
17. Ibid.
18. Justin Martyr, *Dialogue with Trypho*, chap. 32 (Washington, DC: Catholic University of America Press, 2003).

19. Tertullian, *The Five Books of Quintus Sept. Flor. Tertullianus Against Marcion* (London: Ante-Nicene Library, 1909.) chap. 32; Tertullian *Against Marcion* chap. 32 (London: Kessinger, 2004).
20. Tertullian, *Against Marcion* (V, 16).
21. Much of the material in this chapter I have gleaned from the Rev. P. Huchede, *History of Anti-Christ* (New York: 1884) 20. I have also used William C. Weinrich, "Anti-Christ in the Early Church," *Concordia Theological Quarterly* 49 (1985) 135–48.
22. Cyril of Jerusalem, *The Catechetical Lectures* (Lund: Lund Theological Books, 1885) lecture 15.
23. Ibid.
24. Cyril of Jerusalem, *Catechetical Lectures* (15:12).
25. Ibid.
26. *A Select Library of Nicene and Post-Nicene Fathers of the Christian Church*, series II, vol. 2.
27. Ibid.
28. Quoted in P. Huchede, *History of Anti-Christ*, 15.
29. Ibid., 16.
30. Quotes by McGinn, *The Anti-Christ*, 71.
31. Ibid.
32. Quoted in James Ratton, *Anti-Christ: An Historical Overview*, 120–21.
33. Ibid., 121.
34. Ibid.
35. Irenaeus *Against Heresies* book 5. The edition I have used for this chapter is published by Kessinger, 2004.
36. Irenaeus *Against Heresies* (V.25:1–2).
37. Ibid.
38. Ibid., V.30:4.
39. Ibid., chap. 26.
40. Ibid.
41. Ibid., chap. 30.
42. Ibid.
43. Hippolytus *Refutations of all Heresies*. The translation of Hippolytus I have used for this chapter is the *Ante-Nicene Fathers* edited by Alexander Roberts and James Donaldson, reprinted 1866–1872, 5 vols. (Grand Rapids: Eerdmans, 1981).
44. Huchede, *History of Anti-Christ*, 24.
45. Hippolytus, "Of the Anti-Christ" (Section six).

46. Hippolytus, *Anti-Christ* (Eastern Orthodox Books, 2001) sec. 25.
47. Ibid., sec. 26.
48. Ibid. 58–59.
49. Ibid. 70.
50. Hippolytus, *Treatise on Christ and Anti-Christ*, sec. 25.
51. Lightfoot, *The Apostolic Fathers*, vol. I, part ii.
52. Quoted in Huchede, *History of Anti-Christ*, 27.
53. Ibid.
54. Ibid., 24.
55. Cyprian, *Testimonies* book IV. The edition I have used in this chapter is *Treatise XII: Three Books of Testimonies Against the Jews* (London: Kessinger, 204).
56. Robin Daniel, *This Holy Seed: Faith, Hope, and Love in the Early Churches of North Africa* (New York: Tamarisk, 1993). Also see Dom John Chapman, *Cyprian On the Nature of the Church and Papacy* (London, 1912).
57. David Dunbar, "Hipplytus of Rome," *Vigiliae Christianae* 37 (1983) 313–27.
58. Lactantius, *Divine Institutes*. Edited by Anthony Bowen and Peter Garnsey. (Liverpool: Brown, 2003).
59. Lactantius Firminianous, *Divine Institutions*, book VII, chap. 25.
60. P. Huchede, *History of Anti-Christ*, 127–28.
61. Merrill C. Tenny, *New Testament Survey* (Grand Rapids: Eerdmans, 1985) 409.
62. *The Letters of Saint Jerome*. Translated by C. C. Mierow in Ancient Christian Writers Series (New York: Newman, 1963) 70–73.
63. Ibid., 127–33.
64. Saint Jerome, *De Anti-Christo in Danielem*, CCL 75A, p. 914.
65. Thomas Aquinas, *Summa Theologica*, Part Three, Question 8, Article 8.
66. Jerome, *Commentary on Daniel* edited by F. Glorie in *Sancti Hieronymi Presbyteri Opera* (Turnhout: Brepols, 1964). Also see, J. N. D. Kelly, *Jerome* (New York: Harper & Row, 1975).
67. Huchede, *The Anti-Christ*, 40.
68. Ibid.
69. Ibid.
70. Victorinus, *Commentary on the Apocalypse of Blessed John* (London: Kessinger, 2004).
71. Huchede, *History of Anti-Christ*, 59.
72. Saint Jerome, "The Anti-Christ in Maccabees, in Daniel, and in Revelation 13," in *The New Jerome Bible Commentary*, edited by Raymond E. Brown. (Englewood Cliffs: Prentice Hall, 1989).

73. Ibid., 40.
74. Christine M. Thomas, *The Acts of Peter, Gospel Literature, and the Ancient Novel* (Oxford: Oxford University Press, 2003).
75. Jerome, "Letter to Ageruchia," in *Thirty-Three Letters of St. Jerome*. (New York: Paulist, 1962).
76. Huchede, *History of Anti-Christ*, 72.
77. Richard K. Emmerson and Bernard McGinn, *Anti-Christ in the Middle Ages* (Ithaca: Cornell University Press, 1992) 65.
78. Augustine, *City of God*. In this chapter I have used the translation by Marcus Dods (New York: Modern Library, 1950) 665.
79. Ibid., 730–31.
80. Augustine, *City of God*, XX:19.
81. Ibid. 738–41.
82. Ibid.
83. Ibid., 748–49.
84. Ibid.
85. Ibid., 749.
86. Augustine, *City of God*, XX:23.
87. Ibid., chap. 19.
88. Ibid., 758–62.
89. Augustine, *Tractates on the Gospel of John and the First Epistle of John*, trans. John W. Rettig (Washington, DC: Catholic University of America Press, 1995) 167.
90. Ibid., 166.
91. Ibid., 216.
92. Ibid., 218.
93. Ibid., 211–12.
94. Ibid., 221.
95. Ibid., 215.
96. Ibid., 167.
97. Quoted in Huchede, *History of Anti-Christ*, 76–77.
98. Ibid., 14.
99. Ibid., 128.
100. Emmerson and McGinn, *Anti-Christ in the Middle Ages*, 83.
101. *De errore profanorum religionum*, trans. Clarence A. Forbes as *The Error of the Pagan Religion* (Bryan, TX: Newman, 1970). I have also consulted David

McCann's *Profile of a Roman Astrologer* (London: Healy, 1889); and Otto Bardenhewer, *Patrologie* (London, 1901) 354.

102. Saint Augustine, *The City of God*, XXXII:30.
103. Ibid.
104. Ibid.
105. Margaret M. Mitchell, *The Heavenly Trumpet: John Chrysostom and the Art of Pauline Interpretation*. (Louisville: Westminster John Knox, 2002) 353. Also see Wendy Mayer, ed., *John Chrysostom: Early Church Fathers* (London: Routledge, 1999).
106. Saint John Chrysostom, *Homilies on the Epistles of Paul* (London: Kessinger, 2004) 107.
107. Ibid.
108. Gregory the Great, *Dialogues*. The edition I have used in this chapter is London: Burns & Oates, 1874.
109. Gregory the Great, *Moralia on Job*, ed. Manilo Simonetti (Downers Grove, IL: InterVarsity, 2006). Also see McGinn, *Anti-Christ*, 80–82.
110. Ibid.
111. Ibid.
112. Ibid., 82.
113. Quoted in Emmerson, *Anti-Christ in the Middle Ages*, 91.
114. Quoted in Huchede, *History of Anti-Christ*, 44.
115. Ibid., 44–45.
116. Quoted in Norman Geisler and Ralph McKenzie, *Roman Catholics and Evangelicals* (New York: Baker, 1995) 206.
117. *Oxford Dictionary of the Popes* (Oxford: Oxford University Press, 2005) 67.
118. Geisler and MacKenzie, *Roman Catholics and Evangelicals*, 204–8.
119. Huchede, *History of Anti-Christ*, 14.
120. Ibid.
121. Quoted in ibid., 27.
122. Ibid., 34.
123. McGinn, *Anti-Christ*, 8–92. Several other Christian thinkers in the Dark Ages have made comments on the Anti-Christ. For the most part, these come in connection with commentaries on the Book of Revelation. Among these thinkers are Beatus of Liebana, an eighth-century Spanish monk; Ambrosius Autpertus, an eighth-century Italian abbot; Alcuin of York, an eighth- and ninth-century British scholar (PL100: 1087–156); Haimo of Auxerre, a German scholar from the ninth century (PL117: 937–1220); and Berengaudus

of Ferrieres, a French scholar who produced a commentary on the Apocalypse around 860 (PL17: 843–1058).

124. Gregory of Tour, *History of the Franks*, trans. L. Thorpe (New York: Penguin, 1974) book 1, p. 34.

125. Ibid.

126. Odo of Cluny, *Occupatio*, ed. F. Swoboda (Berlin, 1900).

127. Procopius, *The Secret History*, trans. by G. A. Williamson (Harmonds-worth: Penguin, 1966).

128. "Anti-Christ," in *Encyclopedia of the Middle Ages*, ed. Andre Vauchez. (London: Routledge, 2001) vol. 1, 73.

129. Robert G. Hoyland, *Seeing Islam as Others Saw It* (Princeton: Darwin, 1997.)

130. Andrew Palmer, *The Seventh Century in West-Syrian Chronicles*. (Liverpool: University of Liverpool Press, 1993).

131. Ibid., 7–10. Also see Paul Alexander, "The Medieval Legend of the Last Roman Emperor," *Journal of the Warburg and Courtauld Institutes* 41 (1978) 1–15; John V. Toland, *Saracens: Islam in the Medieval European Imagination* (New York: Columbia University Press, 2002).

132. Benjamin Thorpe, *The Homilies of the Anglo-Saxon Church* (London: Richard and John E. Taylor, 1844) vol. 1, homilies 2 and 21.

133. Ibid.

134. Ibid.

4

The Anti-Christ in Islamic Thought

Given the connections, especially the shared apocalyptic mentality, between Islam and both Judaism and Christianity, it is not surprising to find an Anti-Christ-like figure called the *Dajjal* in the new monotheistic religion that came out of the Arabian desert in the seventh century.
—Bernard McGinn, *Anti-Christ*

Also to while away the time of waiting, I explored a little island named Cassel, which belonged to King Mihrage, and which was supposed to be inhabited by a spirit named Dajjal. Indeed, the sailors assured me that often at night the playing of timbals could be heard upon it.
—*The Arabian Nights*, Sinbad's First Voyage

He who recites three verses at the beginning of the Al-Kahf will be protected from the trial of Djaal.
—Al-Tirmidhi

INTRODUCTION

THE NAME FOR THE Anti-Christ in Islam is the *Dajjal*. Zeki Saritoprak, an American scholar, speaks about the origin and functions of the term, *Ad-Dajjal*: "The term *Ad-Dajjal* originally comes from the Syrian language and is used in Arabic. According to some Arabic lexicons, *al-Masih* means the one who has no eyebrows and a single eye on one side of his face. This characteristic is found in *Ad-Dajjal*, the pseudo-messiah."[1]

Saritoptrak continues:

> Ibn Manzur, author of the famous Arabic lexicon, indicates that *al Masih* as two opposite meanings applied to two personalities. Ad

Masih is used to describe ad-Dajjal, as well as Jesus. Al-Masih can mean the beautiful one, Jesus, as well as his opposite, Al-Dajjal, the ugly one. Al-Masih can also mean the one who is blind, therefore, this title is given to the blind al-Dajjal. Accordingly, al-Masih, Isa is the opposite of Al-Masih Ad-Dajjal, i.e. Jesus the Christ is the opposite of the Anti-Christ.[2]

The word comes from the Arabic verb "to deceive," "to cheat," or "to smear with tar." The word Dajjal does not appear in the *Qu'ran*. But it is to be found in all the major collections of *hadith*. Hadith are collections of sayings and deeds related to the prophet Mohammed. They are regarded as important tools for determining *Sunnah*, or the Moslem way of life. The Arabic plural is *Ahadith*. In English, the word hadith is sometimes used as a singular or as the plural.

Generally, Islamic scholars classify hadith into four kinds. *Qawl*, the first variety, is what Mohammed said. *Fi'l*, the second kind of hadith, is what Mohammed did. Actions of others that Mohammed approved are called *taqrir*. There are also hadith related to the words and deeds of the companions of Mohammed, but they generally are not given the same weight as the other three kinds.

Two of the most important collections of hadith are the works of Imam al-Bukhari and Imam Muslim. Bukhari was a ninth-century scholar. His dates are generally given as 810–870. Abul Husayn Muslim ibn Al-Hajjaj is also a ninth-century Islamic scholar. His dates are generally given as 821 to 875. In addition to these collections by Bukhari and Muslim, there are also other compilations of hadith that mention the Dajjal. Among these are Al-Mishkat Al-Masabith, "The Gardens of Righteousness," and "Al-Muwatta," by Imam Malik, an eighth-century Islamic scholar who was born and lived in Medina.

Our principal goal in this chapter is to describe and discuss these major hadith on the figure of Dajjal. In Islam, there are three different aspects to Dijjal. The first is Dajjal, the individual. The second is Dajjal as a world-wide social and cultural phenomenon. The third aspect of Dajjal is as an unseen force, an agent of destruction at the end of the world. Most Islamic scholars believe that Dajjal will not appear until his support system is in place throughout the world.

The Legend of the Anti-Christ

PROTECTION FROM THE DAJJAL

The prophet Mohammed told his followers to recite the first and last ten verses of surah Al-Kahf "the Cave" in the *Qu'ran*, as protection from the Dajjal. Mohammed Marmaduke Pickthall offers this translation of the opening ten verses of The Cave, Surah 18:

1. Praise be Allah Who hath revealed the Scripture until His slave, and hath not placed therein any crookedness.
2. But hath made it straight, to give warning of strong punishment from Him, and to bring unto the believers who do good words the news that theirs will be fair reward.
3. Wherein they will abide forever.
4. And to warn those who say "Allah has chosen a son."
5. A thing wherein they have no knowledge, nor had their fathers, Dreadful is the words that come out of their mouths. They speak naught a lie.
6. Yet it may be, if they believe not in this statement, that thou (Mohammed) will torment thy soul with grief over the footsteps.
7. Lo! We have placed all that is on their earth as an ornament thereof that We may try them, "Which is best in conduct?"
8. And lo! We shall make all that is thereon a barren mound.
9. Or deem though that the People of the Cave and the Inscription are a wonder among our portents.
10. When the young man fled for refuge to the Cave and said, "Our Lord! Give us mercy from Thy presence, and shape for us right conduct in our plight.[3]

The closing ten verses of Surah 18 are rendered this way by Pickthall:

101. Those whose eyes were hoodwinked from My reminder and could not bear to listen.
102. Do the disbelievers reckon that they can choose My bondmen as protecting friends beside Me? Lo! We have prepared hell as a welcome for the disbelievers.

103. Shall We inform you who will be the greatest losers by their work?

104. Those whose effort goes astray in the life of the world, and yet they reckon that they do good work.

105. Those are they who believe in the revelations of their Lord and in the meeting with Him. Therefore, their work are vain, and on the Day of Resurrection, We assign no weight to them.

106. That is their reward: hell, because they disbelieved, and made a Jest of Our revelations and Our messages.

107. Lo! Those who believe and do good works, theirs are the Gardens of Paradise for welcome.

108. Wherein they will abide, with no desire to be removed from there.

109. Say, "Though the sea became ink for the Words of my Lord. Verily the sea would be used up before the words of my Lord were exhausted, even though We brought the like thereof to help."

110. Say, "I am only a mortal like you. My Lord inspires me that your God is only One God. And whoever hopes for a meeting with his Lord, let him do righteous work, and make none sharer of the worship due unto his Lord."[4]

In the opening ten verses of the Cave, Mohammed makes a distinction between those who go straight, and those who are crooked. In the closing ten verses, Mohammed points out that Allah has prepared hell for disbelievers. Indeed, their works will be in vain on the Day of Resurrection. These words were clearly designed as a warning against those who choose to follow Dajjal. Al-Tirmidhi agrees with this tradition of reading the Cave as protection from the Dajjal: "Allah's messenger said, "He who recites three verses at the beginning of the Al-Kahf will be protected from the trial of Dajjal."[5]

THE NATURE AND END OF DAJJAL

In Islamic tradition, the Dajjal will come along with the appearance of the Imam Mahdi (the messiah), who will rally the faithful to oppose Dajjal. Eventually, Isa (the Arabic name for Jesus) will return from heaven and slay the Dajjal. Many Moslem interpreters say this will occur near the Gate of Ludd (the ancient city of Lydda). The defeat of Dajjal and his followers will be followed by a Golden Age for Islam, in which there are only true believers and Jews and Christians have converted to Islam. This scene is very similar to the Christian apocalyptic vision in which Jesus returns to earth and defeats the Anti-Christ and his followers. In the meantime, no one is advised to combat Dajjal because his killing will be accomplished by Jesus.

Moslem literature tells of false messiahs (*mesihu 'd-dajjal*), who will overrun the earth for forty days and leave only Mecca and Medina unharmed. After this reign of forty days or forty years, he will be destroyed by the Mahdi and Jesus. In the *Qu'ran* Dajjal is described as a plump, one-eyed man, with a ruddy face, and the letters KFR on his forehead. These letters are the root of the Arabic word for "unbelief," *kafir*.

Tradition suggests that Dajjal will arrive during a time of tribulation. He will work false miracles, and most people will be deceived by him. Tradition also suggests that Dajjal will appear in the East, possibly near Khorasan, or in the West, somewhere in the East Indies. This Eastern view suggests the Dajjal lives on an island, from which sounds of dancing and the playing of timbals can be heard. An alternative Islamic version is possibly connected to the Greek myth of Prometheus. In this version of the tale, Dajjal is bound to a rock on an island in the sea, and is fed by demons. Some Moslem traditions suggest that Dajjal is of enormous size, and travels at the speed of the clouds. They suggest that the distance between Dajjal's ears is 40 arms spans. The deepest parts of the sea reach up to his ankles.[6]

This Eastern view is supposed by Tamim Al-Dari, an early Christian convert to Islam. McGinn talks about him "meeting the Dajjal chained to a monastery on an island in the sea, and the monster predicted he would soon be loosed upon the earth."[7]

This view that suggests that Ad Dajaal lives on an island where he is shackled is repeated in a number of ahadith. One narrated by Fatimah, the daughter of Qays, tells us this:

> Then we hurried on till we came to a monastery and found a well-built man with his hands tied to his neck and iron shackles gripping his legs by the ankles. We said, "Woe to you, who are you?" He said: "You will soon come to know about me, but tell me who you are." We said, "We are people from Arabia, and we embarked upon

a boat but the waves had been driving us for one month and they brought us to this island."[8]

The narration continues: "We took to the rowing boats and landed on this island. Here a beast with profusely thick hair met us, and because of the thickness of his hair his face could not be distinguished from his back. We said: 'Woe to you. Who are you?'"[9] The chained man on the island responds:

> I am the Dajaal and will soon be permitted to leave. So I shall leave and travel in the land and shall not spare any town where I shall not stay for forty nights, except Mecca and Medina. These two places are prohibited areas for me, and I shall not attempt to enter either of them. An angel with a sword in his hand will confront me and bar my way, and there will be angels to guard every road leading to it. Then Allah's apostle striking the pulpit with the help of the end of his staff said: "This implies Tayba, meaning Medina. Have I not told you an account of the Dajjal like this?"[10]

The same account of the Dajjal being a beast chained on an island can also be seen in an account from the *Arabian Nights* used as an epigram to this chapter.

Other Moslem traditions on the Dajjal tell us that "The time between the great war and the conquest of the city of Constantinople will be six years, and the Dajjal will come forth in the seventh." Mu'adh ibn Jabal, a young boy in Medina when Mohammed began his teachings, concurs: "The prophet said, 'The greatest war, the conquest of Constantinople, and the coming forth of the Dajjal will take place within a period of seven months.'"[11]

These many references to a relationship between the Dajjal and the conquering of the city of Constantinople by Moslem warriors are most likely related to Islamic attempts to conquer the city by sieges between 673 and 678, and 717 and 718.

Hudhayfah ibn al-Yaman, a seventh-century companion of Mohammed's, and one of the earliest converts to Islam, tells us that: "The Dajjal will come accompanied by a river of fire. He who falls into this fire will certainly receive his reward, and have his load taken off him, but he who falls into this river will have his load retained and his reward taken off him. I then asked, 'What will come next?' He said, 'The last hour will come.'"[12]

Anas ibn Malik, another well known eighth-century *sahabi* (companion) of the prophet Mohammed, tells us: "The Dajjal will be followed by 70,000 Jews of Isfahan wearing Persian shawls."[13]

Amr ibn al-A'as, a contemporary of Mohammed's and an Arab military commander who led the forces to conquer Egypt, writes of signs of the coming of the Dajjal: "I committed to memory a hadith from Allah's apostle Mohammed, and I did not forget it after Allah's apostle Mohammed said, 'The first sign (out of the signs of the appearance of Dajjal) would be the appearance of the sun from the West. The appearance of the beast before the people at noontime, and whichever happens first, the other will occur immediately.'"[14]

But a tradition from Abu Harayrah, the seventh-century narrator of hadith most often quoted by Sunni Moslems contradicts this account: "Allah's messenger Mohammed said, 'Dajjal will come from the Eastern side with the intention of attacking Medina until he will get down behind Uhud. Then the angels will turn his face toward Syria and there he will perish.'"[15]

Uhud was a seventh-century city near Medina. It was the site of a famous battle on March 23, 625 between armies from Mecca and Medina. Tradition has it that the battle was won by the Meccans, though Walt W. Montgomery's *Mohammed at Medina* came to the opposite conclusion.

The Dajjal is often associated with Medina in various Moslem traditions. A hadith from Bukhari and narrated by Abu Said, a fourteenth-century ruler of the state of Ilkhanate, tells us:

> One day Allah's apostle Mohammed narrated to us a long story about Ad-Dajjal and among the things he narrated to us was "Dajjal will come, and he will be forbidden to enter the mountain pass of Medina. He will encamp in one of the salt areas neighboring Medina, and there will appear to him a man who will be the best or one of the best of the people. He will say, 'I testify that you are Ad-Dajjal whose story Allah's apostle has told us. Ad Dajjal will say to his audience, 'Look if I kill this man and then give him life, will you have any doubt about my claim?' They will reply, 'No.' Then Ad Dajjal will kill that man and then will make him alive. The man will say, 'Now I recognize you more than ever!' Ad-Dajjal will then try to kill him again, but he will not be given the power to do so."[16]

Other hadith of Bukhari also refer to this tradition. "Allah's apostle Mohammed said, 'There are angels at the mountain passes of Medina, so that neither plague nor Ad-Dajjal can enter it.'" And "The prophet Mohammed said, 'Ad-Dajjal will come and encamp at a place close to Medina. Then Medina will shake three times, and then every *kafir* (disbeliever) and hypocrite will go out of Medina towards him.'"[17]

These stories are most likely related to two traditions from Christianity. First, that the Anti-Christ will have power enough to bring forth miracles and wonders. And second, at the end of time, the Anti-Christ will be the ruler of liars, hypocrites, and non-believers.

One other tradition involving Ad-Dajjal comes from a hadith by Abu Dawood, narrated by Hudhayfah ibn al-Yaman. Dawood tells us: "Then the Anti-Christ (Dajjal) will come forth accompanied by a river of fire. He who falls into his fire will certainly receive his reward, and have his load taken off him; but he who falls into this river will have his load retained and his reward taken off him. I then asked, 'What will come next?' He said, 'The last hour will come.'"[18]

Abu Dawood seems to suggest here that believers will be rewarded in the afterlife simply for being an enemy of Ad-Dajjal. Another Islamic tradition that appears among hadith on Ad-Dajjal is the view that there are angels placed by Allah at the mountain passes of Medina, so that neither plague nor Ad-Dajjal can pass. A hadith from Bukhari tells us precisely this: "There are angels at the mountain passes of Medina so that neither plague nor Ad-Dajjal can enter it."[19]

In another hadith, Bukhari appears to be referring to the same thing when he says: "The Prophet said, 'Ad-Dajjal will come and encamp at a place close to Medina, and then Medina will shake three times, whereupon every *Kafir* (disbeliever) and hypocrite will go out of Medina toward him.'"[20]

Thus, the Islamic tradition seems to believe in a version of the fallen angels story, where Ad-Dajjal and Shaytan, two evil angels, will be banned from entering the holy city of Medina. Ad-Dajjal will not enter the city because Allah has appointed good angels to guard the mountain passes leading to the city.

In another hadith, Muslim, narrated by Abu Harayrah, tells us that Ad-Dajjal will come from the eastern side with the intention of attacking Medina. He will get behind Uhud (a mountain) and then the angels will turn his face toward Syria and there he will perish.[21]

The Legend of the Anti-Christ

DAJJAL WITH ONE EYE

Among Islamic hadith there are many accounts that Dajjal has only one eye. Bukhari, narrated by Abdullah ibn Umar, a prominent seventh-century authority in hadith and the law, tells us: "Allah's apostle Mohammed stood up amongst the people and then praised and glorified Allah as He deserved and then He mentioned Ad-Dajjal and said, 'I warn you of him, and there was no prophet but warned his followers of him; but I will tell you something about him which no prophet has told his followers. Ad-Dajjal has one eye, while Allah does not.'"[22]

In another hadith by Bukhari, narrated by Abdullah ibn Umar, they repeat the same claim, "While Al-Masih Ad-Dajjal is blind in the right eye, and his eye looks like a protruding grape."[23] This same tradition is repeated in hadith by Abu Harairah and ibn 'Abbas. It can also be found in another hadith of Bukhari, narrated by Malik ibn Anas, one of the most highly respected scholars of *fiqh*, the study of Islamic law. Malik ibn Anas' traditional dates are 715–796. He tells us: "The Prophet Mohammed said, 'No prophet was sent but that he warned His followers against the one-eyed liar (Ad-Dajjal). Beware! He is blind in one eye, and your Lord is not so. And there will be written between his eyes the word *kafir*.'"[24]

This story of the Djaal being one-eyed is repeated in a number of ahadith. A hadith from Bukhari narrated by Anas ibn Malik tells us, "Ad Djaal will come and encamp at a place close to Mahdina and the city will shake three times, whereupon every non-believer and hypocrite will go out of the city to meet Djaal." He adds, "I will tell you something about him which no prophet has told his followers: "Ad-Djaal is one eyed, whereas Allah is not."[25] In another passage of Bukhari narrated by Abdullah, Muhammed says, "Ad-Djaal is blind in the right eye, and his eye looks like a protruding grape."[26]

It is not entirely clear how this tradition that Dajjal is blind in one eye arose, but not all Moslem scholars see it as physical blindness. One contrary view says this:

> The word "one-eyed" is not to be taken literally. Allah says in the holy *Qu'ran* "Whoever is blind in this world will be blind in the hereafter." (17.72) Blindness here evidently means spiritual blindness. Thus, the word under discussion will mean that Dajjal will have no spiritual sight, although his worldly sight will be very sharp; and along with it, he will discover such subtle methods resulting in such wonderful performances, that he will almost

appear as one claiming Divinity. But he shall have no spiritual vision whatsoever, as is the case of people of America and Europe today, who have carried the physical side of life to perfection.[27]

Whether or not the blindness of Dajjal is physical or spiritual is not clear; but what is clear is those who believe it refers to spiritual blindness also believe that the Dajjal will be able to execute "wonderful performances" in the final days. Another thing that is clear is that Dajjal is associated with Gog and Magog in some Islamic traditions.

The *Qu'ran* refers to Gog and Magog in two places. The first reference is at 18:94, the second at 21:96. We will look at these two sections of the *Qu'ran*, and their relationship to the legend of Dajjal, in the next section of this chapter.

In addition to the ahadith about Djaal having one eye, there are also a number of other traditions that speak of the Anti-Christ's physical description. Most of these traditions can be found in the work of the ninth-century collector of hadith, Abul Husayn Muslim, who, in different narrators says that Djaal will be "a young, fat man, with wheatish complexion, with a broad chest."[28] Other traditions recorded by Muslim say that Djaal will be from the tribe of Khuza'a, he will have curly hair, his head will be covered, and he shall have a shiny forehead.[29] Muslim also says that Djaal will have defects in both eyes. His left eye will have a swelling pupil, while he will be blind in the right eye.[30] Muslim adds: "He has a brisk walk, and no children."[31]

Abu Bakara Tirmidhi even goes so far as to describe Ad Djaal's parents: "His father will be tall and thin and his nose will be pointed like a beak, while his mother will be fat with two long hands. They will both remain thirty years without a child. After thirty years, a one-eyed son with biting teeth and of little benefit will be born to them. His heart will remain awake while his eyes will sleep."[32]

Abu Huraira also offers a description of Djaal, "The color of his hair will be reddish white."[33] Ibn Abbas and Bukhari report, "He will be well built and his hair will be soft and reach down to his ears. When he lowers his head, beads of perspirations will fall from it, and when he raises his head, beads like pearls will scatter from it."[34]

Abu Hurayrah also writes about the description of Ad Dajaal: "When you see him, recognize him: a man of medium height, reddish hair, wearing two light, yellow garments, looking as if drops of water were falling from his head though it will not be wet. He will fight the people for the cause of Islam."[35]

Hurayrah continues: "He will break the cross, kill all the swine, and abolish jizah. And Allah will abolish all religions but Islam. He will destroy Ad-Dajaal and will live on the earth for forty years. Then he will die, and Moslems will pray over him."[36]

Ubadah ibn Saamit also describes Ad-Dajaal: "I have explained Dajaal to you, but I fear that you might not have understood. Maseeh-ud-Dajjal will be short and his legs will be crooked. The hair on his head will be extremely twisted. He will have one eye, while the other eye will be flat. It will be neither deep, nor protruding."[37]

Ibn Umar, seventh-century writer of a hadith, disagrees: "Regarding Ad-Dajaal . . . he will have a red complexion, fat, with curly hair, blind in the right eye which looks like a bulging grape."[38]

Subay Ibn Khalid, narrated by Hudhayfah ibn al-Yaman suggests that if Allah has on earth a leader who flays your back and takes your property, the believer must follow him, otherwise, he says, "die holding on to a tree stump."[39] Khalid goes on to say, "Ad-Dajaal will come forth accompanied by a river and fire": "He who falls into the fire will certainly receive his reward, and have his load taken off him; but he who falls into the river will have his load retained and his reward taken off him."[40]

DAJJAL, GOG, AND MAGOG

In Ezekiel 38–39, the cities of Gog and Magog are mentioned nine times. They are portrayed by Ezekiel as the leaders of a confederation of Israel's enemies. At some future time when Israel will be united, these forces of Gog and Magog will war against the Israelites. In the New Testament, in Revelation 20:8, for example, Gog and Magog are given as two examples of rebellious nations. They will be deceived by Satan and/or the Anti-Christ, after the former's release from prison, or the latter's appearance on earth. In some Christian traditions, Gog and Magog will be the armies of the Anti-Christ. This view is adopted in Islam.

The *Qu'ran* refers to Gog and Magog (*Yajooj and Majooj*) twice. The first comes near the end of the Cave, Surah 18. Rashad Khalifa's translation of 18:93–99 goes like this:

> 18.93   When he reached the valley between two palisades, he found people whose language was barely understandable.

> 18.94 They said, "Dhul-Qarnain, Gog and Magog are corruptors of the Earth. Can we pay you to erect a barrier between us and them?"
>
> 18.95 He said, "My Lord has given me great bounties. If you cooperate with me, I will build a dam between you and them."
>
> 18.96 "Bring me masses of iron." Once he filled the gap between the two Palisades, he said, "Blow! Once it is hot, help me pour tar on top of it."
>
> 18.97 Thus, they could not climb it, nor could they bore holes in it.
>
> 18.98 He said, "This is mercy from my Lord. When the prophecy of my Lord comes to pass, He will cause the dam to crumble. The prophecy of my Lord is truth."
>
> 18.99 At that time, we will let them invade with one another, then the horn will be blown and we will summon them all together.[41]

Dhul Qarnain, ("the one with two horns") is to be identified with the beasts in Daniel and Revelation. It also refers to the Dajjal, the Moslem version of the Anti-Christ. In Islam, it is the Dajjal that builds the wall. Dajjal constructed the wall out of iron, and then poured molten copper over it, making it difficult to climb or dig under it. Various Islamic scholars locate this wall in various places. Some say it is in the Caucasus Mountains, at Dariel Pass. One Moslem scholar, mufti Ebrahim Desai, the Dear Abby of the Moslem world, calls it "the land of ice."[42]

This same tradition suggests that Gog and Magog attempt every evening to break through the wall, but when it gets late they say, "It's late, we'll finish tomorrow." The next day, when they wake up, they see that all the work they had done the night before had become undone while they slept. This scenario repeats itself, until the day when they finally say, "*in sha Allah*," meaning "by the will of Allah." Then they were able to break through and escape.

The other mention of Gog and Magog in the *Qu'ran* comes in Surah 21, verse 96. Khalifa's renders the passage this way:

> 21.95 It is forbidden for any community we have annihilated to return.
>
> 21.96 Not until Gog and Magog reappear, will they then return— they will come from every direction.

21.97 That is when the inevitable prophecy will come to pass, and the disbelievers will stare in horror, "Woe to us, we have been oblivious. Indeed, we have been wicked."[43]

In Islam, the reappearance of Gog and Magog is a sign that Doomsday is near. The age of Dajjal will be instituted, and he will be defeated by the Second Coming of Jesus. Other Islamic hadith have it that "Gog and Magog are the progeny of Adam,"[44] and "Verily I have created some of My servants whom no one can destroy but Myself."[45] In the same hadith, it is expressly stated that Gog and Magog are the progeny of Adam, which may be connected to another story that Gog and Magog will drink up all the water in the world: "They will drink the water of the world so much so that when some of them (the inhabitants of Gog and Magog) will pass by a stream, and they will drink all that is in it and leave it dry."[46]

Another hadith has it that the advance guards of Gog and Magog will cross the Gulf of Tiberius, and they will drink the whole mass of water in it. In the hadith of Tamim Dari, Dajjal also asks Tamim Dari about the Gulf of Tiberius, "Tell me about the Gulf of Tiberius, is there any water in it?"[47]

SIGNS OF THE COMING OF THE DAJJAL

In a hadith by Bukhari and narrated by Abu Hurairah, we can find eleven signs of the arrival of the Dajjal. Bukhari tells us:

The hour will not be established until:

1. Two big groups fight each other, whereupon, there will be a great number of casualties on both sides and they will be following one and the same religious doctrine.
2. About 30 Dajjals (liars) will appear, and each one will claim that he is Allah's apostle.
3. Until religious knowledge is taken away the death of religious scholars.
4. Earthquakes will increase in number.
5. Time will pass quickly.
6. Afflictions will appear.
7. Al-Harj (killing) will increase.
8. Until wealth will be in abundance—so abundant that a wealthy person will worry lest nobody should accept Zakat, and whenever he will present it to someone, that person (to whom it is offered) will say, "I am not in need of it."

9. Until people compete with each other in constructing high buildings.
10. Until someone passing by a grave of someone will say, "Would that I were in his place."
11. Until the sun rises in the West.[48]

Bukhari completes this hadith this way:

> So when the sun will rise and the people will see it (rising in the West) they will all believe (embrace Islam); but that will be the time when, as Allah said "No good will it do to a soul to believe then, if it believed not before, nor earned good (by deeds of righteousness) through its faith. And the hour will be established while two men spreading a garment in front of them but they will not be able to sell it, nor fold it up; and the Hour will be established when a man has milk in his she-camel and has taken away the milk but he will not be able to drink it; water (his animals) in it; and the Hour will be established when a person has raised a morsel (of food) to his mouth, but he will not be able to eat it.[49]

It should be clear that the mentions of plagues, pestilences, earthquakes, etc. are directly related to prophecies in Daniel and Revelation. Many of the other signs outlined by Bukhari are unusual or impossible events, suggesting that the end of time will only be brought about by the actions of some powerful figure.

Another tradition of Jabir bin Samurah, narrated by Nafi'bin Utbah, also enumerates signs of the coming of Dajjal, Mohammed tells Jabir: "You will invade the Arabian Peninsula and Allah will grant it to you. Then you will conquer Persia and Allah will grant it to you. Then you will invade Ar-Rum and Allah will grant it to you. Then you invade the Dajjal, and Allah will grant him to you. We do not believe that the Dajjal will appear until Ar-Rum is conquered."[50]

The land of Ar-Rum is Europe. Mohammed suggests that Islam will conquer Rome, after they have conquered the city of Constantinople. In a hadith from Abdullah bin Amir bin Al-Aas, narrated by Imam Ahmad, concurs: "While we were around the Messenger of Allah, we ask, 'Which of these two cities will be conquered first?' Constantinople or Romiyah (Rome). He said, 'The city of Heraclius will first be conquered.' He meant Constantinople."[51]

Another hadith from An-Nuwas ibn Sam'an tells us of a conversation about the Dajjal between Mohammed and his followers. He tells us:

> One morning the Prophet spoke about the Dajjal. Sometimes he describes him as insignificant, and sometimes he describes him as so dangerous that we thought he was in a clump of date-palms nearby. When we went to him later, he noticed the fear in our faces and asked, "What is the matter with you?"
>
> We said, "O Messenger of Allah, this morning you spoke of Dajjal; Sometimes you describe him as insignificant and sometimes you describe him as so dangerous that we thought he was in a clump of date-palms nearby.
>
> The Prophet said, "I fear for you in other matters besides the Dajjal. If he appears while I am among you, I will contend with him on your behalf. But if he appears while I am not among you, then each man must contend with him on his own behalf, and Allah will take care of every Muslim on my behalf.[52]

In this same hadith, Mohammed goes on to describe the Dajjal: "The Dajjal will be a young man, with short, curly hair, and one eye floating. I would liken him to Abdul Uzza ibn Qatan. Whoever amongst you lives to see him should recite the opening *ayat* (verses) of Surah al-Kahf. He will appear on the way between Syria and Iraq, and will create disaster left and right. O Servant of Allah adhere to the Path of Truth."[53]

Mohammed's disciples respond by asking how quickly he will be upon the earth. Mohammed answers:

> Like a cloud driven by the wind. He will come to the people and call them to a false religion, and they will believe in him and respond to him. He will issue a command to the sky, and it will rain; and to the earth, and it will produce crops. After grazing on these crops, their animals will return with their utters full and their flanks stretched. Then he will come to another people and call them to his fake religion, but they will reject his call. He will depart from them; they will suffer famine and will possess nothing in the form of wealth. Then he will pass through a wasteland and will say, "Bring forth you treasures," and the treasures will come forth, like swarms of bees. Then he will call a man brimming with youth; he will strike him with a sword and cut him in two, then place the pieces at the distance between an archer and his target. Then he will call him, and the young man will come running and laughing.[54]

Mohammed continues:

> At that point Allah will send the Messiah, Son of Mary, and he will descend to a white minaret in the East of Damascus, wearing two

garments dyed with saffron, placing his hands on the wings of two angels. When he lowers his head, beads of perspiration will fall from it. Every *kafir* (non-believer) who smells this fragrance will die, and his breath will reach as far as he can see. he will search for the Dajjal until he finds him at the Gate of Ludd (biblical Lydda), now known as Lod, where he will kill him.

Then a people that Allah has protected will come to Jesus, the son of Mary, and he will wipe their faces, and tell them of their status in Paradise. At that time Allah will reveal to Jesus, "I have brought forth some of My servants whom on one will be able to fight. Take my servants safely to at-Tur."[55]

Nuwas Samas also sees a role for Gog and Magog for the End Times:

Then Allah will send Gog and Magog, and they will swarm down from every slope. The first of them will pass by the Lake of Tiberius, and will drink some of its water; the last of them will pass by and say, "There used to be water here." Jesus, the Prophet of Allah and his companions will be besieged until a bull's head will be dearer to them than 100 dinars are to you now."

Then Jesus and his Companions will pray to Allah, and He will send insects who will bite the people of Gog and Magog on their necks, so that in the morning they will all die as one. Then Jesus and his Companions will come down and will not find any nook or cranny on earth which is free from their putrid stench. Jesus and his Companions will again pray to Allah, Who will send a bird like the necks of camels; they will seize the bodies of Gog and Magog, and throw them wherever Allah wishes.

At that time, Allah will send a pleasant wind which will soothe them even under their arm pits, and will take the soul of every Muslim. Only the most wicked people will be left. They will fornicate like asses. Then the Last Hour will come upon them.[56]

Another hadith from Ibn Mas'ud also discusses the role of Jesus in the End Times. Mas'ud was a seventh-century Moslem scholar who had administrative and diplomatic duties under Caliphs Umar ibn al-Khattab and Uthman ibn Affan. Mas'us is also one of the four people whom Mohammed said one should learn the *Qu'ran*. Mas'ud's hadith tells us:

The Prophet said, "On the Night of the Isla (the Night Journey), I met my Father Abraham, Moses, and Jesus, and they discussed the Last Hour. The matter was first referred to Abraham and Moses, and both said, "I have no knowledge of it."

The Legend of the Anti-Christ

> Then it was referred to by Jesus who said, "No one knows about its timing except Allah; what my Lord told me was that the Dajjal will appear, and when he sees me he will begin to melt like lead. Allah will destroy him when he sees me. The Moslems will fight against the *Kafirun*, and even the trees and rocks will say, "O Muslim, there is a *kafir* hiding behind me. Come kill him!" Allah will destroy the *Kafirun*, and the people will return to their own lands.[57]

Ibn Mas'ud, through a narration by Ahmad ibn Hanbul, the ninth-century founder of the Hanibal School of *Fiqh* (Law) completes the narrative:

> Then Gog and Magog will appear from all directions, eating and drinking everything they find. The people will complain to me, so I will pray to Allah, and He will destroy them, so that the earth will be filled with their stench. Allah will send rain which will wash their bodies into the sea.
>
> My Lord has told me that when that happens, the Last Hour will be very close, like a pregnant woman whose time is due, but her family does not know exactly when she will deliver.[58]

The most contemporary account of the Djaal in Islam is given by Ahmed Thomas in his book, *The King without Clothes*.[59] Thomas suggests three principal signs of Djaal. First, he will be a human individual. Second, he will be the head of a world-wide social and cultural phenomenon; and third, he will be an "unseen force." In the course of his book, Thomas suggests various candidates for the Anti-Christ, including the possibility that the Djaal will come from UFOs who abduct humans on Earth.

The following hadith describes the defeat of Ad-Dajjal by Jesus at the end of time.

> It will at this very time that Allah will send Christ, son of Mary. He will descend at a white minaret on the eastern side of Damascus, wearing two garments lightly dyed with saffron and placing his hands on the wings of two angels. When he lowers his head, there will fall beads of perspiration from his head, and when he raises it up, beads like pearls will scatter from it. Every non-believer who smells the odor of his body will die and his breath will reach as far as he is able to see. He will then search for him (Dajjal) until he catches hold of him at the gate of Ludd and kills him. Then a people that Allah has protected will come to Jesus, son of Mary, and he will wipe their faces and inform them of their ranks in

Paradise. It will be under such conditions that Allah will reveal to Jesus these words: I have brought forth from among my servants such people against whom none will be able to fight; you take these people safely to Tur, and then Allah will send Gog and Magog, and they shall swarm down from every slope. The first of them will pass the lake of Tiberius and drink out of it. And when the last of them passes, he will say, "There was once water there."[60]

Muslim continues in the same hadith:

> Jesus and his companions will then be besieged here (at Tur) and they will be so hard-pressed that the head of an ox will be dearer to them than 100 diners. Allah's apostle Jesus and his companions will supplicated Allah Who will send to them insects which will attack their necks, and in the morning they would perish as one single person. Jesus and his companions will then beseech Allah who will send birds whose necks will be like those of Bactrian camels and they will carry them away and throw them wherever Allah wills.[61]

Muslim finishes his hadith:

> Then Allah will send rain which no house of mud bricks or tent of camel hair will keep out and it will wash the earth until it resembles a mirror. Then the earth will be told to bring forth its fruit and restore its blessing and, as a result there will grow such a big pomegranate that a group of people will be able to eat it and seek shelter under its skin; a dairy cow will give so much milk that a whole party will be able to drink it. The milking camel will give such a large quantity of milk that the whole tribe will be able to drink from it; and the milking sheep will give so much milk that the whole family will be able to drink from it. At that time, Allah will send a pleasant wind which will soothe people even under the armpits. He will take the life of every Muslim and only the wicked will survive who will commit adultery like asses and the last among themselves; after having their swords by the olive trees, Satan will cry, "The Dajjal has taken your place among your families." They will then come out, but it will be of no avail. When they reach Syria, he will come out while they are preparing themselves for battle, drawing up the ranks. Certainly, the time of prayer will come and then Jesus, son of Mary, will descend and lead them in prayer. When the enemy of Allah sees him, it will disappear, just as salt dissolves in water. And if Jesus were not to confront them at all, even though it would dissolve completely. Allah will kill them

by his hand, and He will show them their blood on his lance (the lance of Jesus).[62]

ISLAM AND THE BEASTS OF DANIEL AND REVELATION

Like the Jewish and Christian traditions, the Islamic faith posits a number of traditions about a "beast" or "beasts" in its ahadith. Many of those traditions are recorded in a book by Michael Fortner entitled, *The Scarlet Beast: Islam and the Beast of Revelation*.[63] Fortner points out that the coming of the Beast is to be a major sign of *Qiyamah*, the Arabic word for the end of the world. A hadith from Surah An-Naml reports "And when the word is fulfilled concerning them. We shall bring forth a Beast of the Earth to speak unto them because man has no faith in our revelation."[64]

Abdullah-b-Umar tells us: "I memorized a hadith from the Messenger of Allah which I have not forgotten. 'The first of the signs that will come is the rising of the sun from the place of its setting and the emergence of the Beast upon the people. Which ever of these two events comes first, the other will be sure to follow.'"[65]

Ibn Kathir tells us that the beast will appear very near the end of time when disintegration, corruption, disbelief, and evil prevail. Commands of Allah will be ignored, the Deen changed and made a mockery of, it is then that Allah will take out the Beast from the Earth.[66]

There are also varied opinions in Islam about where the Beast will appear. Al-Tabrani suggests it shall come out from Al-Masjid Al-Haraam, near Makkah (Mecca). Other traditions agree with the location, but suggest the Beast will appear on three separate occasions. There are also varying opinions about what kind of animal the Beast shall be. Some say it will be a big, hairy man. Others suggest a she-camel. The prophet Salih says, "The first opinion regarding the Beast is that it is the young of the she-ass camel, this the most correct opinion."[67] Still others hold that the Beast to come is an animal that has the features of many different animals.

This last opinion was held by Abu Zubair, who, describing the Beast says: "Its head is like that of a bull, eyes like that of a pig, ears like that of an elephant, horns like that of a stag, neck like that of an ostrich, chest like a lion, color like that of a tiger, flanks like a cat, tail like that of a ram, feet and legs like that of a camel, and a distance of twelve cubits between every two joints."[68]

One final opinion on the nature of the Beast is that the animal is a snake. This tradition holds that when Ibrahim and Ismail built the Ka'bah, after it was complete, Allah sent a snake to guard it. Ibn Abbas, and others, suggest that the Djaal will appear at the end of time, looking like a similar giant snake.[69]

Another authentic hadith about the relationship of Ad-Dajaal to the Beast points out that a number of Muslim scholars disagreed over whether the Beast is to be understood as a vision or as something that exists in reality. The hadith in question is told by Fatima bint Qays, one of the early immigrant women from Medina. Fatima points out that in her day, some believed the Beast to be a literal creature, while others thought the Beast to exist in an allegorical sense.[70]

Subsequent Islamic scholars have questioned the reliability of this narrative, such as A. J. Jenkinson, who states that this story is influenced by Greek tales of the God Zeus, who chained Prometheus to an island, in the same way that Fatima bint Qays suggests that the Dajjal is chained on an island as well.[71]

Other disagreements abound in Islamic literature over the ontological status of Dajjal. Some traditions place the Anti-Christ and Iblis on the same level. Others that Ad-Dajjal is a sort of unseen devil or demon. In still other commentators, Ad Dajjal is seen as a human being, who will lead a human army at the end of time.

OTHER AHADITH ON THE DAJJAL

Other Ahadith regard the Dajjal and inform us that he will emerge between Shaam (Syria) and Iraq, and he will be known when he is in Isfahan (a city in Persia) at a place called Yahudea (Judea). The Jews of Isfahan will be Dajjal's main followers. Dajjal will also have a great number of women followers. He will charm them with his greatest attributes.[72]

Other Ahidith claim the Dajjal will appear with both fire and water, but in reality the fire will be cold, and what appears to be cold water will in fact be a blazing fire. He will travel at great speeds, and his means of travel will be a great mule. He will send down rain to those who believe in him, and cause famine and drought to those who do not.[73]

Some ahadith suggest that hidden riches will spill forth at the command of Dajjal. He will stay on earth for a period of forty days, and the length of the first day shall be a year. The second day will be equal to a month; the third day to a week; the remaining days will be normal. Some say the Dajjal will have thick fingernail in his left eye. He will claim to be both a prophet, and to be God.[74]

Other important Ahadith tell us that Dajjal has other names, including "the Sick Man of Humanity."[75] He will be the embodiment of all that denotes unbelief. When the Mahdi (the Messiah) and Dajjal meet, at the end of time, all human beings will have a choice to follow one or the other. Those who follow the Mahdi will enter Paradise at the end of time. Those who follow the Dajjal will experience the torments and fires of hell.

Jabir bin Samurah tells a tale of Nafi bin Utbah who was traveling with Muhammed. Some people from the west of Madinah came to the prophet wearing clothes made of wool. They met Muhammed next to a mound. The prophet says to them: "You will invade the Arabian Peninsula and Allah will grant it to you. Then you will conquer Persia and Allah will grant it to you. Then you will invade Ar-run (Europe), and Allah will grant it to you. Then, you will invade the Djaal and Allah will grant him to you."[76]

Then Nafi said to Jabir, "We do not believe that the Djaal will appear until Ar-Rum is conquered."[77] In a hadith narrated by Imran Ibn Hussain, he tells us, "From the birth of Adam until the advent of *Qiyaamah* (Judgment Day) there is no *fitnah* (tribulation) greater than that of Djaal." Hussain adds, "Those who hear about Djaal should stay away from him. By Allah, a person will approach him thinking he is a believer, but after seeing his amazing works he will become his follower."[78]

Other hadith on the Djaal suggest that when he takes over the world, "his voice will be heard all over the world simultaneously." Abu Dawood narrated by Abdullah Ibn Busr, tells us, "The time between the great war and the conquest of the city of Constantinople will be six years, and the Djaal will come forth in the seventh year."[79] But another hadith of Dawood narrated by Mu'adh ibn Jabal says, "The greatest war, the conquest of Constantinople, and the coming of the Djaal will take place in a period of seven months."[80]

Another Islamic tradition on the Anti-Christ is narrated by Hadhrat Anas. He suggests that the Djaal will reach the outskirts of Mahdina (Medina), and there will be three tremors. Then all the disbelievers and hypocrites will flee from Madina. Another narration of Hadhrat Asma bin Yazeed tells the tale that when the Djaal appears, there will be three spells of drought, in one year the skies will withhold one third of its rain, causing the earth to withhold one third of its produce. In the second year, the skies will withhold two thirds of its rain, causing the earth to withhold two thirds of its produce. In the third year, the skies will withhold all rain and there will be no crops that year. All animals, whether hooved or toothed, will die as a result.

The story goes on to suggest that the Djaal shall approach someone and ask, "Would you like me to bring your camel back to life?" The person will reply, "Certainly." Then Shaytan, who always accompanies the Djaal will appear before the person as a camel with a fat hump and utters full.[81]

In another version of the same tale, the Djaal approaches a man whose father and brother had recently died. The Djaal says, "If I bring your father and brother back to life will you believe that I am your master?" The man replied, "Why not?" And Shaytan once again took the form of the man's brother and father.[82]

Other Islamic traditions on the Djaal suggest that the main followers of the Djaal will be Jews, specifically Jews from Isfahan, and that many women will also be among his followers. The Djaal will have fire and water with him, but in reality the fire will turn out to be cool water, while what appears to be cool water will actually be a blazing fire. A final tradition on the Djaal says he will not be able to enter Mecca nor Medina at the end of time because Allah will guard those cities with angels to protect the true believers within. Indeed, this story even goes so far to say all seven entrances to Medina will be guarded.

This notion that Ad-Dajjal will not be permitted to enter Mecca and Medina is repeated in a number of ahadith. This entry narrated by Abu Said Al-Khudri is an illustrative example: "Allah's apostle told us a long story about Ad-Dajjal, and among the many things he mentioned was his saying, 'Ad-Dajjal will come and it will be forbidden for him to pass through the entrances of Medina.'"[83]

THE DAJJAL IN LATER ISLAM

The figure of the Dajjal also appears in the number of imperial prophecies in some late sixteenth-century Ottoman traditions. The sources of this tradition go all the way back to the Old Testament prophet, Ezekiel, who foretold of a great military power "in the latter times" that would mount an invasion against Israel. The invasion was to be led by Gog (what some interpreted as Russia) together with Persia (modern day Iran).

Ezekiel speaks of a people from the extreme north known as Gog: "I will turn you around, put hooks into your jaws, and lead you out ... In the latter years, you will come into the land of those brought back from the sword, and gathered from many people on the mountains of Israel, which had long been desolate. They were brought out of the nations, and now all of them dwell safely."[84]

This prophecy has been used by various Islamic prognosticators between the sixteenth and nineteenth centuries. All of them tie the events of Ezekiel to the Ottoman Empire and the coming of the end of the world. One good example is Bahaullah, in the Bahai tradition, who predicted that Sultan Abdul Aziz will lose control of the Ottoman Empire. Bahaullah mentions two signs of the end times. He writes: "We have appointed two signs for the coming of the End Times. The first is the development of a single language, and the adoption of a common script. The second sign is the emergence of a Divine philosophy, which will include the discovery of radical approaches to the study of nature."[85]

Many Islamic scholars see this prophecy, and others like it in the Ottoman Empire in the sixteenth to nineteenth centuries, to refer to the coming of the Dajjal, who will convert Moslems to his false religion, and will possess powers over nature not normally associated with human beings. Other Islamic prophecies tie the Ezekiel quote to Mehmed II (reigned 1451–140), who recaptured the city of Consantinople in 1451 at the age of nineteen. There had been twelve previous attempts by Muslim armies to conquer the city, and in the course of those attempts a considerable body of prophetic literature arose that promised the Byzantine Empire would fall to Islam, just before the end of the world, and the coming of the Dajjal. Often these prophecies linked the fall of Rome with the fall of Constantinople and the End Times.

More recently, in 1838 a Millerite leader named Josiah Litch, on the basis of his understanding of Revelation 9:15 suggests that the Ottoman Empire would fall on August 11, 1840. A scholar named Ellen White gave a glowing endorsement of Litch's prediction in his book, *The Great Controversy*: "In the year 1840, another remarkable fulfillment of prophecy excited widespread interest. Two years before, Josiah Litch, one of the leading ministers preaching the Second Advent, published an exposition of Revelation nine, predicting the fall of the Ottoman Empire."[86]

The Anti-Christ in Islamic Thought

Some who knew of Litch's prophecy also knew of the many Islamic predictions of the fall of the Ottoman Empire, the coming of Dajjal and the drawing of the End Times. One of the great ironies of Litch's prediction is that Russia already had defeated the Ottoman Empire in 1829, when they signed a treaty to protect the Turks.

AD-DAJAAL AND CONTEMPORARY ISLAM

Among some circles in contemporary Islam, particularly among British believers in the Islamic faith, is a conspiracy theory that circulates, regarding the Catholic organization Opus Dei and the coming of the Dajaal. One advocate of this theory is Ahmad Thomson, a British writer whose *Dajjal: The King Who Has No Clothes*[87] sketches out the connection in minute detail. Thomson had developed the theory in an earlier book called, *Blood on the Cross: Islam in Spain in the Light of Christian Persecution through the Ages,* published in 1989.[88]

Thomas uses documents from Rome and Spain, as well as Papal encyclicals and European history to set forth a conspiracy theory not altogether different from the plot of the contemporary 2006 film, *The Da Vinci Code*, starring Tom Hanks and Audrey Tautou. The theory is also held by Robert Hutchison in his *Their Kingdom Come: Inside the Secret World of Opus Dei.*[89]

Hutchison argues that many of Pope John Paul II's closet advisors were members of Opus Dei. He also claims the organization has overturned governments and controls the F.B.I., the C.I.A., and banks throughout western Europe.

In her recent biography of Muhammed, Karen Armstrong suggests that the origins of the idea that the prophet (or Islam in general) is the Anti-Christ is two Spanish thinkers, Eulogio and Alvaro. Armstrong writes: "Eulogio and Alvaro both believed that the rise of Islam was a preparation for the advent of Anti-Christ, the great pretender described in the New Testament, whose reign would herald the Last Days."[90]

A few paragraphs later, Armstrong speaks more about the Spanish tradition of seeing Muhammed or Islam as the Anti-Christ: In relationship to the Crusades, Armstrong tells us:

> The apocalyptic view of Islam promoted by the martyrs of Cordova had continued during the Crusading Period, though it was not a major issue. In 1191 when Richard the Lionheart had been trav-

eling to the Holy Land with the Third Crusade, he had met the celebrated Italian mystic Joachim of Fiori at Messina in Sicily. Joachim had told Richard that he would certainly defeat Saladin. He was wrong, but he made some other interesting observations. He believed that the end of the world was at hand and that resurgent Islam was one of the chief instruments of Anti-Christ, but he added that Anti-Christ himself was already alive in Rome and was destined to become the Pope.[91]

Armstrong goes on to point out that Luther and many of the reformers held the Islam as Anti-Christ view. She quotes R. W. Southern as saying that when Luther was asked if Muhammed and the Muslims were the Anti-Christ, Luther replied that "Islam is too gross to fulfill this terrible destiny."[92]

Armstrong points out that Zwingli and some of the other reformers "put forth similar ideas, seeing Rome as the 'head' of Anti-Christ and 'Muhammadans' as the body."[93]

A number of other contemporary debates about the Dajaal can be found in Islamic Literature. Much of those debates center on whether the figure is real, or is best thought of as a mythological figure. Zeki Saritoprak has given a detailed analysis of the adherents to these two points of view.[94]

CHRISTIAN THINKERS ON ISLAM AND THE ANTI-CHRIST

The earliest Christian critic of Islam was John of Damascus (675–749), an Arab Muslim in Syria who worked for the Umayyad Caliphs. John's polemics against Islam tended to deprecate the prophet Muhammad and ridicule the Qur'an, in order to elevate the status of Christ and Christianity. John of Damascus established the tradition that Muhammad was an imposter, the Anti-Christ.

Saint Eulogius of Cordoba flourished during the reigns of the Cordovan Caliphs, Abd-er-Rahman II and Muhammad I, who lived from 822 to 886. Eulogius, like John of Damascus, deprecated the life of the prophet Muhammad, and suggested he was the Anti-Christ. The first real attempt to communicate and understand Islam from a Christian perspective came late in the Middle Ages with missionaries such as Francis of Assisi and Raymond Lull.

Raymond Lull (1236–1315) was a Christian philosopher and missionary. He was born in Palma, Majorca, Spain, and taught for several years at the University of Paris. His stated goal was to describe the fundamentals of Christianity so succinctly that the Moslems to whom he ministered could not possibly deny the faith. To this end, Lull wrote the *Ars Magna*, that uses a method that exhaustively covers a particular topic. This method requires three concentric circles, each divided into compartments. One circle is divided into nine relevant subjects; the second into nine relevant predicates. The third is divided into nine questions: whether? What? Why? How large? Of what kind? Whence? When? And how?

In Lull's system, one circle is fixed, while the others rotate, providing a complete set of questions and statements in relation to the issue at hand. Among the topics that Lull explores are the prophet Muhammad and the Anti-Christ.

Ramon Lull (1236–1315) discusses the Anti-Christ in two of his works. The first of these is *Doctrina pueril* ("The Childish Doctrine") in which Lull portrays the Prophet Muhammed and the Anti-Christ as having the same characteristics. Lull arrives at the same conclusion in his *Libre contra Anticrist* ("Book Against the Anti-Christ"). Lull was one of the first Christian European thinkers who knew both Judaism and Islam well. In his work, elements from the Christian tradition live alongside Moslem and Jewish sources.[95]

Martin Luther wrote five different pieces of literature on Islam between 1528 and 1542. *On War Against the Turks* (1528); *A Sermon Against the Turks* (1529); *A Book on the Life and Customs of the Turks* (1530); *An Appeal to Prayer Against the Turks* (1451); and *A Refutation of the Qur'an* (1452).[96]

In *A Book on the Life and Customs of the Turks*, Luther wrote about Islam's view of Jesus: "Muhammad denies that Christ is the son of God. He denied that He died for our sins. He denied that He rose for our life. He denies faith in Whom remits our sins and justifies us. He denies His coming judgment of the living and the dead, though he does not believe in the resurrection of the dead and the day of judgment. He denies the Holy Spirit and His gifts."[97]

In comparing Catholicism to the Turks, Luther said that the two were the enemies of Christ and his Holy Church. The Turks were the body of the Anti-Christ, while the Pope was the head.[98] This view of Islam was held by a number of Christian reformers, well into the eighteenth century.

Contemporary scholar from Tripoli, Sheik Sobhi Saleh, in his *Manhal al Waridin*, gives a number of ahadith on Ad-Dajjal. Among these are number 1812, that from Adam until the Day of Resurrection of the Dead there will be no important matter than Ad-Dajaal. Saleh also suggests that the Anti-Christ at first will be a believer, and that the most important apparition of Ad-Dajaal appeared on May 13, 1970. In item 1818, Saleh identifies Ad-Dajaal with Zionism, and he tells us in the same item that Ad-Dajaal will perish in the city of Jerusalem.[99]

Saleh also confirms that as II John 7 tells us, "There will be many Anti-Christs," and he identifies many different possibilities for the identities of Gog and Magog. In item 1815, Saleh confirms that Ad-Dajaal will be one-eyed and he will be a liar. In item 1806, Saleh also confirms that Ad-Dajaal will be misleading, and that he will perform miracles in order to get others to follow him.[100]

MORE ON CONTEMPORARY ISLAMIC VIEWS OF THE ANTI-CHRIST

Among modern Islamic scholars in the nineteenth to twenty-first centuries there has been considerable debate over the figure of Ad Dajjal. The most central issue in these debates has been over the ontological status of the Islamic Anti-Christ. Some traditional modern scholars like Siddiq Hassan Khan, in the late nineteenth century, held the view that Al-Dajjal will emerge as a human being as described in the prophetic traditions. Other scholars disagree.[101]

Some contemporary Moslem thinkers identify the Anti-Christ with Western civilization, or more particularly with the United States. Muhammed Asad, an Austrian convert who died in 1992, saw the U.S. and the West in general, as a society incapable of understanding the spiritual nature of life. Asad influenced a number of other scholars, such as Egyptian columnist, Mustafa Mahmud.[102]

Still other contemporary Islamic thinkers identify Ad-Dajjal with the Jewish people. Rashid Rida, for example, believes that the trials of the Anti-Christ in Moslem literature describe a Zionist king and his followers. This theory goes all the way back to Medieval scholar Muhammed Al-Ghazali, who claimed that a Jewish genius will claim divinity, and will be followed by a great army. Al-Ghazali also suggests that Isa (Jesus) will eventually return to earth and defeat Ad-Dajjal and his "red army," the people of Gog and Magog.[103]

Some contemporary popular authors believe that the Anti-Christ will not be a human being, but rather a demonic figure who will emerge as a personification of evil at the end of time. Others say the Anti-Christ shall be a genie, an invisible creature who exists parallel to humans. These thinkers point out that genies can live without eating or drinking, yet they have a mode of transportation that allows them to levitate and fly wherever they wish.[104]

SOURCES FOR THE DJAAL

It should be clear from the discussion in this chapter that the principal sources for the idea of the Djaal are the Old and New Testaments. From the Old Testament, Islamic traditions have adopted the idea of the beast, the war of Gog and Magog, and the resurrection at the end of time in Daniel 12.

It should be just as clear that Islam adopted many aspects of the Christian idea of the Anti-Christ in its own explications of the End Times. Among apocalyptic New Testament ideas that Islam adopted in its development of the idea of the Djaal were: that the Djaal will have powers beyond normal human abilities; that he will use these powers to perform miracles and to bring beings to his movement; that he will be full of lies and deceit—that the Djaal will be defeated by Jesus and the Messiah at the end of time. Like the New Testament's Anti-Christ, the Djaal will call people to a false religion. Among the physical powers the Djaal will possess in Islam is the ability to get time to travel quickly, the ability to bring fast changes in the weather, the ability to bring new diseases to human beings, and the ability to have the sun rise in the West.

Other Christian ideas on the Anti-Christ adopted by Islam is the claim that the followers of the Djaal will have a physical mark. In the New Testament, it is the number 666. In Islam, it will be the letters K F R written between the eyes on the foreheads of nonbelievers.

Islam also adopted the early Christian idea that the followers of the Anti-Christ will be Jews, perhaps from the tribe of Dan, and that the Anti-Christ will have superior powers, including the ability to control the weather and to bring people and animals back from the dead.

The Islamic traditions also concur with the idea that the Djaal will have some sort of physical disability. Often the descriptions refer to him having one eye, but in all accounts of the Djaal something is unusual about the body of the Anti-Christ, like the various descriptions of the beasts in Daniel and Revelation. Finally, like traditions in the Old and New Testaments, in Islam the Djaal will only come in a time of tribulation that will be preceded by earthquakes, famine, war, and destruction.

ISLAM AS THE ANTI-CHRIST

When the Moslem armies broke out of the Arabian Peninsula and began to spread throughout North Africa and much of the Middle East, many Christian thinkers began to associate the Islamic faith with the Anti-Christ and the End Times. Many events in Spain and Portugal in the seventh and eighth century were interpreted that way.

Emmerson suggests that both John of Damascus and Alvarus of Cordoba were early Christian identifiers of the Anti-Christ with Islam. Emmerson writes:

> Other writers, such as John of Damascus (d. 749) and Alvarus of Cordova, also identify Islam as the Anti-Christ. In his *Indicolus luminosus* (845), Alvarus discusses the prophecies of Daniel 7 to argue that although the little horn originally represented Antiochus Epiphanes, the type of Anti-Christ, it now also represents Muhammed, the precursor of Anti-Christ. Like the little horn, Islam grows in power and overcomes three nations—the Greeks, the French, and the western Goths. Islam also proudly fights against the faith of the trinity. Poets and exegetes continued the identification of Islam with Anti-Christ.[105]

Emmerson continues by pointing out: "During the crusades and long after the crusading spirit had died, the Saracens were described as Anti-Christs and the forces of Gog and Magog. They were also associated with the other symbols of Anti-Christ. To Joachim of Fiori, for example, the Saracens represented the fourth and sixth heads of the dragon and the persecutors of the church to appear at the time of the opening of the fourth seal (Apocalypse 7:7–8)."[106]

Pope Innocent III also associated the Moslem armies with the seven-headed beast of Revelation 13. Innocent also interpreted the number 666 as the number of years Islam is to remain powerful. The fall of Constantinople to the Turks in 1453 was thought to be the culmination of the Moslem Anti-Christ idea.[107]

Englishman Roger Bacon (ca. 1214–1294), also interpreted the number 666 as the number of years Mohammedanism would rule before being destroyed by God.[108]

Many Christians in the seventh and eighth centuries began to see Islam, not as another faith, but as a personification of the last of the great heretics. Like many Christian thinkers before them, who regularly identified with Anti-Christ with various contemporary heretics, Christians in the seventh and eighth centuries began to do the same thing. The rise of Islam came to be seen as another sign of the end of the world.

From this period on, the restraining force of 2 Thessalonians 2:6 began to be identified with the Moslem armies, changing the early Christian view that it was the Roman Empire. By the time of Paulus Alvarus in the ninth century, he argues that Mohammed was not only a heretic, he was also a precursor to the Christian Anti-Christ. Alvarus believed there was no truth outside the Christian tradition, thus people must choose either Christ or Anti-Christ. Alvarus suggests that the fourth beast found in the Book of Daniel describes the Anti-Christ. Alvarus says Mohammed rejected the divinity of Christ and therefore represented the Anti-Christ.[109]

Alvarus took his analysis one step further by rewriting the death of Mohammed, claiming that Islam expected Mohammed to be resurrected at the End of Time. But Alvarus claims that Mohammed's body began to rot, and was eaten by dogs, thus confirming Mohammed as the Anti-Christ.[110]

Around the year 1200, Pope Innocent III called for the Fourth Crusade and suggested that Mohammed was the Anti-Christ. Innocent had intended to recapture the Holy Land. He directed his call toward the knights and nobles of Europe, rather than to kings, for he wished neither Richard I of England, nor Philip II of France, to participate in the Crusade. In order to get the knights and nobles to participate, Innocent repeatedly claimed that Mohammed was the Anti-Christ.

By the fourteenth century, many of the reformers of the Christian Church began to believe that the Pope was the Anti-Christ in the West, and Islam was the Anti-Christ in the East. This view was held by many Protestant thinkers well into the eighteenth century, when it was applied to the Turkish Empire.

Among late Middle Ages thinkers who believed that Muhammed was the Anti-Christ was William Langland and his *Piers Plowman*. In section 10.334–335 and 18.156, Langland describes Mohammed as a forerunner of Anti-Christ. Richard Emmerson comments on this phenomenon: "The poem in the C version may also develop Mohammed as a forerunner of Anti-Christ, for he was popularly understood as the Anti-Messiah of the Saracens and the Jews."[111]

During the Reformation, John Calvin, using Revelation 17 and 18, suggests that "Mohamet and the pope are the two horns of Anti-Christ." Martin Luther also believed that the Turks were the small horn that grew out of the fourth beast in Daniel 7:8 and 24. Heinrich Bornkamn argues that Luther also connected the Turks with Gog and Magog of Ezekiel 38 and 39: "He [Luther] found them described very accurately in the vision of Ezekiel about Gog (Ezekiel 38 and 39), the vision which seemed to him particularly confirmed because of its role in the eschatological drama."[112] Bornkamn continues:

> During his quiet days at Coburg, Luther first started work on a small tract with the translation of Ezekiel 38 and 39 because he was impressed with the danger by the Turks, and wanted to direct the attention of the whole world to this danger. Gog has tasted German blood; he intends to drink his fill of it.
>
> But at the same time, he [Luther] also wanted to uncover the true reason for the Turkish power; our sins "which have awakened God's fury and have hidden his countenance from us, and allow Gog to rage so horribly."[113]

Richard Emmerson sums up the Protestant position on the Anti-Christ: "According to the Protestant interpretation Anti-Christ may be a specific pope, the institution of the papacy, all Roman Catholics, or more generally, all, including Mohammedans, who persecute the Christian church."[114]

After the time of Luther and Calvin, with the European expansion by the English and French into the Middle East, the idea of Muhammed, and or Islam in general, as the Anti-Christ began to fade. By the late nineteenth century, the view was no longer found among Christian exegetes.

Luther may well have believed, as Calvin did, that Islam and the Turkish Empire of his day, were representations of the Anti-Christ; but Luther also believed, as we shall see in a later chapter, that the Anti-Christ is to be identified with the papacy, and this was the reformer's predominant view on the matter.

As Richard Emmerson tells us:

> According to Luther, the attack of the Turks, the immoralities of the Epicureans who live as those in the days of Noah (Matthew 24:37–39) and the heretics of the Anabaptists also are signs of the end. These contradictory perceptions of the times—the simultaneous growth of truth reflected in gospel preaching and opposition to the papacy, and of wickedness reflected in wars, immorality, and heresy—led Protestants to confidently believe that Christ's Second Advent was imminent.[115]

In Emmerson's view, Luther saw the army of the Turks in his day, as well as the heresy of the Anabaptists, as evidence in his own day that the End Times were approaching.

Many Christian thinkers between the 17th and 20th centuries have continued to hold the Islam as Anti-Christ Theory. Most recently, author Joel Richardson in his book, *Anti-Christ: Islam's Awaited Messiah*, has argued not only is Islam the awaited Anti-Christ, but also that the Djaal will be the Messiah of the Moslem faith. Richardson makes these claims in two chapters of his book, 8 and 12. The former is entitled, "The Dajjal: Islam's Anti-Christ," while the latter is named, "The Anti-Christ Spirit of Islam."[116]

SOME PARALLELS BETWEEN CHRISTIANITY AND ISLAM ON THE ANTI-CHRIST

From the materials in all the previous sections of this chapter, we may draw a list of the parallels between Christianity and Islam on the Anti-Christ. First, the New Testament suggests the Anti-Christ will be an unparalleled political, military, and religious leader that will emerge in the End Times. Similarly, Islam believes the Mahdi is an unparalleled political, military, and religious leader who will emerge in the last days.

In the New Testament the idea of false prophets that will emerge at the end of the world is a prominent theme. These false prophets, in the New Testament will support the Anti-Christ. In early Christian sources the Anti-Christ and the false prophets will have a powerful army that will do great damage to the earth, in an effort to subdue the nations of the earth. Among Moslems, Isa or Jesus is a secondary figure who will emerge in the final days who will fight against the Djaal and his armies.

Daniel in the Apocalypse describes the Anti-Christ as a dragon in lamb's clothing. In Islam, the figure of Jesus literally comes bearing the name of the one that the world knows as the Lamb of God. Yet the Muslim Jesus comes to kill all those who do not submit to Allah.

In the early Christian sources, the Anti-Christ is to establish a new world order, which is also true of the Mahdi, the Muslim Jesus. The Anti-Christ will establish new laws over the earth, and Jesus will establish Islamic law over the whole earth. In the New Testament materials the Anti-Christ is to perform great miracles and signs as a way of showing his power. In Islam, the Djaal is said to control the weather and crops, as well as performing great wonders at the end of time.

When the Anti-Christ appears, there will already be a system in place that will be poised to receive him as the Savior, while Islam awaits the Mahdi who will convert everyone to Islam. The New Testament tells us that the Anti-Christ and his followers will attack and seize the city of Jerusalem, setting himself up in the Temple, while the Mahdi is to reconquer and seize the city and the Temple for Islam.

These sources also became an influence in the late Middle Ages and the Reformation to see Islam, and or Muhammed, as the Anti-Christ. We see this position in Wycliffe and John Huss, as well as reformers like Luther and Calvin.

THE LAST WORLD EMPEROR AND ISLAM

The notion of a last world emperor and its relationship to the Anti-Christ and Islam is another important theme in understanding the figure of Ad Dajaal in the Islamic faith. In the eleventh and 12th centuries, a number of thinkers on the Anti-Christ developed the idea that the last of all Christian emperors will defeat the forces of Islam, while uniting the Christian Church.

This idea of a Last World Emperor was developed in the seventh-century *Apocalypse of Pseudo-Methodius*. Indeed, this document shaped the eschatological imaginations of Christian scholars throughout the Middle Ages. The work was written in Syriac toward the end of the seventh century, the same time that Islamic forces were beginning to conquer the Middle East and North Africa.

The *Apocalypse of Pseudo-Methodius* is falsely attributed to a fourth-century church father, Methodius of Olympus. The document depicts many Christian eschatological images and themes, including the rise and fall of Anti-Christ, the invasions of Gog and Magog, and the Tribulation that will precede the end of the world.

Although this idea of a Last World Emperor is not a Biblical idea, the author of the *Apocalypse of Pseudo-Methodius*, nevertheless, found Biblical warrant for the idea. The text selected is II Thessalonians 2:7, concerning the "restrainer" who must be "removed from the middle." *Pseudo-Methodius* also cites Matthew 24:37, which speaks of Christ handing over his kingdom to the Father.

Pseudo-Methodius also quotes Psalm 68:31, that suggests that "Cush will hand over messianic rule to God." *Pseudo-Methodius* believes this refers to the Ethiopian ancestry of the Byzantine Last World Emperor, who will recapitulate all earthly rulers into himself as Christ's immediate apocalyptic predecessor.

The *Apocalypse of Pseudo-Methodius* most likely adopted from the *Triburtine Sibyl*, the idea of a Last World Emperor, who will be a figure to unite Christianity, while defeating the Islamic forces. This idea of a Last World Emperor was then adopted by subsequent Christian thinkers from the tenth to twelfth centuries, beginning with Adso's use of the idea in his essay on the Anti-Christ.

The re-conquest of the Spanish city of Granada and expelling of the Moors from Spain in 1492 was seen by some thinkers in western Europe in the late fifteenth century as signs that the End Times were at hand. Like many other thinkers of their day, Ferdinand and Isabella believed that Muhammed was the Anti-Christ, and the Moors were his followers.

ISLAM AS GOG AND MAGOG

Richard Emmerson suggests that not only was Islam identified as the Anti-Christ in the Dark Ages and High Middle Ages, the Islamic faith was also in this period identified with the armies of Gog and Magog. Indeed, Emmerson suggests this belief may have arisen as the Christian Sibylline Oracles as their source. Emmerson comments: "Although having a wide-ranging influence upon the whole Anti-Christ tradition, the sibylline literature made its most important contribution to the political legends associated with Anti-Christ. Elaborations of Medieval legends of *Nero redivivus* (Books III, IV, and V), the Last World Emperor, and Gog and Magog are due largely to the Oracles and later Sibylline literature."[117] Emmerson goes on to point out that Pseudo-Methodius' commentary on Revelation, and the late seventh century, *Tiburtine Oracle*, "were particularly influential in expanding the exegetical interpretation of Anti-Christ."[118]

Whether or not Emmerson is correct about the origins of the idea, the notion that the armies of Gog and Magog from Ezekiel chapters 38 and 39, became identified with Islamic forces from the Dark Ages until the fall of Constantinople in the fifteenth century. Indeed, this view was also popular in Reformation thinkers. The Geneva Bible, for example, identifies the seven-headed beast with Rome, and the two horned beast with Anti-Christ. Some Protestant thinkers, like Luther for example, identified the two heads as the Papacy and the Turks. This view is particularly evident in interpretations of Gog and Magog. Emmerson tells us: "Napier explains, for example, that Gog signifies a 'covered' enemy of God—that is, the hypocrisy of the Pope—whereas Magog signifies a 'discovered' enemy of God—that is the open hostility of the Muhammedeans."[119]

Christian identifications of the Anti-Christ with Muhammed, as well as his armies with Gog and Magog, begin in the eighth century when Islam invaded the Iberian Peninsual, and continued well into the period of the Protestant Reformation.

In recent years, discussions of the Anti-Christ and the End Times have often had both religious and political implications. The Moslem understanding of Ad Dajaal has been informed by the Arab-Israeli conflicts over the lands of Palestine, and it is also fueled by other associations between Jews and Ad-Dajaal. Zeki Saritoprak speaks of the implications of some of these conflicts:

> The emigration of Russian Jews to Israel was said by some authors to be a sign of his (Ad-Dajaal's) emergence. The mention of specific places where the Anti-Christ will emerge and be killed, such as Jerusalem and the Gate of Lydda (formerly Lod) have added to tensions between Arabs and Jews by attributing religious significance to the lands over which these people dispute; and by giving the dispute itself a special religious significance as part of the final battle between Christ and his forces and the Anti-Christ and his forces.[120]

Saritoprak points out that accusations concerning the Anti-Christ are hurled from all sides in the contemporary Middle East, as are the identifications of the armies of Gog and Magog in those traditions. Saritoprak continues: "Thus, each description or portrayal of the Anti-Christ also has political implications, which are not limited to the Arab-Israeli conflict. For example, Muhammed Asad associated western civilization with the Anti-Christ, portraying political tensions between Muslims and the West. British military forces colonizing the Sudan were associated with Ad-Dajaal, during the war between the Sudanis and the United Kingdom."[121]

Indeed, Saritoprak points out that the leader of one Sudani sect was called the *Mahdi of Sudan*. This same man, Saritoprak tells us, also identified the British troops with Ad-Dajaal and the armies of Gog and Magog. Throughout the modern period, as Saritoprak points out, political ideologies against Islam, and those who support them, are equated with evil, Shaytan, and Ad-Dajaal.[122]

CONCLUSIONS

In this chapter we have explored the many uses of the concept of the Dajjal, the Arabic word for the Anti-Christ. Like Judaism and Christianity, we have seen that Islam has a number of beliefs about the End Times, and a body of stories about those End Times. Islam has its own version of Apocalyptic Literature. Many of these traditions were borrowed from Judaism and Christianity. Chief among these are a final judgment at the end of time, and a battle between the Messiah and the Anti-Christ.

As we have seen, Islam also inherited a number of ideas from the Old Testament, like the coming of the Messiah at the end of time, and the idea of Gog and Magog being cities full of nonbelievers. We have also seen in this chapter that Moslem scholars are in agreement with New Testament writers that the Anti-Christ will have powers that go beyond the norm. Powers like controlling the weather, powers of persuasion, and the power to perform miracles are all abilities of the Moslem figure of Dajjal.

As we have seen, the Islamic tradition also adopted the early Christian ideas that the Anti-Christ will be associated with the armies of Gog and Magog from Ezekiel 38 and 39, and the notion that the Djaal will be able to control the weather and to perform miracles like those performed by Jesus in the gospels, as well as the idea that the main followers of the Djaal will be Jews, another idea found in the early Church.

We also have explored in this chapter a number of signs that Moslem scholars believe will be evidence that the coming of Dajjal is near. Among these were rumors of wars, wars, earthquakes, famine and pestilences, not unlike those in Daniel and the Book of Revelation.

We also have seen in this chapter that Islam has an analogue to the mark of 666 from the Book of Revelation. In Islam, the mark is the letters K F R, the root for the Arabic word for nonbeliever, which will appear on the Dajjal's forehead at the end of time.

Above all, we have seen that the concept of the Dajjal in the Islamic tradition is a moral one. He stands for much that is evil, and that is held by the *Fakirun*, the nonbelievers. We have also seen that Jesus serves a role in the Moslem idea of the End Times. For Islam, Jesus is to be identified with the Messiah, and at the end of time, Jesus will defeat the Dajjal, and bring about judgment for all.

Bernard McGinn sums up his comments on the Anti-Christ in Islam this way: "The description of Anti-Christ as a one-eyed monster riding on an ass as large as himself and leading the Jews against Islam, appear to have been wide spread in both Sunni and Shiite Islam from the eighth or ninth century CE. Like the Christian accounts (and at least some Jewish ones), Muslim texts also speculate about the miracles that he will or will not be able to perform."[123]

Islam's fascination with the Dajjal is akin to Judaism and Christianity's fascinations with evil matters in their apocalyptic literature. And Islam does not come up short in regard to a wealth of stories, descriptions, and explanations for their version of the Anti-Christ, the Dajjal.

In chapter five, we explore the image of the Anti-Christ in the High Middle Ages in the Christian tradition. As we shall see, there is a wealth of information from the tenth to the fifteenth century on the Christian Anti-Christ.[124]

NOTES

1. "The Legnd of Al-Dajjal (Anti-Christ): Personification of Evil in the Islamic Tradition," *The Muslim World* 93 (April, 2003) 291.
2. Ibid.
3. The *Qu'ran* 18:1–10 translated by Mohammed Marmaduke Pickthall. (New York: Kazi, 1996.) Unless otherwise stated, all other Arabic translations are those of the author. For primary sources in this chapter, I have used notes 2 through 10. For secondary sources, I have used the following: Yahya ibn Sharaf, *Forty Ahadith* (London: Islamic Text Society, 1997); Bernard McGinn, *Anti-Christ*, 111–13; the Article by A. Abel on the Dajjal in *The Encyclopedia of Islam* Volume II. (Leiden: Brill, 1965), 76–77; David J. Halparin, "The Ibn Sayyad Tradition and the Legend of the Ad-Dajjal," *Journal of the American*

Oriental Society 96 (1976) 213–25; Gustave E. Von Grunebaum, *Medieval Islam* (Chicago: University of Chicago Press, 1953); and Richard Martin, *Islam: A Cultural Perspective* (Englewoof Cliffs, NJ: Prentice Hall, 1982).

4. Ibid. 18:101-10. I have used a number of translations of the *Qu'ran* for this chapter, including Yusef Ali, *The Koran* (Washington, DC: American International Printing Company, 1946); A. J. Arberry, *The Koran Interpreted* (London: Allen & Unwin, 1955); Richard Bell, *The Qu'ran Translated with a Critical Rearrangement of the Surahs*, 2 vols. (Edinburgh: T. & T. Clark, 1937–1939); and T. B. Irving, *The Qu'ran* (Brattleboro, VT: Amana, 1985).

5. John O'Kane, *The Concept of Sainthood in Early Islamic Mysticism: Two Works by Hakim Al-Tirmidhi* (London: Routledge, 1996) 178.

6. Ahmad Thomson, *Dajjal: The King Who Has No Clothes* (London: Ta-Ha, 1986) 17.

7. Bernard McGinn, *Anti-Christ*, 112.

8. *Al Hadith* (London: Kessinger, 2004) Book 40, Number 7028.

9. Ibid.

10. Ibid.

11. Ibid.

12. N. K. Singh, *The Prophet Mohammed and his Companions* (Delhi: Global Vision, 1996) 137.

13. Eerik Dickenson, *The Development of Early Sunnite Hadith Criticism* (London: Brill, 2001) 97.

14. Thomson, *Dajjal*, 21.

15. Ibid.

16. Charles F. Horne, *The Sacred Books and Early Literature of the East: Medieval Arabic, Moorish and Turkish* (London: Kessinger, 1997) 131.

17. Ibid., 132.

18. Abu Dawood, *Hadith* number 4232.

19. Bukhari, *Hadith* number 9.247.

20. Ibid., 9.239.

21. Muslim, *Hadith* number 3187.

22. Thomson, *Dajjal*, 27.

23. Ibid., 25.

24. O'Kane, 179.

25. Bukhari, *Hadith* 9.239.

26. Ibid., 9.241 and 9.504.

27. Ibid. p. 180.

28. *Al-Hadith* 4 vols., translated by Al Haj Maulana Fazlul Karmin (Lahore: Islamic Book Service, 2001) vol. 77.
29. Ibid., 78.
30. Ibid., 77.
31. Ibid.
32. Ibid., vol. 2, 144.
33. Karmin translation, vol. 2, 233.
34. Ibid.
35. Sunan Abu-Dawud, Book 37, *Battles* (Kitab Al-Malahim, number 4310.)
36. Ibid.
37. A. Guillaume, *The Life of Muhammed* (Oxford: Oxford University Press, 1955) 163.
38. Ibid., 164.
39. Sunan Abu-Dawud, Book 37, *Battles* (Kitab Al-Malahim, number 4282.)
40. Ibid.
41. Thomson, *Dajjal*, 58.
42. Ibid., 111.
43. Qu'ran 21:95–97.
44. S. S. Hasan, *Christian Versus Muslims in Modern Egypt* (Oxford: Oxford University Press, 2003) 19.
45. Thomson, *Dajjal*, 18–19.
46. Ibid.
47. Ibid.
48. Ibid.
49. Ibid., 27–28.
50. Ibid., 30.
51. Ibid., 31.
52. Ibid., 32–33.
53. Ibid.
54. Ibid., 33–34.
55. Ibid.
56. Ibid., 37.
57. Ibid., 37–38.
58. Ibid.
59. Ahmed Thomas, *The King Without Clothes* (Karachi: Sunni Books, 2003.)
60. Muslim, *Hadith* number 7015.

61. Ibid.
62. Ibid.
63. Michael Fortner, *The Scarlet Beast: Islam and the Beast of Revelation* (Denver: White Stone, 2006)
64. Karmin translation, vol. 3, 234.
65. Ibid., 235.
66. Ibid., vol. 4, 77.
67. Ibid.
68. Ibid.
69. Ibid., vol. 1, 98.
70. Muslim, *Fitan* number 119, 120, and 121.
71. A.J. Jenkinson. "The Moslem Anti-Christ Legend," *Muslim World* 20 (1950) 50–55.
72. Ibid., 42–43.
73. Ibid.
74. Ibid., 45.
75. Ibid., 47–48.
76. Jabir Ibin Samurah, *Hadith* Number 2028.
77. Ibid.
78. Ibid.
79. Abu Dawood, number 4283.
80. Ibid, number 4282.
81. Muhammed Ali ibn Zubair Ali, "Signs of Qiyamah."
82. Ibid.
83. *Al Hadith* (London: Kessinger, 2004) vol. III, book 30, number 106.
84. Ezekiel 38:4a and 8b (author's trans.).
85. Bahaullah, *Tablets of Bahaullah Revealed After the Kitab-i-Aqdas* (Wilamette, IL: Bahai Publishing Trust, 1994) 97.
86. Ellen G. White, *The Great Controversy* (Mountain View, CA: Pacific Press, 1950) 335.
87. Thomson, *Dajjal*.
88. Ahmad Thomson, *Blood on the Cross: Islam in Spain in Light of Christian Persecution Through the Ages* (London: Ta Ha, 1989).
89. Robert Hutchison, *The Kingdom Come: Inside the Secret World of Opus Dei* (London: Dunne, 1999).
90. Karen Armstrong, *Muhammad: A Biography of the Prophet*. (San Francisco: HarperCollins, 1992) 24.

91. Ibid., 33.
92. Ibid., 34.
93. Ibid.
94. Zeki Saritoprak, "The Legend of al-Dajjal," 300–304.
95. I have developed these observations on Ramon Lull from materials at the Instituto Brasileiro de Filosofia e ciencia Raimundo Lulio. The Institute has a collection of articles in several European languages.
96. Albert Habib Hourani, *Wester Attitudes Toward Islam* (London: Southampton University Press, 1974) 9.
97. Ibid., 10.
98. Ibid.
99. John Burton, *The Collection of the Qur'an* (Cambridge: Cambridge University Press, 1997) 17–21.
100. Ibid.
101. Zeki Saritoprak, "The Legend of Al-Dajjal (Anti-Christ): Personification of Evil in the Islamic Tradition," *Moslem World* (April 2003) 291–307.
102. Ibid., 301.
103. Ibid., 302.
104. Ibid.
105. Richard Emmerson, *Anti-Christ in the Middle Ages*, 67.
106. Ibid.
107. Ibid., 67–68.
108. Roger Bacon, *Opus Majus* Edited by John Henry Bridges. (London: Adamant Media, 2000) p. 266.
109. For more on Alvarus, see Jessica Ferree, "The Approach of Christian Polemicists Against Islam," *Macalester Islam Journal* 1.1 (2006) 24–28.
110. Ibid., 25.
111. Richard Emmerson, *Anti-Christ in the Middle Ages*, 196–97.
112. Heinrich Bornkamn, *Luther and the Old Testament* (Philadelphia: Fortress, 1969) 68.
113. Ibid.
114. Richard Emmerson, *Anti-Christ in the Middle Ages*, 211.
115. Richard Kenneth Emmerson, *Anti-Christ in the Middle Ages* (Seattle: University of Washington Press, 1984) 220–21.
116. Joel Richardson, *Anti-Christ: Islam's Awaited Messiah* (Enumclaw, Washington: Win Press Publishing, 2006)
117. Richard Emmerson, *Anti-Christ in the Middle Ages*, 212.

118. Ibid., 212–13.
119. Ibid., 212.
120. Zeki Saritoprak, "The Legend of Ad-Dajaal," 303.
121. Ibid.
122. Ibid.
123. Bernard McGinn, *The Anti-Christ: Two Thousand Years of the Human Fascination With Evil* (New York: Harpers) 110–11.
124. For more on these texts about the End Times, the Ottoman Empire, and the Dajjal, see Arthur Jeffrey, "The Descent of Jesus in Mohammadan Eschatology," in *The Joy of Study: Papers to Honor Frederick Clifton Grant* edited by Sherman F. Johnson (New York Macmillan, 1951) 107–26.

5

The Anti-Christ in the High Middle Ages

> The prediction concerning Anti-Christ is indeed very obscure. This, however, is the nature of prophetic language, which, in general, deals much in allegorical and figurative terms.
>
> —Rev. P. Huchede, *History of Anti-Christ*

> Like Christ is the king of all faithful, the Anti-Christ is the king of all heretics and unbelievers.
>
> —Bruno of Segni

> Joachim of Fiori and Matthew of Janov radically changed the traditional interpretations of the Anti-Christ.
>
> —Richard K. Emmerson, *Anti-Christ in the Middle Ages*

INTRODUCTION

THE EARLIEST REFERENCE TO the Christian Anti-Christ after the Dark Ages comes in a German text discovered by German scholar Johann Andreas Schmeller in 1817 and subsequently published in 1832, it is called *Muspilli*. The word *Muspilli* is Old High German, relating to some cataclysmic event at the end of time.

The *Muspilli*, one of the two surviving pieces of Old High German poetry, is a text from the late ninth century. The text focuses on the fate of the soul after death. The hosts of Heaven and Hell do battle and the winners will carry it off in victory. Then, attention shifts in the text to a battle between Elijah and the Anti-Christ, which the text tells us will precede the Last Judgment. The Anti-Christ will eventually fall to Elijah, but the prophet will be wounded in battle. The Anti-Christ's blood falls to the earth and sets it ablaze.

The Anti-Christ in the High Middle Ages

The *Muspilli* describes the Anti-Christ standing with Satan:

> The Anti-Christ stands with the old fiend.
> With the Satan, whom he will ruin:
> On the battlefield, he falls wounded
> And in battle without victory
> But many men of God ween
> That Elijah will be wounded in that battle
> When the blood of Elijah drips onto the soil
> The mountain will burn, no tree will stand,
> Not any on earth, water dries up,
> Sea is swallowed, flaming burn the heavens,
> Moon falls, Midgard burns.[1]

In this chapter we also explore the image of the Anti-Christ in the High Middle Ages, the tenth to the fifteenth centuries. We begin the chapter with an analysis of *Letter on the Origin and Time of the Anti-Christ*, a tenth-century Latin text written by Adso of Montier-en-der, a French monk born in the Jura mountains. We then explore the many uses of Adso's text among later Christian commentaries of the High Middle Ages.

Among later Medieval scholars who wrote about the Christian Anti-Christ were: Hildegaard of Bingen (1098–1179); Bruno of Segni, a twelfth-century Benedictine bishop who served as the Vatican librarian in the mid-eleventh century; Joachim of Fiori, a Cistercian abbot and mystic from Italy in the twelfth century; Richard of Saint-Victor, a Scottish monk and mystic of the late twelfth and early thirteenth century; Martin of Leon, a Spanish priest from the thirteenth century; and William of Langland, the fourteenth-century Welsh priest who wrote *Piers Plowman*.

In addition to these thinkers, we shall also explore a number of comments made by Thomas Aquinas, the greatest of later Medieval scholars. Thomas Aquinas made at least four references to the Christian Anti-Christ, all of which we shall examine in this chapter.

In addition to the material mentioned above, we shall also look at a German play written about the Anti-Christ. It is a Latin text, completed around 1160. It survives in a number of manuscripts.

The Legend of the Anti-Christ

ADSO OF MONTIER-EN-DER AND ARNULF OF RHEIMS ON THE ANTI-CHRIST

Adso was the son of an aristocratic family and oblate in the monastery of Luxeuil in France. In 934, Adso became the school director at the monastery of Saint Evre of Toul. In 935, he moved to Montier-en-der ("in the wood" Der). Eventually, Adso became Abbot there around 968. In the 980s, Adso was called to help reform a monastery in Saint Benigne near Dijon, where he only stayed for two years.

Adso is most known for rewriting many of the lives of the saints, and collections of miracles from earlier in the Middle Ages. Adso's most important work is his treatise on the coming of the Anti-Christ, which he wrote at the request of the Queen Gerberga, the wife of King Lothar (Louis IV of France), and the sister of Otto the Great, the German ruler that reconstituted the Holy Roman Empire.

The *Lebellus de Antichristo* is a kind of narrative biography that uses many of the conventions that are typical of Medieval lives of the saints. Adso gives the Anti-Christ a literary life of his own free of biblical exegesis. The text survives in nearly 200 manuscripts, with many textual variants.

Adso begins the *Libellus de Anti-Christo* by following the Medieval tradition of the *Golden Legend*, where each calendar entry begins with an etymological essay on the nature of the saint of the day's name. Thus, Adso's letter begins with some linguistic comments on the word, *Anti-Christo*. He points out that Anti-Christ, in Greek and Latin, means contrary to Christ. Adso follows the Medieval tradition by telling us that anything the Anti-Christ does will be against Christ.

Adso's letter continues by raising the question of whether there is one or many Anti-Christs. Ados tells us that the Final Opponent to come has "many ministers of his malice." Many of these, in Adso's view, already have existed like Antiochus IV, Nero, and Domitian. Speaking of his own time, Adso tells us: "Even now in our own time, we know there are many Anti-Christs. For anyone, layman, cleric, or monk, who lives contrary to justice and attacks the rule of his way of life and blasphemes what is good (Romans 14:16) is an Anti-Christ."[2]

Adso goes on to give a vita of the Anti-Christ. He will be born in Babylon, and will come from the tribe of Dan, among the Jews, a belief we saw earlier in chapter four. Much of Adso's description on the Anti-Christ is mimetic of the life of Jesus. After receiving an education from magicians and sorcerers, the Anti-Christ will go to Jerusalem where he will rebuild the Temple of Solomon.

About the origins of the Anti-Christ, Adso tells us that: "My authorities say that Anti-Christ will be born from the tribe of Dan, according to the words of the prophet: 'Dan is like a snake by the road side, an adder on the path.' For he will sit like a serpent by the road side, and he will be on a path to strike those who walk on the path of righteousness and kill them with the venom of his malice."[3]

About Anti-Christ's abilities, Adso adds: "Anti-Christ will have magicians, criminals, soothsayers, and wizards, who, with the Devil's inspiration, will bring him up and instruct him in every iniquity, trickery, and wicked art."[4]

Adso also speaks of the Anti-Christ conquering Jerusalem: "Then he will come to Jerusalem, and all the Christians whom he cannot convert to his side, he will kill by various torments, and he will place his own throne in the holy temple. He will restore the Temple now in ruins, which Solomon built to God into its original form, and will circumcise himself and give out the lie that he is the son of the almighty God."[5]

A little later on, Adso again speaks of Anti-Christ's abilities: "He will also make many signs, great and unheard of miracles. He will make fire come terribly from the sky, he will make trees suddenly bloom, and dry up, the sea rage and then become calm, natural objects will change their forms, rivers change their courses, the sky tremble with winds, and storms and other countless and stupendous things. He will even bring the dead to life in the sight of men."[6]

Adso also points out that the tribulation of the Anti-Christ, as per the Scriptures, will last three and a half years: "The awful and terrifying tribulation will last for three and one half years in the whole world. But then the days will be cut short, for the sake of the elect. For unless the Lord cuts the days short, none of the flesh would be saved. Thus, the apostle Paul has revealed the time when Anti-Christ will come and when the day of judgment will appear."[7]

Adso tells us that the Anti-Christ will declare himself the Messiah. He will circumcise himself and pretend that he is the Son of God.[8] Adso goes on to suggest that the Jews will be converted to this false Messiah.[9] He will do this by performing miracles. Adso then summarizes the final days of the Anti-Christ. Rhoads and Lupton describe them this way: "His reign of terror will endure for three and half years; he will assassinate Enoch and Elijah; he will either martyr the faithful or bring about the apostasy."[10]

Adso adds that the Anti-Christ followers will be physically marked on their foreheads. Eventually, either Christ or the Archangel Michael will kill the Anti-Christ, after which the elect will receive a forty-day reprieve following Judgment Day.[11] The Anti-Christ will lay his crown and scepter down at the Mount of Olives.[12] This will pave the way for what Adso calls "the Last World Emperor," a doctrine that greatly influences later Medieval eschatological thinking.

Adso's view of the Anti-Christ can be summed up by the following points. First, the Anti-Christ shall be born from the Jewish tribe of Dan in a perverse parody of the Virgin Birth of Christ. Second, the Anti-Christ shall be conceived by Satan entering the mother's womb. Third, the birth will take place in Babylon. Fourth, he will visit the cities of Berthsaida and Crozain. Fifth, he will form an army of magicians, enchanters, diviners, and wizards. Sixth, he will overtake the Temple at Jerusalem, and set himself up on the throne. Seventh, the Anti-Christ shall circumcise himself, suggesting an affinity with Jews and Moslems.

Adso makes some other conclusions about the Anti-Christ. Eighth, he will raise the dead, sending the natural world into mayhem. Ninth, at first earthly kings and rulers will acknowledge him. Tenth, two prophets, Enoch and Elijah, will preach against the Anti-Christ. Eleventh, these prophets will preach for three and a half years until the Anti-Christ slays them. And finally, the Anti-Christ will be destroyed by Jesus on the Mount of Olives.

THE LAST WORLD EMPEROR

Another late Medieval legend related to the Anti-Christ is the myth of the "Last World Emperor." It began to be formed as early as the fourth century. The seventh century was reformed by Pseudo-Methodius, who wrote in response to Islam spreading into Christian territories. Pseudo-Methodius was translated into Greek and Latin, and his work became the basis for further re-working of the legend in the tenth and eleventh centuries.

The legend itself describes the deeds of the last emperor of the world, who will arise to fight the great armies of the faithful. The last emperor will establish peace before fighting and defeating the armies of Gog and

Magog. The last emperor will then travel to Jerusalem, where he will offer up his crown to Christ, who will bear it, and the last emperor's soul to Heaven. After this, the Anti-Christ will appear in Jerusalem, where the final battle between good and evil will be fought.

This theme of the Last World Emperor was also employed by Adso, and it became popular by the eleventh century. The *Chanson de Roland*, written at the end of the eleventh century, depicted Charlemagne as a messianic ruler who triumphed over Muslims and pagans. Count Emich of Leisingen, a leader of the First Crusade, killed Jews who refused to convert because he was convinced that God had appointed him to be the Last World Emperor. The idea of the Last World Emperor was adopted by the Spiritual Franciscans, principally by Francis of Assisi (1182–1226) and his followers.

Saint Francis also adhered to the idea of Christianity being in the sixth age, as does Franciscan, Peter Olivi (1248–1298), who wrote a lengthy commentary on the Book of Revelation. Olivi's view of the End Times was largely based on Joachim of Fiori, though he added some Franciscan emendations provided by his mentor, Saint Bonaventure.

At the same time, tensions between national and Church rulers were waxing, and many kings and emperors used Adso's vision of the End Times to argue against Count Emich. The idea of the Last World Emperor began to wane in the fourteenth century, and by the Reformation, it was no longer advocated by Christian thinkers.[13]

Arnulf of Rheims (died 921) was a Carolingian Emperor and King of the East Franks. Arnulf was the illegitimate son of Carolman of Bavaria. In 887, Arnulf led a rebellion of the East Franks (Germans) against his uncle, Charles III of Gaul. Arnulf repulsed a Norse invasion of 891, and later attacked Italy in 894. He was the last direct male heir to Charlemagne.

In 991, Arnulf wrote a treatise on the Anti-Christ. He reiterates many of the traditional views of the Anti-Christ, including the view that the Anti-Christ may be associated with political leaders of his own day. About one contender to the Carolingian throne, Arnulf wrote: "What do you estimate this to be reverend fathers? When you see him sitting on a lofty throne flittering in purple and gold. What do you estimate this to be, I say? Without a doubt, if he lacks love, and is only swelled up and lifted up, must he not be the Anti-Christ, sitting in the temple of God, and also showing himself as god?"[14]

Like Adso's treatise on the Anti-Christ, Arnulf reiterates many of the tenth-century beliefs about the Anti-Christ: that he will rule from a lofty throne; that he will lack love; that he will be full of himself; that he will reign from the Temple; and that he will show himself as God.

Adso's letter was partially supplanted by several chapters on the Anti-Christ in Hugh Ripelin's popular handbook, *Compedium theologicae veritatis (Compendium of Theological Truth)*,[15] written around 1260. Ripelin was from Strasbourg. He was among the first of High Middle Ages thinkers to suggest that the Anti-Christ is a parody of the life of Christ. Thus, Christ was born of a virgin, and the Anti-Christ from a prostitute.

Ripelin also held the view that both Christ and Anti-Christ are Jews, the latter coming from the tribe of Dan, the lost tribe known for their apostasy. Ripelin uses Genesis 49:17's reference to "the viper in the road" as an indication of the Anti-Christ. Like Christ, the Anti-Christ will grow up in obscurity, and will begin his ministry at the age of thirty. He will gain followers by performing signs and miracles; but as part of the parody, Anti-Christ's miracles will in reality be tricks.[16]

Adso also addresses the problem of whether the Anti-Christ is a single figure or multiple figures already at large in the world. Adso settles on a final and full Anti-Christ who nevertheless has precedents. Rhoads and Lupton agree: "Adso reconciles these notions by proposing a final and full Anti-Christ who nonetheless has precedents, a mode of interpretation familiar from Christian typology, in which Moses, David, and Solomon, for example, are seen as antecedents of Christ. Just as the Old Testament prefigures the New, so ancient and modern avatars of evil—garden variety of Anti-Christs, selected from Jewish and Roman history as well as everyday life—predict the Final Enemy to come."[17]

LAMBERT OF SAINT OMER AND THE ANTI-CHRIST

In addition to Adso and Arnulf, a third Medieval monk, Lambert of Saint Omer, developed a number of observations on the Anti-Christ. Lambert (1061–1250) was a French Benedictine monk, chronicler, and abbot. Lambert is most known for his *Liber Floridus* ("The Book of Flowers"), an encyclopedia of various forms of knowledge of the day: biblical, historical, astronomical, geographical, philosophical, and theological.[18]

The *Liber Floridus* was begun in the year 1090 and completed around 1120. It was written in Latin, but later translated into French. Lambert saw the contents of the book as a bouquet of flowers plucked from the heavenly meadows. At least nine manuscript copies dating from the twelfth to sixteenth centuries are known to exist, including one at the University Library at Ghent.[19]

Rosemary Muir Wright devotes a significant portion of her *Art and Anti-Christ in Medieval Europe* to Lambert. Wright tells us that "The most arresting image of Anti-Christ, perhaps of all the twelfth-century sources, is that of Anti-Christ riding Leviathan on folio 62v."[20]

Wright refers to an illustration Lambert's *Liber Floridus* in which the Anti-Christ rides the beast Leviathan. Wright describes the image: "At first sight, the image of Anti-Christ on Leviathan is reminiscent of the historiated initial of Romanesque Bible illustrations, a seated frontal figure easily adapted to the enframing shape of its letter, as in the image of the man resting with his feet on a dragon beast in the opening initial to the seventh Homily on Ezekiel by Gregory the Great, in a manuscript produced in southwest France around 1110."[21]

Wright suggests that Lambert had access to an illustrated version of Gregory's *Moralia on Job*, or, she says "a Greek cantena on Job, dating from before the twelfth century."[22] At any rate, in addition to this illustration of Anti-Christ, Lambert also provides details on the nature of the Anti-Christ. He is essentially the opposite of Christ." Lambert continues: "A parodic imitation of the Saviour in order more effectively to deceive the world."[23]

It is also clear that Lambert knew of Adso's treatise on the Anti-Christ, for he seems to quote it verbatim frequently, including a passage translated from the Latin by Wright: "Anti-Christ, son of perdition, will be born of the tribe of Dan, who was the son of Jacob by Pala, the handmaiden of Rachel. Anti-Christ will be born in Corozaim nurtured in Bethsaida, and reign in Capernaum. He will make his way to Jerusalem and sit in the temple of God, as if he were God himself."[24]

It is clear from the use of this quotation that Lambert shared many of the early Church views of the Anti-Christ with Adso and others of the time. Chief among these ideas were that the Anti-Christ is identified with the "Son of Perdition"; that the Anti-Christ shall be a Jew from the tribe of Dan; and that the Anti-Christ will rule from the Temple at Jerusalem, pretending to be God.

Adso's treatise not only became a source for Lambert's view of the Anti-Christ. The text also had a profound effect on the views of the Anti-

Christ among other twelfth and thirteenth-century Christian thinkers, as we shall see in the next section of this chapter.

HILDEGAARD ON THE ANTI-CHRIST

Hildegaard of Bingen, monastic leader, mystic, and author, was born in Germany on September 16, 1098. Most of what we know of her life comes from a biography written by two German monks, Godefrid and Theodoric.[25] From the time Hildegaard was young she had mystical visions. She received a prophetic call five years after her election as magistra in 1141, demanding that she "write down what she sees." At first she was hesitant, but eventually she began to write down the visions.

Hildegaard collected her visions into three books. The first and most important of these is the *Scivias* ("Know the Way") completed in 1151. The second, *Liber vitae meritorum* ("The Book of Life's Merits"), and the third collection, *Liber divinorum operum* ("the Book of Divine Works"), were written over the course of her life until her death in 1179. In these works, she describes each vision and then interprets them.

In her *Scivias*, Hildegaard describes a vision of the end of the world. In this vision, she describes five beasts standing off to the north: a fiery hound, a tawny lion, a pale horse, a black pig, and a grey wolf. Hildegaard suggests that each of these beasts represent the "five ferocious epochs" to come.[26] In the *Liber divinorum operum* (vision III.10) the descriptions of these eras are expanded, and ages of justice and reformation are posited between the eras of misrule.

All the beasts appear in the north because they belong to Satan's kingdom. Hildegaard says that the world is now in its seventh age, "approaching the end of time."[27] In the sixth age, Jesus was made man, just as Adam was made on the sixth day. The seventh age will be the age of the Sabbath, which Hildegaard believes will be indefinitely delayed.

Like Adso and many of her contemporaries, Hildegard believed the beast in the Book of Revelation was the Anti-Christ. And like many of her contemporaries, Hildegard thought that the life of the Final Enemy will be a parody of the life of Christ, but in a demonic form. For Hildegard, the source of the Anti-Christ's evil power will be in Judaism. The Anti-Christ shall be a Jew from the tribe of Dan, and his followers shall also be Jews.

In the *Scivias*, Hildegaard introduces the Anti-Christ as a parody of Jesus. The Anti-Christ is born of a harlot, who feigns she is a virgin. He will be possessed by the devil in this mother's womb and trained by her in the magical arts. Through feigned teachings and false miracles, the Anti-Christ will make many converts. In Hildegaard's view, the Anti-Christ will feign his own death and resurrection, and promulgate his own scriptures. For a time, the Anti-Christ will be opposed by two witnesses, Enoch and Elijah, whom God is saving in heaven for the end times, but eventually they will suffer martyrdom for the faith.[28]

The most extraordinary aspect of the vision is the Anti-Christ's rape of the Church. The Mother Church's private parts become visible and the monstrous head of the Anti-Christ appears as her genitals, for he is both her son and her seducer. After enduring persecution and martyrdom, she will be vindicated by her Bridegroom, Jesus Christ, and united with him in marriage. Scatology and eschatology merge at the end of Hildegaard's vision as The Anti-Christ, self-exalted on a mountain of excrement, likely the Mount of Olives, is struck down by a thunderbolt from on high.[29]

ANTI-CHRIST IN OTHER TWELFTH-CENTURY THINKERS

In the twelfth century there were a number of other commentators on Adso's letter. Of these scholars, the four most important are Joachim of Fiori, Bruno of Segni, Martin of Leon, and Richard Saint-Victor. Not surprisingly, these thinkers affirmed that the Anti-Christ will be born from the Jewish tribe of Dan, and that the Anti-Christ's principal followers will be Jews.

Saint Anselm, in his *Elucidations* tells us that Anti-Christ's eloquence will surpass all possible realization known or imagined. He will know by heart all the sacred scriptures, and possess a perfect knowledge of the arts.[30] Later, in the same work, Anselm suggests that the Devil will show the Anti-Christ all the money on the earth that is hidden, and that all the mines of precious metals will become money minted for the Final Enemy. These immense riches, which he will have distributed among his followers, will soon bring countless numbers to rally round his standard. And they shall faithfully carry out his designs in all things.[31]

Anselm (1033–1109) was one of the most outstanding of Christian philosophers and exegetes in his day. He is most known for his versions of the ontological argument for God's existence; but he also wrote a great deal on the fall of the Devil and the end of the world. The best resource for this material is Anselm's *De casu diaboli* ("On the Fall of the Devil").[32]

This essay can be found in Brian Davies, ed., *Anselm of Canterbury: The Major Works* (Oxford: Oxford University Press, 1998).

Anselm also suggests in his *Elucidations* that the Anti-Christ will come on Easter Sunday, another parody of the life of Jesus. There will be an interval of forty-five days between the death of the Anti-Christ and the Second Coming of Jesus. The death of Anti-Christ, then, must take place during the days of debauchery which precedes, Anselm says, the holy days of Lent.[33]

William of Paris (1105–1202), a French-born churchman of Denmark, speaks of the nature of Christ's return at the end of time. William describes it in much the same terms as Saint Anselm, who in his *Elucidations* suggests that the earth that contained the body of Christ, which was sprinkled with the blood of God will perpetually produce fragrant flowers, with roses and violets that shall never wither. Huchede tells us: "William of Paris speaks in similar terms; stating that the Fathers the most renowned for their profound erudition hold that the earth shall be forever clothed with verdure and charming flowers, which shall never fade."[34]

On Adso's idea that Gog and Magog will be the armies of the Anti-Christ, Bruno says that some understood Gog and Magog as "Goths," and others that they are the armies of Alexander the Great, but Bruno suggests that any attempt to identify them would be pointless.[35] Both Bruno and Martin of Leon ascribe to the idea that contemporary heretics are to be associated with the Anti-Christ. Bruno, commenting on the relationship of the Anti-Christ to heretics says: "Like Christ is the king of all the faithful, thus is the Anti-Christ the king of all heretics and unbelievers."[36]

Richard Saint-Victor also makes the same association. He calls those who have left the Church in his own day, "dogs who bite the faithful, and pigs that soil the faith of false Christians."[37] Bruno of Segni suggests that the beast from the sea in Revelation 13 is about "heresies and pseudo-prophets."[38]

Ludus de Antichristo is an anonymous drama completed in Germany between 1147 and 1187. The play mirrors interior Christian dissent and political proto-national polemics. *Ludus de AntiChristo* has an obvious anti-French tone. The role of the Synagogue in this play is personified by a woman. She is the last to fall under the Anti-Christ's spell in this drama, and likely plays the part of the Whore of Babylon.[39]

In *Ludus de Anti-Christo* there are roles for the kings of Germany and France. Synagogue's false steps cause the necessity of the intervention of the prophets Enoch and Elias through which the souls of the Jews are redeemed; but their lives are not saved, for the Anti-Christ eventually kills the prophets, Synagogue, and all faithful Jews.[40]

This German drama is also called the *The Appearance and Disappearance of the Anti-Christ* and *The Roman Emperor of the German Nation and Anti-Christ*. It is regarded as an Easter play because the arrival of the Anti-Christ, like the resurrection of Jesus, was expected at Easter.[41]

The *Glossa Ordinaria*, an orthodox exposition of biblical traditions from the twelfth century suggests that the Anti-Christ's coming is imminent, and it will be characterized by violence. The Glossa was the most important Medieval glossed Bible and had a huge influence on both secular and religious literature of the late Middle Ages and the Renaissance. It is essentially a presentation of Saint Jerome's Vulgate, as well as a network of texts connected by a complex system of marginal and interlinear notations.

The most original and influential of twelfth-century Christian writings on the Anti-Christ was the work of Joachim of Fiori. Joachim was a Cistercian abbot and mystic who was born in Italy in 1132. Dante called Joachim "an endowed prophetic spirit." Joachim wrote an exposition of the Book of Revelation. His comments on the Anti-Christ are to be found in this work.

Richard Emmerson agrees with McGinn about the role played by Joachim of Fiori in the Anti-Christ Legend. Emmerson points out the late interest in the Middle Ages of a new interpretation of apocalyptic sources. Emmerson adds: "Perhaps the best example of this transformation is found in the exegesis of Joachim of Fiori, one of the most influential visionaries of the later Middle Ages."[42]

Emmerson goes on to point out that Joachim "refashions contemporary ideas into a revolutionary philosophy of history."[43] Emmerson also maintains that Joachim "makes use of many of the features of the Anti-Christ tradition, yet develops an eschatology that differs in important respects from the earlier exegetical interpretations."[44] One of the most important differences in Emmerson's view of Joachim in that the former tells us that the latter places the defeat of the Anti-Christ long before the end of the world.[45] Emmerson also points out that Joachim did not have a place for the Last World Emperor in his eschatological scheme.[46]

Bernard McGinn comments on the importance of Joachim's view of the Anti-Christ:

> What makes Joachim of Fiori so significant in the history of apocalypticism? First, the tendency to link apocalyptic symbolism with concrete past and present events reached a new level in the Calabrian abbot. Despite his politeness to Augustine, Joachim's theology of history is fundamentally at odds with that of the bishop of Hippo in its conviction that God has revealed history's plan in Scripture . . . The abbot of Fiori broke with Augustine and the Tyconian tradition in his return to millenarianism.[47]

The Tyconius to whom McGinn refers is a fourth-century Donatist who first introduced a number of postmillennial eschatological views that Saint Augustine later adopted. Tyconius' most famous work is "Seven Rules of Interpretation," which is quoted extensively in Augustine's *De doctrina Christiana*.[48] Tyconius also wrote a commentary on the Apocalypse that is quoted by Bede, among others.[49]

McGinn goes on to suggest two other reasons why Joachim's work on the Anti-Christ was original—that the forty-five day discrepancy in Daniel would come after the defeat of the Anti-Christ and that Joachim gives a Trinitarian grounding to his view of the Anti-Christ.[50]

Like many Christian exegetes before him, Joachim tied the coming of the Anti-Christ to contemporary events in his day. He also believed that the end was near, as did many other twelfth-century exegetes. Joachim thought the rebuilt temple was not the Temple in Jerusalem, but a representation of the Church. Commenting on Revelation 5:7, Joachim points out that Christ's opening of the seven seals symbolizes the uncovering of the mysteries of the resurrection. Anti-Christ, in Joachim's view, will give false directions to deceive, while Christ reveals deep spiritual understandings.[51]

Again, McGinn sums up Joachim's contribution to the history of the Anti-Christ: "Joachim of Fiori's new view of Anti-Christ was to prove influential over many centuries. By placing it within the context of twelfth-century debates over the nature of apocalyptic reform and its attendant fears of Anti-Christ, we can judge the roots of its power in later ages. The Calabrian abbot summed up a century of debate over the meanings of the last events and their relation to the current state of the Church."[52]

One of the most important observations made by Joachim about the Anti-Christ is that the Cistercian divided history into seven epochs. This enabled Joachim to go beyond the present, and not to talk about the Anti-Christ simply in terms of contemporary heretics. Joachim also talks about the "Age of the Father," the "Age of the Son," and the "Age of the Holy Spirit." Joachim treated the Book of Revelation allegorically. The "Age of the Father" corresponds to the period of the Old Testament; the "Age of the Son" roughly covers the period of the New Testament to the middle of the thirteenth century; these will be followed by the "Age of the Holy Spirit," which will last for 1,000 years and will culminate in the Earth's destruction.

With knowledge of the first two ages, Joachim thought he would be able to predict what will happen in the third. Joachim saw this third age, the "Age of the Holy Spirit," as a spiritual age. In describing this third age, Joachim constantly uses terms like the "Spiritual Church," and "spiritual men."

By Joachim's account, the second age, the "Age of the Son," was to end around the year 1260, with the completion of the 42nd generation from the birth of Christ. Joachim predicted that the years 1200 and 1260 would be filled with the evil doings of the Anti-Christ. In the Third Age, Joachim also predicted a spiritual renewal of the Church that could be exemplified, in his view, by people like Saint Francis (1182–1226), as well as other Spiritual Franciscans.

At the end of this Third Age, the Age of the Holy Spirit, which will last 1,000 years, shall come the End Times. Joachim uses a number of the traditions we have seen in western Christianity to describe the Anti-Christ. Chief among these are the Anti-Christ will be a political leader. Indeed, Joachim's followers identified the Anti-Christ with Christian Emperor Frederick II.

Frederick II (1194–1250) was a pretender to the king of Rome. He was also king of Germany, Italy, and Burgundy. His empire was frequently at war with the Papal States, so it was not surprising that he was excommunicated twice. Frederick was often vilified in the chronicles of the day. In addition to the followers of Joachim calling him the Anti-Christ, Frederick was also identified that way by Pope Gregory IX (Pope from 1227 to 1241).

Joachim's eschatological teachings become some of the most influential in the later Middle Ages. He also makes an important departure from the Augustinian tradition of re-emphasizing the predictive value of Scripture, particularly in Daniel and Revelation. Joachim saw history as an ascent through three successive ages (the Ages of Father, Son, and

Holy Spirit). He believed that his age was in the Age of the Son, and he predicted the Age of the Spirit would begin around 1260.

Frederick (1194–1250), was Holy Roman Emperor from his coronation in 1220 to his death. He was known in his own time as *Stupor mundi*, "wonder of the world," because he was competent in nine languages, at a time when many monarchs were illiterate. Frederick II is also important for the history of the west because he founded the University of Naples in 1224.

Joachim also admits the coming of many Anti-Christs, with the main one he calls "the Great Anti-Christ," which will be preceded by an age of spirituality. Joachim's conception was radically utilized in numerous political and theological polemics that were born between the thirteenth and fifteenth centuries.

The Calabrian Joachim saw the coming of the Anti-Christ as imitative of Christ's roles of priest, king, and prophet. As McGinn tells us: "This triple formula provides the key to the Calabrian's thought on the nature of the seven-headed Anti-Christ and also an explanation for some of the problems found in his presentation."[53]

In this section of his book, McGinn is discussing Joachim's view of the seven-headed beast. He points out, as Robert Lerner does, that Joachim's comments on the tail of the seven-headed beast is one of the twelfth-century Italian's most novel ideas.[54]

Joachim also is important for our purposes because it appears as though he advocated the Papal Anti-Christ Theory at the end of the twelfth century. Bernard McGinn in an article for *Church History* suggests that Roger Howden gave an account of Richard the Lionhearted's meeting with Joachim in the winter of 1190 and 1191. In this meeting between King and Abbot, Joachim is said to have told the King that "The Anti-Christ of this period will obtain the Chair of Peter."[55]

If McGinn is correct about this account of the meeting between King Richard and Joachim of Fiori, then the origins of the Papal Anti-Christ Theory is not to be found in the fourteenth century, with John Hus and John Wycliffe, but rather it stretched all the way back to Joachim in the late twelfth century. More is said about the Papal Anti-Christ Theory at the end of this chapter, as well as in the next chapter on the Anti-Christ and the Reformation.

McGinn points out that the theory may even be older than Joachim when he writes: "The earliest glimmerings of the Papacy's role in the drama of the last days comes from the pen of a choleric reformer in the 1160s, Gerhoh of Reichersberg in his *De quarta vigilia noctis*."[56]

McGinn tells us that Gerhoh was disgusted with the trafficking of money that had become part of Papal operations in his day.[57] This led the German to propose that the Pope is the Anti-Christ.

Dominican friar Vincent of Deauvais (ca. 1190–1264) was the author of the *Speculum historiale*, which contains a history of the world from creation to Vincent's time. It is a massive work, running 1,400 large double-column pages in the 1627 printing. The *Speculum* contains in chapters 108 and 109 an account of the Anti-Christ and his career. Chapter 110 of the same work contains a description of fifteen signs before Doomsday. The *Speculum* appears to have been influenced by the accounts of Joachim of Fiori, Hildegard, and maybe even Adso in its description of the Final Enemy and his times.[58]

LATER MEDIEVAL VIEWS OF THE ANTI-CHRIST

Although Thomas Aquinas, the greatest of all Medieval Churchmen did not write any independent tract on the Anti-Christ, he did, nevertheless, make a number of observations about the End Times. In discussing where Enoch and Elijah reside while waiting for the end of the world, Thomas suggest they are in heaven, eating from the Tree of Life, "which was Adam's food before he sinned."[59] In discussing the Anti-Christ's coming, Thomas agrees with Jerome and Ambrose that he will ascend from the top of a mountain into the air as did Simon Magus in Rome.[60] Commenting on Matthew 25:30, Thomas interprets the "sign of the Son of Man" as a "luminous cross miraculously formed in the air."[61]

Thomas Aquinas mentions the Anti-Christ in his *Commentary on the Epistle to the Romans*. While discussing the conversation of the Jews in the End Times, Thomas writes:

> The blindness of the Jews will endure until the fullness of the Gentiles have accepted Christ in accord with what the apostle says below about the salvation of the Jews, namely, that after all nations have entered, "All of Israel will be saved," not individually as at present, but universally.
>
> What, I say, will such an admission effectuate, if not that it bring the Gentiles back to the believers whose faith has grown cold, or even that the totality, deceived by the Anti-Christ, will return to their pristine fervor and convert the Jews.[62]

Thomas appears to believe that eventually the Jews will be brought to Christ, and the method for their conversion may be the followers of Anti-Christ.

Thomas Aquinas, like the Venerable Bede and Richard Saint-Victor before him, sees the open book of Revelation chapter ten, points out that the open book signifies the deeds of men. As the sun renders all things visible on earth, so too Jesus by his presence shall disclose to the views of all men the consciences of every single person.[63]

Peter Lombard, in his *Sentences*, suggests that secret but pardoned sins of the just will not be revealed on the last day, on account of the shame and confusion that would cause them. Saint Augustine, on the other hand, agrees with Thomas, that the consciences of the just as well as the reprobate will be revealed on the last day.[64]

The High Middle Ages also saw a number of thinkers who were concerned about the differences between the miracles of Jesus and those that will be possessed by the Anti-Christ. Among these thinkers is Thomas Aquinas who suggests that since human beings are by nature deceived easily, the pseudo-Christ will only appear to be dead and then return to life. The Anti-Christ will also appear to be able to resurrect other members of the dead, but he won't really have that skill.

Another thinker in the High Middle Ages who speaks of the contrast of the miracles of Christ and Anti-Christ is Bernardino of Siena (1380–1444). The fifteenth-century Franciscan insists, "there is a great difference between the true miracles of God and the false miracles of Anti-Christ."[65]

Another thirteenth-century text that deals with the Anti-Christ is "The Prophecy of the Sons of Agap," a text associated with the Fifth Crusade (1217–1221). The Fifth Crusade was called by Pope Innocent III. It was a primary reason for which Innocent held the Fourth Lateran Council of 1215 to 1216, the year of Innocent's death.[66]

Innocent III was succeeded by Honorius III, who sent an army to Syria in 1217 that accomplished nothing. A year later, an expedition was sent to Acre, and then on to Damietta, in the Nile Delta.

The *Prophecy of the Sons of Agap* exist in both Latin and French manuscripts. It is a series of prophecies developed by scholars associated with the Papal Legate, Cardinal Pelagius. The text predicts a series of victories for Christianity over Islamic forces, including the conquest of the city of Mecca before the coming of what the text calls the Mexadeigan, the Anti-Christ.[67]

Matthew of Paris, a thirteenth-century English historian, who was a monk of Saint Albans, became the historian of the convent after the death of his mentor, Roger of Wendover around 1236. Wendover had begun a *Chronica majora* (Great Chronicle), which was completed by Matthew of Paris. The *Chronica majora* is a history of the world, completed with a description of the coming of the Anti-Christ:

> When twelve hundred years and fifty
> After the birth from the dear Virgin are completed,
> Then will be born the demon-filled Anti-Christ.[68]

Matthew of Paris (ca. 1200–1259) was an English born Benedictine monk, chronicler of history, and illuminator of manuscripts. His major work is the *Chronica Majora*.[69] Corpus Christi College, Cambridge owns a copy of the manuscript. The text contains 100 marginal drawings, some fragmentary maps, and an itinerary. The text also contains a number of comments on the Anti-Christ, including a prediction that the Anti-Christ will appear in the year 1250.

The Latin text tells us:

> Cum fuerint anni transacti mille ducenti
> Et quinquaginta post partum Virginis almae
> Tunc Anti-Christus nascetur daemone plenus.[70]

A number of other twelfth to fifteenth-century Christian thinkers also predicted the arrival of the Anti-Christ. Manfred of Vercelli, for example, suggests the arrival of the Final Enemy in 1417–18. Richard Emmerson writes of a "certain Friar Richard who preached through France that Anti-Christ already had been born."[71] Emmerson adds: "In Italy chroniclers recorded prophets who predicted devastations for the last two decades of the fifteenth century."[72]

Stories that circulated about Savonarola in Florence in the 1490s and his preaching about the imminence of Dooms Day, may have put the Anti-Christ on the minds of many Italians. Other thinkers, like Vincent Ferrer (1350–1419) and Bernadino of Siena (1380–1444), point out that no human being can know the day, hour, month, or year of the advent of the Anti-Christ.[73]

Emmerson mentions an early thirteenth-century text called *Pictor in carmine*. Emmerson quotes M. R. James on this text. "It is the largest known collection of types and anti-types intended to be used by artists." The text contains 138 images of scenes from the New Testament from the Annunciation to Doomsday. Emmerson tells us: "However, it does conclude with eschatological subjects drawn from Apocalypse interpretations, including six suggested types for heretics in the church, four types for Anti-Christ's claim to be God, and eight types for the conversion of the Jews by Enoch and Elias."[74]

An edition of the *Pictor in carmine* recently has been edited and published by German scholar Karl August. The original manuscript from which he worked is owned by Corpus Christi College, Cambridge University (Ms. 300), which contains one image of the Anti-Christ.

Another thirteenth-century Englishman, Roger Bacon (1214–1294) was one of the most well-known Franciscans of the late Middle Ages. Bacon, who was also known as "Doctor Mirabilis" ("Astounding Teacher") is credited with the modern scientific method. In his *Opus majus* ("Major Work"), written in 1266 and 1267, he included a number of astrological calculations related to the end of the world. Among Bacon's predictions were the defeat of the Saracens and the coming of the Messiah and the Anti-Christ.[75]

In his *History of Magic and Experimental Science*, Roger Bacon points out that he believes the Anti-Christ will be imminent, and wrote to the pope for the purpose of convincing him of the kinds of study that would be needed for the protection of Christendom. Bacon believes that the Anti-Christ will have magical powers and writes of the danger of the Final Enemy:

> not only for the consideration of the wise, but because of the dangers which are now arising and will arise for Christians and the Church of God, from infidels, and most especially from the Anti-Christ, because he will use the power of wisdom, and will turn all things to evil; and by the words of this sort and stellar work and with great desire for doing evil compounded with absolutely certain intentions and very strong confidence, he will fascinate and cause misfortune to befall not only individuals but also cities and regions. And in this wonder-working, he will do what he wishes without war, and men will obey him as beasts, and he will cause realms and cities to fight each other for him, as friends destroy friends, and thus he will have his will with the world.[76]

Bacon believes that Christendom will be threatened by the coming of the Anti-Christ, primarily because of his magical abilities. Luckily, Bacon knew the means to combat the magic, and he wrote the pope accordingly.

One other collector of late Medieval literature on the Anti-Christ is related to the movement of the papacy from Rome to Avignon in the middle of the fourteenth century. During this period, the Avignon popes began to be identified with Babylon of the Book of Revelations. Robert Rusconi writes of the coming of a false pope, the "*Anti-Christos misticus*,"[77] perhaps a fore-runner to the papal Anti-Christ theory of the Reformation. Indeed, Rosconi identifies three other elements related to these fourteenth-century views of the Anti-Christ. He calls these "fear of an imminent schism, expectations of a heaven-sent *pastor-angelicus*, and finally: "conviction that the persecution of the *Anti-Christus magnus* could not be far behind."[78]

McGinn points out that some thinkers of the day also made connections between the expectations of the End Times and the coming of the Black Death, the Great Plague, in 1348 and 1349. McGinn points to John of Rupescissa (1310–1365) as a fourteenth-century apocalyptic thinker who makes that connection.[79] Bacon also discusses the Anti-Christ in his *Opus Majus*, where he writes of "future perils for the Church in the times of Anti-Christ."[80]

In 1267, Roger Bacon wrote that forty years before it had been prophesied that a Pope would come who would reform the Church, heal the schism with the Eastern Church, and then will convert the Tartars and Saracens, so that there will be a one World Order. In an article for the journal *Church History*, Bernard McGinn suggests that Bacon and other thirteenth-century thinkers may have been one of the causes of the early Papal Anti-Christ Theory, a theory we take up in a later chapter.[81]

DANTE ON THE ANTI-CHRIST

A number of contemporary scholars have suggested that Dante in his *Divine Comedy* has the Anti-Christ appear in at least two places. The first is in the "Inferno," Cantos XVI to XIX, and the other is in the "Purgatorio," in Cantos XVI and XVII. In the latter passage, Dante and Virgil ride on the back of the monster, Geryon on their journey to Malebolge.

John Block Friedman in an article for the *Journal of the Warburg and Courtauld Institutes*, develops this idea of Geyron as the Anti-Christ in some detail. Friedman points out that unlike other monsters in the *Divine Comedy*, Geryon does not seem to embody the sin with which he is identified, "the foul image of fraud."[82]

Friedman goes on to argue that the description that Virgil gives Geryon reminds us of a passage from Ezekiel 38, where the armies of Gog and Magog are described. "By Dante's time," Friedman tells us, "Anti-Christ was not merely one of thousands enclosed by Alexander's gate, Gog and Magog were his minions."[83]

Friedman goes on to suggest that the face of Geryon and his paws are connected to lines from Revelation, particularly the Beast from the Sea in chapter 12:1–2. He also identifies Geryon as a Draconpede, a common High Middle Ages image of the Anti-Christ. He identifies the beast that Anti-Christ is riding on in the *Liber Floridus* and other Medieval manuscripts is also a Draconpede. Friedman also suggests that the description of Leviathan in the book of Job is another image in the High Middle Ages often identified with the demonic and the Anti-Christ. In short, Friedman makes a compelling argument that Geryon in Canto XVII of the "Purgatorio" is nothing more than a representation of the Anti-Christ.

Canto XIX of the "Inferno" has also been pointed to as another embodiment that Dante may have given in relation to the Anti-Christ. Again, Canto XIX contains those sinners who are guilty of fraud, whom tradition has long associated with the Anti-Christ. Bernard McGinn speaks of Canto XIX: "This Canto might be called the inversion Canto, suffused as it is with images of the reversal of values and historical types long associated with the Anti-Christ."[84]

McGinn goes on to point out that one of the figures in Canto XIX is Simon Magnus, who has been considered an Anti-Christ figure for millennia in the Christian tradition.[85]

LATE MEDIEVAL OPINIONS ON THE ANTI-CHRIST

There are a number of late Medieval thinkers who have dealt with the Anti-Christ in the Christian tradition from the fourteenth and fifteenth century. Among these are William Langland and his *Piers Plowman*, which contains a vision of the "Harrowing of Hell," and the coming of the

Anti-Christ. Both John Wycliffe and John Hus, two fourteenth-century reformers also expressed a number of views on the Anti-Christ.

William Langland's *Piers Plowman* is a poem about the perfection of man through the Christian way of life. Langland's dreamer/narrator, Will, has asked Scripture how he might achieve perfection. Instead of directions for how to achieve the moral and spiritual life, Will complains he receives a lesson in theology. Will says that many scholars gather knowledge, as other men accumulate property, but at the end, they find themselves bereft of grace. Langland says:

> But I suppose it will be many Christian teachers and scholars as it was in Noah's time when he made the ship of planks and boards; no carpenter or workman who worked on the ship was saved, only birds and beasts, and blessed Noah, and his wife with their sons and their wives; of the carpenters that wrought if none were saved. God grant that it not be so for the folk who teach the faith of the Holy Church, which is a harbor and God's house within which we are saved and shielded from sin, as Noah's ship protected the beasts; and the men who made it drowned in the flood . . . On Doomsday there shall be a flood of death and fire together; therefore, I counsel you clerks, the carpenters of Holy Church, do such deeds as you see prescribed in Scripture lest you not be within.
>
> On Good Friday, I find a thief who had lived all his life by lies and theft and was saved; and because he confessed on the cross to Christ, he was saved sooner than Saint John the Baptist, and either Adam or Isaiah, or any of the prophets who had lain with Lucifer many long years. A robber was released to eternal joy sooner than any of them without any penance in purgatory.[86]

In addition to the "Harrowing of Hell," Langland also offers a vision of the coming of the Anti-Christ:

> When Nede hadde undernome me thus, anoon I fil aslepe,
> And mette mereillously that in mannes forme
> Antecrist cam thane, and al the crop of truthe
> Toned it up-so-doum, and overtilte the roote,
> And made fals sprynge and sprede and spede mennes nedes.
> In ech contree ther he came he kutte awey truthe.
> And gerte gile growe tghere as he a god were.
> Freres folwede that fend, for he gaf hem copes,
> And religious reverenced hym and rongen hir belles,
> And al the covent cam to welcome that tyraunt,
> And alle hise as wel as hym—save oonly fooles;

> Whiche fooles were wel gladdere to deye
> Than to lyve lenger sith Leute was so rebuked,
> And a fals fend Antecrist over alle folk regnede.[87]

A modern translation of this Middle English goes something like this:

> When need had reproached me thus, I soon fell asleep.
> And dreamed full marvelously that in man's form
> Anti-Christ came then, and all the crop of truth
> Turned it upside down, and upturned the root
> And made false spring and spread and prospered men's needs.
> In each country there he came and called away truth
> And made guile grow as if he were a god.
> Friars followed that fiend, for he gave them copes
> And religious reverenced him and rang their bells.
> And all the covent came to welcome that tyrant
> And all his as well as him—save only fools;
> Which fools were more glad to die
> Than to live longer since Fidelity was so rebuked,
> And a false fiend Anti-Christ over all folk reigned.[88]

In section 19.219–26 of *Piers Plowman*, Langland gives a prophecy of the future, where the coming of the Anti-Christ is predicted. In this passage, the Anti-Christ is associated with many of his traditional companions, and it predicts the future corruption of the Church and its leaders.[89]

Richard Emmerson points out that *Piers Plowman* has a number of evil characteristics that remind him of the Anti-Christ: "*Piers Plowman* describes many other evil characters, and some of these may be understood as forerunners of Anti-Christ. For example, False, who is described as the son of the devil (3.143–44) has much in common with Anti-Christ, whereas Cain (10.334–35) may prefigure Anti-Christ's followers in the last days, the friars."[90]

The final section of *Piers Plowman* opens with the attack of Anti-Christ, the last things figure who comes before the Second Advent of Christ (20.52–79). Langland tells us the Anti-Christ "comes in many forms" (20.52); that he will be a "false fiend" (20.53–55.); and that he will have control over many forces of nature, such as crop production (20.56–57).[91] It should be clear that Langland incorporates many of the traditional characteristics of the Anti-Christ from a number of the Church Fathers, as well as material from Adso, Joachim, and Hildegard of Bingen.

Langland uses many of the traditional elements of the Christian Anti-Christ legend. The Anti-Christ uses guile, and calls himself a God. He is called a tyrant and a fiend. He has the ability to turn things upside down, and the only people who will not follow him will be fools who still hold to the faith.

Richard Emmerson describes the image of Anti-Christ in *Piers Plowman*: "Will's physical impotence mirrors the vitiated state of his soul. Weakened in body and spirit, the end of his long quest is to seek a dubious refuge in the doomed house of Unity. On the contrary, the house of Unity though weakened, is not doomed. As the attack of Anti-Christ emphasizes, the 'fools' that Conscience calls into Unity do withstand Anti-Christ."[92]

Emmerson points out that Will's entrance to Unity is the most positive element of *Piers Plowman*. It points to the climax of the poem, when the attack of the Anti-Christ begins. In the end of the poem, Conscience sets out to find Piers, who represents an "Angelic Pope," a term most likely borrowed from Joachim.[93]

The work of John Wycliffe, fourteenth-century English scholar also plays a key role in the development of attitudes toward the Anti-Christ. His principal contribution to the Anti-Christ Legend is that he is the first thinker to identify the Anti-Christ with the papacy. Indeed, after the year 1360, Wycliffe continuously ridicules the doctrine of transubstantiation, and assails the pope as the Anti-Christ. As Herbert Workman, a Wycliffe scholar, puts it, "The Anti-Christ became for Wycliffe the source or symbol of all evil, and as such identified with the pope, though Wycliffe is careful to point out that it does not follow that because one pope is the Anti-Christ that all popes are such."[94]

Among Wycliffe's political works is an elaborate contrast between Christ and the pope. Workman calls it a "contrast that amounts to an antagonism so complete that the pope thereby becomes the Anti-Christ."[95] J. Loserth, in his *Wiclif und Hus*, also comments on Wycliffe's view of the papacy. "For Wycliffe, sanctity is the sign of authority, the true papacy consists in service, and a pope that departs from the ways of the apostles is the Anti-Christ, upon whose characteristics Wycliffe dwells."[96]

Another Wycliffe scholar, William Farr quotes Wycliffe on the same point: "The temporal lords have power given to them by God, so that where the spiritual arm of the Church does not suffice to convert the Anti-Christs by evangelical preaching, ecclesiastical admonition, or the examples of virtues, the secular arm may help its mother by severe coercion."[97]

Wycliffe clearly refers to the papal authorities who cannot suffice to bring nonbelievers to salvation. The principal reason this is true for Wycliffe is that the papacy is the Anti-Christ. Gotthard Lechler, commenting on Wycliffe and the papacy, makes this comment: "The Pope's claims to absolute power, and to a heaven entirely special to himself, appeared to Wycliffe all the more astounding."[98]

Lechler continues: "But now he regards the assumption of such absolutism as the very kernel of the papacy itself. For the claim to the dignity of a viceregent of Christ upon earth, taken along with the strongest contrast to Christ in all respects—in character, teaching, and life—was a combination which appeared to him only fully expressed in the idea of the Anti-Christ."[99]

Commenting on the Babylonian Captivity when two popes were competing against each other, Lorimer says, "We see how neutrality toward the two popes was converted into a renunciation in principle of the Popedom itself, which ended in the conviction that the Papacy is the Anti-Christ, and its whole institution of the wicked one."[100] Lorimer adds, "From the year 1381, we find this opinion repeatedly expressed by Wycliffe."[101]

Even earlier, in 1376, when Wycliffe wrote his *On Civil Lordship*, he expressed the view that power, whether religious or civil, was God's to extend to faithful stewards, as was the use of temporal property. Wycliffe argues the Church should not own property, nor gather wealth, nor could it inflict the punishment of excommunication. Even as warrants for Wycliffe's arrest were issued, he suggests the pope who grasps after worldly power is of the Anti-Christ and could be deposed. In fact, as early as 1360 there is evidence that Wycliffe believed that the pope was the Anti-Christ.[102]

In 1382, in a Bull written by Pope Gregory XI, Wycliffe was finally condemned for claiming the Pope was the Anti-Christ.[103] Two years later, Wycliffe responded to the Pope's request that he be summoned to the Papal Court in Rome. In the first half of his remarks, Wycliffe suggests that the life of Christ should be the measure of who is a Christian, and who is the Anti-Christ; but in the final paragraph of his remarks, Wycliffe says that if Gregory XI does lead a Christ-like life, "then, I suppose, of our pope he will not be Anti-Christ."[104]

Wycliffe's view that the papacy is the Anti-Christ had repercussions, for his contemporaries, as well as for later reformers in the sixteenth to 18th centuries. In his own time, John Hus adopted Wycliffe's view. Workman argues that in 1361, while teaching at Oxford, Wycliffe began purporting this view.[105] When he became rector at Fillingham, Workman suggests, Wycliffe also expressed the view in some of his sermons.[106]

Wycliffe's view that the pope was the Anti-Christ had repercussions in his own time, as well among subsequent reformers in the sixteenth to 18th centuries. It was John Hus who carried on Wycliffe's teachings in Bohemia. John Hus was a theologian at the University of Prague, and a preacher at Bethlehelm Chapel in the fifteenth century.

Wycliffe's writings came to the attention of Hus around the turn of the fifteenth century. Bohemia was torn between German and Slavic interests. Hus, unlike Wycliffe, accepted the doctrine of transubstantiation, but he accepted Wycliffe's view on the nature of the Church, with Christ as its head, and not the papacy. Hus challenged the doctrine of indulgences in 1412.

John Hus also adopted Wycliffe's view that the papacy is the Anti-Christ. Hus was called to the Council of Constance, where he was questioned about his opinion that the pope is the Anti-Christ. McGinn describes his ambivalent response: "I did not say this, but I did say that if the pope sells benefices, if he is proud, avaricious, or otherwise morally opposed to Christ, then he is the Anti-Christ."[107]

Hus goes on to say: "But it should by no means follow that every pope is Anti-Christ; a good pope, like Saint Gregory, is not the Anti-Christ, nor do I think he ever was."[108] This ambivalent response was not enough to save Hus' life. He was burned at the stake by the Inquisition on July 6, 1415.

The Taborite Rebellion in the early fifteenth century set up a radical wing of the Hussite, Bohemian Church. Taborites held that their time was the last days, and the Church of Rome was the Whore of Babylon, and the Pope the Anti-Christ. The Taborites declined rapidly after their army was defeated by more moderate Hussites in 1434.

In the late fifteenth century, Girolamo Savonarola, who lived from 1452 to 1498, and worked as a Dominican preacher at San Marco in Florence, appears to have said or taught little about the Anti-Christ. But Savonarola is important for our purposes because many in his day believed he was the Anti-Christ. Leonardo of Fivizzano, for example, called Savonarola "an agent of the Anti-Christ," as did Marsilio Ficino.[109]

Other fourteenth and fifteenth-century thinkers who believed that the papacy is the Anti-Christ include: Michael of Cesena, Francisco Petrach, John Milicz, Matthew of Janow, John Purvey, and Walter Brute.

Michael of Cesena (1270–1342) was a Franciscan and General of the Order. He was a strong advocate of ecclesiastical poverty, and was involved in a number of conflicts with Pope John XXII, causing him to believe that the pope was the Anti-Christ. Matthew of Janow (d. 1394), was a fourteenth-century Bohemian reformer. He composed and collected several treatises under the title *Regulae veteris et novi testamenti*. Later parts of this manuscript were falsely attributed to John Hus, particularly sections advocating the pope as the Anti-Christ, and were published among Hus' writings.

Joshua Trachtenberg, in his classic, *The Devil and the Jews*, suggests that Matthew of Janow wrote that the Anti-Christ was so universally and thoroughly discussed that when he will appear, even the little children will know him instantly.[110] From Matthew and others we get the sense of just how ubiquitous thoughts of the Anti-Christ were in late Medieval Europe.

John Purvey (1353–1428) was one of Wycliffe's leading followers. He undertook a project of revising the 1380 translation of the Bible into English. Other followers of Wycliffe, whom also believed that the papacy was the Anti-Christ include Nicholas of Hereford and John Aston. Nicholas of Hereford assisted Purvey in the revision of the Bible. John Aston was appointed Warden of Thela College, Oxford in November of 1386. It is likely Aston knew Wycliffe and Purvey at Oxford, and that he shared their view of the papacy as the Anti-Christ.

Walter Brute, a Lollard and a follower of Wycliffe, sent a manuscript to the Papal Court in response to being summoned to Rome. Brute wrote, "Rome is the daughter of Babylon, the great whore sitting upon the many waters, with whom the kings of the earth have committed fornication, with her enchantments, witchcraft and Simon Magnus' merchandise. The whole world is infected and seduced. The identity of the Pope with the Anti-Christ."[111]

Francesco Petrarch (1304–1374) was an Italian philosopher. He is sometimes called "The Father of Humanism," because he was one of the early Italian Renaissance thinkers. He is the author of *Rerum vulgarium fragmenta*, which is usually called in English, "The Song Book,"[112] a collection of 266 sonnets to his wife, Laura. A collection of his letters also is extant.[113] Petrarch is important for our purposes because, like his contemporary John Wycliffe he too believed in the Papal Anti-Christ theory.

The *Fortalicium fidei*, the *Fortress of Faith* by Alfonso de Espina, bishop of Orense, contains an account of the Anti-Christ. The text was written around 1470, and it appeared in seven German editions between 1471 and 1525. In the text, Alfonso has the "Queen of the Amazons" guard the "sons of Israel," who are enclosed between two camps or fortresses (*castra*) called Guth and Maguth, an obvious reference to Gog and Magog.

These enclosed Jews are endowed with horrible characteristics of "unclean peoples." In Alfonso's view, when the Anti-Christ appears, these Jews will join him and accompany him to Jerusalem, where he will reign as a mighty king. All other Jews on earth will also gather in Jerusalem. The Anti-Christ will then be circumcised, and he will claim to be the Jewish Messiah. He will then claim that Jesus was a great deceiver who will be defeated at the end of time.

Like many other thinkers of his day, as well as in the Christian tradition in general, Alfonso not only identified the Anti-Christ with the Jews, he also suggests that the Final Enemy is to be identified with various heresies and heretics of his day.

Emmerson claims this work "particularly plays up Anti-Christ's devilish connections and close association with the Jews."[114]

Robert Ripon, a fifteenth-century sub-prior of the Durham Cathedral, wrote a number of sermons. The biggest issue of Ripon's day was the "antipope" at Avignon. Robert of Ripon claims that the Avignon pope was the Anti-Christ. Altogether, the Harley Manuscript (Ms 4894) has sixty-six of Robert's homilies. It is owned by the British Library. Folio 6v. contains the homily on the Anti-Christ, and the Avignon popes identification with the Anti-Christ.

Andrew Gow, in a recent article for the *Journal of Millennial Studies*, explores a number of other late Medieval texts on the Anti-Christ. Among these is *The Byrth and Lyfe of the Moost and Deceytfull Antechryste*, an early sixteenth-century English text. Gow suggests that this text is based on the German *Anti-Christ* drama mentioned earlier in this chapter.[115]

Gow also mentions a mid-fifteenth-century Flemish block book that depicts a number of apocalyptic figures as Jews. The locus from the bottomless pit of Revelation 9:3–11, appears much as it is described in the

Biblical text, but in the place of crowns of gold, they wear pointing rabbi's caps of the late Medieval period.[116]

A third late Medieval Anti-Christ text mentioned by Gow is University of Paris master Peter Comestor's *Historia Scholastica*. Comestor's text identifies the armies of Gog and Magog with the Jews, as do many other late Medieval writers on the Anti-Christ.[117]

Finally, the Fifth Lateran Council in December of 1516, along with a number of other provisions, condemned all attempts to fix the end of the world and the coming of the Anti-Christ. Other decrees from the Fifth Lateran Council included: the institution of Church regulated pawn shops, and the printing of books, without ecclesiastical permission.

ANTI-CHRIST IN FOURTEENTH-CENTURY DRAMA

Twenty-five scriptural mystery plays were performed in the city of Chester, in northern England. They are traditionally dated around 1325, though some scholars put them as late as 1375. They were presented on three successive days on the feast of Corpus Christi, a summer feast day. On the first day were performances of plays 1–9, which include the fall of Lucifer, Old Testament narratives, and the Nativity. The second day brought performances of plays 10–18, including the flight into Egypt, Jesus' public ministry, the Passion, and the Crucifixion. Finally, the third day brought performances of plays 19–25 that included the resurrection, the Ascension, the descent of the Holy Spirit to earth, the coming of the Anti-Christ, and the Last Judgment.

The Chester plays are much simpler than the other surviving cycles in York and Wakefield. The Chester Cycle has been preserved from five manuscripts that are owned by the Bodleian Library, Oxford. In the Anti-Christ play of the Chester Cycle, the Last Enemy performs self-resurrection when the people ask for proof of his power. He eventually brings all men to worship him. After a long disputation, Michael and his angelic minions kill the Anti-Christ, and he is carried off by two demons.

The "Doomsday" play completes the Chester Cycle. In this drama, a pope, a king, and an Emperor are judged and saved, while similar characters confess their sins and are carried off to Hell.

The York Cycle of mystery plays included 48 dramas from Creation to Judgment Day, but the cycle contains no Anti-Christ play. The Wakefield Cycle consists of 32 scriptural dramas, dating from the early fifteenth century. These texts have been preserved in the Towneley Manuscript, named after an old family from Burnley in Lancester. The manuscript is owned by the Huntington Library in San Marino, California. The Wakefield Cycle includes 32 plays from Creation to Judgment Day, with no drama of the Coming of the Anti-Christ.

The fourteenth and fifteenth centuries were also a period of the flourishing of iconography, particularly illustrations of the End Times. Illustrated bibles, and particularly illustrated Apocalypses, were frequent in this period. We discuss a number of these iconographic images in a later chapter on "The Anti-Christ in Art."

OTHER EARLY ADVOCATES OF THE PAPAL ANTI-CHRIST THEORY

In addition to the analyses of Wycliffe and Huss, there is further early evidence in western Christianity of the Papal Anti-Christ theory, going all the way back to the tenth century. Bishop Arnulf of Orleans, for example, "deplored the Roman popes as 'monsters of guilt' at the end of the tenth century."[118] Philip Schaff, writing on Arnulf, tell us he: "Declared in a council called by the King of France in 991, that the Pontiff, clad in purple and gold, was 'Anti-Christ sitting in the temple of God, and showing himself as God himself.'"[119]

Eberhard II, archbishop of Salzburg and a Benedictine, at a synod of bishops held in Regensburg in 1240 or 1241, tells us that people of his day were "accustomed to calling the Pope the Anti-Christ."[120] By the time of Wycliffe, when the western church was divided for forty years between two rival popes, one in Rome and one in Avignon, France, each called the other pope the Anti-Christ. Wycliffe is reported to have said that they were both correct: "two halves of Anti-Christ, making up the perfect Man of Sin between them."[121] Thus, there is evidence in the High Middle Ages, in France, Germany, and England of the belief that the Anti-Christ is to be identified with the Bishop of Rome.

Indeed, the belief appears to have been held by a host of other Christian thinkers in the late Middle Ages. Michael of Cesena, John Milicz, Matthew of Janow, R. Wimbledon, and John Purvey were among this number.

Michael of Cesena was an Italian Franciscan theologian in the fourteenth century. Cesena accused the Pope of heresy and being in league with the Anti-Christ in three separate bulls in the late 1320s.[122] Matthew of Janow was a fourteenth century Bohemian who contributed the church's woes to the split of the papacy at the time. Between 1388 and 1392, he composed several treatises, which he later collected in a single work. In this work, he also indicated a belief in the papal Anti-Christ theory.[123]

John Purvey was a countryman and associate of John Wycliffe's. His dates are generally given as 1353 to 1428. For a time, Purvey lived with Wycliffe at Lutterworth. He also appears to have done a revision of Wycliffe's English translation of the Bible around 1380. In the 1390s, he wrote a number of treatises on the corruption of the Roman Church that included a number of references to his belief in the Papal Anti-Christ identification.[124]

CONCLUSIONS

In this chapter we have explored the image of the Christian Anti-Christ from the tenth to the fifteenth centuries. We began the chapter with an analysis of Adso of Montier-en-der's letter on the Anti-Christ, written at the end of the tenth century. As we have argued, this letter served as a template for future, late Medieval discussions of the Anti-Christ. Indeed, comments on the Anti-Christ by Hildegaard of Bingen, Richard of Saint Victor, and Joachim of Fiori, were more like commentaries on Adso's letter than they were original material.

Adso and his commentators adopted many of the themes from earlier Medieval Christian traditions on the Anti-Christ, including that the Anti-Christ will come from the lost tribe of Dan, and that his followers will be Jews. Adso saw the Final Enemy as a being of guile, capable of powers beyond human abilities. For Adso, the Anti-Christ will declare himself the Messiah and reign over all the peoples of the earth.

We also have explored in this chapter some observations from Thomas Aquinas on Judgment Day and the Coming of the Anti-Christ. We also have explored other thirteenth-century thinkers on the Final Enemy, including observations by Roger Bacon. In the next section of this chapter we looked carefully at the role the Anti-Christ plays in William Langland's *Piers Plowman*. Finally, we ended the chapter with an analysis of contributions to the Anti-Christ Legend from fourteenth and fifteenth-century reformers. Chief among these were John Wycliffe, John Hus, and their followers.

The most important contribution to the Christian tradition of the Anti-Christ made by these reformers, as we have seen, is the notion that the Anti-Christ is to be identified with the Roman papacy. This idea had enormous repercussions for several Christian denominations in the sixteenth to eighteenth centuries. This tradition also will be developed more fully in the following chapter on "The Anti-Christ in the Reformation."

NOTES

1. Gustav Grau, *Quellen und Verwandtschaften der älteren germanischen Darstellungen des Jüngsten Gerichtes* (Halle: Niemeyer, 1908).
2. Adso of Montier-en-Der, *De Ortu et Tempore Anti-Christi*, edited by D. Verhelst (Brepolis: Turnholti Typographi Brepolis Editores Pontifici, 1976). This text is translated as "Letter on the Origin and Time of the Anti-Christ," in Bernard McGinn, *Apocalyptic Spirituality* (New York: Paulist, 1979) 81–88.
3. Robert Fuller, *Naming the Anti-Christ: The History of An American Obsession* (Oxford: Oxford University Press, 1995) 1292.
4. Ibid., 1293.
5. Ibid.
6. Ibid.
7. Ibid., 1294.
8. Ibid.
9. Bonita Rhoads and Julia Reinhard Lupton, "Circumcising the Anti-Christ: An Ethno-Historical Fantasy," in *Jouvert* 3.1 (1999).
10. McGinn, *Apocalyptic Spirituality*, 88.
11. Ibid.
12. Ibid.
13. For more on this material, see the following: McGinn, *Apocalyptic Spirituality*; David Burr, *The Spiritual Franciscans* (University Park: Pennsylvania State University Press, 2001); Malcom D. Lambert, *Medieval Heresy: Popular Movements From the Gregorian Reform to the Reformation* (Oxford: Blackwells, 2002); and David Saville Muzzey, *The Spiritual Franciscans* (Washington, DC: American Historical Association, 1914).
14. *History of Christian Church Volume IV: Medieval Christianity, 590–1073*, 199.
15. Kees Schepers, *Het Compendium theologicae veritatis van Hugo Ripelin van Straatsburg* (Amsterdam: Ons Geestelijk Erf, 1999) 17.
16. Ibid., 18.
17. Rhoads and Lupton, "Circumcising the Anti-Christ," 90.

18. Lambert of St. Omer, *Liber Floridus*, Codex Autographus Bibliothecae Universitatis Gandavensis, edited by A. Derolez (Ghent, 1968).
19. Ibid., 83.
20. Rosemary Muir Wright, *Art and Anti-Christ in Medieval Europe* (Manchester: University of Manchester Press, 1995) 64.
21. Ibid, 66.
22. Ibid., 68.
23. Lambert, *Liber Floridus*, 84.
24. Wright, *Art and Anti-Christ*, 69.
25. Hildegaard of Bingen, *Scivias* (Mahwah, NJ: Paulist, 1990) ix.
26. Ibid., 41–42.
27. Ibid., 42.
28. Ibid.
29. Ibid.
30. Quoted in Huchere, *History of Anti-Christ*, 19.
31. Ibid., 21.
32. Ibid., 19.
33. Ibid., 76.
34. Huchede, *History of Anti-Christ*, 104–5.
35. Bruno of Segni, in Migne, *Patrologia Latina*, vol. 164, cols. 603–736.
36. Ibid.
37. Richard of Saint-Victor, in Migne, *Patrologia Latina*, vol. 195, cols. 683–888.
38. Bruno of Segni.
39. *Ludus de Anti-Christo* (ca. 1150–1160). This text was developed during the reign of Emperor Frederick Barbarossas in the Monastery Tegernsee. It suggests a fight between the Emperor and an Anti-Christ figure with magical powers. Also see McGinn, *Apocalyptic Spirituality*, 133–35.
40. Ibid.
41. Ibid.
42. Richard Emmerson, *Anti-Christ in the Middle Ages*, 60.
43. Ibid.
44. Ibid.
45. Ibid.
46. Ibid., 61.
47. Bernard McGinn, *Anti-Christ: Two Thousand Years of Human Fascination with Evil* (San Francisco: HarperCollins, 1994) 136–37.
48. *Patrologia Latina*, vol. 24, cols. 81–90.

49. *Patrologia Latina*, vol. 93, cols. 130–32.
50. Ibid., 137.
51. Ibid., 140.
52. Ibid., 142.
53. McGinn, *Anti-Christ*, 140.
54. Ibid., 140–41.
55. Bernard McGinn, "Angel Pope and Papal Anti-Christ," *Church History* 47 (1978) 155–67.
56. Ibid., 157.
57. Ibid., 158.
58. Emmerson, *Anti-Christ in the Middle Ages*, 159.
59. Thomas Aquinas, quotes in P. Huchede, *History of Anti-Christ*, 53.
60. Ibid., 72.
61. Ibid., 60.
62. Thomas Aquinas, "Commentary on the Epistle of the Romans," in *Thomas Aquinan's Aristotelean Commentaries Series* (New York: Saint Augustine's Dumb Ass Books, 1993) vol. 7, 179.
63. Quoted in Huchere, *History of Anti-Christ*, 96.
64. Ibid., 97.
65. Emmerson, *Anti-Christ in the Middle Ages*, 93.
66. McGinn, *Anti-Christ*, 150–51.
67. Ibid.
68. Ibid., 183.
69. Matthew of Paris, *Chronica Majora*. Ms 26 16., Corpus Christi College, Cambridge.
70. Quoted in Emmerson, *Anti-Christ in the Middle Ages*, 55.
71. Ibid., 56.
72. Ibid.
73. Ibid.
74. Emmerson, *Anti-Christ in the Middle Ages*, 119.
75. Ibid., 152.
76. Roger Bacon, *History of Magic and Experimental Science*, 4 vols. (London: Kessinger, 2003). This quotation is in vol. 1, 399. The Latin Text reads: "Non solum pro consideratione sapientiali haec scribo, sed propter pericula quae contingent et contingent Christianis et ecclesiae Dei per infideles, et maxime per Antichristum, quia ipse utetur potestate sapientiae, et omnia convertet in malum. Et per hujusmodi verba et opera stellificanda, et magjo desiderio

malignandi componenda cum intentione certissima et confidential vehement, ipse infortunabit et infascinabit non solum personas singulares, sed civitates et regions. Et per hanc viam magnificam faciet sine bello quid voles, et obedient homines ei sicut bestiae, et faciet regna et cititates pugnare ad invicem pro se, ut amici destruant amicos suos, et sic de mundo faciet quod desiderabit."

77. Robert Rusconi, *L'attaesta*, quoted in McGinn, *Anti-Christ*, 174.
78. Ibid.
79. Ibid., 174–75.
80. Roger Bacon, *The Opus Majus*, trans. Belle Burke (Oxford: Oxford University Press, 1928) vol. 2, 634.
81. McGinn, "Angel Pope and Papal Anti-Christ," 161.
82. John Block Friedman, "Anti-Christ and the Iconography of Dante's Geryon," *Journal of the Warburg and Courtauld Institutes* 35 (1972) 108–22.
83. Ibid., 110.
84. McGinn, *Anti-Christ*, 170.
85. Ibid., 171.
86. Milton McC. Gatch, *Death: Meaning and Morality in Christian Thought and Contemporary Culture* (New York: Seabury, 1969) 107–8.
87. McGinn, *Anti-Christ*, 190.
88. Author's translation.
89. Emmerson, *Anti-Christ in the Middle Ages*, 196.
90. Ibid., 196–97.
91. Ibid., 198.
92. Ibid., 203.
93. Ibid.
94. Herbert Workman, *Christian Thought to the Reformation* (New York: Scribners, 1911) 113.
95. Ibid.
96. Johann Loserth, *Wiclif and Hus* (London: Hodder & Stoughton, 1884) 78.
97. William Farr, *The Waning of the Renaissance* (New Haven: Yale University Press, 1994) 53.
98. G. Lechler and Peter Lorimer, *John Wycliffe and the English Precursors* (London: Religious Tract Society, 1878) 317.
99. Ibid.
100. Ibid.
101. Ibid.
102. Ibid., 318 and 366.

103. Oliver J. Thatcher, editor, *The Library of Original Sources* (Milwaukee: University Research Extension, 1907) 378–82.
104. Ibid., 382.
105. Workman, *Christian Thought to the Reformation*, 115.
106. Ibid.
107. McGinn, *Anti-Christ*, 184.
108. Ibid.
109. Ibid., 188.
110. Joshua Trachtenberg, *The Devil and the Jews* (New York: Jewish Publication Society, 2002) 37–38.
111. "The Lollards," quoted in *Truth for Today*, 12/29/06.
112. Francesco Petrarch, *The Song Book* (Tempe: Medieval and Renaissance Texts, 1995).
113. Francesco Petrarch, *Oeuvres completes de Petrarque* (Rome: Italica, 2001). Also see James Harvey Robinson, *Petrarch: The First Modern Scholar and Man of Letters* (Los Angeles: University Press of the Pacific, 2003).
114. Emmerson, *Anti-Christ in the Middle Ages*, 165.
115. Andrew Gow, "Jewish Shock-Troops of the Apocalypse: Anti-Christ and the End, 1200–1600," *Journal of Millennial Studies* 1.1 (1998) 1–18.
116. Ibid., 4.
117. Ibid., 2.
118. Philip Schaff, *History of the Christian Church*, 8 vols. (London, 1910; reprinted, Grand Rapids: Eerdmans, n.d.).
119. Ibid.
120. LeRoy Edwin Froom, *The Prophetic Faith of Our Fathers* (Washington, DC: Review and Herald, 1954) vol. 1, 79.
121. Ibid.
122. Michael of Cesena, "Ad perpetuam rei memoriam innotescat quod ego," "Christiane fidei fundamentum," and "Ad Conidorem Canonum." See article in *Catholic Encyclopedia*, vol. 10 (Rome, 1911).
123. Ibid.
124. Matthew of Janow, "Regulae Veteris et Novi Testamenti." The work has never been published.

6

The Anti-Christ in the Reformation

Martin Luther is in relation to the Reformation rather like the opening notes of some piano concerto—say Beethoven's Fourth—which states the theme, which is then taken up by other instruments, and finally lost in the developing pattern of music.

—Gordon Rupp, "Luther and the Reformation"

It is heretical for the pope whose power is spiritual to become a prince. If he does this, he is the Anti-Christ. This is a term that comes from the Bible and was used during the Reformation. It has been used in Church history, especially by sectarians in their criticisms of the Church. They said that if the pope claims to represent Christ, but is actually a ruler of this world opposed to Christ, then he is the Anti-Christ.

—Paul Tillich, *A History of Christian Thought*

I hope that the last day is at hand; things surely cannot possibly grow worse than what the conduct of the papacy has brought to pass. It has suppressed God's commandments, replacing them with their own. If this is not the Anti-Christ, let someone else say what it is.

—Martin Luther, *Against the Execrable Bull of Anti-Christ*

INTRODUCTION

The idea of John Wycliffe and John Huss that the Anti-Christ is to be identified with the Roman papacy was a notion adopted by most of the principal reformers of the Christian Church from the sixteenth to the eighteenth centuries. In this chapter, we take a close look at the development of this idea in the work of Martin Luther, John Calvin, John Knox,

The Anti-Christ in the Reformation

Thomas Cranmer, John Wesley, Roger Williams, Cotton Mather, Ian Paisley, and many others.

In a second section of this chapter, we explore the responses of the Counter-Reformation to the Protestant claim that the pope is the Anti-Christ. As we shall see, among Counter-Reformation Roman thinkers who respond to the papal Anti-Christ theory are Robert Bellarmine (1542–1621), Francisco Ribera (1537–1591), and Luis De Alcazar (1554–1613). The late eighteenth century brought another Counter-Reformation thinker that responded to the papal Anti-Christ theory. A Chilean Jesuit names Lacunza wrote a book entitled, *The Coming of the Messiah in Glory*, that deals with the pope as the Anti-Christ point of view. At the end of this chapter, we also make some general conclusions about the role the Anti-Christ has played for Reformation and Counter-Reformation theology. We will begin this chapter with a discussion of several dates in the life of Martin Luther more fully to understand his view of the Anti-Christ.

KEY DATES IN LUTHER'S EARLY CAREER

In order fully to understand Martin Luther's view of the pope as the Anti-Christ, we must recall some important events in Luther's life. The first of these is in July of 1505, when Luther had a religious experience during a great storm. At the time, he vowed to become a monk. At around the same time, Luther came to the Pauline view of salvation by faith. Luther came to understand that "At last, by the mercy of God, I began to understand the justice of God, and by which God makes us just in his mercy and through faith, as it is written, "By faith the just man shall live . . ." and at this I felt as though I had been born again, and had gone in through open gates into Paradise itself."[1]

The importance of this discovery was not that it was new, but that it was new for Luther. As Gordon Rupp comments, "What he saw in the Bible with fresh eyes, he was able to teach others to understand, so that this doctrine of justification by faith had a new importance."[2]

The next important date for understanding Luther's early career is October 31, 1517, when Luther tacked his *95 Theses* to the Wittenberg Cathedral door. It was with this event that Luther first broke with the Roman Church. A third series of events are several disputations Luther had with officials of the Roman Church, including a dispute with Thomas

Cajetan at Augsburg in 1518, and disputations with John Eck at Leipzig in 1519. These disputes were followed by a Bull of Excommunication of Luther by the Roman Church in 1520.

In a letter to his friend Wenceslaus Link in December, 1518, written shortly after the debate with Cardinal Cajetan at the Diet of Augsburg, Luther already wonders whether "The true Anti-Christ according to Paul is reigning in the Roman curia."[3] In March of 1519, in another letter to Georg Spalatin, Luther writes, "I scarcely doubt that the pope is properly that Anti-Christ which by common consent the world expects; everything which he lives, does, speaks, and establishes fits so well."[4]

By 1520, nearly all of Luther's major works express the same notion. In his *Address to the Christian Nobility*, Luther speaks of "storming the walls of the Romanists in order to reveal the Anti-Christ within."[5] A few months later, in *The Babylonian Captivity of the Church*, Luther tells us that "The papacy is indeed nothing more but the kingdom of Babylon and of the true Anti-Christ."[6] These works were followed by *Against the Execrable Bull of Anti-Christ*.

Luther responded to the Bull by writing the *Execrable Bull of Anti-Christ*, the first time that Luther in public claims that the pope is the Anti-Christ is in November of 1520. This is followed a month later, when Luther burned the Bull with his students. Luther's translation of the New Testament from Greek to German in 1523 is the next event in Luther's life for understanding his view of the Anti-Christ. This is eventually followed by the publication of Luther's entire German Bible in August of 1534, the first great modern vernacular translation of the biblical text.

In a letter to Spalatin on October 10, 1520, Luther talks of rumors of the Bull: "The Bull condemns Christ himself. I summons me not to an audience but to a recantation. I am going to act on the assumption that it is spurious, though I think it is genuine ... I feel much freer now that I am certain the pope is Anti-Christ."[7]

At the same time Luther arrived at justification by faith, he had also been reading the words of John Huss. Indeed, Luther found his view of justification in the Bohemian reformer as well. Luther says, "We have all, Paul, Augustine, and myself been Hussites, without knowing it. God will surely visit it upon our world, that the truth was preached to it a century ago, and burned."[8] Many years later, in 1561, when commenting on Daniel 12:4f, Luther was to say that "the burning of Huss in 1415 was a clear sign that the papacy was the Anti-Christ."[9]

Before the writing of the *Execrable Bull of Anti-Christ* in November of 1520, there is also evidence that Luther already believes in the theory of the papacy as Anti-Christ. Leroy Froom quotes Luther from August 18, 1520, where Luther says, "We here are of the conviction that the papacy is the seat of the true and real Anti-Christ."[10]

During the disputations with John Eck, Luther and Eck debated the importance of Wycliffe and Huss. After Eck had accused Luther of being a Bohemian, Luther responded, "I repulse the charge of Bohemianism. I have never approved of the schism."[11] In another letter to Spalatin from March 1519, Luther refers to a letter from Eck to Luther: "I am sending Eck's letter in which he already boasts of having won the Olympic. I am studying the papal decretals for my debate. I whisper this in your ear, "I do not know whether the pope is the Anti-Christ or his apostle, so does he in his decretals corrupt and crucify Christ, that is, the truth."[12]

Roland Bainto suggests this reference to Anti-Christ is "ominous." Bainton continues: "Luther was to find it easier to convince men that the pope was the Anti-Christ than the just shall live through faith. The suspicion which Luther did not yet dare breathe in the open, links him unwittingly with the medieval sectaries who had revived and transformed the theme of the Anti-Christ."[13]

Bainton is clearly referring here to Wycliffe and Huss, but again, he continues: "A figure invented by the Jews in their captivity to derive comfort from calamity on the ground that the coming of the Messiah is retarded by the machinations of the Anti-Messiah, whose raging must reach a peak before the Saviour should come."[14]

Bainton suggests that Luther believed that the Anti-Christ was a Jewish invention developed during the Babylonian Captivity. He may be referring here to the early Christian view that the Anti-Christ will come from the lost tribe of Dan, and that Jews will be his most important followers. Whether or not this is the proper interpretation of this passage, Bainton continues his comment about the early history of the Anti-Christ: "The gloomiest picture of the present thus becomes the most encouraging for the future. The Book of Revelation made of the Anti-Messiah an Anti-Christ and added the details that before the end two witnesses must testify and suffer martyrdom."[15]

The comment on two witnesses refers to two figures mentioned in Revelation 11, where it is said they will prophesy before the world for three and a half years (1,260 days) [11:3]. During this time, they can strike the earth with whatever sickness they desire, and cannot be harmed by their enemies [11:5–6]. Ultimately, they will be killed by the beast [11:7] but they will rise to life in three and a half days [11:11].[16]

This mention of two witnesses in Revelation 11:3 is most likely connected to an Old Testament passage, Zechariah four. Revelation describes the two witnesses as two olive trees and two lamp stands standing before the Lord (11:4). In the Zechariah passage, the prophet saw a vision of a solid gold lamp stand, with a bowl at its top with seven lights. Also, on either side of the bowl are two olive trees (Zechariah 4:2–3). Zechariah asks an angel for the meaning of the olive trees. The angel's answer: "These are the two anointed to serve the Lord of all the earth (4:14), that is, they are two prophets of the Lord."

This identification of the two witnesses in Revelation 11 with two prophets in Zechariah 4 has led various biblical exegetes to identify who these prophets are. Some say they are Moses and Elijah, and that is the principal way they are identified in the Reformation period. Some say Elijah and Elisha, or Elijah and Enoch.

LUTHER'S TRADITIONAL VIEW OF THE ANTI-CHRIST

In his book, *Here I Stand*, Roland Bainton speaks about Luther's adopting of the Wycliffe/Huss papal Anti-Christ theory: "The theme became very popular in the late Middle Ages among the Fraticelli, Wycliffites, and Hussites, who identified the pope with the Anti-Christ soon to be overthrown. Luther was unwittingly in line with these sectaries with one significant difference. Whereas they identified particular popes because of their evil lives with Anti-Christ, Luther held that every pope was Anti-Christ."[17]

From the materials in the previous section of this chapter, it is clear that Luther held the view that the papacy is the Anti-Christ long before his disputations with John Eck. In addition to Luther's *Execrable Bull of the Anti-Christ*, he also developed this view in a number of other works. The best places to see this view are Bainton's *History of the Reformation in the Sixteenth Century*, comments on these exegetical works: "Luther proved by the revelations of Daniel, and Saint John, by the epistles of Saint Paul, Saint Peter, and Saint Jude, that the reign of Anti-Christ, predicted and described in the Bible, was the papacy ... And all the people did say 'Amen!' A holy terror seized their souls. It was Anti-Christ whom they beheld seated on the pontifical throne. This new idea, which derived greater strength from the prophetic descriptions, launched forth by Luther into the midst of his contemporaries, inflicted the most terrible blow on Rome."[18]

In his introduction to the New Testament, Luther comments on the ability to change water to wine: "It is said that the pope has the power to do it. I say that is all fiction. The pope does not have a hair's breadth of power to change what Christ has made; and whatever of these things he changes, that he does as a tyrant and Anti-Christ, I should like to hear how they will defend themselves."[19]

In commenting on Daniel 11, Luther points out that the writer of Daniel identified the Anti-Christ with Antiochus IV, but he leaves open the possibility that there may be other embodiments of the Final Enemy as well.[20] In his preface to the First Book of Maccabees, Luther again makes the identification of Antiochus and the Anti-Christ, regarding Daniel 11:32–34, but also leaves open the possibility that this is not the only identity of the Anti-Christ.[21]

In his preface to Second Thessalonians, Luther says that the Roman Empire must pass away before the Anti-Christ sets up himself with a false religion, implying that the establishment of the papacy of Gregory the Great was the first manifestation of the Anti-Christ in Medieval Christianity. In his preface to the epistles of John, Luther identifies the references to the Anti-Christ as referring to Cerinthians, a Gnostic heretic around 100 CE[22]; and in his preface to the New Testament, Luther identifies Gog as identical with Magog. Luther implies that these terms are to refer to the Moslem Turks then threatening western Europe. Indeed, Luther identifies Gog and Magog with earlier Tartar forbearers, going all the way back to Genghis Khan.[23]

In 1525, Pope Hadrian uses a reverse Anti-Christ argument against Luther. Writing to Frederick the Wise about the Counter-Reformation, Hadrian says of Luther: "He [Luther] has committed the decretals of the Holy Fathers to the flames. Does this sound to you like Christ or Anti-Christ? Separate yourself from Martin Luther, and put a muzzle on his blasphemous tongue."[24]

Two other places where Luther's view of the Anti-Christ can be seen are two related works published around 1545, *Against the Roman Papacy: An Institution of the Devil*, and a pamphlet, *The Depiction of the Papacy*. The latter work was accompanied by nine eschatological woodcuts, depicting the pope as the Anti-Christ. *Against the Roman Papacy* is an attack on Pope Paul III. It is Luther's last great testimony against the papacy, which he calls "*Meine grosse Anfechtung*," ("My great anguish."). In the opening paragraph of *Against the Roman Papacy*, Luther writes: "The most Hellish Father, Saint Paul III, in his supposed capacity as the bishop of the Roman Church."[25] Later, he adds: "The pope is the head of the accursed Church of all the worse scoundrels, on earth, a vicar of the devil, an enemy of God, an adversary of Christ, a destroyer of Christ's churches, a teacher of lies ... a brothel keeper over all brothel keepers, even that which cannot be named; an Anti-Christ."[26]

In *Against the Roman Papacy*, Luther says he deals with three main questions: "(1) Whether it is true that the pope is supreme lord over Christendom, councils, angels, and everything else; (2) Whether it is true that no one can judge or depose him; and (3) Whether it is true that he brought the reign of the Roman Empire from the Greeks to the Germans, that is, whether German emperors could receive the title of 'Holy Roman Empire of the German Nation' only from the pope."[27]

Needless to say, Luther answers all three questions in the negative. The treatise is full of invectives and scatological references to the pope, but nevertheless, Luther identifies the pope with 2 Peter 2:14's "insatiable for sin," and with 2 Thessalonians 2:8 Anti-Christ. About the latter, Luther says: "I only deride with my weak derision, so that those who now live and those who come after us should know what I thought of the pope, the damned Anti-Christ, and so that whoever wishes to be a Christian may be warned against such an abomination."[28]

Later in *Against the Roman Papacy*, Luther identifies Saint Paul's "Man of Sin" and "Son of Perdition" with the papacy and the Anti-Christ. Luther comments: "In Hebrew 'Man of Sin' means one who is not only a sinner in his own right, but who through false doctrines causes others to sin with him, as Jeroboam the King of Israel sinned [1 Kings 14:16], or, as Scripture says, made Israel to sin, through his idolatry."[29]

Luther seems to be agreeing here with the long-standing Christian tradition, going all the way back to Paul and the Johannine epistles, that the Anti-Christ will be a false prophet, one who convinces others to join his ranks, and is possessed with supernatural powers of persuasion. John Calvin, in March of 1545, also produced a propaganda tract on Pope Paul III. This text uses many of the same arguments against the pope that

Luther uses in *Against the Roman Papacy*. This work is called, *Admonitio Paterna Pauli III Romani Pontificis,* and was published in Geneva.[30]

One interesting aspect of Luther's view of the pope as the Anti-Christ is the fact that several German artists, including Luther's friend Lucas Cranach, provided illustrations to Luther's translations of the Bible. Roland Bainton writes of these illustrations: "Unfortunately, the illustrations for the Book of Revelation were made all too contemporary. The temptation was too strong to identify the pope with the Anti-Christ. In the first edition of the New Testament, in September of 1522, the scarlet woman sitting on the seven hills wears a papal tiara. So also does the great dragon. The beast of the abyss has a monk's cowl. Fallen Babylon is clearly Rome."[31]

More is said about these illustrations in the next chapter, "The Anti-Christ in Christian Art." It is enough now to say that Luther's many illustrators shared his view of the identification of the Anti-Christ with the papacy.

G. C. Berkouwer has argued that the real impetus for Luther identifying the Anti-Christ with the Papacy was the rediscovery of justification of faith through grace. Berkouwer writes:

> Luther felt himself surrounded by great eschatological tensions, and part of this for him included the role played by the Anti-Christ. For Luther, the Anti-Christ was not a remote figure of some future end time, but a threatening and dangerous possibility each and every day ... The major point was that the danger was present, not relegated to the future.
>
> Clearly, the actuality of the Anti-Christ as portrayed by John, accords with the entire eschatological proclamations of the New Testament. Althaus correctly observes that the New Testament proclamation of the Anti-Christ is not an irrelevant prediction of some remote future, but an alarm signal. "The church must always look for the Anti-Christ as a reality present or as an immediately threatening future possibility ... The recognition of the Anti-Christ is a deadly serious matter; and all other talk about Anti-Christ is idle and irresponsible play.[32]

Berkouwer warns us that for Luther the Anti-Christ is a present phenomenon, at work in the world already. He suggests that Luther discourages us from seeing the Final Enemy as an End Time phenomenon. The

Anti-Christ is more present in the evil acts of contemporary people than it will be in an eschatological End Time event.

THE ANTI-CHRIST IN LUTHER'S TABLE TALKS

In addition to mentions of the pope as the Anti-Christ in Luther's major works, he also speaks of the papal Anti-Christ in his *Table Talks*, collections of dinner conversations between Luther and his students, taken down by various students during Luther's theological career.

The Lutheran Publication Society published a collection of Luther' *Table Talks*, translated and edited by William Hazlitt. Hazlitt's edition contains 111 references that Luther makes to the papacy and the Anti-Christ. In all of them, Hazlitt argues, the two are synonymous. Typical of these comments is Hazlitt's entry number 326: "Anti-Christ is the pope and the Turk together; a beast full of life must have a body and soul; the spirit or soul of Anti-Christ is the pope."[33]

In item 327 of Hazlitt's edition, Luther says, "This prophecy, in the book of Daniel, as all teachers agree, point directly to the Anti-Christ." A few paragraphs later in the same entry, Luther says, "If this sin of Anti-Christ be not a sin against the Holy Spirit, then I do not know how to define the distinguish sins."[34]

In item 3330 of the Hazlitt edition, Luther again reiterates his belief that Islam is related to the Anti-Christ:

> Someone speaking of the signs and marvels which are to herald the coming of Anti-Christ, when he shall present himself prior to the Last Judgment, said he was to be armed with a breath of fire, which would overthrow all who might seek to oppose him. Dr. Luther observed: these are parables, but they agree in a measure with the prophecies of Daniel; for the throne of the pope is a throne of flame, and fire is his arm, as scimeter is the Turk's. Anti-Christ attacks with fire, and shall be punished with fire. The villain is now full of fear, crouching behind his mountains, and submitting to things against which heretofore he would have hurled his lightning and his thunder.[35]

Luther confirms a number of elements in traditional Christian views of the Anti-Christ, like the notion that Anti-Christ will come prior to Judgment Day, and the Anti-Christ is to be identified both with the papacy and with the Turkish Empire. Other editions of the *Table Talks* make these same associations, including this entry from an edition of the

Table Talks by William J. Peterson and Warren A. Hutchinson: "If the pope will throw away his crown and descend from his throne and primacy, and confess that he has erred, has destroyed the Church, and poured out innocent blood, then we will receive him into the Church. Otherwise, we must always regard him as Anti-Christ."[36]

Luther in his view of the Anti-Christ has not brought anything that is new to the Christian tradition. A century before Luther, both Wycliffe and Huss already had made the association of the Anti-Christ to the papacy. What Luther did that was new is that he popularized this notion among Protestant thinkers in the sixteenth to nineteenth centuries. Along the way, Luther also extended a number of elements in the traditional Christian view of the Anti-Christ. Among these elements are that the Anti-Christ will come prior to Judgment Day, that the Anti-Christ will be a man of persuasion, that the Anti-Christ is to be identified with Paul's Man of Sin and Man of Perdition, and that the Anti-Christ might also be associated with Moslem Turks. Many of these ideas are further developed in the Reformed Traditions, as we shall see in the next section of this chapter.

James Ratton quotes Moses Stuart who sums up Martin Luther's view of the Anti-Christ:

> This Reformer, when he published his German translation of the New Testament, thrust the Apocalypse from the canon and printed it merely in the way of an Appendix and an apocryphal book. His main reason was the book is unintelligible, and that there was no Christ in it. Subsequent writers, more keen sighted than Luther, found, or thought they found, good reasons for applying John's description of the beast to the Pope and his adherents. As the contest waxed warmer, Luther perceived the advantage of such an ally, and it was not long before consent was given to the reception of the Apocalypse. Thus the book was restored to its place of honor at the close of the canon, and John was converted into one of the most formidable assailants of the Roman camp.[37]

Ratton goes on to say that after the *Articles of Schalkald*, the Papal Anti-Christ was an article of faith, and "from that time until the last quarter of the nineteenth century, Anti-Christ was used as a polemical weapon against the Catholic Church."[38]

THE ANTI-CHRIST IN LATER LUTHERAN DOCTRINE

Luther's view of the papal Anti-Christ is reflected in many of the founding documents of the Lutheran Church. The *Book of Concord* published in 1580 is the historic doctrinal standard of the Lutheran Church. It consists of ten creedal documents recognized as authoritative in Lutheranism since the sixteenth century.

The *Book of Concord* was compiled by Jakob Andreae and Martin Chemnitz. It was published in Dresden, fifty years to the day of the presentation of the Augsburg Confession to Emperor Charles V. at the Diet of Augsburg.

The *Book of Concord* tells us this about the Anti-Christ: "The pope is the real Anti-Christ who has raised himself over and set himself against Christ ... Accordingly, just as we cannot adore the devil himself as our Lord or God, so we cannot suffer his apostle, the pope or Anti-Christ, to govern us as our head or Lord."[39]

The *Smalcald Articles*, is a summary of Lutheran doctrine written by Martin Luther in 1537. Luther's patron, Elector John Frederick of Saxony, had asked Luther to prepare these articles for a meeting of reformers in Schmalkalden. In the *Smalcald Articles*, Luther again summarizes the chief doctrines of the Lutheran Church, including the judgment in articles 2:4, 10, and 14 that the office of the papacy is synonymous with the Anti-Christ.[40]

In 1546, Luther wrote an essay shortly before his death entitled "Against the Roman Papacy: An Institution of the Devil," in which he also describes the pope as the Anti-Christ. Among these comments, Luther calls the pope "a Vicar of the Devil, an enemy of God, an adversary of Christ, a destroyer of Christ's churches, a teacher of lies ... a brothel keeper over all brothel keepers and all vermin, even that which cannot be named, an Anti-Christ."[41]

Emmerson points out that Protestants replaced the notion that Anti-Christ has a "life," like the Anti-Christ will be a Jew and shall come from the tribe of Dan, with the history of the Papacy. The Reformation thinkers also add new details, like Luther's insistence that "the Church of the Pope is the Synagogue of Satan."[42]

Richard Emmerson tells us that "The Protestant identification of Anti-Christ with the papacy and Catholicism in general is much more revolutionary. It represents a change in doctrine in which not merely some specific papal proms, but the papacy itself is repudiated."[43]

Emmerson quotes Hans Preuss, "Luther attacked the teachings and beliefs, not just the life and actions, of the pope.[44]

Emmerson continues: "A similar shift is evident throughout most Protestant tracts of the early Reformation. In *The Image of Both Churches*, Bale insists that 'in naming the pope we mean not his person, but the proud degree of abomination of the papacy.'"[45]

Emmerson goes on to say that John Foxe, another Protestant holder of the Papal Anti-Christ theory, that "Anti-Christ is not one person against Christ, but doctrine against doctrine, faith against faith, church against church."[46] Early Reformation thinkers, then, went quickly from damning particular popes to an entire institution, the Papacy.

Perhaps the most fervent English Reformation thinker on the Anti-Christ was John Jewel (1522–1571), Bishop of Salisbury. Jewel fled England during Mary's reign to escape persecution. He returned in 1559 and was then made Bishop of Salisbury. In 1560, Jewel published the first methodical statement of the position of the Church of England against the Church of Rome, *Apologia pro Ecclesia Anglicana* ("Apology for the Church of England").

Jewel also wrote an extensive commentary on the Epistles to the Thessalonians. In this work, Jewel sums up various Reformation beliefs about the Anti-Christ in his day. Jewel tells us:

> Some say he should be a Jew of the tribe of Dan; some say he shall be born in Babylon; some that he will be bred up in Bethsaida and Corazin; some that he should rise up in Syria; some that Mahomet is Anti-Christ; some that he should overthrow Rome; some that he shall be born of a friar and a nun; some that he should continue but three years and a half; some that he should turn threes upside down, with the tops in the ground, and should force the roots to grow upward, and then should flee up into heaven, and fall down and break his neck. These tales have been craftily devised to beguile our eyes, that, whilst we think upon these guesses, and so occupy ourselves in beholding a shadow or probable conjecture of Anti-Christ, he which is Anti-Christ indeed may unawares deceive us.[47]

Like the Reformers, for Bishop Jewel the Pope is the Anti-Christ, but he nevertheless seems to ridicule many of the elements of the Medieval

Roman Anti-Christ tradition. At any rate, Jewel tells us that "there is none, neither old nor young, neither learned nor unlearned, but he hath heard of Anti-Christ."[48]

CONTEMPORARIES OF LUTHER ON THE ANTI-CHRIST

The Geneva Bible, a Protestant translation of the Bible into English in the sixteenth century, makes a number of references in its notes to the idea of the Anti-Christ. It points out that the seven-headed beast of Revelation is ancient Rome, and that the Whore of Babylon is the "New Rome," or the institution of the Papacy, "the Anti-Christ, that is, the pope with the whole bodie of his filthie creatures . . ."[49] The Geneva Bible makes a number of other references to the Anti-Christ, and in all of them it is identified with the Papacy.

The Geneva Bible's note on the number 666 suggests that it may refer to "666 years after the writing of the Apocalypse." This is when the "Pope or Anti-Christ began to manifest himself in the worlde."[50] Elsewhere, the Geneva Bible again identifies the seven-headed beast with pagan Rome, and the two-horned beast with the Anti-Christ, whose two horns symbolize the "pope's religious and temporal powers."[51]

The sixteenth century saw a number of Protestant advocates of the Protestant Papal-Anti-Christ theory besides Luther and Calvin. Among these thinkers were Nicholas Ridley (d. October 16, 1555). Ridley was from a prominent family from Northumberland. He was educated at the Royal Grammar School of Newcastle, and in Cambridge. In his *Piteous Lamentation of the Miserable State of the Church of England*, Ridley clearly advocates the Papal Anti-Christ view when he writes:

> The head, under Satan, of all mischief is Anti-Christ and his brood; and the same is he which is the Babylonian beast. The beast is his whereupon the whore sitteth. The whore is that city saith John in plain words, which hath empire over the kings of the earth. This whore hath a golden cup of abominations in her hand, whereof she maketh to drink the kings of the earth, and of the wine of this harlot all nations have drunk; yea, the kings of the earth have lain by this whore; and merchants of the earth, by virtue of her pleasant merchandise, have been made rich.
>
> Now what city is there in the whole world, that when John wrote, ruled over the kings of the earth? Or what city can be read of in any time, that of the city itself challenged the empire over the

The Anti-Christ in the Reformation

kings of the earth, but only the city of Rome; and that since the usurpation of that See hath grown to her full strength?"[52]

Henreich Bullinger (1505–1575), Swiss reformer and successor to Zwingli as head of the Swiss church, is another contemporary of Luther's that held the Papal-Anti-Christ theory. In discussing the little horn of Daniel, Bullinger writes: "By the little horn many understand the kingdom of Muhammed, of the Saracens and the Turks... But when the apostolic prophecy in Second Thessalonians 2 is more carefully examined, it seems that the prophecy of Daniel and that prophecy of the apostle belong more rightly to the kingdom of the Roman Pope, which kingdom has arisen from small beginnings and has increased to an immense size."[53]

A third contemporary of Luther and Calvin's who advocated the Papal-Anti-Christ theory is John Hooper (1495–1555), English clergyman, Bishop of Gloucester and martyr. Two volumes of Hooper's writings are included in the Parker Society's publications, and another edition appeared at Oxford in 1855. In 1550, Hooper translated Tertullian's *Ad Exorem*, which is the first translation of Tertullian in English.

In writing about the Apocalypse, Hooper tells us: "Because God has given this light unto my countrymen, which be all persuaded (or else God send them to be persuaded), that the bishop of Rome nor none other is Christ's Vicar upon the earth; it is no longer any need to use any long or copious oration; it is so plain that it needs no probation; the very properties of Anti-Christ, I mean of Christ's great and principal enemy, is so openly known to all men, that are not blinded with the smoke of Rome, that they know him to be the beast that John describes in the Apocalypse."[54]

Huldreich Zwingli (1483–1531), another great Swiss reformer, on December 28, 1524 says this about the Pope and the Anti-Christ: "I know that in its works the might and power of the Devil, that is, of the Anti-Christ... The Papacy has to be abolished... But by no means can it be more thoroughly routed than by the word of God (2 Thessalonians 2), because as soon as the world receives this in the right way, it will turn away from the Pope without compulsion."[55]

THE ANTI-CHRIST AND OTHER REFORMERS

We already have pointed out in the preceding section of this chapter, that John Calvin shared with Luther a repugnance for Pope Paul III, as well as an identification of the Anti-Christ with the papacy. Indeed, Calvin called

Luther "My respected father who has denounced the darkness of the papacy."[56] Calvin continuously made this same identification throughout much of his theological writings. Commenting in his *Institutes of the Christian Religion*, Calvin tells us: "Some person think us too severe and censorious when we call the Roman pontiff the Anti-Christ. But those who are of this opinion do not consider that they bring the same charge of presumption against Paul himself, after whom we speak and whose language we adopt. I shall briefly show that Paul's words in II Thessalonians 2 are not capable of any other interpretation than that which applies to the papacy."[57]

Calvin also identifies the Anti-Christ with the papacy in a number of other places in the *Institutes*. He also makes the same claim in his *Commentary on Daniel*. At vol. IV, 7:25 of the *Institutes*, Calvin again identifies the papacy with the Anti-Christ: "To some we seem slanderous and petulant, when we call the Roman Pontiff Anti-Christ. But those who think so perceive not that they are bringing a charge of intemperance against Paul, after whom we speak, nay, in whose very words we speak. But lest anyone suggest that Paul's words have a different meaning, and are wrestled by us against the Roman Pontiff, I will briefly show they can only be understood of the Papacy. Paul says that Anti-Christ would sit in the temple of God (2 Thess 2:4)."[58]

Later, in the same section of the *Institutes*, Calvin again suggests that Daniel 7:9 is further evidence that "He that would rob God of his honor and take it for himself is the Anti-Christ."[59] He adds, "This is the leading feature which we ought to follow in searching out Anti-Christ."[60] Calvin's conclusion is clear: "Seeing then it is certain that the Roman Pontiff has impudently transferred to himself the most peculiar properties of God and Christ, there cannot be a doubt that he is the leader and standard bearer of an impious and abominable kingdom."[61]

In another section of the *Institutes* in regard to prophecies, Calvin tells us this:

> Daniel and Paul had predicted that Anti-Christ would sit in the temple of God. The head of that cursed and abominable kingdom, in the Western church, we affirm to be the Pope. When his seat is placed in the temple of God, it suggests that his kingdom shall be such, that he will not abolish the name of Christ or the church. Hence, it appears that we by no means deny that church may exist, even under his tyranny; but he has profaned them by sacrilegious

impiety, afflicted them by cruel despotism, corrupted and almost terminated their existence by false and pernicious doctrines; like poisonous potions, in such churches Christ lies half buried, the gospel is suppressed, piety exterminated, and the worship of God almost abolished; in a word, they are altogether in such a state of confusion, that they exhibit a picture of Babylon, rather than of the holy city of God.[62]

Calvin often used 2 Thessalonians 2 and I John 2:18 and 4:43 as clear signs and proof texts that the pope is the Anti-Christ. Calvin also thought the burning of John Huss in 1415 was a clear sign that the papacy was the Anti-Christ. Commenting on Daniel 12 in 1561, Calvin remarks, "At the present time in the papacy, . . . impiety and the Anti-Christ prevail."[63]

In Calvin's treatise *The Necessity of Reforming the Church*, written in 1544, the reformer repeats his view of the papal Anti-Christ: "I deny that See (the Roman Catholic's throne of authority) to be Apostolical, wherein naught is seen but a shocking apostasy. I deny him to be the Vicar of Christ, who furiously persecuting the gospel, demonstrates by his conduct that he is Anti-Christ."[64]

Calvin's students were expounded in Britain by his student John Knox. In his *Zurich Letters*, Knox speaks of "that tyranny that the pope himself has for so many ages exercised over the Church . . . As with Luther, I conclude that the papacy is the very Anti-Christ, and Son of Perdition, of whom Paul speaks."[65]

Like Martin Luther, John Calvin believed that the pope and Islam were two horns of the Anti-Christ. Calvin tells us: "The Pope is the spirit of the Anti-Christ, and the Turk is the flesh of the Anti-Christ. They help each other in their murderous work. The latter slaughters bodily by the sword, and the former spiritually by doctrine."[66]

In another of his published sermons, Calvin tells us about the Pope, "I deny him to be the vicar of Christ . . . He is Anti-Christ. I deny him to be the head of the church."[67]

Even scientist Sir Isaac Newton, in his *Observations on the Prophecies*, suggests: "But if the Papacy was a kingdom of a different kind from the other ten Kingdoms [referring to Daniel 7:7–8] . . . And such a seer, prophet, and King is the Church of Rome [referring to the little horn of Daniel]."[68]

Phillip Melanchton (1497–1560), reform follower of Luther and a key leader in the Lutheran Reformation, confirms Luther's identifying the pope with the Anti-Christ, when he writes: "It is most manifest, and true without any doubt, that the Roman pontiff with his whole order and kingdom, is the very Anti-Christ."[69]

In his essay, "On Matrimony," Melancthon also speaks of the Papal Anti-Christ: "Since it is certain that the pontiffs and the monks have forbidden marriage, it is most manifest, and true without any doubt, that the Roman pontiff, with his whole order and kingdom, is very Anti-Christ. Likewise, in 2 Thessalonians 2, Paul clearly says that the man of sin will rule in the Church exalting himself above the worship of God, etc."[70]

A group known as the Centuriators of Magdeburg, a group of sixteenth-century Lutheran scholars, wrote a twelve volume work called *The Magdeburg Centuries*. For the purpose of discrediting the Roman Papacy, and identifying the Anti-Christ with the Pope. The group was led by Matthias Flacius (1520–1575). Flacius also applies the titles "Son of Perdition" and "Man of Sin" to the Roman Papacy.[71]

The *Magdeburg Centuries* is divided into thirteen centuries, covering 1,300 years from the birth of Jesus to the year 1298. The work was first published in 1559 to 1574. In addition to identifying various popes with the Anti-Christ, it also speaks of a legend related to the female Pope Joan. Donald Kelly, in his recent book, *Faces of History*, writes extensively on Flacius and the Centuriators of Magdeburg.[72]

Samuel Lee, a seventeenth-century Rhode Island preacher, in his *The Cutting Off of Anti-Christ* also makes the papal Anti-Christ identification. Lee writes, "It is agreed among all main lines of the English Church that the Roman pontiff is the Anti-Christ."[73]

The Luther-Calvin-Knox view was reflected in the First and Second Scots Confessions of 1560 and 1580, as well as in the 1646 Westminster Confession of Faith. The First Scots Confession of 1560 speaks of "The true Kirk distinguished from the filthy Synagogues of Romanism."[74] The Second Scots Confession, also known as the Scottish National Covenant, denounces "all kinds of papistry in general." "We detest and refuse the usurped authority of that Roman Anti-Christ. Many are stirred up by Satan and that Roman Anti-Christ to subvert secretly God's true religion."[75]

The 1646 Calvinistic Westminster Confession of the Faith denounces "popish monastical vows." It denies the pope "the power and jurisdiction" over magistrates, citing II Thes. 2:4 and the 666 passage of Revelation 13:15–17 as proof texts. It calls "papists . . . idolators." And it describes "the popish sacrifice of the mass ... as most injurious to Christ's own sacrifice."[76]

Finally, the Presbyterian Westminster Large Catechism suggests that the portion of the Lord's prayer that mentions, "Thy Kingdom come," is a plea for the destruction of the ecclesiastical Anti-Christ, and it uses Thessalonians, Revelation, and Romans 16:20 to prove that point.[77]

Other early reformers that believed that the pope is the Anti-Christ are Thomas Cranmer, Roger Williams, Cotton Mather, and John Wesley. Thomas Cranmer (1489–1556) was the Archbishop of Canterbury during the reigns of English kings Henry VIII and Edward VI. He is also credited with the compiling of first two Anglican Books of Common Prayer. Crammer was also one of the first Anglican martyrs. He was burned at the stake for heresy in 1556. In volume one of Cranmer's *Collected Works*, the Anglican Bishop tells us, "Whereof it followeth Rome to be the seat of Anti-Christ, and the pope to be the very Anti-Christ himself, I could prove the same by many other scriptures, old writers, and strong reasons."[78]

Crammer combines the prophecies of Daniel seven and 2 Thessalonians two when he wrote: "After all these sprung up the pope, that triple-crowned monster, and great Anti-Christ, which took upon his authority, not only over the clergy, but also climbed above kings and emperors, disposing of them at his pleasure, and settled himself in the temple of God, that is, in the consciences of men, extolling himself above God, dispensing with good laws, and giving men leave to break them and to regard more his decrees than the everlasting commandments of God."[79]

Richard Emmerson tells us that Cranmer, in his *Confutation*: "Argues that the miracle of the real presence in the sacrament is the delusion of the Devil, and notes that Anti-Christ is to work false miracles."[80]

Emmerson also points out that other Protestant era thinkers also equated the veneration of saints with Anti-Christ's false miracles and doctrine. Other thinkers, Emmerson adds, thought the mass and other Catholic doctrine are "spiritual witchcraft."[81]

Thomas Cranmer was burned at the stake for his testimony in favor of the Papal Anti-Christ theory, as were Hooper, Ridley, Bradford, and many others.

Philip Melancthon (1497–1560) professor of Greek and follower of Luther at Wittenberg, also held the Papal-Anti-Christ view. In his "On Matrimony" Melancthon tells us this: "Since it is certain that the pontiffs and monks have forbidden marriage, it is most manifest, and true without any doubt, that the Roman Pontiff, with his whole order and kingdom, is the very Anti-Christ."[82]

A little later on, in the same work, Melancthon adds: "That both of them belong to the Roman Pontiff, who does not clearly see? The idols are clearly the impious masses, the worship of saints, and the statues which are exhibited in gold and silver that they may be worshipped."[83]

Again, in his "On Matrimony," while referring to the prophet Daniel, Melancthon says: "The prophet Daniel also attributes these two things to Anti-Christ; namely that he shall place an idol in the temple, and worship it with gold and silver; and that he shall not honor women."[84]

Roger Williams (1603–1683), governor of the state of Rhode Island and first Puritan minister in America, also held the pope as Anti-Christ view. Leroy Froom, in Volume III of his *The Prophetic Faith of Our Fathers*, quotes Williams: "The pope is the pretended Vicar of Christ on earth, who sits as God over the Temple of God, exalting himself not only above all that is called God, but over the souls and consciences of all his vassals, yea over the Spirit of Christ, over the Holy Spirit, yea, and God himself . . . speaking against the God of heaven, thinking to change times and laws; but he is the Son of Perdition (II Thessalonians 2)."[85]

Cotton Mather (1663–1748), was a Harvard educated, influential Puritan preacher. He was also a prolific writer and pamphleteer. Some estimates have it that Mather authored more than 450 books and pamphlets. In his work, *The Fall of Babylon*, Mather mentions the pope as Anti-Christ theory: "The oracle of God foretold the rising of the Anti-Christ in the Christian Church: and the pope of Rome, all the characteristics of that Anti-Christ are so marvelously answered that any who read the Scriptures do not see it, there is a marvelous blindness upon them."[86]

Froom also reports that Cotton Mather on three different occasions predicted the coming of the End Times, and the reign of the Anti-Christ. Mather's three prophecies of 1697, 1716, and 1736 did not materialize.

John Wesley (1703–1791) was an eighteenth-century Anglican clergyman, Christian theologian, and founder of Methodism. In his *Anti-Christ and His Ten Kingdoms*, Wesley devotes considerable time and space to his view of the Anti-Christ. About the Final Enemy as the pope, Wesley wrote: "He is in an emphatical sense, the Man of Sin, and as he increases all manner of sin above measure. And he is, too, properly styled the Son of Perdition, as he has caused death of numberless multitudes, both of his opposers and followers . . . He is it . . . that exalteth himself above all that is called God, or that is worshipped . . . claiming the highest power and highest honour . . . claiming the prerogatives that belong to God alone."[87]

In his commentary on the Second chapter of second Thessalonians, Wesley tells us this about 2 Thessalonians 2:2: "But the man of sin, the son of perdition—eminently so called, is not yet come. However, in many respects, the Pope has an indisputable claim to those titles. He is, in an emphatic sense, the man of sin, as he increases all manner of sin above measure. And he is, too, properly styled the son of perdition, as he has caused the death of numerous multitudes, both of his oppressors and followers, destroying innumerable souls, and will himself perish everlasting."[88]

About 2 Thessalonians 2:8, Wesley suggests: "And then when every prince and power that restrains is taken away will that wicked one—emphatically so called, be revealed. Whom the Lord will soon consume with the spirit of his mouth—His immediate power. And destroy—with the very first appearance of His glory."[89]

McGinn comments on Tyndale's view of the Anti-Christ: "William Tyndale (1494–1536), the Bible translator, held a general spiritual view of Anti-Christ, one that included the papacy, but only as part of the growing force of evil through history."[90]

King James (1566–1625) himself held the Papal Anti-Christ theory, as evidence by this comment: "'The faithful praise God for the Popes destruction and their deliverance,' and for "the plagues which are to light on him, and his followers. The Pope by his pardons makes merchandise of the souls of men: Heaven and the Saints rejoice at his destruction, albeit the earth and the worldlings lament for the same."[91]

Perhaps the most important early English Protestant thinker on the Papal Anti-Christ was John Bale (1495–1563). Bale was a Carmelite friar turned reformer, writer, and later bishop. Bale's *The Image of Both Churches*, written in 1548, includes a commentary on the Apocalypse based on Joachim of Fiori's understanding of the text.[92]

In the late sixteenth and early seventeenth centuries, fascination with the figure of the Ant-Christ was at its height. The 1260 days/years of Daniel and the Apocalypse were calculated so that they were related to contemporary events, including the defeat of the Spanish Armada.

Some Catholic thinkers responded to these claims, including Englishman Henry Smith who in the *Sermons* of 1631 tells us, "He who can swear that the Pope is Anti-Christ and that flesh is good on Fridays is a Protestant."⁹³

William Tyndale in his *The Obedience of a Christian Man*, makes the identification of the Whore of Babylon with Rome. Tyndale says Catholics "set up that great idol, the Whore of Babylon, Anti-Christ or Rome, whom they call the pope."⁹⁴ Later, some Roman authorities, like Thomas More, for example, called Tyndale's English translation of the Bible, "The Testament of Anti-Christ."

A number of other reformers also identified the Whore of Babylon with the Roman Church. John Bale (1495–1563), English playwright, a convert to Protestantism around 1535, identifies the Whore of Babylon as the "hypocritical church, the Roman religion" whose golden cup contains false religion.⁹⁵

Pamphilus Gengenbach (ca. 1480–1525) a printer from Basel and an early advocate of the Reformation, wrote a series of morality plays, including his "Nolhart," completed in 1517. The "Nolhart" contains a number of prophecies about the end of the world, including an analysis of the Anti-Christ.⁹⁶ Later Gengenbach completed his "*Die Totenfresser,*" *The Devourers of the Dead*, completed in 1521. This latter play, contains a theological critique of Papal masses for the dead, and strongly identifies the Anti-Christ with the Roman Church and the Papacy.⁹⁷

A number of other sixteenth-century dramas, in both Latin and the vernacular, attacked the Pope as the Anti-Christ. McGinn tells us this: "At least fourteen other Anti-Christ dramas of the sixteenth century in Latin, German, English, and Italian, attacked the pope as the Final Enemy. Most of these were morality plays based on the Antitheses of Christ's virtues and the vices of the Papal Anti-Christ."⁹⁸

McGinn goes on to discuss a number of these dramas, including the 1538 Latin play, *Pammachius* by Thomas Kirchmaier.⁹⁹ Emmerson also discusses a number of these dramas.¹⁰⁰

John Knox took Daniel seven and identifies the four kingdoms there as Babylon, Persia, Greece, and Rome. Knox then shows that Daniel's "little horn" is identical to Paul's "man of sin," and John's "Whore of Babylon" as symbols of one Anti-Christ. Knox understood every prophetic day as a year. "A prophetic week is a week of years," and a Jewish or Greek common year is a year of "360 days." Knox quotes Numbers 14:34 and Ezekiel 4–6 and cites the seventy weeks as evidence of fulfillment. "In the seventy weeks of Daniel, a day is to be taken for a year, extending in the whole to 460 years;

otherwise, that prophecy of the Messiah's coming, would not fall upon the just time of Christ's coming, as necessarily it ought to do."[101]

Wesley makes similar comments in his commentaries on Daniel seven, First John, and Revelation. In all these comments he points out that the Anti-Christ is to be identified in general with the Roman Church, and in particular with the Papacy.

Ellen G. White (1827–1915), was an American religious leader whose prophetic ministries were instrumental in the establishing of the Seventh-Day Adventist Church. White's principal work was *Christian Education*, where she writes of the "Compromise between paganism and Christianity resulting in the 'Man of Sin' foretold in prophesy as opposing and exalting himself above God. That gigantic system of false religion is a masterpiece of Satan's power—a monument of his effort to seat himself upon the throne to rule the earth according to his will."[102]

PAPAL ANTI-CHRIST AND OTHER PROTESTANT CONFESSIONS

Formal statements of doctrinal belief ordinarily intended for public avowal, by an individual, a group, a congregation, a synod, or a Church, have existed primarily since the beginning of the Protestant Reformation, particularly those denominations associated with the great leaders of the Protestant Reformation: Luther, Calvin, Zwingli, and Wesley.

In the seventeenth to nineteenth centuries the creeds or confessions of faith of various Protestant denominations suggest that the Roman pontiff is the Anti-Christ. The London Baptist Confession of 1689, is quite clear about the identity of the Anti-Christ. It tells us: "The Lord Jesus Christ is the head of the Church, in whom, by the appointment of the Father, all power for the calling, institution, order or government of the Church, is invested in a supreme and sovereign manner; neither can the Pope or Rome in any sense be heard thereof, but is that Anti-Christ, that man of sin and son of perdition."[103]

The Westminster Confession of Faith, written in 1646, makes the same identification: "There is no other head of the Church but the Lord Jesus Christ, nor can the Pope or Rome in any sense be the head thereof; but is the Anti-Christ, that man of sin and son of perdition, that exalts himself in the Church against Christ, and all that is called God."[104]

Similar identifications of the Anti-Christ with the Roman papacy can be found in Lutheran Augsburg Confession of Faith, and in the original version of the Methodist Confession of Faith.

The *Smalcald Articles*, a summary of Lutheran doctrine, written in 1537 by Luther himself after he had been asked by Prince John Frederick for the meeting of the Smalcald League in that same year. The League had been organized in 1531 as a union for Lutheran believers. In these articles Luther summarized the major tenets of the Lutheran Reform Movement. Among these articles is the claim that the bishop of Rome is not Christ's representative on earth. Indeed, he is the Anti-Christ.[105]

In the Dutch Reform tradition, after the meeting of the Synod of Dordrecht in 1618–19, the Synod set forth the Canons of Dort, which included one provision that the Pope is indeed the Anti-Christ. Among the words of the Canons of Dort are "The Reformation Against Anti-Christ. Against the Papacy (Roman Catholicism), the Jesuits, Islam, etc."[106]

By the year 1900, these confessions began to change, so that by the year 1950, none of these Protestant Confessions mention the figure of the Anti-Christ. In the days of the original sixteenth-century reformers, however, it would be hard to find a Protestant Confession that did not identify the Anti-Christ with the papacy.

Nevertheless, the belief of the Papal Anti-Christ has not died out completely. The view is still sometimes heard in various Protestant denominations, particularly those associated with Evangelical movements. Although the belief is no longer as widespread, it is still deeply held in some quarters.

In 1959, the Wisconsin Evangelical Lutheran Synod formally issued its *Statement on the Anti-Christ,* a doctrinal statement that says, "We affirm the statement of the Lutheran Confession that 'the Pope is the very Anti-Christ.'" Another place the Papal Anti-Christ theory can still be seen is the resolution unanimously passed by the South Atlantic Presbytery at a Presbyterian Church meeting in Charlotte, North Carolina on March 25, 2000. After several whereases, the resolution concludes: "Therefore: The South Atlantic Presbytery of the Bible Presbyterian Church ... resolves and warns the Roman Catholic Church, Mystery, Babylon the Great, Mother of Harlots and abominations of the earth (Revelation 17:5) constitutes the greatest threat to fundamental Christianity in the 21st century."[107]

The resolution continues:

The Anti-Christ in the Reformation

> The Roman Catholic Church has long forsaken the Bible alone, Grace alone, faith alone, and Christ alone. There should be no confraternity with this apostate church in ministerial associations, community Easter sunrise services, Thanksgiving services, mass evangelism, or common social endeavors. We admonish devout believers to lovingly and firmly win Roman Catholics to Christ and urge new converts to obey Revelation 18:4. "And I heard another voice from heaven, saying, come out of her, my people, that ye be not partakers of her sin, and that ye receive not her plagues."[108]

Francis Pieper sums up the Papal Anti-Christ Theory in the sixteenth to eighteenth centuries: "There can be no greater enemy of the church of God than the Papacy. In and by the doctrine of justification the church lives ... Can anything worse befall the Church than being robbed of the doctrine of justification by which alone she lives and exists? When the enemy takes my earthly life, he can do me no greater harm in earthly matters. And when the Pope has taken away the spiritual life of the church by robbing her of the doctrine of justification, the climax of harm has been reached."[109]

Pieper, like Luther, seems to suggest that at the core of the Papal-Anti-Christ Theory was the Roman Church's denial of justification by faith through grace. Pieper argues that the Roman Church puts its emphasis on salvation by works and the "treasury of merit," and thus denies the most fundamental doctrine of Christianity.

H. G. Guinness, noted nineteenth-century expositor, also summarizes the Papal Anti-Christ Theory of the sixteenth to eighteenth centuries:

> From the first and throughout that movement was energized and guided by the prophetic word. Luther never felt strong and free to war against the papal apostasy till he recognized the pope as Anti-Christ. It was then he burned the papal bull. Knox's first sermon, the sermon that launched him on his mission as a reformer, was on the prophecies concerning the Papacy. The reformers embodied their interpretation of prophecy in their confessions of faith, and Calvin in his *Institutes*. All the reformers were unanimous in the matter ... And their interpretation of these prophecies determined their reforming action ... It nerved them to resist the claim of that apostate church to the uttermost. It made them martyrs. It sustained them at the stake. And the view of the Reformers was shared by thousands, by hundreds of thousands. They were adopted by princes and peoples.[110]

The Legend of the Anti-Christ

THE COUNTER-REFORMATION'S RESPONSE TO THE PAPAL ANTI-CHRIST

Historians used to describe the Catholic response to the beginnings of the Protestant Reformation as the "Counter-Reformation," but the term was surely a misnomer. By 1500 any thinking Christian knew that the Church was in much need of reform. The debates were about what to reform, and not did the Church need reform.

Those who worked for reform within the Roman Church took a number of steps. First, they sought for an end to the worst of Church corruption. Second, in theological circles that culminated in the Council of Trent (1545–1563), they concentrated more clearly on their views of issues the Protestants had brought to the center of attention—Justification, the Sacraments, and the authority of Scripture. Finally, the Roman Church developed a new spirituality, a new language and practices regarding prayer, and a new view of the relationship of discipline to Church institutions. In this section of this chapter, we take a close look at the responses of several Roman Counter-Reformation scholars to the reformer's view that the Pope is the Anti-Christ.

The reformers mentioned above were by no means unified in all points of theology; but one item about which they do seem to be unanimous was that the prophecies of Daniel, Revelation, Paul, and John the Divine made about the Anti-Christ that refer to the papacy. As a response to this theory, the Roman Church ushered some of its scholars to combat this interpretation of the Anti-Christ. Principal combatants on the side of the Roman Church in this battle were members of the Society of Jesus, the Jesuits, an order founded by the papacy in 1540. The chief proponents on the side of the Roman Church were Robert Bellarmine, Francisco Ribera, and Luis De Alcazar.

Through the Jesuit Ribera of Salamanca, Spain, and Bellarmine of Rome, the papacy put forth a Counter-Reformation theory that came to be known as the Futurist Theory. Almost simultaneously, Alcazar, a Spanish Jesuit from Seville, advanced another Counter-Reformation theory that came to be known as the Preterist Theory. Both of these theories were designed to respond to the Protestant churches' claim that the pope is the Anti-Christ.

Ribera in his commentary on Revelation applied the prophesies in the book to the end of time rather than to the history of the papacy. In his view, Anti-Christ shall be a single person who would be received by the Jews at the end of time, when he will rebuild the Temple in Jerusalem.

In his commentary, Ribera makes four major points. First, the Anti-Christ will be a political leader, an individual, who will appear some time in the future. Second, he will arise in the last days and make a covenant with the Jewish nation. Third, he will rebuild the Temple of Solomon in Jerusalem, where the Temple Mount now sits. And finally, he will emerge as a world ruler, with power and authority over all nations, and he shall take control of the churches as well during a time of great tribulation.

Ribera maintained that while the first few chapters of Revelation refer to ancient Rome in the time of John the Divine, the greater part of the prophecies in the book are assigned to the distant future—to events immediately preceding the second coming of Jesus Christ. Ribera's futurism was polished and popularized by the great Papal controversialist, Cardinal Bellarmine. Between 1581 and 1593, Bellarmine published the most detailed defense of the Catholic Church's view of the Anti-Christ.

Robert Bellarmine (1542–1621), was a Saint and Cardinal of the Roman Church. He joined the Jesuits in 1560, and became a lecturer at the new Jesuit College in Rome. Between 1576 and 1589, Bellarmine also lectured to large audiences, often about the Protestants' theory of the papal Anti-Christ. Bellarmine argues that the prophecies of Daniel, Revelation, Paul, and John the Divine have nothing to do with papal power. These lectures came to form the third part of Bellarmine's *Disputatio de controversies christianae fidei Adversus Huius temporis haereticos*,[111] published between 1580 and 1593.

Bellarmine's main criticism of the Protestant views of prophecies was related to the year/day principle, which stood as the basis of the Protestant view. Bellarmine, determined to nullify the day=year prophetic principle which was used as the basis of the 1260 year period of the Anti-Christ's reign, sought to argue against this interpretation by using the fourth chapter of Ezekiel. Bellarmine suggests that in Ezekiel 4, a year equals a day.[112]

Cardinal Bellarmine also pointed out that Luther was at first against Revelation being considered as canonical. He pointed out that Luther, in his preface to Revelation, said, "There is too much lacking in this book to call it apostolic or prophetic."[113] Huldreich Zwingli (1481–1531), great Swiss reformer and author of the Helvetic Confession, also refused to recognize that Revelation was apostolic and canonical. Bellarmine uses these rejections as arguments in his Futurist Theory.

The Legend of the Anti-Christ

Bellarmine thinks the apocalyptic symbols of Daniel and Revelation refer to the distant past and the distant future, thus the name of the theory. Bellarmine maintained that the little horn of Daniel seven, as well as the end power in Daniel eleven were a single king, who, like Antiochus IV, would take away three kings and subdue seven others. For Bellarmine, then, Antiochus IV was the Anti-Christ of the distant past.

In Bellarmine's view, the Anti-Christ of the distant future is the one described in the prophecies in Thessalonians and John's epistles, where the Cardinal points out that all the verbs about the Anti-Christ are in the future tense. If the Anti-Christ is to come, Bellarmine says, then he cannot already be here. Thus, the Protestant view of the pope as the Anti-Christ makes little sense.

Cardinal Bellarmine also points out, as Francisco Suarez and others do, that the Devil has the power to produce illusions. Anti-Christ will not be a devil, born of a fantastic virgin, clothed in flesh and blood, as it was believed by Hippolytus and others.[114] Bellarmine also suggests that Gog will be the Devil himself, and Magog will be his army because Ezekiel 38 and 39 designates Gog as a leader and Magog as a region.[115]

Cardinal Bellarmine tells us that Providence restored the Roman Empire in the person of Charlemagne. It then passed from France to Germany, and thus the temporal succession of Roman emperors has been perpetuated to the time of the Reformation. Thus, Bellarmine points out, the Papacy had some breaks in its history, so the pope cannot be the Anti-Christ.[116]

Bellarmine was also adamant against the idea that the Anti-Christ is the son of the Devil. But both Bellarmine and Suarez maintain that the Devil has the power to produce illusions, and these powers will be passed on to the Final Enemy.[117]

Bellarmine's position on the Anti-Christ also can be seen in his treatment of the number 666 in chapter nine of Revelation. After providing a survey of many traditional Christian views of the Anti-Christ, the Cardinal notes that Luther's name in Hebrew, Greek, and Latin means the number 666.[118]

Cardinal Bellarmine argues that scriptures tell us that Anti-Christ will be a single man, while the Papal-Anti-Christ theory of the reformers suggests it is a series of men. Bellarmine writes: "For all Catholics think thus that Anti-Christ will be one certain man; but all heretics teach ... that Anti-Christ is expressly declared to be not a single person, but an individual throne or absolute kingdom, and apostate seat of those who rule over the church."[119]

Bellarmine also points out that Anti-Christ is to rule for three and a half years, while popes have ruled for centuries: "Nor can anyone be pointed out who has been accepted for Anti-Christ, who has ruled exactly for three and one half years; therefore, the Pope is not Anti-Christ. Then it follows that Anti-Christ has not yet come."[120]

Bellarmine makes a third argument by pointing out that the Anti-Christ's throne is neither in Jerusalem, nor in the Temple of Solomon if the papacy is the Anti-Christ.[121]

Francisco Ribera's 500-page commentary on the book of Revelation concurs with Bellarmine's theory. Ribera assigned the first few chapters of the Apocalypse to the fall of ancient Rome in John's own time. The remainder of the commentary, Ribera believes, is related to the three and a half year reign of the Anti-Christ. Ribera taught that Anti-Christ will be a single man, who would rebuild the Temple in Jerusalem, abolish the Christian faith, deny that Christ is God, pretend to be like God, revered by the Jews, and conquer the world.

Among Ribera's other beliefs about the End Times are that: the Anti-Christ will come at the close of the seventh seal; the Anti-Christ will place trumpets beneath the seventh seal; the Anti-Christ's reign will be in literal days; and that Babylon stands for Rome, past and future, not present. This Futurist view was also adopted by a third Jesuit, an eighteenth-century Chilean named Manuel Lacunza (1731–1801), who wrote a book entitled, *The Coming of the Messiah in Glory*. In this work, Lacunza attempted to show that the Second Advent of Christ will be preceded by the coming of the Anti-Christ, and that the Final Judgment will follow both these events.

The Futurist School, in addition to Ribera, also included Tristam Viegas, Antoon Sanderus, and Sieur de Remond. Like Ribera, these thinkers see the Anti-Christ as coming at the end of time. He will rebuild the Temple at Jerusalem. Like Ribera, they also saw much of Revelation as a commentary on Matthew eleven. They also believed that the two witnesses of Revelation eleven will be slain in Jerusalem.

Over and against this Futurist view is the work of another Spanish Jesuit, Luis de Alcazar (1554–1613). Alcazar produced a tract called, "Investigations of the Hidden Sense of the Apocalypse," a 900-page commentary on the book of Revelation. In the commentary, Alcazar proposed that all of Revelation applied to the first five centuries of the Common Era in the Roman Empire, and not to contemporary popes.

Alcazar maintains that chapters one through eleven of the Apocalypse describes the rejection of the Jews and the destruction of the Temple in Jerusalem by the Romans. Chapters 12 to 19 of Revelation, Alcazar argues, are about the overthrow of Roman paganism (the Whore of Babylon), and the conversion of the Empire to Christianity. For Alcazar, chapter 20 of the Apocalypse describes the final persecutions by the Anti-Christ, who is identified with Caesar Nero; and chapters 21 and 22 of Revelation are the triumph of the New Jerusalem, the Roman Church.

Other elements of Alcazar's scheme include: the seals are the early expansion of the Church; the trumpets are God's judgment on fallen Judaism; the first beast in Revelation 13 is the arrogance of pagan Rome, and the second beast stands for carnal Wisdom.

Alcazar's Preterist School suggests that the fall of kingdoms in Revelation refers to the fall of Jerusalem in 70 CE, or as the fall of Rome around 410. Alcazar maintained that Revelation chapters 1 to 11 refer to the destruction of Jerusalem by the Romans and rejection of the Jews. Chapters 12 to 22, in Alcazar's view, refer to the overthrow of paganism, and the establishment of the empire of the Roman Church over Rome and all the world. Alcazar was fully aware that his view contradicted some of the thinkers who held the Futurist theory like Ribera and the Portugese Alexandre Claudio De Sena Viegas, and was in conflict with approving of the concept of spiritual resurrection held contended against his view of the binding of Satan, as well as Viegas.[122]

A final Jesuit Counter-Reformation thinker who wrote about the Anti-Christ was Spaniard Francisco Suarez (1548–1617). Suarez suggests that everything about the New Testament depictions of the Anti-Christ is obscure. Like Bellarmine, Suarez's goal was to counteract the Protestant view of the papal Anti-Christ. And like Bellarmine's view, Suarez believed that the Anti-Christ will come in the distant future.[123]

Suarez maintains that scripture and the faith show us that the Anti-Christ will be one individual, a signal enemy of Christ. This excludes those who contend that Anti-Christ is either a whole collection of those who oppose Jesus Christ, or as the Papacy. Suarez says that the Waldensian and Albigensian heretics, as well as Wycliffe and Hus called the Pope the Anti-Christ; but this expression, Suarez suggests, was only a metaphor.

Suarez says the Anti-Christ will be one individual person, not a demon. He will not be the figure of Satan incarnate in a human being. He will perhaps be of Jewish distraction. As per Genesis 49:17, he will be from the tribe of Dan. Suarez also agrees with Bellarmine that Gog will be the Anti-Christ and Magog his army.[124]

Francisco Suarez also tells us in his *Memorati* that the Anti-Christ shall never do a good act. Being the counterpart of our Savior, who never did an evil deed, Suarez says the Anti-Christ shall be like the Devil, buried in wickedness.[125] Suarez also believes that when Elias was carried off to heaven, it was more probable that he was conveyed to a part of Earth as yet unexplored, "a delightful Paradise that will not be discovered until the end of the world."[126]

Protestant scholars had mixed reactions to Alcazar's Preterist Theory. Most rejected it, as well as the futurist point of view, but others did not. Thomas Brightman gives a typical reaction from most Protestant thinkers about these Jesuit theories on the Anti-Christ. In his *Revelation of Saint John*, published in London in 1609, Brightman tells us:

> But mine anger and indignation burst out against the Jesuits. For when I had by chance light upon Ribera, who make a commentary on this same holy Revelation, is it even so? Said I. Do the Papist take heart again; so as that book, which of a long time before they were scarce suffer any man to touch, they dare not take in hand, to intreat fully upon? What! Was it but a vain image or bug, at the sight whereof they were wont to tremble a few years since, even in the dim light, that now they dare be bold to look wishly upon this glasse in the clear sunshine; and dare to proclaim to the world that any other thing rather is pointed at in it than their Pope of Rome.[127]

Other writers, such as Nicholas Vignier, the younger, rose up to answer the expositions put forth by the Roman writers. Vignier's *The Theatre of Anti-Christ* is a response to Cardinal Bellarmine. At any rate, the Protestants continued to maintain that the Book of Revelation was now being fulfilled, while the Romanists thought it is either in the past or the future.

Another good example is Hugo Grotius (1583–1645), who had a Jesuit friend, named Dionysius Petavius (1583–1652), who convinced Grotius to read Alcazar's theory. Eventually, in 1620, Grotius wrote his own treatise on the Anti-Christ, arguing that the pope was not related to any of the prophecies of Daniel, Revelation, Thessalonians or the epistles of John. In his *De veritate religionis Christianae* (*On the Truth of the Christian Religion*), published in 1632, Grotius devotes a section of the book to the papal Anti-Christ theory, rejecting it in its entirety.

Perhaps the greatest irony of responses to the Futurist Theory and the Preterist Theory now dominate contemporary Protestant thinking. Almost all Protestant scholars agree that the Anti-Christ is to come at the End of Time. The Futurist Theory is the major one among Protestant thinkers. Thus, the notion of the pope as the Anti-Christ began to fade in the seventeenth century, and was nearly extinct by the nineteenth century.

One final Counter-Reformation thinker who wrote a great deal about the Anti-Christ was Thomas Malvenda (1566–1628). Malvenda was a Spanish Dominican whose *On Anti-Christ* was published in 1604. He also translated the entire Old Testament into Latin, and did commentaries on each of the Old Testament books. Malvenda also appears to have known both Hebrew and Greek. Like many of his Catholic contemporaries, Malvenda placed the coming of the Anti-Christ into the distant figure. He also developed a series of arguments against the Papal Anti-Christ theory.[128]

Richard Emmerson sums up the differing views of the Anti-Christ in the Reformation period: "Since Protestants and Catholics differ in their definitions of the true church, however, in specifics their identifications of Anti-Christ's supporters and opponents differ radically. For example, even though Medieval commentators repeatedly emphasize that many Christians will be misled by Anti-Christ, and that kings and political leaders will be among Anti-Christ's first converts, in the Middle Ages the most important supports of Anti-Christ are the Jews."[129]

Throughout Christian history, many thinkers believe that having rejected Jesus Christ as the Messiah, and having crucified Christ, thus the Medieval vitae of Anti-Christ often emphasizes the Jews as deceivers and chief supporters of the Anti-Christ.

During the period of the Enlightenment, Revelation 13:3, where one of the heads of the beast becomes wounded and then is healed, was used by a number of thinkers in the late eighteenth century as thought referring to a resurgence of the Papacy. More specifically, it was believed by some to refer to French General Louis Berthier's capture of Pope Pius VI in 1798, and the Pope's subsequent death in 1799.

Subsequent thinkers believe that the line refers to some figure in most of the major wars in Europe and America from the eighteenth century to the present. Thus, Napoleon, Peter the Great, Kaiser Wilhelm, Hitler, and others have all been described as the Anti-Christ.

THE PAPAL ANTI-CHRIST IN THE NINETEENTH CENTURY

The identification of the Anti-Christ with the papacy continued in the Protestant Churches well into the nineteenth century. In his book, *The Church of Rome: The Apostasy*, published by Presbyterian Board of Publications in 1841, William Cunningham identified the papacy with both the Anti-Christ and Paul's Man of Sin. He suggested that the Roman Church is guilty of idolatry, and that the call to come out of Babylon in Revelation 18:4–5 is a call out of the Roman Church.[130]

Presbyterian pastor Samuel J. Cassels from Norfolk, Virginia, in his book, *Christ and Anti-Christ*,[131] presented one of the most comprehensive reviews of the Papal Anti-Christ theory. Cassel's book was thoroughly endorsed by Presbyterian, Episcopal, Methodist, and Baptist leaders of the day.

In his book, *Christianity and Anti-Christianity in the Final Conflict*, Samuel J. Andrews identified the beast of Revelation 13 as a cruel and oppressive secular leader. Andrews' book originally published in the late nineteenth century recently has been reissued by Kessinger Publications.[132]

In rare instances, the Papal Anti-Christ theory continued into the early twentieth Century. The theory can be found in Fred J. Peters' *The Present Anti-Christ*, which was published in 1920. Peters cites Huss, Jerome, Luther, Calvin, Newton, Latimer, and Bunyan, as thinkers who believed the theory before him.[133] But by and large, by the end of the nineteenth century, the identification of the Anti-Christ with the Papacy had begun to wane.

The nineteenth century also saw a number of proponents to the Futurist Theory. John Quincy Adams' *His Apocalypse* held the theory,[134] as did F. M. Messenger in his 1928 work, *The Coming Superman*.[135] More recently, Herman Hoyt's *The End Times* has revived a Protestant version of the Futurist Theory.[136]

THE PAPAL ANTI-CHRIST THEORY AND CONTEMPORARY THEOLOGY

Among contemporary believers of the Papal Anti-Christ theory there are a number of proponents, including F. M Messenger, Herman Hoyt, and Ian Paisley. Messenger's 1928 book, *The Coming Superman*, was the first of twentieth-century tracts on the Papal Anti-Christ Theory. Messenger's principal candidates for the Papal Anti-Christ were Pope Pius X and Pius XI.

More recently, the Papal Anti-Christ theme has been revised by Herman A. Hoyt in his book, *The End Times*, published by Moody Press in 1969, and reissued by BMH Books in the year 2000.[137] Hoyt is a strong advocate of both the Papal Anti-Christ Theory and the Futurist Theory of Counter-Reformation thinkers.

Ian Richard Kyle Paisley (1926–) is Pastor of a noted Free Presbyterian Congregation in Ireland. In 1946, at the age of twenty, Paisley accepted a call from the Ravenhill Evangelical Church in Belfast. By 1969, Paisley had built the largest Protestant Church in the British Isles. In that same year, Paisley was arrested in Vatican Square for handing out copies of the King James Version of the Bible. In October of 1988, Paisley was beaten and forcibly removed from a European Parliament meeting in France. The occasion was a speech made by Pope John Paul II before the Parliament.

As the Pope began his talk, Ian Paisley stood up in the crowd and held up a red sign painted with black letters that read: JOHN PAUL II ANTICHRIST. Paisley shouted, "I refuse you as Christ's enemy and Anti-Christ with all your false doctrines." These same words had been spoken by Archbishop Cranmer before he was burned at the stake. Also in 1988, Paisley preached a sermon called "None Dare Call Him Anti-Christ," at the Martyrs' Memorial Free Presbyterian Church.[138]

By 1989, Paisley publicly opposed Billy Graham's ecumenical crusade in London because of the open participation of Roman Catholics in the ceremonies. He turned down a luncheon invitation from Graham, saying he would have no fellowship with those who associate with deniers of the faith. Needless to say, Paisley has become the most virulent advocate of the Papal Anti-Christ Theory in contemporary theology.

CONCLUSIONS

In this chapter we began by looking carefully at Martin Luther's view of the relationship of the papacy to the Anti-Christ. We developed this theme by examining Luther's view in a number of his exegetical works, in his *Table Talks*, and in a number of his other works. In general, Luther furthered the Wycliffe and Huss view that the pope is the Anti-Christ, but he also developed a starting point for later reformers on the Anti-Christ

In a second section of this chapter, we examined the views of several other reformers on the Anti-Christ. Among these were John Calvin, John Knox, John Wesley, Roger Williams, Thomas Cranmer, and Cotton Mather. As we have seen in this chapter, each of these thinkers shares Luther's view of identifying the papacy with the Anti-Christ.

In a third section of this chapter, we have explored the Counter-Reformation's arguments against the reformers' papal Anti-Christ view. The three most important Roman thinkers in this section of the chapter were Cardinal Robert Bellarmine, Francesco Ribera, and Luis de Alcazar. Each of these three thinkers developed arguments to respond to the Reformation papal Anti-Christ theory. In its stead, these three Jesuits suggest two theories: Futurism and Preterism. In these theories, Bellarmine, Ribera, and Alcazar make a number of observations about various biblical prophecies, concluding that the papacy could not be the Anti-Christ.

At the close of this chapter, we have shown that the reformers' responses to these Counter-Reformation thinkers were mixed. Some reformers rejected these Roman claims out of hand; but other reform thinkers, like Hugo Grotius, for example, were convinced by the claims of the Counter-Reformation.

One development in the Reformation period regarding the Christian Anti-Christ is that the Reformed Churches began to see a number of illustrations of the Anti-Christ, many in Germany. Most artistic depictions of the Anti-Christ in Western Christianity were developed from the 8th to the sixteenth centuries. In the following chapter, "The Anti-Christ in Christian Art," we shall explore these images.

NOTES

1. Roland Bainton, *Here I Stand: A Life of Martin Luther* (New York: New American Library, 1950) 49. Secondary sources I have used in preparing this chapter include: Elmer Kiessling, *The Early Sermons of Luther* (Grand Rapids:

Zondervan, 1935); Arthur Cushman McGiffert, *Martin Luther, the Man and His Work* (New York: Century, 1911); Philip S. Watson, *Let God Be God: An Interpretation of the Theology of Luther* (London: Epworth, 1954). Rudolf Thiel, *Luther*, 2 vols. (1936–37). Joseph Leo Koerner, *The Reformation of the Image* (Chicago: University of Chicago Press, 2004); Francois Wendel, *Calvin* (New York: Harper & Row, 1950); Edward A. Dowey, *The Knowledge of God in Calvin's Theology* (New York: Columbia University Press, 1952); Thomas Tentler, *Sin and Confession on the Eve of the Reformation* (Princeton: Princeton University Press, 1977); and Michael Walzer, *The Revolution of the Saints: A Study in the Origins of Radial Politics* (Cambridge: Harvard University Press, 1965). For more on the life of Luther, see Heiko A. Oberman, *Luther* (New York: Image, 1992). For more on Luther's theology, see Bernhard Lohse, *Martin Luther's Theology* (Minneapolis: Fortress, 1999); and Paul Althaus, *The Theology of Martin Luther* (Minneapolis: Fortress, 1966).

2. Gordon Rupp, *The Patterns of Reformation* (Philadelphia: Fortress, 1969) 131.
3. Scott Hendrix, *Luther and the Papacy: Stages in Reformation Conflict* (Philadelphia: Westminster, 1981) 97–98.
4. Quoted in Bernard McGinn, *Anti-Christ* (Chicago: University of Chicago Press, 1994) 203.
5. Martin Luther, "Address to the Christian Nobility," in *Three Treatises: Martin Luther*, edited by Charles Jacobs (Philadelphia: Fortress, 1970) 27.
6. Quoted in Hendrix, *Luther and the Papacy*, 111.
7. Bainton, *Here I Stand*, 84.
8. Ibid., 128.
9. Ibid.
10. Leroy Froom, *The Prophetic Faith of Our Fathers* (Washington, DC: Review and Herald, 1954) vol. 2, 121.
11. Bainton, *Here I Stand* 89.
12. Ibid., 84.
13. Ibid., 86.
14. Ibid., 84.
15. Ibid.
16. Ibid.
17. Ibid.
18. J. H. Merle D'Aubigne, *History of the Reformation in the Sixteenth Century* (London: Kessinger, 2003) bk. VI, chapter 13, 215.
19. *Luther's Works* (Philadelphia: Muhlenberg, 1960) edited by E. Theo-dore Bachmann, 107.

20. Ibid., 306.
21. Ibid.
22. Ibid., 393 n. 42.
23. Ibid., 407.
24. Bainton, *Here I Stand*, 193.
25. Martin Luther, *Against the Roman Papacy: An Institution of the Devil* in *Luther Werks für das Christliche Haus* edited by Georg Buchwald (Braunschweig, 1889–1892) vol. 41, 259–90.
26. Ibid., 260.
27. Ibid., 263.
28. Ibid.
29. Ibid.
30. John Calvin, *Paternal Admonition of Pope Paul III* (Geneva, 1545).
31. Bainton, *Here I Stand*, 53.
32. G. C. Berkouwer, *The Return of Christ* (Grand Rapids: Eerdmans, 1972) 268–69
33. Luther, *The Table Talks*, trans. and ed. William Hazlitt (Philadelphia: Lutheran Publication Society, 1997) 1. I have used several other editions of the Table Talks, as well, including: Helmut T. Lehmann, *Luther's Works: Table Talks* (Philadelphia: Fortress, 1967); and Thomas S. Kepler, *The Table Talks of Luther* (New York: Dover, 2005). I have also consulted Preserved Smith, *Luther's Table Talks* (New York: AMS, 1970).
34. Luther, *The Table Talks*, trans. and ed. William Hazlitt, 8.
35. Ibid.
36. Luther, *Table Talks* (New Canaan, CT: Ketats, 1979) 149.
37. James J. L. Ratton, *Anti-Christ: An Historical Review* (London: Burns & Oates, 1917) 152–53.
38. Ibid., 153.
39. *The Book of Concord: The Confessions of the Lutheran Church* (Min-neapolis: Fortress, 2002).
40. *The Smalcald Articles* (London: Kessinger, 2004).
41. Eric W. Gritsch, *Against the Roman Papacy: An Institution of the Devil*, Luther's Works 41 (Philadelphia: Fortress, 1966) 295–301.
42. Richard Emmerson, *The Anti-Christ in the Middle Ages* (Seattle: University of Washington Press, 1981) 215.
43. Ibid., 206–7.
44. Ibid., 207.
45. Ibid.

46. Ibid.
47. Quoted in Emmerson, *Anti-Christ in the Middle Ages*, 8.
48. Ibid.
49. *1559 Geneva Bible*, edited by Marshall Foster (London: Tolle Lege, 2006), commentary on First John.
50. Ibid.
51. Ibid.
52. Nicholas Ridley, *A Piteous Lamentation of the Miserable Estate of the Church of England, in the Time of the Late Revolt From the Gospel* in *Works*, 53.
53. Henreich Bullinger, *Daniel Sapientissimus Dei Propheta* (Author's translation from the German), chapter seven, folio 78v.
54. John Hooper, *Declaration of Christ and His Office*, chapter 3. In *Wiorks*, vol. 1, 22–23.
55. G. W. Bromiley, *Zwingli and Bullinger* (Philadelphia: Westminster, 1953) 143.
56. Bretta Martyn, *The Life and Times of Luther* (London: St. Martin's, 1989) 372–73.
57. John Calvin, *The Institutes of the Christian Religion* (Paris, 1859). Quoted in Froom, *The Prophetic Faith of Our Fathers*, vol. 2, 121.
58. John Calvin, *The Institutes of the Christian Religion* (Paris, 1859) vol. IV, 7:25.
59. Ibid.
60. Ibid.
61. Ibid. I have also consulted a number of more modern interpretations of the *Institutes*, including Donald K. McKim, ed., *Calvin's Institutes: Abridged Edition* (Louisville: Westminster John Knox, 2000); Benjamin A. Reist, *A Reading of Calvin's Institutes* (Louisville: Westminster John Knox, 1991); and Tony Lane, *Calvin's Institutes Abridged* (Grand Rapids: Baker, 1986).
62. John Calvin, *Institutes of the Christian Religion* (Philadelphia: Westminster, 1960) bk. 4, chap. 2, sec. 12.
63. Ibid.
64. John Calvin, *The Necessity of Reforming the Church* (Dallas: Protestant Heritage, 1995) 27.
65. John Knox, quoted in Froom, 199.
66. *The Sermons of M. John Calvin Upon the Fifth Booke of Moses Called Deuteronomie*, trans. Arthur Golding (London, 1583; reprinted by Banner of Truth Trust, 1987).
67. John Calvin, *Tracts and Treatises of John Calvin* (Eugene, OR: Wipf & Stock, 2004) vol. 1, 219–20.

68. Isaac Newton, *Observations Upon the Prophecies of Daniel and the Apocalypse of John* (London: Kessinger, 2003) 98.
69. Samuel Lee, *The Cutting Off of Anti-Christ* (Boston, 1694) 1.
70. Philipp Melancthon, "De Matrimonio," in *Opera Corpus Reformation*, vol. 12, col. 535.
71. Donald R. Kelly, *Faces of History*. (New Haven: Yale University Press, 1999) 173.
72. Ibid.
73. Ibid.
74. First Scots Confession (Edinburgh, 1560).
75. Second Scots Confession (Edinburgh, 1580).
76. Westminster Confession (Geneva, 1646).
77. Presbyterian Large Catechism (London, 1647).
78. Thomas Cranmer, *Works by Cranmer* (London, 1716) vol. 1, 6–7.
79. Ibid., 116.
80. Emmerson, *Anti-Christ in the Middle Ages*, 305.
81. Ibid.
82. Philip Melancthon, "De Matrimonio," *Disputationes*, Number 56, in *Opera*, vol. 12, cols. 535–36.
83. Ibid.
84. Ibid.
85. Quoted in Froom, vol. 3, 52.
86. Quoted in ibid., 113.
87. John Wesley, *The Anti-Christ and His Ten Kingdoms*, quoted in Froom, *The Prophetic Faith of Our Fathers*, vol. 3, 110.
88. John Wesley, *New Testament Commentary* (London: Baker, 1966) 143.
89. Ibid., 144. Wesley also mentions the Papal Anti-Christ Theory in a number of his journals and diaries. See *The Works of John Wesley: Journals and Diaries* (Nashville: Abingdon, 1988).
90. Bernard McGinn, *The Anti-Christ*, 218.
91. James I, "Paraphrase," in *Workes*, 47 and 57.
92. Ibid., 220.
93. Ibid.
94. Emmerson, *Anti-Christ in the Middle Ages*, 205.
95. Ibid.
96. Pamphilus Gengenbach, *Nolhart*, quoted in McGinn, *Anti-Christ*, 212.
97. Ibid.

98. McGinn, *The Anti-Christ*, 212.
99. Ibid.
100. Emmerson, *Anti-Christ in the Middle Ages*, 146–203.
101. Quoted in Friedrich Brandes, *John Knox: Der Reformer Schottlands* (Berlin, 1889) 191.
102. Ellen G. White, *True Education* (Vancouver: Pacific Public Relations Publications Association, 2000) 105.
103. Samuel E. Waldron, *Modern Exposition of the 1689 Baptist Confession of Faith* (New York: Evangelical Press, 2005) 79.
104. James E. Bordwine, *A Guide to the Westminster Confession of Faith* (Philadelphia: Trinity Foundation Press, 1991) 63.
105. Martin Luther, *The Schmalkald Articles*, trans. William R. Russell (Minneapolis: Fortress, 1995).
106. C. Bouwman, *Notes to the Canons of Dort* (Spindle Works, 1996) 49.
107. "The Threat of the Roman Catholic Church in the 21st Century," South Atlantic Presbytery, Bible Presbyterian Church, Charlotte, North Carolina, March 25, 2000.
108. Ibid.
109. Francis Pieper, *Christian Dogmatics* (St. Louis: Concordia, 1950) vol. 2, 553–54.
110. H. Grattan Guinness, *Romanism and the Reformation* (Toronto: S. R. Briggs, n.d.) 150–260.
111. John Olin, *The Catholic Reformation: Savonarola to Ignatuis Loyola* (New York: Fordham University Press, 1992) 73.
112. Ibid.
113. Ibid, 75.
114. Quoted in Huchere, *History of Anti-Christ*, 40.
115. Ibid.
116. Huchede, *History of Anti-Christ*, 54.
117. Ibid., 13–14.
118. Robert Bellarmine, *Controversies* III.3.
119. Bellarmine, "De Summo Pontifici," *Disputationes*, bk. 3, chap. 2, 190.
120. Ibid., 195.
121. Ibid.
122. L. E. Froom, *The Prophetic Faith* (Washington: Review and Herald, 1948) vol. 2, ddd 509.

123. Francisco Suarez, "Commentaries and Disputations on the Summa of Thomas Aquinas," in *Francis Suarez's Opera Omnia* edited by Charles Bertin (Paris: Vives, 1860) 1025–44.
124. John Marenbon, *Medieval Philosophy*, vol. 3 (London: Routledge, 2006).
125. Huchede, *History of Anti-Christ*, 18.
126. Ibid., 54.
127. Thomas Brightman, *Revelation to Saint John* (London, 1609) 149.
128. Thomas Malvenda, *De Anti-Christo: Libri Undecim* (Rome: Vulliettus, 1604).
129. Emmerson, *Anti-Christ in the Middle Ages*, 217.
130. William Cunningham, *Church of Rome: The Apostasy* (New York: Presbyterian Board of Publications, 1841).
131. Samuel J. Cassels, *Christ and Anti-Christ* (Norfolk, 1846).
132. Samuel J. Andrews, *Christianity and Anti-Christianity in the Final Conflict* (London: Kessinmger, 2003).
133. Fred J. Peters, *The Present Anti-Christ* (New York, 1920).
134. John Q. Adams, *His Apocalypse* (New York, 1824).
135. F. M. Messenger, *The Coming Superman*; quoted in Colin D. and Russell R. Standish (New York: Russell Standish, 1996) 168.
136. Herman A. Hoyt, *The End Times* (London: BMH, 2000).
137. Ibid.
138. This sermon was delivered on October 16, 1988.

7

Anti-Christ in Christian Art

> Underlying it all was a deep indignation against the corruption of the Church. Again and again the pope was shamed by a comparison with Christ. This theme went back through Hus and Wycliffe.
>
> —Roland Bainton, *Here I Stand: A Life of Martin Luther*

> Anti-Christ iconography flourished as never before between 1335 and 1500. Especially significant was the rich development of the illustrated cycles of the life of the Final Enemy in manuscripts and early printed books. The period closed with the supreme monumental presentation of Anti-Christ in art, Luca Signorelli's fresco in the San Brixio Chapel in Orvieto.
>
> —Bernard McGinn, *The Anti-Christ*

> Within a few years, Catholics consolidated their critical gestures in a printed image of infamy, the *Seven-Headed Martin Luther*.
>
> —Joseph Leo Koerner, *The Reformation of the Image*

INTRODUCTION

IN THIS CHAPTER, WE will explore the Anti-Christ as an iconographic image in Western Christianity. The earliest extant images of the Anti-Christ in western art come from the Dark Ages, and are usually depictions of the Psalms.[1] Several images are extant from the 9th to 11th centuries. We will begin the chapter with an analysis of these images. Ahuva Belkin, in an interesting paper in the *Florilegium*, suggests that a number of 12th century works in Christian art are depictions of the Anti-Christ. In the second section of this chapter, we shall look at Belkin's work.

In a third section of this chapter, we shall explore the image of the Anti-Christ in Christian art in the 14th and 15th centuries. The primary materials examined in this section are a series of images developed by the Master of the Marienkirche, a late 14th century German artist. These images are done in stain glass and are very provocative. A number of 15th century extant images of the Anti-Christ will also be discussed in the second section of this chapter. A number of images owned by the New York Public Library, mostly from the late 15th century, will be examined in this section.

In a fourth section of this chapter, we will examine a number of 16th century German woodcuts of the Anti-Christ made by Lucas Cranach, George Lemberger, an illustrator of the Nuremberg Chronicle, and the work of a number of other 16th Century Reformation artists. In a fifth section of this chapter, we shall take a close look at the Orvieto frescoes of Lucas Signorelli, one of the great painters from the Italian Renaissance, as well as the work of Master Vergillius, who painted a miniature of "The Judgment of the Devil and Anti-Christ," in 1410–1412.

There are very few extant images of the Anti-Christ from the 17th and 18th centuries; there are a few from the 19th century, and an abundance of depictions in the 20th century. In the penultimate section of this chapter, we shall explore these more modern Anti-Christ images in the 19th and 20th centuries; and we shall bring the chapter to a close with some general conclusions about the iconography of the Anti-Christ in western Christianity.

ANTI-CHRIST AND EARLY ILLUSTRATIONS OF THE PSALMS

Most of the earliest Christian extant images of the Anti-Christ are connected to illuminated manuscripts of the Psalms. These books, which are called Psalters, also contain other devotional material. They often contain canticles from the Old and New Testaments.

Psalters are also part of either the Horologion, the breviary, or both. They were used to say the Liturgy of the Hours in both the eastern and western churches.

It was common for early Christian artists to illuminate certain of the psalms with colorful depictions. These early depictions of the psalms sometimes have images of the Anti-Christ. The psalms most often depicted as the Anti-Christ were psalms 10, 14, 51, and 52. Psalm 10 is divided into four sections: 1) The cry of the remnant (verse 1); 2) the character of the wicked (verses 2–11); 3) the cry of the remnant (verses 12–15); and 4) the confidence of the remnant (verses 16–18). The opening verse speaks of "the times of trouble," followed by a particular "Wicked One," which led many scholars to see this description as the Anti-Christ.

Psalm 14 speaks of a fool in his heart that there is no God. Again, some identify this fool with the Christian Anti-Christ. Psalm 51 contains the description of a sinner whose transgressions are tied to an evil figure called "Doeg, the Edomite."[2]

Among the earliest depictions of these Psalms is the Corbie Psalter, an illuminated text from around 800. The Corbie Monastery, founded by the Benedictines around 660, contained one of the earliest and best scriptoriums in western Europe. In an illumination of Psalm 51, the initial letter Q contains an enthroned figure, accompanied by two wild beasts, perhaps Behemoth and Leviathan.[3] Earlier, Cassiodorus (ca. 485–585), in his commentary on Psalm 51, had suggested that Doeg the Edomite may be the Anti-Christ, so this may be what the illuminator had in mind.

The Utrecht Psalter was created at the Benedictine Abbey Hautvillers in northern France, between 816 and 834. Around 970, the Utrecht Psalter had made its way to the scriptorium at Christ Church in Canterbury, where three identical copies were made. The Utrecht Psalter has illuminations for both Psalm 13 and 52 of some importance to our study. The first contains an enthroned figure beneath a small domed structure to whom soldiers are bringing heads that have been lopped off with swords. In the center of the image stands a figure with outstretched arms, lecturing to a crowd. A number of scholars have identified this second figure as the Anti-Christ. The image that accompanies Psalm 51 also contains an evil figure pontificating before his colleagues. This figure appears to be identical to the one in Psalm 13.[4]

In addition to these depictions of the Psalms, early Christian representations of the Anti-Christ can be seen in illuminations of the Book of Revelation. Among the earliest of these are a group of illuminated texts related to Beatus of Liebana, an 8th century Spanish monk and theologian. Beautus is best known for his *Commentary on the Apocalypse*, completed around 775. This commentary was popular in the Middle Ages, and it survives in 30 manuscripts from the 10th to the 13th centuries. Among these extant manuscripts are *The Illustrated Beatus Manuscripts and Manchester Codex*, the *Illustrations of the Beatus Manuscripts and the Apocalypse of*

Lorvao, and the *Morgan Beatus*, which is owned by the Pierpont Morgan. Each of these texts illustrates Revelation 11:7, where the Anti-Christ is shown as a giant figure, slaying the two witnesses. The Lorvao illustrates the attack of Jerusalem in Revelation 20:7–9, with a nearly identical giant tyrant. These Beatus manuscripts are dated from the mid-10th century.[5]

Another illuminated Apocalypse from the early 11th century, the Bamberg Apocalypse, was produced in southern Germany on Reichenau Island in Lake Constance. It was commissioned by Otto III, and completed for Henry II, who donated it to the Abbey of Saint Stephan at Bamberg. The manuscript contains a number of illustrations of the Apocalypse, including the victory over the Beast (19:19-20), and the binding and loosing of Satan (20:1–10). Other illuminated manuscripts of the Apocalypse include: the Valladolid Apocalypse (ca, 970), the Gerona Apocalypse (ca. 975), and the Burgo de Osma Apocalypse (ca. 1086).[6]

The Gerona Apocalypse is a Beatus manuscript which is owned by the Gerona Cathedral in Spain. The text is illuminated with 131 miniatures of many themes in Revelation. The Valladolid Apocalypse is also an illuminated Beatus manuscript. It is owned by the Biblioteca de la Universidad in Valladolid, Spain. The Osma Apocalypse is a third illuminated Beatus Apocalypse, which also contains a number of depictions of the Book of Revelation.[7]

Another 12th century image is "Anti-Christ Seated on the Coiling Tail of a Dragon-like Leviathan," an illumination in the *Liber Floridus*. In this depiction an Anti-Christ with crown and a staff in his right hand and seated on a Leviathan-like beast appears to be making pronouncements to his followers.[8] The *Liber Foridus* is one of the most famous encyclopedias from the Middle Ages, and was copied down to the 16th century.

ANTI-CHRIST IN 13TH CENTURY ART

Ahuva Belkin, in a very perceptive article, argues that several illuminated manuscripts from the 13th century contain depictions of the Anti-Christ. The first of these is an illuminated Bible from around the year 1200, which is owned by the Boulogne Municipal Library. The image to which Belkin refers is

> A cross-legged seated figure holding a scepter in his left hand while his right hand is raised in a conversational gesture, with a the Devil standing off to the left.[9]

A second manuscript, owned by the Musee Plantin in Antwerp, contains many of the same elements. Belkin argues that both of these images are representations of the Anti-Christ conversing with the Devil. He also mentions similar figures in a Paris Bible, known as the Mazarine,[10] and a Bible owned by the National Library in Palermo.[11] Belkin claims that a fifth text, owned by the British Library, and called the Arsenal, is also a depiction of the Anti-Christ. Belkin says this about the Arsenal:

> The Arsenal depicts a seated, cross-legged ruler attired in a royal wrap, holding a scepter in his left hand, and pointing upwards with his right.[12]

Belkin goes on to discuss how this image is different from the others in two important ways:

> In addition to the Devil confronting the ruler, there is a second small devil, hovering next to the ruler's ear. And, the ruler is wearing the pointed Jewish cap.[13]

Belkin continues by pointing out that many of these themes can also be seen in a Bible from Clairvaux, Troyes, which is owned by the Municipal Library, as well as in the Evesham Psalter, a mid-13th century English psalter, and in another manuscript owned by the British Library, which comes from Lyre. All of these manuscripts mentioned above are illuminations of Psalm 52, which begins this way, "The fool says in his heart 'there is no God.'"[14] Belkin makes this conclusion:

> The presence of the Anti-Christ is consistent with Psalm 52, the opening of which deals with the denial of God. All sources describe the Anti-Christ as a rebel who negates the sanctity of God and desecrates his Name. Thus, in the Christian catechism, as well as in folk tales and mystery plays, the Anti-Christ is represented as a heretic tyrant.[15]

The Abingdon Apocalypse from the late 13th century contains an image of the Anti-Christ at folio 72 r. This Apocalypse contains the Latin text of Revelation, with a commentary in French on the facing rectos. The Anti-Christ holds a sword and directs his followers to demolish a church in which there are several monks praying at an altar. The Abingdon Apocalypse is owned by the British Library (MS42555).

The Getty Museum in Los Angeles owns a 13th century illuminated manuscript of the Apocalypse. It contains a number of illustrations of materials from Revelation, including: the war in heaven (12:7–8); the dragon cast into the earth (12:9–11); the dragon persecuting the woman and flies into the desert (12:13-16); the seed of the woman fighting the dragon (12:17–18); the dragon delegating power to the beast (13:2); the worship of the beast (13:3–4); the false prophet rising from the earth (13:11–13); and the false prophet causing men to be marked (13:15–17).[16]

In this latter image, two false believers already have been marked on their foreheads. The image also contains a group of well to do ladies, and a group of dead lying at the bottom right who have been slain for refusing to adore the beast.[17] In the other, the false prophet rises from the earth as a monster rises from the earth and commands the people to adore the beast. This beast is a small blue-grey image, half animal with small horns, and half man. To show his power, he brings down fire from the heavens. John of Patmos appears upper left in the illumination. He looks toward the beast with a fixed gaze.[18]

The dragon delegating power to the beast who comes from the sea features a seven-headed best emerging from the sea and given power by a dragon. The commentary of this manuscript tells us that this beast from the sea is the Anti-Christ.[19]

The war in heaven is the depiction of a heavenly battle. Michael and two other angels spear the seven-headed dragon, as other followers are cast down to Hell. This image is very similar to an illumination at the British Museum, where the small dragons cast to Hell are supplemented with figures of devils.[20]

ANTI-CHRIST IN THE 14TH AND 15TH CENTURIES

The 14th century saw a number of artistic representations of the Anti-Christ, including a collection of stain glass windows at the late 14th century German Church, Marienkirke. The anonymous creator of these images include 16 representations of the Anti-Christ, Enoch, and Elijah. Among the Anti-Christ images "The Advent of the Anti-Christ to Jews Waiting at the Water's Edge," "The Anti-Christ Blessing and Rewarding His Apostles," "Anti-Christ Giving Gold to His Apostles to Bribe People," "Anti-Christ Preaching to the Nations," and "Anti-Christ Turning Stones to Bread."

These images reflect a number of traditional theological beliefs about the Anti-Christ, such as the Anti-Christ will first be accepted by the Jews, the Anti-Christ will use trickery to convert people, the Anti-Christ will preach to all nations, and the Anti-Christ will be capable of performing miracles like those of Jesus.

Rhoads and Lupton have identified a number of Anti-Christ images that are owned by the New York Public Library. Among these are: "Mock Annunciation of the Anti-Christ," a 1467 wood cut.[21] In the scene a monk demon announces the female Mary-like figure, the coming of the Anti-Christ. A second manuscript identified by Rhoads and Lupton is from the same text. It is a depiction of "The Anti-Christ Rebuilding the Temple," a reference to 2 Thessalonians 2:4. A third image discussed by Rhoads and Lupton is from a 1482 woodcut called "Circumcising the Anti-Christ," an apparent reference to the early Christian belief that the Anti-Christ will be a Jew.[22] A similar image from Martinez Martin, entitled, "Circumcising the Anti-Christ," is from a late 15th century manuscript, *Libro del AntiChristo*, published in Zaragoza in 1496.[23]

The *Velislai biblia picta* is an early to mid-14th century manuscript which, in effect, is a picture book of the Bible. The manuscript is on 188 folios, and is owned by the Czech National Library. The manuscript contains one image called "The Anti-Christ Having the Scholars Beheaded." In the image, the Anti-Christ observes from the left, as his minions lop off the heads of scholars. Presumably, these are Christian scholars familiar with Biblical materials and theology.

Other late 15th century depictions of the Anti-Christ can be found in Lucas Cranach's 1493 "The Anti-Christ," also discussed by Rhoads and Lupton. "The Reign of the Anti-Christ," also a 1498 illumination for the *Liber Chronicarum* by Michael Wogelmut or Wolgenmuth.[24] The Wolgemut illustration features a seven-headed beast hovering above a mountain. At the base of the mountain stands a crowd that seems to be worshipping the beast. The Strassburg Anti-Christ Book, produced around 1480, contains a number of scenes related to the Anti-Christ. Folio 4v depicts scenes of Anti-Christ's birth and early education.[25] In the latter image, a young man holds a chalice, while being taught by an older man, perhaps a magician.

The Nuremberg Blockbook (folio 5v), produced around 1465, contains the images of the Anti-Christ performing miracles. In one, he seems to be healing or blessing a fig tree, while in the other, the Anti-Christ seems to be inflicting a paralytic, as a winged demon rests on his left shoulder.[26] Earlier 15th century depictions of the Anti-Christ are: "A False German Pope Crowns Frederick III: The Mystical Anti-Christ," from Munich around 1431;[27] the "Anti-Christ and Harlot in the Chariot of the Church," a late 14th century depiction of Dante's *Purgatorio*, owned by the Bodleian Library;[28] an early 14th century "Crowning of the Anti-Christ," from a manuscript in the Vatican Library;[29] and "Anti-Christ's Conception and Birth," from the Velislaus Bible, a late 14th century Czech manuscript.[30]

Many of the early Christian themes on the Anti-Christ can be seen in a 15th Century Dutch woodcut entitled, "Anti-Christ Condemns Enoch and Elias Causing the Faithful to be Beheaded." This anonymous image is owned by the Minneapolis Institute of the Arts. In the top of the image, a papal figure with staff in his right hand condemns Enoch and Elias with his left. In the bottom of the two images, a papal Anti-Christ directs the executions of the faithful.[31]

A 15th century illuminated manuscript produced in Florence has a series of visions and accompanying illustrations. Prophecy number XV, and its accompanying illustration, depicts Pope Urban VI in the form of a two-headed dragon, his front head as a tiara-crowned human. The head on the tail is that of a beast that stands on a sea of flames.[32]

The Paris Netherlandish Apocalypse, a French manuscript from the early 15th century, features Saint John on the left receiving from the Lord the rod to measure the Temple. On the right, Saint John is purifying the Temple by throwing out an impure Jew. In the lower part of the miniature, on the right, Anti-Christ sits enthroned in Solomon's Temple, giving money to those who believe in him.[33]

The illustrator of Lambert of Saint Omer's *Liber Floridus*, a French manuscript from around 1460, produced an "Anti-Christ Sitting on Leviathan."[34] The image looks much like those discussed by Ahuva Belkin discussed earlier in this chapter. A kingly tyrant adorned with a crown, sits on a dragon-like Leviathan. The king's right hand holds a scepter, while the left hand is in a conversational gesture.

The Pierpont Morgan Library owns a number of Medieval and Renaissance images of the Anti-Christ. MS. M0894, folio 202r includes three miniature images of the Anti-Christ painted on vellum. The first is "Anti-Christ Distributing Gifts." It is a depiction of five men wearing hats, some gesturing, one standing with a staff, flanked by Anti-Christ, the Final Enemy wears a pointed hat with a jewel. With his left hand, he gestures, while his right hand points to three men. One offers a platter of gold coins. One stands in a pool of gold coins, while the third bends at the waist, while pouring a cauldron full of coins.

In the same manuscript is "Anti-Christ's Persecution of the Faithful." Three men wearing hats stand behind Anti-Christ. He looks on while three men are being tortured. The third image in this late 15th century manuscript features "Anti-Christ's Fall." Six men wearing hats witness the destruction of Anti-Christ who kneels with his arms raised to protect his head from thunderbolts.

MS M 0514, folio 07r is from a mid-13th century manuscript. It shows the Anti-Christ, wearing a hat, and armed with a sword in his right hand. He raises his left hand toward two male executioners. One holds a bloody sword, with his left foot on the body of Enoch. The other man raises an axe while grasping the hair of Elijah, kneeling with his hands raised. This appears to be an illustration of Revelation 11:7.

In a second image from the same manuscript, the Anti-Christ makes the roots of a tree flower. The Anglo-Norman manuscript seems to illustrate the Anti-Christ's ability to perform miracles outside the bounds of the laws of nature. In a third image from this 13th century manuscript, "Anti-Christ in the Temple," one of four kneeling men receives a money bag and a ring. In the background stand two soldiers in battle dress. One raises a sword at a mitered bishop.

In a third manuscript from Holland from the early 15th century (MS M. 0691, folio 180 v.) an Anti-Christ figure sits on a dragged altar with retable and looks down on six Jews, who wear peaked caps and sit on the floor. The Anti-Christ appears to be preaching to these non-believers.

The Morgan Library also owns two other manuscripts with depictions of the Anti-Christ. These are designated as MS. M. 429 (folios 109v and 110r) and MS. M 644 (folio 171 v.). Both images are miniatures, and both depict the Anti-Christ ruling from an altar table.

A 15th century French manuscript owned by the Bodleian Library at Oxford University has an illumination called "Anti-Christ," on folio 4r of this text. This manuscript (MS Douce 134) is dated from the 1400s. In the upper register center stands the Anti-Christ. He holds a scepter in his right hand, a horned demonic figure rests on his head. In the lower register, a young noble woman stands conversing with two men, probably peasants.[35] The *Apocalypse Blockbook, Schreiber* III, owned by the Kongelige Bibliotek in Copenhagen, contains two images related to the Anti-Christ. In the first of these the Anti-Christ stands with a sword in

Anti-Christ in Christian Art

his right hand, as two followers lop off the head of a believer. In the other image, the Anti-Christ orders the beheading of a bishop. These images are also from a 15th century block book from the Low Countries, perhaps the Netherlands.[36]

Albrecht Durer (1471–1528) produced a number of drawings illustrating the Apocalypse, including the "Four Horsemen," "The Seven Angels with Trumpets," "The Seven-Headed Beast" the "Beast with the Lamb's Horns," and "The Whore of Babylon and the Seven-Headed Beasts." These works were completed between 1496 and 1498. In the latter work, one of the seven heads breathes fire at the feet of the Whore of Babylon, while God and his angels reign above. In "The Seven-Headed Beast and the Beast with the Lamb's Horns," the large seven-headed beast preaches to a crowd, while a lion with a lamb's horns looks on the scene. Again, above these figures sits God on some clouds, surrounded by his angels.[37]

Durer also completed "The Woman Clothed with the Sun the Seven-headed Dragon," in 1497–1498. This is the only illustration of Durer's on the Apocalypse that might be related to the Anti-Christ. The woman clothed with the sun, a radiant, winged creature stands opposite the seven-headed beast. In the background, God peers down from the heavens, angels to his right and left aiming arrows at the heart.

ANTI-CHRIST IN 16TH CENTURY CHRISTIAN ART

There are two major sources for 16th century Anti-Christ art. The first of these is Lucas Signorelli (1455–1523), an Italian Renaissance painter, who was most likely a student of Piero della Francesca. Signorelli's masterpiece, some frescoes on "The End of the World" and "The Last Judgment," was produced between 1499 and 1502. These frescoes are in the chapel of Saint Brizio in the Orvieto Cathedral. These images, which greatly influenced Michelangelo, are crowded with powerful nudes painted in many different postures that accentuate the musculature. One section of Signorelli's "Last Judgment" contains a scene called, "The Deeds and Preaching of the Anti-Christ."[38]

Some critics have argued that these images refer to Savonarola, the Dominican hanged and burned at the stake in Florence on May 23, 1498, a few months before Signorelli began his work on the frescoes. This identification of Signorelli's Anti-Christ with Savonarola is bolstered by two facts. First, that Signorelli saw himself as a victim of persecutions by the

Florentine government; and second, Marsilio Ficino, in his *Apologia*, published in 1498, also identifies Savonarola with the Anti-Christ.

In the Signorelli images, all sorts of miraculous events are taking place. The Anti-Christ orders some people to be executed. He raises one man from the dead, while a group of clerics huddle by. Signorelli also shows us that the age of the Anti-Christ is at hand, with false prophets being hurled down from the heavens by an Angel. Many of these elements, of course, are traditional Christian ideas about the Anti-Christ, like performing miracles, and raising people from the dead.[39]

Another Italian Renaissance painter, Vicente Carducho (1476–1538), completed a number of paintings with biblical themes in the 1520s and 30s. Among these paintings is one striking image of the Anti-Christ. Later on, when Carducho was defending Michelangelo against the onslaughts of Caravaggio, Carducho called the latter, "A monster of genius and talent, Anti-Michelangelo and Anti-Christ."[40]

The other source for 16th century images of the Anti-Christ are the many illustrations of Martin Luther's Bible from the mid to late century. Writing about these illustrations, Bainton tells us:

> An interesting development to be observed are the illustrations, from one artist to another in the successive editions of the Luther Bible, notably from Cranach to Lemberger. One senses something of the transition from the Renaissance to the Baroque.[41]

The Cranach to whom Bainton refers is Lucas Cranach, the Elder (1472–1553). Joseph Koerner describes the relationship between Luther and Cranach:

> Cranach and Luther were also linked by professional bonds. Over three decades, the artist produced scores of paintings, broadsheets, and book illustrations for the reformer's cause.[42]

Koerner continues:

> In 1521 his woodcuts for the *Passional Christi und Anti-Christi* gave visual form to Luther's attacks on the papacy.[43]

In *Passional Christi und Anti-Christi*, Luther hoped to shame the pope by comparing the pontiff to Christ. Cranach's images for the book are in pairs, one sketch of Christ, and a corresponding image of the Anti-Christ. In one pair, Jesus washes the disciples' feet, while the pope is having his feet kissed; in another pair, Christ enjoins his followers to keep the faith, while the pope declares that no faith is required. In a third pair of Cranach's illustrations of Luther, Christ is crowned with thorns, while the pope is crowned with a tiara. In a fourth pair, Jesus is mocked and his tormentors say, "Hail King of the Jews," while the pope is being worshipped on his throne.

Again, Koerner speaks of the juxtaposing of these images:

> In the *Passional*, Cranach negates the likeness asserted formally between Christ and the pope, by exposing the worldliness of the latter's pursuits . . . The clash between humility and vanity is so clear that Cranach needs hardly to work to make it speak.[44]

Countless other images illustrating Luther's Bible were produced in the 16th and 17th centuries. The Lemberger mentioned by Bainton above is Georg Lemberger (1490–1540), who completed 100 woodcuts for an edition of Luther's Bible. Twenty-six of these illustrations are full page, and some of them are colored. This manuscript is owned by the Kessler Collection of Emory University.[45] Among these illustrations are a number of depictions of the pope as the Anti-Christ. In addition to the depictions by Cranach and Lemberger, there are also extant a number of anonymous artists' depictions of the pope as the Anti-Christ. Usually, these images are called "Anti-Christ," and are attributed to an "unknown master connected to the Protestant Reformation Era writings."[46] In all of these anonymous Protestant images they are called "The Anti-Christ," and the pope is in the center of each image.

Another image of the papal Anti-Christ was done by Melchior Lorch in 1545. Lorch, a German artist who lived from 1526 to 1585, presents the Anti-Christ as an enormous beast, with a papal crown, a twisting tail, and a trident in his right hand. At the figure's feet are souls claimed by the Anti-Christ, and from his mouth comes forth a great wind, bringing destruction to those below.[47] Another image from the same text in which Lorch's depiction of the Anti-Christ can be found is a depiction produced around 1540, where two demons attempt to revive a papal Anti-Christ. In the right part of the image, two other demons are torturing souls locked in a giant vat.[48]

The Pope as Anti-Christ continued in Christian art well into the 17th century. "The Pope as Anti-Christ Riding the Beast of the Apocalypse," is a fine example from the early 17th century. The pope, with jeweled tiara and a staff in his right hand and a sign in his left that reads, "Go kill your prince," sits atop a seven-headed beast. Three penitents stand to the right of the beast. The beast has cloven hoofs and a long, serpentine tail. Evil invectives spew from the mouth of the pope and enter the mouths of the penitents. This image comes from the book, *Fierie Tryall of God's Saints*. It was published in 1611, and is owned by the Folger Shakespeare Library.[49]

CATHOLIC RESPONSE TO THE PAPAL ANTI-CHRIST

In addition to these images of the pope as the Anti-Christ, Catholic responses to Luther were also angry at representations of Martin Luther from this same period. A woodcut by Hans Baldung Grien, a Reformation artist, depicts Luther nimbused like a saint, and with the Holy Spirit overhead, affirming his Divine election as interpreter of the Bible. Joseph Koerner picks up the story:

> Catholics were scandalized by this and similar prints, and accused its purchasers of idolatry "kissing it and carrying it." At the Diet of Worms papal authorities banned Baldung's woodcut, and burned and mutilated extant impressions. One surviving example displays such a defacement, including, in addition to the mocking moustache, the marks on the eyes that cancel Luther's heavenward gaze.[50]

Koerner continues his analysis:

> Within a few years, Catholics consolidated their critical gestures in a printed image of infamy, the *Seven-Headed Martin Luther*.[51]

This image was probably designed by Hans Brosamer, a 16th century, German Catholic artist. It shows the Reformer as the dragon or Anti-Christ described in Revelation 13. The seven heads are: a doctor, a saint, an infidel, a priest, a fanatic, a Church supervisor, and Barrabas, the prisoner released by the Roman's during Jesus' trial in Matthew 27:16.

Protestants responded with their own image, the *Seven-Headed Papal Beast*. This image is an effigy of an effigy on several levels. It gives the Anti-Christ the heads of the pope and his officials. It mocks the Catholic mockery of Luther's portraits. An accompanying text for this piece of art tells us, "the papacy places itself in the temple of God and thereby declares itself to be God."[52]

Again, Koerner comments on this series of events:

Anti-Christ in Christian Art

> The Protestant woodcut strikes a blow against the things it depicts and against the framing depiction it parodically appropriates . . . Imitating such pictures in medium, layout, and composition. The *Seven-Headed Papal Beast* disfigures their model from within. Christ, whom the target pictures make multiply present, as vanished.[53]

ANTI-CHRIST IN THE 17TH AND 18TH CENTURIES CHRISTIAN ART

One of the earliest 17th century images of the Anti-Christ comes from a text entitled, *Fierie Tryall of God's Saints*, a 1611 image owned by the Shakespeare Library. A papal Anti-Christ rides on a seven-headed beast. Lethal words spew from the Anti-Christ's mouth and land in the open mouths of supplicants to the right of the beast.

In a separate work I have pointed out how infrequently images of the biblical Job, the man from Uz, can be found in Enlightenment art.[54] This is also true of images of the Christian Anti-Christ. What few images of the Anti-Christ there are in this period are primarily Reformation images of the papal Anti-Christ. One noted exception to this rule is a Russian illuminated manuscript of the Apocalypse. Among these illuminations of the manuscript is an image called, "Peter the Great as Anti-Christ Building Saint Petersburg."[55] In this image, several laborers work on the roof of the St. Petersburg Cathedral, as the Czar looks up toward them from ground level. Another figure at ground level, possibly the architect, gives instructions to the laborers. To the rear of the two workers, on the edges of the roof, are two demons who seem to be influencing the construction. It is clear in this image that, like many emperors and monarchs before him, Peter the Great is being identified with the Anti-Christ; and the construction may refer to the Anti-Christ rebuilding the Temple at the end of time.

Peter the Great (1672–1725) was czar of Russia from 1682 to 1725. He is generally credited with pulling Russia out of the Middle Ages, so that by his death, he had established Russia as a leading Eastern European state. Peter the Great's sheer physical presence seemed to indicate the way he would rule. Like Alexander the Great and Charlemagne, Peter was nearly seven feet tall, and very broad. Peter was also loudmouthed, violent, ruthless, and impetuous. It is not difficult to figure out why some people, in his own time and beyond, thought him to be the Anti-Christ. Similar sentiments were expressed a century later during the time of Napoleon Bonaparte (1769–1821). The French ruler's ruthlessness caused many people to pronounce that he was the Anti-Christ. McGinn refers to the widespread belief in England and the United States that Napoleon was the Anti-Christ. He mentions a friend of Samuel Johnson, named Hester Thrale Piozzi, and David Tappan, a professor at Harvard Divinity School, both maintained the view. McGinn suggests the belief was popular in New England after 1798.[56] This period also saw a plethora of artistic images of Napoleon as Anti-Christ, mostly in England and America. Indeed, these images continue in our own time with Pat Marvenko Smith's "Napoleon and the Anti-Christ," produced in 1992. Smith's image is a multi-headed beast with sharp teeth and royal crowns.[57]

In the early 19th century, Europe became obsessed with Napoleon Bonaparte. To his enemies he was often seen as the Devil incarnate or as the Anti-Christ. But to the French, he represented all of the ideals of the French Revolution. Johann Michael Voltz's "The Triumph of 1813: The Anti-Christ as the Beast of the Apocalypse," Napoleon is depicted as a Death-God. Napoleon's face consists of a number of corpses. James Girtin's "Bonaparte: The Monstrous Beast," also features Napoleon as the Beast of the Apocalypse. Other early 19th century images of Napoleon as the Anti-Christ were done by Pere Lacroix and Jean Louis.

Other images of Napoleon as the Anti-Christ are owned by the Napoleonic Museum on the Island of Aix, as well as by the Napoleon Museum of Arenenberg. These images of the Napoleonic Anti-Christ continued well into the 20th Century. Like Pat Marvenko Smith's 1992 piece, "Napoleon and the Anti-Christ."

ANTI-CHRIST IN 19TH AND 20TH CENTURY CHRISTIAN ART

The 19th and 20th centuries have brought a plethora of artistic depictions of the Anti-Christ and related matters. William Blake completed a number of images of our interests in 1805, and then again from 1808 to the end of 1809. Among the first set are "The Red Dragon and the Beast from the Sea," "The Great Red Dragon and the Woman Clothed with Sun," and "The Number of the Beast 666."[58]

Each of these four images are representations of the Book of Revelation. "The Great Red Dragon and the Beast From the Sea," illustrates Revelation 11:7 and 12:3. Blake presents a multi-headed Red Dragon, standing on the sea, his arms by his sides, and two lamb's horns on the main head of the standing dragon. A second dragon emerges from the sea between the first dragon's legs. The second dragon is also many-headed, and carried a scepter in his left hand and a sword in his right.[59]

Blake's "Great Red Dragon and the Woman Clothed in Sun," is a pen and watercolor work owned by the Brooklyn Museum of Art. The lamb-horned dragon has great wings and a large sweeping tail coming from his hind quarters. We see the Dragon from the rear. He looks down at a woman beneath him, bathed in sun. "The Number of the Beast 666," is also a pen and watercolor creation, produced in 1805 and owned by the Philadelphia Rosenbach Museum. The painting features a lamb-horned well-muscled Anti-Christ, with scepter in his right hand, and his left forefinger pointing away. Above the figure is another well-muscled beast who looks up to the heavens.[60]

The second set of Blake images related to the Anti-Christ and like matters was produced in 1808 and 1809. Among these images are a number of other depictions of scenes from the Apocalypse, including "The Whore of Babylon," and a depiction of the "Last Judgment." In the first of these images, a bare-chested woman with chalice in her right hand, sits atop the back of a multi-headed, well-muscled demon. Out of the chalice, in the woman's hand comes a bad fragrance, perhaps disease. The image was completed in 1809, and is owned by the British Museum.[61]

In Blake's "Last Judgment," God sits on his throne, accompanied by angels on both sides, with a halo of saints above him. Beneath, at the earthly level, and below, are people being carried to Hell, with many trying to escape. In the center of Hell is a figure with two sets of wings, perhaps the Devil or the Anti-Christ.[62]

In the 20th and 21st centuries there are more images of the Anti-Christ than all the other centuries we have discussed. Some of these images are by traditional artists like Arthur Szyk and Duncan Long, while others are commercialized images produced for widespread distribution.

Arthur Szyk (1894–1951) was a Polish born, American artist. After studying at Paris and Krakow, Szyk served in the Russian army during World War I. During the Polish-Soviet War, Szyk served as the artistic director of the Department of Propaganda for the Polish army in Lodz. He moved to Paris in 1921, and in 1934, he came to the United States, running from the Nazis. During World War II, Szyk completed the "Anti-Christ," produced in 1942. In the image, Szyk portrays Adolf Hitler as the Anti-Christ. Szyk shows Hitler as a personification of evil. Under Hitler's raised fist is the twisted Star of David's, whose owners are being enslaved and murdered. The dictator's hair hides the Latin phrase, *Vae Victis*—"Woe to the Defeated." A banner hangs from the top left corner. It reads: "Today Europe, Tomorrow the World."[63]

Arthur Szyk's depiction of Hitler as the Anti-Christ is, of course, part of a long line of ruthless emperors, kings, and czars all thought to be the Anti-Christ, including Antiochus IV, Nero, Domitian, various popes, Peter the Great, Napoleon, and Hitler. In fact, in the Christian tradition in the modern world, whenever a ruler has been thought to be particularly ruthless, that ruler has often been labeled the Anti-Christ.

More recent images of the Anti-Christ and the End Times, include works by Duncan Long, Henryk Baca, Pat Marvenko Smith, and John Steczynski. Long has done a number of illustrations of the Book of Revelation, including "The Fifth Trumpet: Locusts From the Abyss," "The Four Seals," "Another Rider on a White Horse," "The Great White Throne," and "A Woman Sitting on a Beast." All of these images are evocative. The "A Woman Sitting on the Beast," depicts a young woman sitting on the back of a Leviathan-like beast, emerging from the sea. The beast has many heads and sharp teeth. One of the heads to the right of the central head, looks like the claws of a Venus flytrap.[64]

One of Duncan Long's most interesting images is called "The Mark of the Anti-Christ." It features computer bar codes on the foreheads of two figures of the painting, suggesting a new theory of the nature of the Anti-Christ.[65]

Polish painter, Henryk Baca, produced a painting entitled, "Christ-Antichrist," where it is difficult to distinguish between the Christ and the Anti-Christ.

Pat Marvenko Smith is an American artist and born-again Christian. In 1992, she completed a group of paintings illustrating the Book of Revelation. Among these images are "The War in Heaven: Michael Defeats the Dragon," a depiction of Revelation 12:7–12, and "The Three Beasts and 666," a representation of Revelation 13. In the first image, good and bad angels war in the clouds, as a Leviathan-like beast is being cast down. In the other image, a multi-headed lion beast with many sets of sharp teeth. Above this battle, on the horizon, is a God-like figure who is throwing a lightning bolt from the sky, while a group of angels or saved souls looks on.[66]

Smith's "Woman with the Wings of an Eagle," a depiction of Revelation 12:14 and "The Dragon Spewing Water to Overtake the Woman, But the Earth Swallows the Water," a representation of Revelation 12:15–16, are two other of her most evocative images. In the former image, a white-clad woman, with enormous eagle's wings, soars toward the heavens. Her right hand stretches out to something above, and her feet and dress illuminated at the bottom. In the latter image, an enormous dragon spews forth water from the distance. In the fore-ground the woman is being hit by the water, which seems to be pushed into the ground.[67]

John Steczynski, a faculty member at Boston College, has also completed a series of images based on the Book of Revelation. These images include illustrations of Revelation 1:9–10; 4:1; 4:2–8; 5:1–3; 5:6–13; chapters 6, 7, 8, 9, 10, and 12–20. This series contains 42 images of the Book of Revelation, including one of the two witnesses; several of the seven-headed beast; one of the plagues and seven bowls, and several other images.[68]

In addition to the contemporary artists mentioned above, several other painters and artists have completed works about the Anti-Christ, the Apocalypse, or both. Among these artists are: McKendree Robins Long, A. J. Meyer, physicist and painter, Peter Olsen, David Miles, Robert Roberg, and Basil Wolverton. David Miles' images are digitally produced. Peter Olsen has done a series of 45 images on the Apocalypse. Robert Roberg has 24 paintings that illustrate Revelation; and Basil Wolverton's collection of 16 "Horrifying scenes from the end of the world," were colorized by his son, Monte.[69]

In the early 1950s, evangelist Herbert Armstrong asked Basil Wolverton to create a series of horrifying scenes of the end of the world. The corresponding work is a combination of science fiction, horror, and comics. Wolverton's *Apocalypse* includes images entitled: "Famine," "Scorching Heat," "Darkness and Boils."[70]

One other contemporary piece of art on the Anti-Christ is Henryk's Baca's "Christ-Anti-Christ." The painting features four panels. The first and fourth are images of Christ and Anti-Christ. Between them, in panels two and three, are scenes of the End Times, while off in the distance is a rising sun.

The Legend of the Anti-Christ

ANTI-CHRIST AND THE OTHER ARTS

In addition to the mentions of Anti-Christ in Literature in the past 500 years, there have also been a number of works that deal with the Anti-Christ as a drama, or even as an opera or piece of music. We will explore some of these uses of the Anti-Christ in the remainder of this chapter.

ANTI-CHRIST IN DRAMA

In addition to the Mystery and Morality plays mentioned in earlier chapters, a number of other 16th century dramas on the Anti-Christ are extant. Perhaps the most interesting of these is John Bale's 1538 drama, *God's Promises*. Mark Pilkinton, writing for the *Journal of Religion and Theatre*, discusses this and other dramas when he writes:

> In these dramas, in the spirit of Reform, the prince becomes God's incorruptible vicar, and he defends God's laws against the world's infidels, whether they be Turks or Roman Catholics. A play like *God's Promises* states clearly that princely infallibility is a tradition established by the great patriarchs of the Bible; thus the play elevates Henry VIII into the company of Moses and David. The prince emerges as the only individual capable of destroying the demonic hierarchy of the Church of Rome, while at the same time, protecting the souls and bodies of his subjects. As God's minister, he no longer freely chooses between good and evil, as does Magnificence in the preceding period; evil prevails only when the formidable strength of the Pope-Anti-Christ triumphs.[71]

Pilkinton suggests that much of 16th century English drama uses the Anti-Christ as one of its characters, and that often in these dramas, a Prince appears who takes the place of Christ, defeating the Anti-Christ by the end.

Since the beginning of the 17th century, a number of writers and playwrights have attempted to turn the saga of the Anti-Christ into a drama. The oldest of these is Florimond de Faemond's *Anti-Christ et L'antipapese*, published in 1599. The drama discusses the traditional Biblical view of the Anti-Christ and argues expressly against the view that the pope is the Final Enemy.

The 18th century saw the emergence of a number of dramas arguing for or against the Anti-Christ as Pope theory. Among these are works by James Winthrop (1795); Richard Hurd (1788); Charles Crawford (1788);

John Stancliff (1784); Silas Mercer (1783); and Joseph Risk (1762). The dramas of Winthrop, Hurd, Crawford, Mercer, and Stancliff all argue for the papal Anti-Christ theory, that of Joseph Fisk against it.

In the 19th century a number of Anti-Christ dramas are extant, including those by Stanley Griswold (1803); William Cummins Davis (1811); William Gregory (1830); and John W. Nevin (1848). The subtitle of Nevin's work is "The Spirit of Sect and Schism." In the final scene of the drama, Christ defeats a Papal Anti-Christ in a cataclysmic battle. Gregory's work is called *the Trial of Anti-Christ*, a court room drama published in 1830. In the final scene, a Papal Anti-Christ is found guilty in a British court room.

Griswold's drama is entitled, *Infidelity is not the only Enemy of Christianity*, published in 1803 and first performed at Yale University in the same year. Davis' drama is called *A Short Sketch of the Rise and Fall of Anti-Christ* which was published in 1830. In this drama, the Anti-Christ is called the "Man of Sin," and is defeated by Jesus and his angels at the end of time.

Both W.W. Greg and Linus Urban Lucken produced 20th century versions of the Anti-Christ play from the Chester Cycle. Greg's version was published in 1935, Lucken's in 1940. Luchen's drama was called "Anti-Christ and the Prophets of Anti-Christ," and Greg's was entitled "Play of the Anti-Christ From the Chester Cycle." A 1967 play called "Ludos de Anti-Christo" by John Wright was produced in Toronto by the Pontifical Institute of Medieval Studies. The drama is the English translation of a Latin text. It was produced several times in Canada in the 1960s and 70s.

German scholar Gottfried Hasenkamp wrote a 1961 drama called, *Spiel vom Anti-Christ*, a modern version of the Old German *Ludens de AntiChristo*. Around the same time, Louis Gros, wrote a modern French version of a late 16th century drama entitled *Etudes sur le mystere de lAntivhrist du judement de Dieu*. The play was produced in Paris in 1962.

More recently, three other Anti-Christ dramas have appeared, one in Germany, one in England, and the third in Rome. Of these, Italian Mario Prosperi's *The Anti-Christ* is the most interesting. It was directed by Ranato Mambor, and performed for the first time in January, 1981 at the Politecnico Theatre in Rome. The work was inspired by Nietzsche's *Der Anti-Christ*. The hero, a man named Federico, is played by Prosperi. He impersonates Nietzsche by spouting his philosophy. Federico lives in an asylum which is also a school. The institution is presided over by a nun, Sister Maria, played by Carla Cassola who also serves as Federico's therapist.

The play is set in the recreation room of the institution on Christmas Eve night, between 11:00 p.m. and midnight. Sister Maria appears in a dim light. She beats a drum and prances like a drum majorette. Federico is in bed asleep. The nun searches the room and discovers that the baby Jesus is missing from his crib. With motherly insistence, Sister Maria asks Federico to go to the sacristy to procure another statue of the baby Jesus. As he is gone from the room, the nun inspects the various hiding places Federico has used to conceal his secrets. She finds the missing statue of Jesus and puts it back in the crib just as Federico returns and announces, "There is no surplus of Jesuses!"

Federico changes into tennis clothes, while Sister Maria becomes seated on a Referee's chair, while they wait for the other player who is late. While they wait, Federico challenges the nun about her belief in God. He tells her, "The Romans had the genius to create an empire, while Christians had the faith to destroy it." Federico's nephew, Giorgio rushes on stage, waving an Italian flag, and announcing a victory of the international Italian soccer team. Sister Maria reminds him that he had promised a racquetball game to his uncle. Then Giorgio leaves the stage to go change. Giorgio returns and demands that the Italian national anthem be played before their match. Sister Maria hands out the balls and then leaves the room. Giorgio begins to give a radio-like account of a soccer match.

As Giorgio continues his account, Federico opens a manhole in the middle of the stage. He lowers himself into the hole, and begins to spout Nietzschean ideas from it. The nun returns and addresses the unseen Federico. She tells him he is ill-constituted for this life, he is far too strong. Federico returns to the stage, revealing to the nun his faith in the soon to come emergence of the Anti-Christ. The clock strikes 11:30, and Federico says, "Yes, in half an hour instead of Christ..."

Left alone, Giorgio finds a golden mask of the Devil. Federico takes it from him and seems to conceal it from Sister Maria. She does not know that Federico and his nephew have been rehearsing a play. Sister Maria pretends to not see the mask and asks Giorgio to show her the costume he wears in the secret play. He resists but says, "I play an angel."

Later uncle and nephew perform their play, it is called "The Catechism." Federico sis in the referee's chair wearing the Devil mask. Federico summarizes the faith of the Anti-Christ using the form of the catechism. Federico dances on stage and tells the nun in his play, she plays the part of Eve. "What kind of costume does she wear?" Giorgio goes off and returns with a life-sized drawing of a nude woman that he places in front of the nun. He offers the nun an apple. She bites it and says, "The Anti-Christ is already in the world!"

Like many Anti-Christ dramas, in Prosperi's play the action mirrors much of the material in the Anti-Christ legend in the West: that he will be the son of Satan; that he will imitate Christ; that he will be born on Christmas, etc. But the play seems to be more about Frederich Nietzsche than about the Final Enemy. Indeed, Nietzsche's ideas are central to this Italian drama.

ANTI-CHRIST AND MUSIC

The idea of the Anti-Christ has also inspired a number of pieces of music in the West in the Modern Period. Some of these are historical pieces, some as appearances in contemporary rock music, and one piece is a full-length opera called *The Prelude to Anti-Christ* by Danish composer, Rued Langgard. The opera was composed from 1921–1923 and the revised between 1926 and 1930. The official Rued Langgaard website describes the opera this way:

> It is a philosophical-religious opera about the decline and spiritual fall of western civilization. It is an atmospheric fantasia over our time, pillorying life style and mentality, and warning against an all-pervasive egoism and materialism at the expense of the spiritual values of existence. The message of the opera is that society and culture are digging their own grave, but that individual human beings can find hope by becoming aware of the state of the world and opening up towards the divine.[72]

The opera has no recurring characters, no traditional plot, and consists mainly of monologues. It is framed by a prologue, where Anti-Christ is sent into the world. In the final scene, the sixth scene, the Anti-Christ is destroyed. The scenes in between these two show the Anti-Christ's negative influence on human kind through tableaux using allegorical or archetypal figures. In Act One, Lucifer causes Anti-Christ to rise from the Pit, and God permits him to be active for a time on earth. The second Act is called, "The Mouth Speaking Great Things." Act three features the allegorical Despair, personified Despondency. Act Four is called "Lust."

It features a soprano sung by "The Great Whore of Babylon" and a tenor sung by "The Scarlet Colored Beast." In the fifth act, Lioe and the Great Whore quarrel over truth and power. Hate intervenes, but cannot settle the dispute.

The sixth and final act is called "Perdition." It is sung by Mystical Voice in baritone. This is the voice of God that comes from within a marble sarcophagus that curses the Anti-Christ and his followers, followed by a mixed choir entitled, "Ephphetha Chorus," where Heavenly peace prevails, and only God has the power to give humans insight, peace and harmony.

In Classical music, composer Igor Stravinsky billed himself as "Wagner's Anti-Christ." Contemporary composer, Daniel Bernard Roumain, Haitian-American violinist and his group of eight other musicians has been called "The Anti-Christ of Classical Music."

Most references to the Anti-Christ in contemporary music come from heavy metal music. Many of these references to the Anti-Christ in contemporary music can be found in chapter ten of this work. Among the groups who have songs with the word "Anti-Christ" in the title are: Marilyn Manson's *Anti-Christ Superstar*; 6Lyrics "Thy Anti-Christ;" Gorgoroth's *Anti-Christ*; and Swedish rock band Dark Funeral's *King Anti-Christ*, a 5 minute song on a CD by the same name. Finally, a group called Akercoke has a 2007 song named "Summon the Anti-Christ." The lyrics of this song go like this:

Summon the Anti-Christ

>Master, take wing over the desert
>And parched land.
>Master, the art of suffering
>A divine dance.
>
>Summon the Master . . .
>
>Mouth incendiary evocation
>Black flame engulfs
>Filth and maggots of humanity
>Hair burning, faces melt.

Summon!
Master!

The inexhaustible beauty
The incomparable gift
Satan has made to the human race
Is his only child
Anti-Christ.

Mouth incendiary evocation
Back flame engulfs
Filth and maggots of humanity
Hair burning, faces melt.

Obscene ritual
Totems sacrosanct
Divine Baphomet
Worship the Goatlord
Divine Lucifer
Worship the Goatlord.

Swarming, the spirits of the pit
Infernal, rise from the abyss
Absonant, within the pentagram
Ritually summon the Anti-Christ,
The wings of the Master . . .[73]

    The Master in this song is clearly the Anti-Christ. The "Baphomet" of the seventh stanza is the name of a pagan god during the 14th century. In the 19th century, this name came into popular English usage with the publication of a number of books about the Knights Templar. The name also became association with a "Sabbatic Goat" image drawn by Eliphaz Levi, a Medieval Cabalistic magician. The word "Absonant" in the eighth stanza. It means "discordant, contrary, or opposed."[74] In this case, to Christ. The other images in these lyrics are to the Anti-Christ being the son of Lucifer whose "incomparable gift" to humanity is the Anti-Christ.

The Legend of the Anti-Christ

ANTI-CHRIST AND POETRY

The earliest account of the Anti-Christ in poetry comes from a 12th century German poet who was called Ava. The *Poems of Ava*, edited by Andrew Thornton, were published by Living Liturgy Press in 2003. This volume contains Ava's 118 line "Der Anti-Christ." The poem deals with the distress that Christians will undergo at the end of time and the coming of the Anti-Christ. In additional to numerous scriptural references in the poem, it also has much in common with other German accounts of the Anti-Christ from the same time.[75]

In the 13th century, Dante associated the Roman Church with the whore of Revelation 17:3 in his *Purgatorio*. *Piers Plowman* mentions the Anti-Christ in a number of places in the poem. Chaucer also mentions the Anti-Christ in his "Pardoner's Tale." And Wordsworth mentions the Anti-Christ in his 1815 "Recluse."

G. K. Chesterton's "Anti-Christ: Or the Reunion of Christendom," calls the poem, "An Ode." It is a poem about Welsh succession and Chesterton suggests it would be the mark of the coming of the Anti-Christ. The poem begins with an epigram, followed by 37 lines:

"A bill which has shocked the conscience of every Christian community in Europe."

Mr. F.E. Smith, on the Welsh
Disestablishment Bill

Are they clinging to their crosses?
                       F. E. Smith.
Where the Breton boat-fleet tosses?
                       Are they, Smith?
Do they, fasting, trembling, bleeding,
Wait the news from this our city?
Groaning "That's the Second Reading!"
Hissing "There is still Committee!"
If the voice of Cecil falters,
If McKenna's point has pith
Do they tremble for their altars?
Do they, Smith?

Russian peasants round their pope
                      Huddled, Smith?
Hear about it all, I hope,
                      Don't they, Smith?
In the mountain hamlet clothing
Peak beyond Caucasian pales,
Where establishment means nothing
And they never heart of Wales,
Do they read it all in Hansard
With a crib to read it with—
"Welsh Tithes: Dr. Clifford Answered."
                      Really, Smith?

In the lands where Christians were,
                      F. E. Smith,
In the little lands laid bare,
                      Smith, O Smith!
Where the Turkish bands are busy
And the Tory name is blessed
Since they hailed the Cross of Dizzy
On the banners from the West!
Men don't think it half so hard if
Islam burns their kin and kith,
Since a curate lives in Cardiff
                      Saved by Smith.

It would greatly, I must own,
                      Soothe me, Smith!
If you left this theme alone,
                      Holy Smith!
For your legal cause or civil
You fight well and get your fee;
For your God or dream or devil
You will answer, not to me.
Talk about the pews and steeples
And the Cash that goes therewith!
But the souls of Christian peoples . . .
                      Chuck it, Smith![76]

The Legend of the Anti-Christ

This poem refers to Frederick Edwin Smith, a Conservative statesman who was staunchly against Irish nationalism, while is favor of Welsh Development. Chesterton castigates Smith for the suggestion, cryptically suggested that Smith might be the Anti-Christ.

More recently, Andrew Huntley's 2001 poem, "The Ballad of Anti-Christ," has six stanzas that go like this:

Midnight—midnight. Millennium.
Now casting all behind,
The noon of zero shuddering:
My light invades mankind!

New century—a namelessness
As heaven disappears—
With Christmas snuffed in unbelief
How start a course of years?

Spring—
Around the point of pain.

Many have found my faithless cause
To tear the creature free,
In Life torn separate at last
To master the agony;

But always love in servile time
Could weave the web anew,
Seeming so weak, proving too strong…
Until a stroke ago.[77]

Contemporary poet, Victoria Austin has a poem called, "Don't Become an Anti-Christ." It says:

Let Jesus into your life
Don't become an Anti-Christ.
Don't let evil into your home.

Lock the door, and don't answer the phone
Keep praying to Jesus for good things everyday
He'll be with you every step of the way
Those who believe has his and God's best love,
And when you die, you're promised heaven above.[78]

    Philip Walton, another contemporary poet, in 2006 wrote a poem entitled, "Anti-Christ." The poem has only three stanzas:

There I sat looking at the Christmas palm
Lights and tinsel on the branches,
Fed plastic roots which searched in vain
For nutrition in a painted table.

Around me fellow beings sitting,
Unmoving in front of a new Christ,
A new Trinity,
Offering comfort in a violent age.

This seasonal outburst of enforced
Merriment
Seems to leave us nowhere:
A mere discord over a ground bass
Which rolls on to an ultimate end
And a silent joyful and holy night.[79]

    In this poem, the Anti-Christ does not appear; nevertheless, that is the title of the poem. Robert Pettit, another contemporary poet, has a poem called, "A San Francisco Anti-Christ." It has only one stanza:

In San Francisco he started his crusade,
To preach the word of God, and all good He made!
His followers even though penurious
Gave him al they had, they were oblivious!
He showed them how to atone for sins and pray,
To a much better life, Jones will show the way!
To South America, they followed Him down,
In the thick, hot jungle, they built their Jonestown!

The Legend of the Anti-Christ

There soon was no peace, no love, no sanctity,
Instead there was pain, deceit and cruelty!
A California congressman was sent there,
To alleviate the relatives' despair!
But his finding down there could not be revealed,
He and His part met their deaths on the field!
Hones tested his children's loyalty later,
By drinking poison they met their creator!
He was once a shepherd, purveying God's grace,
But led most of his flock to death and disgrace![80]

Pettit's poem recalls the November, 1978 at the People's Temple Agricultural Project's massacre of 918 people, members of a San Francisco cult that later moved to the northwestern portion of Guyana. Their leader, Jim Jones had ordered the massacre in which the members drank a fruit drink laced with cyanide. Jones died along with 917 other members of the community. In his poem, Pettit suggest that Jim Jones, whose group began in California, was a "San Francisco Anti-Christ."[81]

Another anonymous poet who called himself "Infidel," posts this poem on the internet:

They were wrong
I am the Anti-Christ
I am the beholder
Of the devastation of the self-proclaimed
Holy nation of incarnation
And it will be grand
Rom a distance we will stand
And watch
As the land of blessings
Tears itself to pieces
And then
I will put her out of her
 Misery and with a
Sly grin I'll decimate
The weak nut I'll
Start with the more fortunate
To start a ruckus

And then at the bottom of my list just as they
Begin to think
They are safe
I will kill all of those
Who have tried to
***k us.[82]

This poem uses some of the traditional beliefs about the Anti-Christ, including the convincing of followers and devastation at the end of time led by the Anti-Christ. In this poem, however, Infidel thinks he is the Anti-Christ. Finally, an entry on the noprose.wordpress.com website, under the heading, "Christian Poetry from the 21st Century," this following poem appears:

On the Anti-Christ

I could write a poem
With cute, sweet lines which rhyme
And dance along their merry way,
Ina perfect simile of time,
To warn you of the man I've seen—
In pages turned aside and warn—
A man who will speak words of peace,
But instead will bring the sword.

But I'd rather not waste my time
For no poem or words will much avail,
On the day he first arrives

For I have thought of that moment often—
When he gracefully takes the stage—
And I know how we all will greet him.
Not with silence. But with praise.[83]

The anonymous writer of this poem seems to be writing about the coming of the Anti-Christ. The author speaks of "a man who will speak words of peace," but will really "bring the sword." Again at the end of the poem, the response to this man, the Anti-Christ will not be "silent" like Jesus, but rather he will be "praised."

ANTI-CHRIST IN FILM

In chapter ten of this study, we have given a discussion of modern films the Anti-Christ. The section speaks at length about a number of films, including *The Seventh Seal* (1957); *Rosemary's Baby* (1968); *The Omen* (1976); *Damien* (1978); and *The Final Conflict* (1981). It also speaks of a number of foreign films that explore the Anti-Christ legend.

More recently, a 2009 feature film called *Anti-Christ* was directed by Danish film maker Lars von Trier that stars Charlotte Gainsbourg and Willem Defoe. Primarily a Danish production, the film was also co-produced with companies from five other countries, including the U.S.

The plot of the film involves a couple who, after the death of their son, retreat into a cabin in the woods were they encounter strange and terrifying things. The film premiered during the Competition portion of the 2009 Cannes Film Festival to a mixed response. Gainsbourg won the best Actress Award at the Festival.

The film has come under attack for its explicit sexuality, including the opening scene that shows a toddler falling to his death, while his parents make love nearby. It has also invited controversy for its graphic sexual violence. In Denmark, the film became an immediate hit with both film critics and audiences. The ecumenical jury at the Cannes Festival gave *Anti-Christ* a special "Anti-Award," and declared the move to be "The most misogynist movie from the self-proclaimed biggest director in the world."[84]

CONCLUSIONS

We began this chapter with an analysis of the earliest extant Christian images of the Anti-Christ. These early images, from the 9th to the 11th centuries, as we have seen, are mostly depictions of the Psalms. Several of the Psalms have been used as models for the nature of the Anti-Christ, along with the accretion of earlier Christian ideas about the Anti-Christ. The most popular of these Psalms that are used to depict the Anti-Christ are 10, 14, 51, and 52.

In a second section of this chapter, we have analyzed and discussed the work of Ahuva Belkin, an Israeli scholar who has written on the image

Anti-Christ in Christian Art

of the Anti-Christ in 12th century French manuscripts. Belkin maintains that many of these manuscripts, which represent Satan talking to another figure, that the second figure, a king holding a scepter on the top of a mountain, is the Anti-Christ.

In a third section of this chapter, we have looked carefully at a number of images of the Anti-Christ from the 14th and 15th centuries. In discussing these images, we have also incorporated the analyses of Rhoads and Lupton, two scholars who have discussed several Anti-Christ images owned by the New York Public Library. In the main section of this section, we have examined several images of the Anti-Christ that come from the Protestant Reformation. Among the Protestant artists that created these images of the papal Anti-Christ were Lucas Cranach and Georg Lemberger. In a following section of this chapter, we have shown something of the Catholic reaction to the pope as the Anti-Christ.

We have brought this chapter to a close by looking at artistic depictions of the Anti-Christ in the modern world. Many of these, as we have seen, are images where the Anti-Christ is identified with some political ruler, including Peter the Great, Napoleon, and Adolf Hitler.

At the very end of the chapter, we have described and discussed a number of 19th and 20th century images of the Anti-Christ. For the most part, these images are either art that follows the tradition of identifying various rulers with the Anti-Christ, like Arthur Szyk's "Anti-Christ," or they are depictions of the Book of Revelation.

In addition to the image of the Anti-Christ in painting and drawing, we have also explored in this chapter the Anti-Christ legend in other arts, particularly in music, drama, poetry, and film. As in the paintings and drawings of the Anti-Christ, the image of the Final Enemy in these other arts tend to feature or emphasize aspects of the Anti-Christ image we have seen earlier in this study. These aspects include: that he will be a political leader; that he will be associated with the demonic; that he may be the son of Satan; and that his defeat will come at the end of time.

In the following chapter, chapter eight, we take up the work of Frederich Nietzsche, who completed a book called *The Anti-Christ* in 1895. As we shall see, Nietzsche has a very different view of the Anti-Christ than anything we have seen so far.

NOTES

1. Bernard McGinn, *Anti-Christ: Two Thousand Years of Human Fascination with Evil* (San Francisco: Harper Collins, 1994) 103–8.
2. "Doeg the Idumean as a Type of Anti-Christ," Corbie Psalter (ca. 800). Bibliotyheque Municipale, Amiens.
3. Ibid.
4. "Anti-Christ and the Last Emperor," (ca. 820) in Utrecht Psalter, found in Ahuva Belkin, "Then Anti-Christ Legend in the Utrecht Psalter," *Revista di Storia Litteratura Religiosi* Volume 23 (1987), plate facing page 280.
5. Peter K. Klein, *Beatus of Liebana: Illustrations of the Beatus Manuscripts and the Manchester Codex.* Manuscript 644, Pierpont Morgan, New York.
6. Bamberg Apocalypse (11th century). Staatsbibliothek Bamberg Ms. 140.
7. The Valladolid Beatus, ms. 433; Burgo de Osma Beatus, Cathedral Archives Codex 1.
8. "Liber Floridus," Chantilly, Musie Condi. Ms. 724, folio 59v.
9. Ahuva Belkin, "Anti-Christ as the Embodiment of the *Insipiens* in Thirteenth Century French Psalters," in *Florilegium* 10 (1988–1991) 65–78.
10. Ibid., 67.
11. Ibid.
12. Ibid.
13. Ibid., 68.
14. Author's translation.
15. Belkin, 66.
16. Nigel Morgan, *The Douce Apocalypse: Picturing the End of the World in the Middle Ages* (Oxford: Bodleian Library, 2007).
17. Ibid., 77.
18. Ibid., 76.
19. Ibid., 74.
20. Ibid., British Library, Add. MS 42555.
21. Bonita Rhoads and Julia Reinhard Lupton, "Circumcising the Anti-Christ: An Ethno-Historical Fantasy," in *Jouvert* Volume 3, number 1. (1999). "Mock Annunciation of the Anti-Christ," (1467) New York Public Library, KB1467.
22. "The Anti-Christ Rebuilds the Temple," (1467). New York Public Library, KB1467.
23. "Circumcising the Anti-Christ," from Martin Martinez, *Libro de Anti-Christo* Zaragosa, (1496). New York Public Library, KB1496.
24. Michael Wolgemut, "The Reign of the Anti-Christ," in *Liber Chronicarum* (1493).

25. Strassburg Anti-Christ Book (1480) Folio4v.
26. Nuremberg Blockbook (1465) Folio rv.
27. "A False German Pope Crowns Frederick III: The Mystical Anti-Christ," (1431) in *The Great Tribulation and the State of the Church* Munich Bayerische Staatsbibliothek. Ms. Clm. 313, folio 26r.
28. "Anti-Christ and Harlot in the Chariot of the Church," (late 14th century) illustration of Dante's *Purgatorio* XXXII. 148–60. Bodleian Library, Mr. Holkam misc. 48, p. 110.
29. "Crowing of the Anti-Christ," (early 14th century). Vatican Library Ms. Lat. 3819, Folio 149r.
30. "Anti-Christ Conception and Birth," (late 14th century). Velislaus Bible, Folio 130r.
31. "Anti-Christ Condemns Enoch and Elias to Death Causing the Faithful to be Beheaded," (15th century Dutch woodcut). Minneapolis Institute of Arts.
32. Pseudo-Joachim, Anselm of Marisco, *Vaticinia de summis pontificibus*. (Florence, ca.1440) Folio 10r.
33. *The Paris Apocalypse*. (ca. 1400) Bibliotheque Nationale, Paris.
34. "Anti-Christ Sitting on Leviathan," *Liber Floridus* (1460). University Library, Ghent, Ms. 92. folio 62v.
35. Bodleian Library, MS Douce 134, folio 4r.
36. Det Kongelige Bibliotek, Copenhagen, Denmark, *The Apocalypse Blockbook*.
37. Albrecht Durer, *The Complete Woodcuts* edited by W. Kurth (New York: Dover Books, 1963). For more on the life of Durer, see Francis Russell, *The World of Durer* (New York: Time-Life Books, 1967); and Marcel Brion, *Albrecht Durer* (London: Tudor Publishing, 1960).
38. Ibid., Durer.
39. Lucas Signorelli, "Sermons and Acts of Anti-Christ," (ca. 1505). Duomo, Orvieto Cathedral.
40. Ibid.
41. Mary Crawford Volk, *Carducho and 17th Century Castillian Painting* (New York: Taylor and Francis, 1997) 167.
42. Roland Bainton, *Here I Stand: A Life of Martin Luther* (New York: New American Library, 1950) 120.
43. Joseph Leo Koerner, *The Reformation of the Image* (Chicago: University of Chicago Press, 2004) 76.
44. Ibid.
45. Ibid., 77.
46. Georg Lemberger Bible. Kessler Collection, Emory University.

47. "Reviving the Papal Anti-Christ," in *The Origin and Heritage of Anti-Christ* (ca. 1545), found in H. Grisar, *Luther's Kapfbilder* Volume 4, folio 3.
48. Meclchior Lorch, "Papal Anti-Christ as Wild Man," in Grisar, folio 2.
49. "The Pope as Anti-Christ Riding the Beast of the Apocalypse," Artist unknown. From *Fierie Tryall of God's Saints* (1611) The Folger Shakespeare Library.
50. Ibid., folio 3.
51. Kroener, 115.
52. Ibid.
53. Ibid., 116.
54. Stephen Vicchio, *Job in the Ancient World* (Eugene, Oregon: Wipf and Stock, 2006) 224–25.
55. Ibid., 117.
56. "Peter the Great as Anti-Christ Building St. Petersgurg," in Michael Cherviavsky, "The Old Believers and the New Religion," *Slavic Review* Volume 25 (1966) plate 8.
57. McGinn, 245.
58. Pat Marvenko Smith, *Thy Kingdom Come* (London: International Branch of Lion of Judah, 1993); David L. Phillips and Pat Marvenko Smith, *Understanding What John Saw* (Los Angeles: Revelation Productions, 1995).
59. William Blake, *The Illuminated Blake* (New York: Courier Dover Books, 1992).
60. Ibid.
61. Ibid.
62. Ibid.
63. Ibid.
64. Arther Szyk, *The Book of God* (New Haven: Yale University Press, 1990). Introduction by Gabriel Josipovici.
65. For Smith, see note 44. Duncan Long, *Breath No Evil* (Bozeman, Montana: Renaissance, 1996).
66. Ibid.
67. See note 44.
68. Ibid.
69. Felix Just, "Art, Images, Music, and Materials Related to the Book of Revelation," http://catholic-resources.org/Art/Revelation.
70. Ibid.
71. Mark Pilkinton, "The Theatrical Process as Priestly Oblation," *Journal of Religion and Theatre* Volume 4, no. 1. (summer, 2005) 29.
72. "Rued Langgard Index" at www.langgard.dk/oversight.htm.

73. Retrieved from www.metrolyics.com/summon-the-antichrist-lyrics-akercoke .html.
74. See http://wordie.org/words/absonant.
75. Ava, "Der Anti-Christ," in *The Poems of Ava*. Edited by Andrew Thornton OSB (Living Liturgy Press, 2003).
76. G. K. Chesterton, "Anti-Christ: Or the Reunion of Christendom; An Ode," at http://poetry.poetryx.com/poems/8608/.
77. Andrew Huntley, "The Ballad of Anti-Christ," at www.ad2000.com.au/articles/2001p18_452.html.
78. Victoria Austin, "Don't Become an Anti-Christ," at http://petrypoem.com/cgi-bin/index.pl?poemnymber=187250&sitename=godspoet&poem.
79. Philip Walton, "Anti-Christ," at http://www.blaristrax.com/Poems.html.
80. Robert Pettit, "A San Francisco Anti-Christ," at http://www.poemhunter.com/poem/an-antichrist-in-guyana/.
81. Ibid.
82. Infidel, "Anti-Christ," at http://www.poemofquotes.com/members/dark-poetry/antichrist.
83. Anonymous, "The Anti-Christ," at http://noprose.wordpress.com/2008/02/01/theanti-christ/.
84. "Anti-Christ Gets Anti-Prize," at www.brietbard.com/article.php?.

8

Frederick Nietzsche and the Anti-Christ

> What is good? All that heightens the feeling of power, the will to power, power itself in man.
>
> —Friedrich Nietzsche, *Der Anti-Christ*

> The title is ambiguous. It first calls to mind the apocalyptic Anti-Christ. And this more sensational meaning is in keeping with the author's intentions to be as provocative as possible.
>
> —Walter Kaufmann, *The Portable Nietzsche*

> In the fall of 1888, he completed the manuscript of *The Anti-Christ*, which was initially intended as the first book of the "Revaluation," but wound up being the entirety of that text.
>
> —Rudiger Safranski, *Nietzsche*

INTRODUCTION

IN THIS CHAPTER, WE take a close look at Frederick Nietzsche's essay, *Der Anti-Christ*[1] ("The Anti-Christ"), written in 1888. We begin this chapter with some background materials on Nietzsche, and a close look at his life leading up to 1888. In a second section of this chapter, we describe and discuss some principal theological and philosophical ideas of *Der Anti-Christ*, that will help us elucidate his understanding of the Anti-Christ. In the main section of this chapter, we explore the text of Nietzsche's *Der Anti-Christ*; and we end the chapter, with some general conclusions about Nietzsche's view. We shall move now to some general introductory remarks on the life and times of Frederick Nietzsche.

THE LIFE AND TIMES OF FREDERICK NIETZSCHE

Friedrich Nietzsche was born on October 15, 1844, in the small town of Rocken in the then Prussian province of Saxony. His father was a Lutheran pastor, his mother a school teacher. Nietzsche was the first of three children. His sister Elisabeth was two years younger; his brother Ludwig was born in 1848, two years after Elisabeth. Nietzsche's father died in 1849, followed by the death of Ludwig a year later.

Nietzsche attended local schools, and then matriculated at the University of Bonn, where he studied theology and classical philology. He studied with the great German philologist Friedrich Wilhelm Ritschl, whom Nietzsche followed to the University of Leipzig. In the mid-1860s, Nietzsche became acquainted with the work of Arthur Schopenhauer. After one year of military service, Nietzsche became acquainted with Richard Wagner and his wife, Cosima.

In the late 1860s, mostly at the efforts of Ritschl, Nietzsche became professor of classical philology at the University of Basel. In this period, Nietzsche also met Franz Overbeck, a professor of theology, who remained his friend for the rest of his life. Nietzsche attended the lectures of the historian Jacob Burckhardt, who also became an influential colleague.

In the 1870s, the Wagners brought Nietzsche into their intimate circle. Around the same time, Nietzsche gave Wagner's wife a draft of his manuscript, *The Birth of Tragedy*, about which his classical colleagues thought very little. In the 1870s, Nietzsche also wrote a number of long essays, including separate pieces on David Strauss, Schopenhauer and Wagner. These later appeared together in a volume entitled *Untimely Meditations*.

In the late 1870s, Nietzsche began to work on a number of philosophical works, including *Human, All Too Human* (1878), and *Mixed Opinions and Maxims* (1879). In these books in the late 1870s, we begin to see the development of Nietzsche's most important philosophical ideas that are enumerated later in this chapter. This period also is the beginning of the split with the philosophy of Wagner and Schopenhauer. In 1879, after a significant decline in his health, Nietzsche had to resign his position at the University of Basel. Since his childhood, various disruptive illnesses had plagued him, including moments of short-sightedness that rendered Nietzsche blind. Nietzsche also suffered in his adult life with migraine headaches and violent attacks of stomach trouble. A serious riding accident in 1868 also had long term effects for the remainder of his life. While at Basel, Nietzsche took longer and longer vacations, until his resignation in 1879.

Beginning in the 1880s, Nietzsche wrote his most important philosophical works. Among these are *The Gay Science* (1882), *Thus Spoke Zarathustra* (1883), *Beyond Good and Evil* (1886), and *The Genealogy of Morals* (1887). In this same period, Nietzsche's sister married the virulent Anti-Semite Bernhard Forster, who began a Germanic colony in Paraguay in 1882. Forster was not only an Aryan, he was also a brother-in-law of Adolf Hitler.

In the *Genealogy of Morals* and *Beyond Good and Evil*, Nietzsche begins his sustained philosophical argument against Christianity and monotheism. In these works, Nietzsche not only argues that God is dead, he also suggests that "only that which has no history can be defined." What he means by this, is there never has been a God. Thus, any attempt to define Him, or to tell His history would be pointless.

In these two works, Nietzsche also begins his lengthy attack on Christian morality, which was taken up again in the *Anti-Christ*. In Nietzsche's view, Christianity has inverted the genuine understanding of ethics. It has stressed a herd morality, when it should have featured a morality of the Hero.

Kaufman describes the content of *Thus Spoke Zarathustra:* "Zarathustra speaks of the death of God and proclaims the overman. Faith in God is dead as a matter of cultural fact, and any meaning in life in the sense of a supernatural purpose is gone. Now it is up to man to give life meaning by raising himself above the animals and the all-too-human. What else is human nature but a euphemism for inertia, cultural conditioning, and what we are before we make something of ourselves? Our so-called human nature is precisely what we should do well to overcome; and the man who has overcome it Zarathustra calls the overman."[2]

Kaufman goes on to point out that George Bernard Shaw has popularized the word "superman," which has since become "associated with Nietzsche and the comics without ever losing its sarcastic tinge."[3] In the present translation [of Zarathustra] "the older term 'overman' has been reinstated."[4]

After severing philosophical ties to Schopenhauer and social ties with the Wagners, Nietzsche had few remaining friends. In these works from the 1880s, Nietzsche's work becomes more and more alienating. The philosopher recognized this and began to maintain his solitude.

In 1886, Nietzsche printed *Beyond Good and Evil* at his own expense. A second edition of *The Birth of Tragedy* was published a year later. *On the Genealogy of Morals* followed six months later in 1887. Nietzsche also had a correspondence with Hippolyte Taine, and another with George Brandes, two other early exponents of existentialism. The following year, 1888, was the most literary productive of his career.

Nietzsche's *Beyond Good and Evil* is the philosopher's first extended analysis of Christianity. In *Ecce Homo*, Nietzsche describes the content of *Beyond Good and Evil*:

> To give some idea of me as a psychologist, I will take an odd bit of psychology from *Beyond Good and Evil*,—incidentally, I won't allow any speculation as to what I am describing here. "The genius of the heart, as it is possessed by that great hidden one, the tempter-god and born pied-piper of consciences, whose voice knows how to descend into the underworld of every soul, whose every word and every glance conveys both consideration and a wrinkle of temptation, whose mastery includes an understanding of how to seem—not like what he is but rather like more compulsion for his followers to keep pressing closer to him, to keep following him more inwardly and thoroughly.[5]

Nietzsche is clearly referring here to Jesus and the former's view of the latter that sees Jesus' work as a compulsion, as a kind of pied-piper who easily hood-winked his followers to follow him.

Beyond Good and Evil consists of about 200 pages of nearly 300 numbered aphorisms, framed by a preface and a poem. The book covers a whole range of Nietzsche's interests in nine chapters, each of which deals consecutively with various topics, including religion and "the natural history of morals." In *Beyond Good and Evil*, Nietzsche suggests it is possible to reduce all systems of morality to either a "master morality," a "slave morality," or a combination of the two. More is said about these ideas in a later section of this chapter.

The *Genealogy of Morals* comprises three essays. The first contrasts good and evil as characteristics of slave morality with good and bad as characteristic of master morality. Nietzsche suggests that slave morality is born of resentment and that evil is its primary concept, with good as an after thought. In the master morality, which is basically affirmative "good" is primary and "bad" is an after thought, a term for anything that is contemptible.

The second essay of the *Genealogy* deals with the ideas of guilt and bad consciences and related matters. The third essay explores the nature and meaning of what Nietzsche calls "ascetic ideals."

Nietzsche wrote *Der Anti-Christ* in 1888, along with four other books. We shall say more about this in the next section of this chapter. On January 6, 1889, Nietzsche experienced some sort of mental breakdown, from which he never recovered. The often repeated tale of the breakdown is that while in Turin Nietzsche witnessed the beating of a horse at the other end of the Piazza Carlo Alberto. The philosopher ran to the horse, threw his arms around it to protect it, and then collapsed. The initial dream sequence in Dostoyevski's *Crime and Punishment* contains just such a scene in which Raskilikov witnesses the whipping of a horse around the eyes.[6] A year earlier, in 1888, while writing *Twilight of the* Idols, Nietzsche called Dostoyevsky "The only psychoanalyst from whom I have anything to learn."[7] After Nietzsche's illness, which incapacitated him, his sister returned to Germany, with whom the philosopher lived the rest of his life.

After Elisabeth and her husband's return to Germany in 1893, she took control of Nietzsche's papers and manuscripts. Nietzsche died on August 25, 1900, after having contracted pneumonia. Nietzsche's sister compiled her brother's *The Will to Power* from notes he had written which she published in 1905. The content of this book, particularly with the emendations from Elisabeth, gave rise to accusations that Nietzsche held similar views to the Nazis, but most Nietzsche scholars disagree with this view.

Nietzsche's influence on literature is impossible to count. It is especially marked in the poetry of Rilke, Stefan George, and Gottfried Benn; in the novels of Thomas Mann, Hermann Hesse, Andre Gide, and Andre Malraux; as well as the works of philosophers and theologians like Camus, Sartre, Max Scheler, Oswald Spengler, and Paul Tillich. At the age of 83, Martin Buber published an autobiography that included "encounters" with two philosophers, Kant and Nietzsche.

In a footnote of this autobiography, Buber reveals that at the age of seventeen the Jewish philosopher was so impressed with *Zarathustra* that he began to render it into Polish. Indeed, he actually did complete the first part. After Sigmund Freud's death, Ernest Jones published a letter in which the doctor from Vienna says of Nietzsche, "In my youth, he signified a nobility which I could not attain."[8]

Today, Nietzsche is quoted by both the right and the left. To use the weighty word he applied to himself in *Ecce Homo*, Nietzsche became for many a "destiny,"[9] including many major thinkers in the twentieth century and beyond.

Under the Nazis an expurgated edition of *Der Anti-Christ*, a few anthologists of Nietzsche's work, and some unconscionable books about him gained currency. Hitler probably never read any of Nietzsche's books, nor could any of them be used effectively in the expurgated form. In fact, very few writers have ever been as hard on nationalism, socialism, labor unions, Germans, or what Nietzsche called "party men." Indeed, in *Der Anti-Christ*, Nietzsche says, "Of necessity, the party man becomes a liar."[10]

1888, THE YEAR OF *DER ANTI-CHRIST*

Aaron Ridley and Judith Norman describe Nietzsche's output in the year 1888:

> The 1888 texts are certainly very diverse. One—*Twilight of the Idols*—proceeds in a distilled version of Nietzsche's established aphoristic manner. Two—*The Anti-Christ* and *The Case of Wagner*—are sustained polemics, directed, respectively, against institutionalized Christianity, and Richard Wagner's musical dramas. One—*Ecce Homo*—is a strange sort of autobiography. And the remaining work—*Nietzsche Contra Wagner*—is an anthology of aphorisms culled, sometimes with minor alterations, from Nietzsche's other books. But variety is hardly a sign of madness.[11]

Walter Kaufman also describes Nietzsche's activity in 1888: "In 1888, Nietzsche dashed off a brilliantly sarcastic polemic, *The Wagner Case*, which was followed by a hundred-page epitome of his thought, *Twilight of the Idols*. Then he gave up his intention of writing *The Will to Power*, and decided to write a much shorter *chef-d'oevre* instead, under the title of *Revaluation of All Values*, and completed the first of four projected parts: *The Anti-Christ*."[12]

Kaufmann continues: "No sooner was this finished on a high pitch of rhetoric than he turned around and, on the same day, wrote the relatively calm preface for the *Twilight of the Idols*; and still, in the same year, one of the world's strangest autobiographical works, *Ecce Homo*. On Christmas Day, 1888, he completed *Nietzsche Contra Wagner*—and less than two weeks later, he broke down insane."[13]

The year 1888 was a productive one for Friedrich Nietzsche. He wrote five books in a six month stretch in the latter part of that year. After that, Nietzsche wrote nothing. Conrad Bonifazi, writing in his *Christendom Attacked: A Comparison of Kierkegaard and Nietzsche*, describes Nietzsche's last period of literary productivity:

> Nietzsche's last works are full of self-assertion and mental exaltation. Believing that the standards which had hitherto passed for truths were on the eve of disintegration, he alone could say, "I alone have the criterion for truths in my possession." He prepared to write a *magnum opus* on the Will to Power, of which the *Anti-Christ* forms the first part. It is a virulent attack upon the Christian religion. All that elevates the Will to Power is good; all that proceeds from weakness is bad.[14]

The first book of 1888 was *The Case of Wagner* (German title, *Der Fall Wagner*) in which Nietzsche set forth his aesthetic objections to the music and writings of his former close friend, who was then leading an ultra-conservative movement devoted to German nationalism and Anti Semitism. This work was subtitled "A Musician's Problem." It announces the philosopher's rupture with the German composer. Nietzsche suggests that Wagner's problems are only one symptom of a broader "disease," which is affecting Europe.

The next work of 1888 was *The Twilight of the Idols*, an obvious parody of Wagner's *The Twilight of the Gods*. In this work, Nietzsche attacks Romanticism, Schopenhauer's pessimism, German culture, and Socrates drinking the hemlock before his death. *Twilight of the Idols* was originally titled, "A Psychologist's Idleness," but renamed "Twilight of the Idols: How One Philosophizes with A Hammer." The "hammer" is a metaphor used by Nietzsche to say that he diagnoses the ill of the idols as a doctor, and as a doctor beats the knees of his patients to test their reflexes; but the noise that Dr. Nietzsche hears is hollow, the hollow resonance of false gods, a corrupt religion.

Nietzsche's fourth work written in 1888 was *Ecce Homo* (English title, "Behold the Man"). This Latin title was taken from the New Testament, where Pontius Pilate is presenting Jesus to the people in John 19:5. *Ecce Homo* is a brilliant autobiographical work, the first of Nietzsche's Anti-

Christian tracts. In this book, Nietzsche gives very thoughtful reviews of each of his previous works.

Nietzsche wrote *Ecce Homo* as what Kaufmann calls "an incomparably sarcastic review of his life and works, including sections on all his books, except *The Anti-Christ*, which he now thought of holding back until *Ecce Homo* has prepared the public for it."[15]

Ecce Homo consists of four chapters, the titles of which suggest Nietzsche's estimation of himself: "Why I am So Wise," "Why I am So Clever," "Why I Write Such Good Books," and "Why My Life is Destiny."

In *Ecce Homo*, Nietzsche reports that he has found the consolation of "a charming Parisian woman." Safranski reports: "This woman was most likely Louise Ott, who had come from a well to do Alsatian family, and had moved to Paris after the German annexation of Alsace. She was a passionate Wagnerian, and had also admired Nietzsche's essay on the composer."[16]

We do not know if the woman he mentions in *Ecce Homo* is Louise Ott, but we do know that this incident is rare in the philosopher's life. There is no evidence that Nietzsche ever had a sustaining relationship with a member of the opposite sex. Many claim that Nietzsche's mental breakdown was caused by syphilis, which he might have contracted in a brothel in his youth, but he appears not to have had a long-standing love relationship.[17]

Nietzsche also had a friendship with a Russian born woman, Lou Salome (1861–1937). She met the philosopher in the winter of 1881–1882. They, with several other people, traveled to Sorrento, Italy, where Nietzsche wrote much of *Ecce Homo*. Later, in 1894, Salome wrote a controversial study, *Friedrich Nietzsche in seinen Werke*, usually translated as *Nietzsche's Personality and Philosophy*.[18] But the exact nature of this relationship is not clear.

Finally, in September of 1888, these books were followed by *Der Anti-Christ*. Unlike many of the other works mentioned above, this work is of exceedingly clear prose, and of seldom-equaled polemics. Even today, the depths of Nietzsche's contempt for all things Christian surprises and shocks many people.

In *Der Anti-Christ*, Nietzsche sets out to denounce and make illegitimate not only Christianity itself as a belief and practice, but also the ethical-moral value system that modern western civilizations have inherited from it. The book is an extension of ideas he worked out in *Beyond*

Good and Evil and *The Genealogy of Morals*, particularly Nietzsche's claim that modern morality is an inversion of noble, true, morality.

Der Anti-Christ is a book of further developments of some ideas on Christianity that Nietzsche developed in *Beyond Good and Evil* and *The Genealogy of Morals*, particularly his ideas about morality. The principal idea about morality explored in these works, as well as in *Der Anti-Christ*, is what is sometimes called a "trans-valuation of all values." We shall explore this idea, as well as other notions of Nietzsche's about religion and ethics, in the next section of this chapter.

OTHER ACTIVITY IN 1888

In the final year of Nietzsche's sanity he also encountered for the first time the work of Fyodor Dostoyevsky. In a letter to Nietzsche from Georg Brandes, he asks the German philosopher to read Soren Kierkegaard. Nietzsche replied that he would come to Copenhagen and read Kierkegaard with him. Before he could fulfill that promise, the German slipped too far into sickness and madness.

In December of that year, Nietzsche began a correspondence with August Strindberg, and told him that short of an international breakthrough, he will attempt to buy back his older writings from the publisher, and have them translated into other European languages.

Around the same time, Nietzsche planned the publication of *Nietzsche Contra Wagner*, as well as his poems, *Dionysian Dithyrambs*. Needless to say, these works were never completed, nor published. In addition to Georg Brandes, Nietzsche also exchanged letters with Hippolyte Taine (1828–1893), French critic and historian.

In the final year of his sanity, Nietzsche was enormously productive, more so than any other year of his adult life. He wrote five books in the last six months of that year, as well as carrying on correspondence with a good number of people.

Nietzsche also appears to have done a tremendous amount of reading in 1888. In a letter on February 26th, Nietzsche mentions that he is reading Charles Baudelaire. He also read Tolstoy's *My Religion*, as well as the German Biblical critic, Julius Wellhausen, Dostoyevsky's *The Possessed*, and Ernest Renan's *Life of Jesus*.

Another polemic that Nietzsche carries out in *The Anti-Christ* is a judgment that science is the biggest enemy of Christianity and the

Church. In section 49 of *The Anti-Christ*, Nietzsche tells us: "I have been understood. At the opening of the Bible there is the whole psychology of the priest. The priest knows of only one great danger: that is science—the sound comprehension of cause and effect."[19]

Throughout section 49 of *The Anti-Christ*, Nietzsche tells us, "The whole moral order of the world was set up against science, against the delivery of man to priests."[20] Nietzsche seems to make the argument that science in the late nineteenth century is the only aspect of western civilization that has wrestled the reins of power away from the Church. Nietzsche believed that in place of God and churches, the west shall see beliefs related to organization devoted to, and centered on, the sciences.

In a recent book by Gregory Moore and Thomas H. Brobjer, these authors explore this view of Nietzsche's. The first part of the book explores Nietzsche's knowledge of the sciences of his day. The second part examines how the philosopher actually incorporates various scientific ideas, concepts, and theories into his philosophy. Many of the observations of Nietzsche's that Moore and Brobjer refer to are from *The Anti-Christ*.[21]

One other development in Nietzsche's life in 1888 was the fact that in the fall of that year, Nietzsche's writings and letters began to reveal a higher estimation of his own status and "fate." He overestimated the increasing responses to his writings, above all for the polemic *The Case of Wagner*. On his forty-fourth birthday, after having completed *Twilight of the Idols* and *The Anti-Christ*, he decided to write the autobiographical *Ecce Homo*. The man to behold was Nietzsche. He is very clear in the preface to point out that he did not want to be misunderstood.

NIETZSCHE'S PRINCIPAL IDEAS

In his preface to *The Portable Nietzsche* Walter Kaufmann suggests that although Nietzsche's ideas may seem contradictory, a thorough understanding of Nietzsche's free-thinking spirit may yield explanations of these apparent paradoxes.[22] Among Nietzsche's principal philosophical ideas are seven of note. Besides the "transvaluation of all values," these are: God is dead; the master and slave morality; Christianity as an institution and the life of Jesus; the eternal recurrence; the overman, and the will to power. Each of these ideas must be understood fully to comprehend Nietzsche's view of the Anti-Christ.

The Legend of the Anti-Christ

The "transvaluation of all values" is an expression that Nietzsche uses in many of his books in the 1880s. It is the goal around which all his other ideas revolve. This central idea was an attempt to break through the traditional understanding of the boundaries that prescribe our intellectual and moral lives, and to establish in its place a new set of higher values. The old values, exemplified by Immanuel Kant, were life-denying. They must be replaced by values that are life-enhancing.

What Nietzsche is proposing is a scraping of our traditional view of both moral and non-moral values. Nietzsche uses names from Greek mythology to describe the old and new values. The Apollonian (named after the God of the Sun) is rational, and Nietzsche argued, "life-denying." In contrast, the Dionysian (named after the God of wine, women, and song) is irrational, passionate, and life-enhancing. Nietzsche did not like Kant primarily because he saw him as a purely Apollonian thinker. In Nietzsche's view, Kant's categorical imperative was one of the most egregious of philosophical inventions.

In Nietzsche's view, the Apollonian point of view gives rise to what he calls "slave morality," a concept discussed below; the Dionysian is akin to the "master morality," in which people adopt a "hero morality" and view themselves as autonomous and free, breaking out of conventional ways of interpreting right and wrong.

Nietzsche's idea that "God is dead," first appeared in section 108 of *The Gay Science*. It also appears in section 125 in a narrative called "The Madman," and even more famously in *Thus Spake Zarathustra*. The expression is typically placed in quotation marks. By it, Nietzsche means to say that the traditional foundations of western religion are no longer viable in the modern world.

Zarathustra centered around the notion of the will to power, radical nihilism, and the eternal recurrence. Pain, suffering, and contradictions are no longer seen as objections to existence, but as expressions of its actual tensions. In a note entitled "Anti-Darwin," Nietzsche stated that "man as a species is not progressing." Nietzsche substituted the normal notion of progress with his doctrine of the eternal recurrence, and he stressed the positive power of heroic suffering.

Walter Kaufman describes the history of *Zarathustra*:

> *Zarathustra* is by far Nietzsche's most popular book, but Nietzsche himself never witnessed its success. The first three parts, each

composed in about ten days, were at first published separately, and scarcely sold at all. Of part four, Nietzsche had only a few copies printed privately; and the first public edition was held up at the last moment in 1891, when his family feared that it would be confiscated on the charge of blasphemy. By then, Nietzsche was insane and unaware of what was happening. Part four appeared in 1892, and it was not confiscated. The first edition of the whole work followed not long after.[23]

Kaufman adds these introductory remarks to the book:

> *Zarathustra* is as different from its reputation as its author is different from the widely reproduced busts and pictures commissioned by his sister. Her grandiose conception of the heroic strikes us as childish, and has provoked the reaction, understandably enough, that Nietzsche was merely a *petit rentier*. But perhaps there are most kinds of valor than are dreamed of by most of Nietzsche admirers and detractors. And the most important single clue to *Zarathustra* is that it is the work of a utterly lonely man.[24]

In *Twilight of the Idols*, Nietzsche wrote of many themes that will appear in *Der Anti-Christ*, such as "I call Christianity the one great curse, the one enormous and innermost perversion, the one great instinct of revenge, for which no means are too venomous, too underhanded and too petty—I call it the one immortal blemish of mankind."[25]

Nietzsche agrees with many theorists of his day, like Marx and Freud, that God is nothing more than a human projection on to an imaginary figure of the highest of human attributes. This, Nietzsche believes, is a projection of man's uneasy conscience, and, as a result, he has developed a propensity for self-torture. It could be that Nietzsche got this idea from German philosopher, Ludwig Feuerbach, whose *The Essence of Christianity* was among the books in Nietzsche's library. Nietzsche's projection theory can be seen clearly in this passage from *Der Anti-Christ*:

> The deity of decadence, gelded in his most virile virtues and instincts, becomes of necessity, the god of the physiologically retrograde of the weak. Of course, they do not call themselves the weak; they call themselves "the good."
>
> The Christian conception of God—God as god of the sick, God as a spider, God as spirit—is one of the most corrupt conceptions of the divine ever attained on earth. It may even represent the low-water mark in the descending development of divine types.[26]

The Legend of the Anti-Christ

In Nietzsche's comments on the master and slave moralities, the philosopher argues that only two types of morality exist for human beings—a master morality that springs actively from the "noble, powerful man," and a slave morality that develops reactively with weak men. These two moralities are not simple inversions of one another, they form two different values systems. Master morality, Nietzsche argues, fits action into a scale of "good" or "bad," whereas slave morality speaks more in terms of "good" and "evil."[27]

In a number of places in Nietzsche's works, he discusses Christianity as an institutional religion. Nietzsche finds it important to distinguish between the life of Jesus and the institutional church. Nietzsche believed that the apostle Paul, and not Jesus, was the real architect of the early church. Beginning with Paul, the institutional church underwent what Nietzsche calls a "transvaluation" of Jesus' healthy, instinctive values, whereby the original teachings of Jesus have been corrupted.[28] This view that Nietzsche had of Paul of Tarsus is very much like the perspective that Thomas Jefferson had on Paul—that the latter had corrupted the true teachings of Jesus, along, Jefferson argued, with many of the early church fathers.

Nietzsche encountered the idea of the eternal recurrence in the works of Heinrich Heine, who speculates that one day a person will be born with the same thought processes as himself. Nietzsche expanded on this idea in *The Gay Science* and *Thus Spake Zarathustra*. Nietzsche also found ideas related to eternal recurrence in Schopenhauer, who maintained that a person who unconditionally affirms life would do so, even if everything that has happened were to happen again repeatedly.

Nietzsche claims that belief in an eternal recurrence would require what he calls an *Amor Fati* (a love of fate) Nietzsche calls belief in fate a "horrifying and paralyzing" idea. He also calls it the "heaviest weight" imaginable (*das schwerste Gewicht*). Critics have debated over what Nietzsche means by these expressions.[29]

Nietzsche presents the idea of the eternal recurrence as an answer to nihilism. He addresses the idea in *Thus Spake* Zarathustra, where Zarathustra finds himself on a path up a mountain, a path that ends with a sign that is marked "This Moment!" Two paths come together at this gate, going in opposite directions, and neither has an end. Zarathustra ponders this and discusses it with a dwarf who has been riding on his shoulders. Together Zarathustra and the dwarf work on the problem of two eternal paths, one of which runs backward, and the other forward. Zarathustra comments about the path running backward. "Must not whatever runs its course of all things have already run this lane? Must not whatever happens of all things already have happened and gone by?" Zarathustra concludes that if everything has already run its course along this eternal path, then everything has already existed, including the gate at which they stand.

Nietzsche believed that his idea of the eternal recurrence was implied by the science of his day. He also held that there is at least partial truth in all the various perspectives humans have entertained in regard to the nature of the universe. Although Nietzsche was fond of the early Greek idea that history is to be understood as cyclical, he nevertheless kept up with various scientific ideas of creation, like Darwin's theory of evolution, for example.

Nietzsche's idea of the Overman, sometimes called the Superman, describes for the philosopher the ideal human being. He will be a person of high integrity, without prejudice, proud, intellectually gifted, and considerate towards those who are inferior.

The Overman will be a lover of solitude. Nietzsche did not see this idea as a transformation from man to Superman. Rather, he introduces the figure as a norm or measure of what human beings are capable. Nietzsche's German for "Overman" is *Ubermensch*. It is a state of being where one is no longer affected by pity, suffering, tolerance of the weak, and the power of the soul over the body.[30]

Finally, Nietzsche's idea of the will to power involves what he thought was the most basic drive of human beings. The will to power is man's will to bring to perfect fruition all of his capabilities. It is the will to be creative, rather than creaturely. From this standpoint, it is possible to see both the master and slave moralities as a falling away from the ideal. If a man fails to actuate his will creatively, it is possible that he would sublimate where he substitutes power over his original goal. For Nietzsche, the master morality, to some extent, fits the description of the will to power.[31]

It is the slave morality, which constitutes the sickness of Europe, for Nietzsche. He believes that a herd morality lulls people into believing a false conception of equality. The result is a loss of standards for excellence, a leveling of humanity to mediocrity, and a widespread moral nihilism.

Nietzsche thought this sickness was present in both democracy and Christianity. The Christian value of humility and self-denial expresses this leveling process. Furthermore, Christianity has made sex unclean and evil, and has wrongly deprecated the value of the human body, in favor of the value of a non-existent soul. All the ideas discussed in this section of the chapter are important in understanding Nietzsche's work *The Anti-Christ*. In the next section of this chapter, we analyze that work.

AN ANALYSIS OF NIETZSCHE'S *DER ANTI-CHRIST*

The original subtitle of *Der Anti-Christ* was "An Attempt at a Critique of Christianity." But Nietzsche struck out the original subtitle and substituted, "Curse on Christianity." The former subtitle seems more appropriate if one considers the content of the work. In the book, Nietzsche delves into his principal idea of the "revaluation of all values," which we shall discuss in a later section in this chapter.

Der Anti-Christ contains some of the most vitriolic prose that Nietzsche wrote about Christianity. The work is sprinkled with aphorisms like "The pure spirit is the pure lie," and "Christianity is the religion of pity ... it has depressing effect." As we shall see in this chapter, like Fyodor Dostoyevsky, Nietzsche believes that Christianity preaches the opposite of what Jesus taught. Where Christianity claims to preach love, Nietzsche says its message is closer to resentment.

Nietzsche believes that the figure of Jesus is more like Prince Myshkin in Dostoyevsky's *The Idiot*, a figure that is wonderfully pure and free of resentment, while at the same time, being profoundly pathological. In Nietzsche's view, Jesus' disciples misunderstood him from the beginning, and thus, from the start Christianity was opposed to the real spirit of Jesus and the gospel message.

Nietzsche considers the attitude that most Christians have toward the founder of their religion is "child-like and a decadent avoidance of pain." Nietzsche's portrait of Jesus, as we shall see in this chapter, is not disrespectful. Indeed, he offers many words of praise for the prophet from Nazareth, like "The bringer of glad tidings died as he lived ... not to redeem man but to show how one must live."

Peerbolte speaks of the two *parousia* in Justin Martyr's *Dialogue with Trypho*. Peerbolte tells us: "In this writing Justin Martyr speaks several times about the two *parousias* of Christ, thereby referring to his earthly ministry and his expected return. A standard feature in the mention of the two *parousias* is the contrast between the two events. The first *parousia* took place unostentatiously, with Christ as a humble man, who was crucified. The second, on the other hand, will be a glorious event in which mankind will recognize Christ as the promised Messiah."[32]

In discussing the second *parousia*, Justin mentions in two places an evil person whose appearance will precede the Second Coming of Christ. The language in both these places look very similar to that in II. Thessalonians 2:3–12.[33]

Walter Kaufman writes of the quality of *Der Anti-Christ*:

> Stylistically, the work is, like most of Nietzsche's books, very uneven. The often clipped cadences offer a refreshing contrast to *Zarathustra*; but frequently the rhetoric gets out of hand. Nietzsche is at his best when he manages to restrain himself; for example, in section 45 and 48 Voltaire and Shaw may have envied him such passages.
>
> Philosophically, his uncritical use of terms like life, nature, decadence greatly weaken his case. Historically, he is often ignorant: the two Hebrew words he sticks in for effect do not make sense, and his conception of Jesus—to mention a more important matter—is quite unconvincing, though no more than most of his portraits. That the book was meant to be shockingly blasphemous scarcely needs saying.[34]

Kaufman sums up *Der Anti-Christ*:

> Like Nietzsche's first essay, *The Birth of Tragedy*, the *Anti-Christ* is so unscholarly and so full of faults that only a pedant could have any wish to catalogue them. But unlike most scholars, Nietzsche sees vital things and has the power to communicate them vividly. And as he himself noted at twenty-three: The errors of great men are more fruitful than the truths of little men.[35]

Ridley and Norman also introduce Nietzsche's *Der Anti-Christ*:

> The *Anti-Christ* is Nietzsche's longest sustained discussion of a single topic since the mid-1870s, when he wrote the *Four Untimely Meditations*. In tone, it is quite like *Twilight* (with which it is often compared). Where *Twilight* is graceful, light, and even effervescent in its intensity, the *Anti-Christ* strikes one as over-emphatic and rather tiring. Nietzsche really hates Christianity, and he make the reader feel it. He hectors; he insists. But it is surely the degree of his antipathy that has got the better of him here, rather than any diminution of his powers.[36]

The Legend of the Anti-Christ

In *Der Anti-Christ* Nietzsche sets out to denounce and make illegitimate Christianity as a belief system, as well as any relationship it may have to morality. Nietzsche suggests that Christianity has made people nihilistic and weak by regarding pity and humility as cardinal virtues. In his *Genealogy of Morals*, Nietzsche had argued that the high elevation of these virtues was begun by the ancient Jews who lived under Roman occupation.

Nietzsche saw the expression of these values as what he calls an "inversion" of the values and virtues that ought most to exemplify humanity. In the place of pity and humility, Nietzsche suggests courage and strength. Nietzsche says in the *Genealogy* that the Jews originally exemplifies these new virtues, only to be corrupted during Roman times and replaced by humility and pity.

In section seven of *Der Anti-Christ*, Nietzsche talks specifically about the role of pity in Christianity:

> Christianity is called the religion of pity. Pity stands opposed to the tonic emotions that heighten our vitality. It has a depressing effect. We are deprived of strength when we feel pity. That loss of strength which suffering as such inflicts on life is still further increased and multiplied by pity. Pity makes suffering contagious.[37]

In Nietzsche's view, pity is nothing more than the multiplication of suffering in that it allows us to suffer right along with the people of whom we feel pity. Pity depresses us. It saps us of our strength and the will to power. Indeed, it is interesting that the German word for pity, *Mitleid*, is made up of the preposition *mit* (with) and the noun *Leid*, the common German word for "pain."

In Nietzsche's terms, then, to feel pity for someone we must suffer along with that person. Thus, in Nietzsche's view, pity serves two purposes. It multiplies suffering, and it requires us to suffer along with those we pity.

The German word for "compassion," *Mitgefuhl*, has a similar connotation in German. It literally means, "feeling with." In other essays, Nietzsche seems to use the terms interchangeably. He never uses either in a positive light.

The *Anti-Christ* was originally published as the first part of a work that Nietzsche was to call *The Will to Power*. Under a heading marked "Revaluation of All Values," Nietzsche describes the planned four parts:

The Anti-Christ. Attempt at a critique of Christianity.
The Immoralists. Critique of the most fatal kind of ignorance, morality.
The Affirmer. Critique of philosophy as a nihilistic movement.
Dionysius. The philosophy of the eternal recurrence.[38]

This book was originally to be called *The Revaluation of All Values*. Only later did Nietzsche change the title of this project to *The Will to Power*.

Needless to say, only the first of these works was completed. After completing *The Anti-Christ* in the fall of 1888, Nietzsche had his breakdown the following January. *The Anti-Christ*, thus represents Nietzsche's most extensive attack on institutionalized Christianity. Lee Spinks in his *Friedrich Nietzsche* suggests that *The Anti-Christ* may be read as a companion piece to the first and third essays of *The Genealogy of Morals*, where themes are discussed in some detail. Rudiger Safranski describes the period:

> In the fall of 1888, he completed the manuscript of *The Anti-Christ*, which was initially intended as the first book of the "Revaluation," but wound up becoming the entirely of that text.[39]

Both *Twilight* and *The Anti-Christ* offer excellent and highly readable examples of the wit and bite of Nietzsche's polemical style. Arthur Danto, in his book, *Nietzsche as Philosopher* agrees with Spink's assessment:

> *The Anti-Christ* is unrelievedly vituperative, and would indeed sound insane were it not informed in its polemic by a structure of analysis and a theory of morality and religion worked out elsewhere and accessible even here to the informed reader.[40]

Danto goes on to suggest if one has followed his book to this point will "easily enough detect the thoughts behind the screen of insult which makes up the following sample passage from the *Anti-Christ*.[41] Danto continues by quoting the *Anti-Christ*:

> Man ought not to ornament and embellish Christianity. It has waged a war to the death against these higher human types, it has placed under ban all the basic instincts of this type, it has distilled evil and the Evil One out of these instincts—the strong man as the typically unworthy man, as refuse. Christianity is the partisan of all that is weak and degraded; it has constructed an ideal out of the negation of the survival-instinct of the strenuous life; it has cor-

rupted the reason of those spiritually strongest through teaching them to interpret the highest values of the spirit as sinful, misguiding, seductive ... It is a sad, awful spectacle which breaks upon me: I draw the curtain back from the corruption of manhood ... All the values that now define what man must find most desirable are decadence-values.[42]

In this short section from the *Anti-Christ* we can see most of Nietzsche's main themes: the transvaluation of values, his view of Christianity as corrupting the most important values of Christ, the nature of the Overman, and the master and slave moralities. There are a number of other paragraphs in Nietzsche's *Anti-Christ*, where all his principal themes can be found in a single paragraph.

Nietzsche begins *The Anti-Christ* with a warning. "This book belongs to the very few, perhaps to no one yet living."[43] He seems to suggest that only those who have mastered the obscure meaning of his earlier works, like *Zarathustra*, could comprehend *The Anti-Christ*. Nietzsche next discusses the idea of declining and ascending life and culture. An animal, a species, a culture, is depraved or decadent, Nietzsche argues, when it loses its instincts. Christianity sets itself up in opposition to those instincts, and thus Christianity is an expression of decadence, a negation of the will to live.[44]

In addition to Christianity, Wagner, and Kant, Nietzsche also criticizes Arthur Schopenhauer in *Der Anti-Christ*. In section seven, Nietzsche has a great deal to say about Schopenhauer's pessimism. Nietzsche suggests that Schopenhauer taught that since it is impossible to satisfy one's desires, one must renounce one's desires and become resigned to unhappiness.

Schopenhauer's point of view was extremely popular among the intellectual elite at the end of the nineteenth century, particularly among the followers of Wagner. Indeed, many argued at the time that Wagner's *Tristan and Isolde* was an expression of Schopenhauer's nihilism, as the lovers sing of the impossibility of earthly happiness, and of an expected mystical union after death.

The opera closes with Isolde's famous *liebedtod*, or "love-death," as she sings of her dead lover transfigured in the afterlife of the netherworld. Like in Christianity, Nietzsche believes that for Schopenhauer, pity becomes a virtue. Schopenhauer's philosophy, for Nietzsche, is no more attractive than Christianity.

Nietzsche then turns his attention to the concept of "pity," which Nietzsche calls "practical nihilism." He says by elevating pity to the highest value, its expressive effects thwart those instincts that reserve life, establishing the deformed or the sick as the standard value.[45]

Nietzsche adds: "Christianity is called the religion of pity. Pity stands opposed to the tonic emotions which heighten our vitality; it has a depressing effect. We are deprived of strength when we feel pity. That loss of strength which suffering as such inflicts on life is still further increased and multiplied by pity. Pity makes suffering contagious."[46]

In Nietzsche's view, pity is nothing more than the multiplication of suffering, in that it allows us to suffer along with those for whom we feel pity. Pity depresses us and saps us of our strength and will to power. Indeed, Nietzsche points out that German word for pity, *Meitleid*, literally means "suffering."[47] Thus, for Nietzsche, to feel pity for someone is to suffer along with him or her.

Some argue that Nietzsche's attack on pity was triggered by his revulsion to Wagner's opera, *Parsifal*, in which the formerly atheist composer returns to his pious Christian roots. In *Parsifal*, a series of misfortunes occur because a once holy knight succumbs to sin of the flesh. Nietzsche found this idea repugnant.

Nietzsche's major criticism of Wagner in the book he wrote about the composer is that Nietzsche thought that Wagner lacked style, or what Ridley and Normal call "the absence of an 'organizing idea' in his works."[48] "Wagner's art is sick," Nietzsche says, "it is a sign of declining life, of life that

> lacks the energy for itself—indeed, that suffers of itself. It is, in a word, decadent.[49]

In section 15 of *The Anti-Christ*, Nietzsche charges that "in Christianity neither morality nor religion come into contact with reality at any point." Christianity deals with imaginary causes (God, the soul, the spirit) and imaginary effects (sin, grace, etc.). Nietzsche argues that Christianity has its own versions of natural science (anthropomorphic) and imaginary psychology based on its beliefs about the soul.[50]

In sections 16 to 19 of *The Anti-Christ*, Nietzsche turns to comparative religion. Nietzsche argues that in a healthy society or religious tradition, its gods represent the highest ideals, aspirations, and sense of competence of that religion or society. Zeus and Apollo were powerful ideas for Greek society, an image that mere mortals projected into the heavens. The Christian god represents the "divinity of decadence," the reduction of the divine into a God who is the contradiction of life. The people who constructed this God cannot call themselves "weak," so they call themselves "good" instead.[51]

Nietzsche also gives a clear view of what he thinks of the Judeo-Christian God in section 18 of *The Anti-Christ*:

> The Christian conception of God—God as god of the sick, God as a spider, God as spirit—is one of the most corrupt conceptions of the divine ever attained on earth. It may even represent the low water mark in the descending development of divine types. God denigrated into the contradiction of life, instead of being its transformation and eternal Yes! God as the declaration of war against life, against nature, against the will to live! God—the formula for every slander against "this world," for every lie about the "beyond"! God—the deification of nothingness, the will to nothingness pronounced holy.[52]

Nietzsche argues that the Old Testament God, a God of a very proud and powerful people, is a healthier conception of God than the Christian view. The Jew's God, Nietzsche suggests, is for them only. This God was one to whom a proud people could give thanks. He points out that the ancient Jews ascribed both good and bad to their God. And thus was consistent with nature; but the Christian God is only good, and thus is contrary to nature.[53]

Nietzsche tells us that the traditional concept of God in the Judeo-Christian tradition "denigrates step by step into a mere symbol a staff for the weary, a sheet-anchor of the drowning." In Nietzsche's view, Christianity has become a religion of the poor and the weak, and thus the concepts of "Savior" and "Redeemer" remain essential in the faith. This God of the sick and the weak will have an appeal to people in subjugation. Thus, Nietzsche argues, it was during the Jews' Roman occupation that this conception of God was devised.

In *The Anti-Christ*, Nietzsche criticizes the Christian conception of God, but he also has little to say that is good about Immanuel Kant and his deontological theory of ethics:

> An action demanded by the instinct of life is proved to be right by the pleasure that accompanies it; yet this nihilist with his Christian dogmatic entrails, considers pleasure an objection. What could de-

stroy us more quickly than working, thinking, and feeling without any inner necessity, without any deeply personal choice, without pleasure—as an automaton of "duty"? This is the very recipe for decadence, even for idiocy. Kant became an idiot. And this man was a contemporary of Goethe! This catastrophic spider was considered the German philosopher—he still is![54]

Nietzsche argues that Kant's moral system also goes against nature. Nietzsche says that the categorical imperative is simply "the Christian God's 'Thou shalt' disguised as an apriori philosophy." Nietzsche seems to imply that the categorical imperative is born from the theologian's instincts. Indeed, German theologians were another of Nietzsche's most important set of enemies.

Nietzsche is also quite clear about his view of theologians, when he writes, "It is necessary to say whom we consider our antithesis: it is the theologians and whatever has theologian's blood in its veins—and that includes our whole philosophy."[55]

Nietzsche again discusses theologians in section 52 of *Der Anti-Christ*, where he writes:

> *incapacity for philology*. What is here meant by philology is, in a very broad sense, the art of reading well—of reading facts without falsifying them by interpretation, without losing caution, patience, delicacy, in the desire to understand. Philology as *ephexis* in interpretation ... The manner in which a theologian in Berlin as in Rome, interprets a verse of Scripture or an event—for instance, a victory of the armies of the fatherland in the higher light of the Psalms of David—is always so audacious that it makes a philologist climb the walls.[56]

Nietzsche suggests that theology has ruined philosophy by poisoning it with its nihilistic rejection of the body in favor of pure spirit. He compares the philosophical Idealist to a priest, in that the former reduces everything to ideas, while the latter reduces everything to spirits that don't exist.[57]

Nietzsche compares Christianity to Buddhism in sections 20 to 22 of *The Anti-Christ*. Both, he argues, are religions of decadence, but Buddhism is a much more wise and realistic religion in Nietzsche's view. Buddhism does not require prayer or asceticism. It demands instead ideas that produce repose or cheerfulness. Buddhism is much more at home in the upper and learned classes, while Christianity represents the revengeful instincts of the subjugated and oppressed.

Although Nietzsche regards both Buddhism and Christianity as decadent and nihilistic, nevertheless, he regards Buddhism as far healthier because the purposes of Buddhism are to reduce suffering; whereas the purpose of Christianity, Nietzsche argues, is to avoid sin. Nietzsche also maintains that Buddhists do not often become angry nor resentful, no matter what others have done against them.

Although Nietzsche believed that both Buddhism and Christianity are both nihilistic and decadent, he regards Buddhism as far healthier and more realistic than Christianity. In contrast to Christianity, where people are always trying to avoid sin, the Buddhist's goal, as exemplified in the Four Noble Truths, is to eliminate suffering and desire. Nietzsche believes that the Buddhist faith does not carry with it any moral presuppositions. The Buddhist achieves this elimination of suffering by leading a passive, non-compulsive life. The Buddhist does not become angry or aggressive, no matter what transgressions have been brought about against him.

In Nietzsche's view, the Buddhist takes measures to avoid anything that excites the senses, while Christianity, on the other hand, does just the opposite. The Buddhist aims for a life of peace and contemplation. In this sense, the Buddhist succeeds, while in Christianity its believers never rid themselves of sin.

In Nietzsche's view, Buddhism promotes hygiene, while Christianity repudiates it. Buddhism is a religion for mature, older cultures, where people grow in gentility and kindness. Christianity, on the other hand, came about by taming barbarians.[58]

In sections 23 to 26 of *The Anti-Christ*, Nietzsche discusses Christianity's origins from Judaism. He says to the Anti-Semites, "You who despise the Jews, why did you adopt their religion?"[59] Nietzsche praised Judaism for its ability to survive. He calls the Jews, the "most powerful vital energy in history."[60]

Nietzsche expresses some degree of admiration for Jesus in sections 40 to 42 of *The Anti-Christ*. He is impressed with the fact that Jesus expressed no bitterness toward those who arrested and crucified him. Nietzsche suggests that the gospels are proof that the corruption of Jesus' ideas already had begun in the early years of Christianity. Nietzsche bitterly complains that they say "Judge not!" then sends to Hell anyone who stands in their way.[61]

Nietzsche sums up his view of Jesus and of Christianity in *Der Anti-Christ*, where he wrote, "In truth, there was only one Christian, and he died on the cross."[62] By this Nietzsche meant that Christianity does not really follow the rules of Jesus because most Christians in Nietzsche's day did not lead the selfless life that the Nazarene gave us as an example. The only person that Nietzsche knew who lived by those principles is Jesus himself.

Nietzsche suggests that the gospels typify a "morality of resentment," a spirit of vindictiveness and covert revenge, common among those who are seething with a sense of their own impotence. Nietzsche says that people should put on gloves before reading the New Testament, for one will be in the proximity of so much "uncleanliness."[63]

In section 35 of *The Anti-Christ*, Nietzsche gives an account of Jesus; he says:

> The "bringer of glad tidings" died as he lived, as he had taught—not to "redeem men" but to show how one must live. This process is a legacy to mankind; his behavior before the judges, before the catchpoles, before the accusers of all kinds of slander and scorn—his behavior on the cross. He does not resist, he doe not defend his right, he takes no step which might ward off the worst; on the contrary, he provokes it. And he begs, he suffers, he loves with those, in those, who do him evil. Not to resist, not to be angry, not to hold responsible—but to resist not event the evil one—to love him.[64]

Nietzsche tells us that this understanding of Jesus is totally alien to the one the Church has promulgated. Nietzsche blames this conception on Paul of Tarsus. In Nietzsche's view, Paul saw Christianity as a religion of shame, when Jesus had made it a religion of love.

In sections 47 to 49 of *The Anti-Christ*, Nietzsche discusses the inevitability of a warfare between Christianity and science. He argues that on countless occasions the Church has clashed with scientific discovery. In doing so, the religious authorities work hard to make and keep people feeling sinful, unworthy, and unhappy.[65]

Toward the end of *The Anti-Christ*, (sections 54 and 55) Nietzsche launches a tremendous defense of skepticism. He argues that "conviction might be more dangerous of truth than lies." He even dares to ask, "Is there any difference between a lie and a conviction?" suggesting that there is none.[66]

In section 57 of *The Anti-Christ*, Nietzsche compares Christianity to another religion, the Law Book of Manu. Unlike the Bible, the Law Book of Manu is a means for "noble orders," to keep the mob under control. Sex is treated not with revulsion, but with reverence and respect. Nietzsche also talks in this and the following sections about why people live the "lie" of religion. If priests lie in order to preserve, as in the Law Book of Manu, then it is a good thing; but if the lie is maintained to destroy, as in Christianity, then the lie is a bad thing.[67]

At the very end of *The Anti-Christ,* Nietzsche discusses the meaning and significance of the Renaissance. The philosopher admired the movement, and thought the Germans were responsible for the Renaissance failing to bring its real effects.

In the final section of *The Anti-Christ*, Nietzsche writes of what he calls "the most terrible charge" against the Church that "any prosecution has ever uttered." He says, "I call Christianity the one great curse, the one great intrinsic depravity,

> The one great instinct for revenge for which no expedient is sufficiently poisonous, secret, subterranean, petty—I call it the one immortal blemish of mankind.[68]

Nietzsche also carries out a polemic against Rene Descartes in *Der Anti-Christ*. The German philosopher faults Descartes for reserving the appellation of the "ghost in the machine" for animals, claiming that Descartes did not go far enough in analyzing human beings in a mechanical sense. Because of this reserve, Nietzsche argues, Descartes was forced to invent an illusory mental substance as the real, essential, human core.[69]

Nietzsche goes on to suggest that many of Descartes' ideas are nothing more than traditional Christian principles in the disguise of European Rationalism. Nietzsche had in mind here souls, salvation, spirits, and immortality of the soul.[70]

EVALUATION OF NIETZSCHE'S ANTI-CHRIST

Stephen Williams, in his *Shadow of Anti-Christ: The Nietzsche Critique of Christianity*, raises the question:[71] "What was it about Christianity that caused Nietzsche's hostility?" Williams answers that question with a careful examination of many of the themes of Nietzsche's that we have discussed in this chapter. Williams also surveys twentieth-century thinkers from Dietrich Bonhoeffer, to Jacques Derrida, who, as Williams puts it, write in Nietzsche's shadow.

Williams points out that Nietzsche's most fundamental criticism of Christianity is that it is Anti-human and Anti-life. It is fatal to genuine life, thriving in a soul-killing atmosphere of shame, guilt, and mediocrity. Williams suggests Nietzsche faults Christianity, not for being false, but for being a dishonest way of life. He sees Nietzsche not so much in error as being in poor taste.[72]

Williams also suggests that Nietzsche misunderstood a number of key theological ideas, particularly the doctrine of the goodness of creation. Williams also maintains that Nietzsche's portrayal of Christians as dogmatic, fearful, herd animals is overblown. Nevertheless, Williams' book is valuable because it sums up the most important ideas about Christianity that Nietzsche saw as objectionable.[73]

It goes without saying that Nietzsche's *Anti-Christ* did not succeed in becoming the dagger to the heart that the philosopher wanted it to be. After finishing the work, and then *Ecce Homo*, the *Anti-Christ* was not published until 1895, seven years after its writing, six years after his breakdown and five years before his death.

One reason that Nietzsche's criticisms of Christianity did not have the impact he believed it would is due to the widespread distortions and misrepresentations of his philosophy. Many of these distortions have been quite deliberate, like the Nazis drawing on the philosopher as support for the Third Reich. Another great damage was done to Nietzsche's reputation by his sister, Elisabeth, who gave a far different view of her brother in her editing of his manuscripts—a view that has Nietzsche looking like the nationalists she and her husband had become.

When Elisabeth returned to Germany her situation looked quite grim. She was middle-aged and a widow, nearly penniless. Her mother was elderly, her brother an invalid. Nevertheless, she perceived a magnificent opportunity. Her brother's books were beginning to attract attention. Elisabeth set out to exploit the situation as best she could. She created a Nietzsche cult in her dead husband's image, bending the brother's philosophy wherever necessary to conform to the husband's point of view. In fact, it is interesting that Elisabeth went back to using her maiden name, so that she would more clearly be identified with her famous brother.

The brother pronounced a hideous curse upon Christianity, but the sister gave him a showy and pious Lutheran funeral. In her old age,

Elisabeth embraced German National Socialism. At her funeral in 1935, Adolf Hitler himself placed the wreath on her casket.[74]

Where Nietzsche's polemics against Christianity have experienced an effect is in the history of western philosophy. He is now counted as one of the great minds of the nineteenth century, as well as one of the founders of a movement that came to be called Existentialism. Like Nietzsche's philosophy, this movement emphasizes individuality, and subjectivity. Nietzsche's influence on Existentialism is only rivaled by that of Soren Kierkegaard, the strange, hermetic Danish philosopher.

One question that remains to be answered about Nietzsche's *The Anti-Christ* is why the philosopher chose this title for the book, which contains no real discussion of the figure in the history of Christianity. Walter Kaufmann, in the preface to his translation of *The Anti-Christ*, suggests three reasons. First, he says, it calls to mind the apocalyptic Anti-Christ; but Kaufman gives other reasons as well. Kaufman writes:

> It is also likely that a parallel to "Anti-Semitic" is intended. Nietzsche's attitude toward anti-Semitism in this work is, at first glance, puzzling. It has even been suggested that his Anti-Christianity might have been motivated by anti-Semitism, but he is as opposed to Anti-Semitism as ever. This is plain in all the other works from 1888.[75]

Kaufmann wrote a biography of Nietzsche in which the subtitle is "Philosopher, Psychologist, and Anti-Christ." Perhaps this alone suggests that Nietzsche chose the title of *Der Anti-Christ* because the man Nietzsche saw himself as the Anti-Christ and Kaufmann understood that clearly.

Kaufmann points out that the words "Anti-Christ," and "Anti-Christian," only appear in two places in the book, one in section 38, and the other in section 47[76]; but these mentions of the word have nothing to do with the traditional Christian views about the Anti-Christ. The final answer, then, about what the title of the work means, is that Friedrich Nietzsche's work would appear to have little to contribute to the history of the Anti-Christ we have been exploring in this volume.

In the following chapter, chapter nine, we will explore the work of the great English cleric, John Henry Newman. As we shall see, Cardinal Newman completed a number of different essays on the Anti-Christ. One of these essays is a response to the Reformation's claim that the pope is the Anti-Christ. The others make some general observations about the theological significance of the Anti-Christ.

THE ANTI-CHRIST IN NIETZSCHE'S OTHER WORKS

In addition to Nietzsche's *The Anti-Christ*, the philosopher also mentions the Anti-Christ theme in a number of other places in his work. The principal place Nietzsche mentions the idea is in his *Die Geburt der Trasgodie aus dem Geiste der musik*, usually translated as *The Birth of Tragedy From the Spirit of Music*, and was written and published in 1872. In this book, Nietzsche suggests that tragedy of the ancient Greeks was the highest form of art. He makes this claim mostly because tragedy is a mixture of the Apollonian and the Dionysian.

The Dionysian element of tragedy is to be found in the music of the chorus, while the more ordered Apollonian is to be found in the dialogue of tragedy. For Nietzsche, the Apollonian spirit was able to give form to the abstract, passionate Dionysian. Nietzsche found the Dionysian in the wild revelry of Greek festivals and in the upper class tendency to drink during parties.

In the midst of *The Birth of Tragedy*, Nietzsche wrote:

> As a philologist and man of words, I baptize it, taking some liberties (For who knew the correct name for the Anti-Christ?), after the name of a Greek god: I call it Dionysian.[77]

The best way to interpret this comment may be to suggest that Nietzsche, in the *Birth of Tragedy*, as well as in *The Anti-Christ*, the German philosopher sees himself as the Anti-Christ, in that Nietzsche saw himself as the most Anti-Christian alive in his day. Nietzsche could not imagine a thinker more against the ideals of Christianity, nor full of the Dionysian spirit.

In the very end of *Beyond Good and Evil*, Nietzsche compares the common man to himself and to others with the will to power. He comments on the latter:

> Meanwhile I have learned much, all too much about the philosophy of this god and, as I have said, from mouth to mouth—I, the last disciple and initiate of the god Dionysius.[78]

In the final analysis, it is clear that Nietzsche saw himself as both a great representation of the Dionysian way of life, as well as the most

Anti-Christian thinker of his time. In this sense, Nietzsche saw himself as the Anti-Christ.

This observation also goes a long way in explaining why Nietzsche was so opposed to the philosophies of Socrates and Immanuel Kant. Nietzsche did not like Socrates and Kant, for the most part, because they exemplified for him the best characteristics of the rational, Apollonian way of life. For Nietzsche, Kant's categorical imperative, as well as Socrates and Plato's theories on virtue, are what he saw as the worst of Apollonian philosophical ideas, primarily because the emphasis in Kant's ethics is on reason, while eschewing passion, while Socrates and Plato put their emphases on virtue, a very Apollonian idea.

NIETZSCHE AND MODERNISM

One other polemic that Nietzsche carries out throughout *Der Anti-Christ* is his dissatisfaction with Modernism. When Nietzsche uses the term "modernism" in *Der Anti-Christ*, he means a kind of compromise position that modern people share. Among the elements of this view are Anti-Semitism, German nationalism, contemporary philosophers from the 18th and 19th centuries, and most forms of liberal Protestant theology.

Sometimes Nietzsche refers to modern as a "lazy peace," "cowardly compromise," "tolerance," and "resignation."[79] In *Der Anti-Christ*, Nietzsche talks specifically about modern people of his day:

> There are days when I am haunted by a feeling blacker than the blackest melancholy contempt of man. And so as to leave no doubt as to what and whom I despise: it is the man of today, the man with whom I am fatefully contemporary.[80]

Nietzsche continues:

> The man of today ... with regard to the past, like all men of knowledge, of a large tolerance, that is to say a magnanimous self-control ... Our age knows what was formerly merely morbid has today become indecent. It is indecent to be a Christian today.[81]

One of the reasons Nietzsche was no longer friends with Wagner is that the former saw the latter as the archetypal example of the modern man. Nietzsche also saw Schopenhauer's philosophy as an example of the modern decadent man, in that knowledge of inner nature of the world and life results in ". . . perfect resignation, which is the inner-most spirit of Christianity."

Another way that Nietzsche's polemic against modernism can be seen is in his remarks on science. The German philosopher claims that prior to the nineteenth century, the method for searching for truth and knowledge have been unscientific. Christianity has made it that human beings are to discover their relationship to divinities, when we are, in Nietzsche's view, far more like animals than gods. This fact led Nietzsche to believe that part of the decadence of modern man is that he often does not realize his true name.

Another way that Nietzsche criticizes modernism in *Der Anti-Christ* is his many comments on contemporary theologians. When referring to them he says, "Pure spirit is a pure lie," a reference to Hegel. Nietzsche calls a priest "a denier, slanderer, and poisoner of life, who is a conscious advocate of nothingness and negation." Theologians, Nietzsche says, turn the truth on its head. He describes theologians as "closing their eyes with respect to oneself and the world."[82]

SUPPRESSED PASSAGES IN *DER ANTI-CHRIST*

In section 35 of the original manuscript of *Der Anti-Christ*, conveyed the idea that to Christ, Heaven is a subjective state of mind. In order to make this point, Nietzsche parodied a passage from the New Testament, which the Nietzsche Archives, through the work of Nietzsche's sister, tried to suppress. Elisabeth Nietzsche-Forster wished to do this, so that there would be no doubts about Nietzsche's use of the Bible.

According to Nietzsche, one of the thieves who was crucified along with Jesus said, "This was truly a divine man, a child of God." Nietzsche had Christ respond, "If you feel this you are in Paradise, you are a child of God." In the actual gospels, only Luke recounts the story. In Luke's account, the thief says, "This man has done nothing wrong," to which Jesus responds, "Today you will be with me in Paradise."

Nietzsche mistakenly had the good thief speak the words that the centurion utters in Luke 23:47, Matthew 27:54, and Mark 15:39. In these passages, Jesus is called the son of God by the Roman soldier. The suppression was lifted in subsequent editions of *Der Anti-Christ*, where the passage now appears exactly as Nietzsche wrote it.

The Penguin edition of *Der Anti-Christ* speaks of this omission. In the "Translator's Notes," it tells us "... omission from the 1889 text were subsequently published and restored in Karl Schlechta's edition." (*Werbe in drei Banden*, Volume II, 1955.)

In Erich Podash's version of *Der Anti-Christ*, published in 1961, Podach restores words that have been omitted in three different places from the 1895 edition.[83] All three come in section 35. The discovery of this mistake was made by Hofmiller in his 1931 edition of the book.[84]

CONCLUSIONS

Our main goal in this chapter has been to examine Frederick Nietzsche's work, *Der Anti-Christ*, written in 1888, and first published in 1895. *The Anti-Christ* is the philosopher's most sustained attack on Christianity. As we have seen, *The Anti-Christ* reflects all of Nietzsche's principal theological and philosophical ideas he had developed in previous books like *Zarathustra, Ecce Homo*, and *Beyond Good and Evil*. Among these ideas were: the master and slave moralities, the Overman, and the will to power.

We have also suggested in this chapter that although Nietzsche's book has little or nothing to do with the theological history of western Christianity, *The Anti-Christ* is, nevertheless, one of the most polemical responses to the main ideas of the Christian church. Nietzsche chose this title for his work because the philosopher thought himself to be the Anti-Christ, in the sense that he was the best example of all that stands against Christianity.

In addition in this chapter, we have explored those major objections that Nietzsche has to the doctrines of the Christian church, and we have enumerated these objections in *The Anti-Christ*. In the place of these traditional values, Nietzsche offers a new view of morality, one based on his notion of the transvaluation of values and his master and slave moralities.

Frederick Nietzsche's philosophy, we have argued in this chapter, has had lasting effects on the histories of philosophy and theology. Many of those effects have to do with the nature and existence of God, the role and meaning of the scriptures, and the relationship of Christianity to Judaism. Other effects involve Nietzsche's grounding of Existentialism and other movements in literary criticism, epistemology, and metaphysics. Although

Nietzsche's *Anti-Christ* did not further our study of the Anti-Christ, he did have a lasting effect on much of intellectual history.

Let us now turn our attention to Cardinal John Henry Newman (1801–1890), a rough contemporary of Frederich Nietzsche's, who has a great deal to say about the Protestant Papal Anti-Chris theory, as well as some general theological ideas about the notion of the Anti-Christ.

NOTES

1. The translation of *Der Anti-Christ* I have used in this chapter is that of Walter Kaufmann, *The Portable Nietzsche* (New York: Viking Press, 1968) pp. 565–656. I also have used R. J. Hollingdale's edition of Nietzsche's *Anti-Christ* (New York: Penguin Classics, 1968).

    I have also consulted the translation of *Der Anti-Christ* completed by H. L. Mencken in 1920. Mencken was one of the great American prose stylists of the twentieth century. In many ways, Mencken's text is far superior to those by Kaufmann and Hollingsdale, primarily because Mencken is able to mimic Nietzsche's acerbic style. See *The Anti-Christ* by Frederich Nietzsche, translated by H. L. Mencken, (New York: See Sharp Press, 1999). Secondary sources I have used for this chapter include Gilles Deleuze, *Nietzsche and Philosophy* (London: Athlone, 1983); Volker Gerhardt, *Frederich Nietzsche* (Munich: Beck, 1995); Karl Jaspers, *Nietzsche* (Tucson: University of Arizona Press, 1965); Joachim Kohler, *Nietzsche and Wagner* (New Haven: Yale University Press, 1998). Theodore Lessing, *Neitzsche* (Berlin: Ullstein, 1925). David B. Allison, *The New Nietzsche* (Cambridge: MIT Press, 1985); Robert Solomon, *Living With Nietzsche* (Oxford: Oxford University Press, 2003); Conrad Bonifazi, *Christendom Attacked* (London: Rockliff, 1954); and Laurence Lampert, *Nietzsche's Task* (New Haven: Yale University Press, 2001). For Nietzsche's biography, I have used the following: Walter Kaufmann, *Nietzsche* (Princeton: Princeton University Press, 1975); Rudiger Safranski, *Nietzsche* (New York: Norton, 2001); Adrian Delcaro, *Grounding the Nietzsche Rhetoric on Earth* (Berlin: Walter de Gruyter, 2004); and Carol Diethe, *Nietzsche's Sister and the Will to Power* (Champaign: University of Illinois Press, 2001); and the collection of essays entitled *Nietzsche*, edited by Bernd Magnus and Kathleen Higgins (Cambridge: Cambridge University Press, 1996).
2. Walter Kaufman, *Portable Nietzsche*, 115.
3. Ibid.
4. Ibid.
5. Quoted in Ridley and Norman, *Nietzsche: The Anti-Christ, Ecce Homo, Twilight of the Idols, and Other Writings*, 106–7.

6. Fyodor Dostoyevski, *Crime and Punishment* (New York: Acclaim Books, 1997.) Part One, chapter 5.
7. The edition of the *Twilight of the Idols* I have used in this chapter is that edited by Michael Tanner. (New York: Penguin Classics, 1990.) Paragraph 45. I have also consulted the Hackett edition, published in 1998, as well as the edition edited by Duncan Large (Oxford: Oxford University Press, 1998).
8. Quoted in Walter Kaufmann's essay, "Frederich Nietzsche" in *The Encyclopedia of Philosophy* (London: Macmillan, 1967) vol. 5–6, 513.
9. Ibid., 514.
10. *Der Anti-Christ*, section 55.
11. Frederich Nietzsche, *The Anti-Christ, Ecce Homo, Twilight of the Idols, and Other Writings*. (Cambridge: Cambridge University Press, 2005.) viii.
12. Walter Kaufman, *The Portable Nietzsche*. (New York: Penguin, 1959).
13. Ibid.
14. Conrad Bonifazi, *Christendom Attacked: A Comparison of Keirkegaard and Nietzsche* (London: Rockliff, 1954) 53.
15. Walter Kaufmann, *The Portable Nietzsche*, 657.
16. Rudiger Safranski, *Nietzsche: A Philosophical Biography* (New York: Norton, 2002) 139.
17. The relationship between Nietzsche's mental breakdown and his subsequent literary work has been treated by many scholars. Many of these are to be found in note one on secondary sources. See Safranski, 13–14; 211, 232, 242, and 286–318; Santaniello, 196–206; and Ronald Hayman, *Nietzsche: A Critical Life* (London: Quartet, 1981) 24–27.
18. Lou Salome, *Nietzsche's Personality and Philosophy*. Translated and edited by Siegfried Mandel. (Champaign: University of Illinois Press, 2001).
19. Frederich Nietzsche, *Der Anti-Christ* (Kaufmann translation, section 49).
20. Ibid.
21. Gregory Moore and Thomas H. Brobjer, *Nietzsche and Science* (Stockholm: University of Uppsala Press, 2004).
22. Kaufmann, pp. 565–66.
23. Walter Kaufman, *Portable Nietzsche*, 103.
24. Ibid.
25. Frederich Nietzsche, *Twilight of the Idols* (Oxford: Oxford University Press, 1996) 151.
26. Kaufmann translation, 585.

27. Frederich Nietzsche, *Beyond Good and Evil* translated by Helen Zimmeran in *The Complete Works of Frederich Nietzsche* (New York: Russell and Russell, 1964) 50.
28. Ibid, 54. For more on Nietzsche and Christianity, see Aaron Ridley, *Nietzsche: The Anti-Christ, Ecce Homo, and Twilight of the Idols* (Cambridge: Cambridge University Press, 2005). Also see Karl Lowith, *From Hegel to Nietzsche* (New York: Columbia University Press, 1991) and Weaver Sananiello, *Nietzsche and the Gods* (New York: SUNY Press, 2001).
29. Nietzsche, *The Anti-Christ*, section 6.
30. For more on Nietzsche's idea of the *Ubermensch*, see Martin Heidegger, *Nietzsche* (New York: HarperCollins, 1991); Gilles Deleuze, *Nietzsche and Philosophy* (New York: Columbia University Press, 1985); and Aryeh Botwinick and William Connolly, *Democracy and Vision* (Princeton: Princeton University Press, 2001).
31. This idea of sublimation is one Nietzsche shared with a number of other German speaking thinkers, including Arthur Schopenhauer, Sigmund Freud and others. For more on the history of this idea, see Norman O. Brown, *Life against Death* (Middletown, CT: Wesleyan University Press, 1959).
32. L. J. Lietaert Peerbolte, *The Antecedents of Anti-Christ*, 89–90.
33. Ibid., 90.
34. Walter Kaufman, *The Portable Nietzsche*, 567.
35. Ibid., 567–68.
36. Frederich Nietzsche, *The Anti-Christ, Ecce Homo, Twilight of the Idols, and Other Writings*. Edited by Aaron Ridley and Judith Norman. (Cambridge: Cambridge University Press, 2005) ix.
37. Nietzsche, *Der Anti-Christ*, section seven.
38. Quoted by Robert Solomon, *Living With Nietzsche* (Oxford: Oxford University Press, 2003) 86.
39. Safranski, 141.
40. Arthur Danto, *Nietzsche As Philosopher* (New York: Macmillan, 1965) 83.
41. Ibid., 84–85.
42. Ibid.
43. Kaufmann translation, 568.
44. Ibid., 569–70.
45. Ibid., 571–72.
46. *The Anti-Christ* (Kaufmann translation) 572.
47. The German word, *leid* means "pain" or "suffering," while *mit* is the preposition "with". Thus, the word literally means "with pain" or "with suffering".

48. Aaron Ridley and Judith Norman, eds., *The Anti-Christ, Ecce Homo, Twilight of the Idols, and Other Writings* (Cambridge: Cambridge University Press, 2005) xxxi.
49. Ibid.
50. Ibid., 581–82.
51. Ibid., 582–86.
52. Ibid., 585.
53. Ibid., 592–93.
54. Ibid., 597.
55. Ibid., 600.
56. Ibid., 635.
57. Ibid.
58. For more on Nietzsche and Buddhism, see Robert G. Morrison, *Nietzsche and Buddhism* (Oxford: Oxford University Press, 1999).
59. Ibid., 590–98.
60. Ibid.
61. Ibid., 614–18.
62. Frederich Nietzsche, *Der Anti-Christ* (Kaufmann translation) 586.
63. Ibid., 608–9.
64. Ibid.
65. Ibid., 627–31.
66. Ibid., 638–42.
67. Ibid., 643–47.
68. Ibid., 655–56.
69. Friedrich Nietzsche, "The Anti-Christ," in *The Portable Nietzsche*. Translation and edited by Walter Kaufman (New York: Penguin Books, 1984) 581.
70. Ibid.
71. Stephen Williams, *Shadow of Anti-Christ: The Nietzsche Critique of Christianity*. (Grand Rapids: Brazos Press, 2006) 17.
72. Ibid., 319.
73. Ibid., 220.
74. For more on the relationship between Nietzsche's sister, Elisabeth Nietzsche-Forster, and the philosopher's late work, see Carol Diethe's *Nietzsche's Sister and the Will to Power: A Biography of Elisabeth Nietzsche-Forster* (University of Illinois Press, 2003). Diethe argues that the edition Elisabeth Forster published of *The Will to Power* was more a function of her anti-Semitism and Fascism than it was the philosophy of her brother.

Frederick Nietzsche and the Anti-Christ

75. Kaufmann, 565.
76. Ibid.
77. The edition of *The Birth of Tragedy* I have used in this chapter is that edited by Peter Gay, with an introduction by Walter Kaufmann. (New York: Modern Library Editions, 2000) 27. I have also consulted the edition edited and translated by H. L. Mencken. (New York: Dover Publications, 1995). I have also extensively used Walter Kaufmann, *Nietzsche: Philosopher, Psychologist, Anti-Christ* (Princeton: Princeton University Press, 1975).
78. Frederich Nietzsche, "Beyond Good and Evil," in *Great Books: Hegel, Kierkegaard, and Nietzsche* (Chicago: University of Chicago Press, 1952) 543.
79. Frederich Nietzsche, *Der Anti-Christ* (Kaufmann's translation) Section 1.
80. Ibid., section 2.
81. Ibid.
82. Ibid., Foreward.
83. Frederich Nietzsche, *Der Anti-Christ*. Edited by Fredrich Podach (Palo Alto: Stanford University Press, 1961).
84. Frederich Nietzsche, *Der Anti-Christ*. Edited by Josef Hofmiller (Berlin: Stromverlag, 1947).

9

The Anti-Christ and John Henry Newman

> I feel at quite a loss how to express my astonishment, that any expositor should have been hardly enough to carry on the interpretation, by applying this part of the prophecy to the facts of the Church of Rome. Strange indeed it will be, if the predicted mark of apostasy should turn out to be a practice commanded in the word of God, recognized as a religious duty by every Christian communion, and placed first and foremost in her list of good works by the purest Protestant Church in the world.
>
> —T. H. Todd, *Discourses*

> Since Newman was thus attaching a tenet that was clearly popular, he had to show why so many weighty authorities had gone wrong on this subject.
>
> —Paul Misner, "Newman and the Tradition concerning the Papal Anti-Christ"

> In fact, Newman was quite certain that he considered Anti-Christ to be a person yet in the future.
>
> —James Tolhurst, Introduction to *Discussion and Arguments on Various Subjects*

INTRODUCTION

IN THIS CHAPTER, WE shall examine the work of Cardinal John Henry Newman on the idea of the Anti-Christ. In November and December of 1835 Newman preached four Advent sermons on the Anti-Christ. James Tolhurst, in the introduction to an edition of these homilies, suggests that the impetus for them may well have been Newman's correspondence with his brother Frank who had joined the Plymouth Brethren in 1831, and had followed the group's leader, J. N. Darby to Persia.[1]

Plymouth Brethren was a Christian Evangelical religious movement that began in Dublin in the 1820s. The movement was divided into "Open Brethren," and "Exclusive Brethren." The latter had a very isolationist and traditional view of religion, with their children being home-schooled, and a strict dress code for attending services. Francis William Newman, the Cardinal's brother, was a member of the Exclusionists. Other prominent members were John Gifford Bellett, classics scholar at Trinity College, Cambridge, historian Edmund Hamer Broadbent, and Dr. Edward Cronin, one of the pioneers of homeopathy.[2]

Before examining Newman's four homilies on the Anti-Christ, we will first examine the Cardinal's life, as well as earlier British thinkers on the Anti-Christ that may have influenced Newman's point of view on the matter. We shall end the chapter with a section of conclusions on Cardinal Newman in relation to the idea of the Anti-Christ.

THE LIFE OF JOHN HENRY NEWMAN

Newman was the son of a banker, John Newman and his wife, Jemima. He entered private school at Ealing in 1808 at the age of seven. Following the failure of his father's bank in 1816, Newman, then in his first year at Ealing, underwent what later he will refer to as his conversion. He came out of this ordeal pledged to a celibate life and committed to evangelism. This experience left him with a hatred of the Roman Church and a personal conviction that the pope was the Anti-Christ. In 1817, he entered Trinity College, Oxford, eventually graduating with third-class honors.

John Henry Newman began his career as an Anglican churchman and ended it as a Roman Catholic cardinal. He was born on February 21, 1801, and at the age of fifteen, he enrolled at Trinity College, Oxford. This began an association with Oxford University that would last for several decades. Newman moved from Trinity to Oriel College after receiving his bachelor's degree in 1820. He was made a fellow at Oriel in 1822, and a tutor in 1826.

In 1828, Edward Hawkins became the new provost of Oriel, but it soon became clear that Newman and Hawkins had differing opinions about the role of a tutor at the University. Newman thought the role had some pastoral duties, while Hawkins maintained the tutor-student relation was strictly an academic one. Newman describes the dispute as one with "a substantially religious nature." As a consequence of the dispute, Hawkins cut off the supply of new students to Newman, leading the latter to resign from his post in 1832.

In December of 1832, Newman traveled with R. H. Froude to southern Europe. The trip was undertaken to improve Froude's health. They visited Gibraltar, Malta, the Ionian Islands, and subsequently to Sicily, Naples, and Rome. In a letter home, he describes Rome as "the most wonderful place on earth," while describing Roman Catholicism as "polytheistic, degrading, and idolatrous."

It was on this trip to Europe with Froude that Newman wrote most of the short poems that were printed as *Lyra Apostolica*. Rather than accompanying the Froudes home in April, Newman went to Sicily alone. While on Sicily, Newman became violently ill, but he recovered from the illness with the conviction that God still has much work for him to do in England. In June of 1833, Newman left Sicily for Marseille in an orange boat which became becalmed in the Strait of Bonifacio. It is then that Newman settled down to write "Lead, Kindly Light," a poem that later became a popular hymn.

Newman's resignation at Oriel did not end his association at Oxford. While at Oriel, Newman also held academic and pastoral posts as fellow of Oriel and curate of St. Clement's, and later as both tutor and vicar at St. Mary's. He remained in his pastoral office until 1843, attracting many students, parishioners, and university officials to his homilies.

The high point of Newman's Anglican career was his influential role in the Oxford Movement, a high church effort to return the church to its conservative roots, and to affirm the Anglican's faith's status as a *via media* (a middle way) between the Roman Church and the rationalism and skepticism of the day.[3]

In 1836, Newman began editing an English version of the writings of the Fathers of the Church. He was determined to prove that the Church of England held a middle way (a *media via*) between the extremes of Popery and Protestantism, and to recapture some of the Catholic doctrine that had been lost during the Reformation.

The middle way was sometimes called the "Branch Theory." In 1837, Newman delivered a series of lectures explaining the *via media*. The true Anglican Church, he maintained, was neither Romanist nor Protestant, and that the true doctrines of the Church were those held before the breakup of the Church into various factions.

The Movement began in July of 1833, when John Keble delivered a sermon entitled, "National Apostasy," from the pulpit of St. Mary's. Newman became involved a few months later, and became the Movement's chief spokesman. Newman also became the editor of the *British Critic*, and he contributed regularly to another journal, *Tracts for the Times*, as well as giving regular homilies at St. Mary's.

The Oxford Movement was also named the Puseyites, after E. B. Pusey, the Regius Professor of Hebrew at Christ Church, Oxford and one of the main leaders of the movement. Pusey began a fifty-volume set of translations of early Christian writers that came to be known as "The Library of the Fathers." Other prominent members of the Oxford movement were Archdeacon Henry Edward Manning, biblical scholar, Richard Hurrell Froude, Robert Wilberforce, and Sir William Powell.[4]

Dean Church describes the beginning of the Oxford Movement: "It was Keble who inspired, Froude who gave the impetus and Newman who took up the work; but the first organization of it was due to H. J. Rose, editor of the *British Magazine,* who had been styled 'the Cambridge originator of the Oxford Movement.'"[5]

In the later 1830s, Newman began to lose confidence in the Anglican Church. In his work, *Tract Ninety*, he argued that the *Thirty-Nine Articles*, the chief doctrinal statement of the Church of England, could be interpreted in such a way that supported Roman Catholic doctrine. The tract was published in February of 1841, and Newman was censured by the Church a month later. Between July 1841 and September 1843, Newman left the *British Critic*, moved from Oxford to a semi-monastic life at Littlemore, and retracted some anti-Catholic statements he had published earlier, including his claim, early on, that the papacy and the Anti-Christ were synonymous.

By the year 1843, Newman placed an anonymous advertisement in the *Oxford Conservative* Journal, in which he retracts all his earlier Anti-Catholic statements. In September of 1843, Newman preached his final Anglican sermon and resigned his position at Saint Mary's. In 1845, he wrote his *Essay on the Development of Christian Doctrine,* in which he reconciles himself to Roman doctrines and creeds. And finally, on October 9, 1845, Newman and several of his followers were received into the Catholic Church. Newman was ordained a Catholic priest two years later.

Among his early work as a Catholic were establishing the Oratory of St. Philip Neri in Birmingham in 1848, and the development of the Catholic University of Ireland, of which he served as rector from 1854 to 1858.

Among Newman's most important publications from his Catholic period were his *Parochial and Plan Sermons* (1868), *The Idea of the University* (1852), the *Grammar of Assent* (1870), and his classic, spiritual autobiography, *Apologia Pro Vita Sua*, published in 1864.

Of these works, *The Grammar of Ascent* was the most closely reasoned. Newman sketches out how his religious beliefs are in full assent with leading Catholic theologians of the day. *The Idea of a University*, written in the early 1850s, contains some of Newman's most effective writing, particularly his views of education. The *Parochial and Plain Sermons* were first published in 1834 and dedicated to E. B. Pusey. These homilies were delivered between 1825 and 1843 and sketch out Newman's evolving views in the period on scripture, God, resurrection, and many other theological issues.

Newman's *Apologia* is his explanation of his religious views from the period of 1833 to the time of the writing of the book in 1864. I use the word "explanation" as Newman's understanding of the Latin *Apologia*, rather than "apology," for Newman explains much in this work, while apologizes for nothing.[6]

In 1858, Newman proposed opening a branch of the Oratory at Oxford. The idea was opposed by Newman's old friend Henry Edward Manning and others who believed it would encourage Catholics to send their sons to Oxford. In association with the Birmingham Oratory, he founded a school in 1859 that provided an education similar to that of the English public schools for the sons of English gentlemen.

In 1864, Newman used Charles Kingsley's attack on Catholic attitudes toward truth to defend his own career and actions before the English people. In his defense, Newman published a brochure, "Mr. Kingsley and Mr. Newman: A Correspondence on the Question whether Dr. Newman teaches that Truth is no Virtue."[7]

The 1870s brought Newman special recognition from both the Anglican and Roman Catholic Churches. In 1877, Newman became the first person ever elected to an honorary fellowship at Trinity College, Oxford. Two years later, Pope Leo XIII awarded Newman a place in the Roman College of Cardinals. Newman died on August 11, 1890, and was buried in Warwickshire. His epitaph reads: *ex umbris imaginibus in veritatem*, "out of the shadows and pictures, and into the truth."

Newman writes in his *Apologia* that during the autumn of 1816, while an undergraduate, he "fell under the influence of a definite creed," and received into his intellect "impressions of dogma, which, through God's mercy, have never been effaced or obscured."[8] The tone of Newman's mind in those days was evangelical and Calvinistic. At the same time, Newman wrote his aunt Elizabeth about his education. "Did you ever read Bishop Newton on the prophecies? I read them a week or two back, they are extremely ingenious and also satisfying. (I mean they account and explain well.)"[9]

Many years later, while writing his *Apologia Pro Vita*, Newman recalls the reading of Bishop Newton:

> I read Newton on the Prophecies and in consequence became most firmly convinced that the Pope was the Anti-Christ predicted by Daniel, Saint Paul, and Saint John. My imagination was stained by the effects of this doctrine up to the year 1843; it had been obliterated from my reason and judgment at an earlier date; but the thought remained upon me as a sort of false conscience. Hence came that conflict of mind, which so many felt besides myself; leading some men to make a compromise between two ideas, so inconsistent with each other, driving others to beat out the one idea or the other from their minds, and ending in my own case, after many years of intellectual unrest, in the gradual decay and extinction of one of them, I do not say in its violent death, for why should I not have murdered it sooner, if I murdered it at all?[10]

Newman spoke again of these early years and his view of the Anti-Christ in his *History of My Religious Opinions*. Newman says:

> When I was young, as I have said already, and after I was grown up, I thought the Pope to be the Anti-Christ ... I considered after Protestant authorities that Gregory I about AD 600 was the first Pope that was the Anti-Christ, though, in spite of this, he was also a great and holy man; but in 1832–1833 I thought the Church of Rome was bound up with the cause of Anti-Christ by the Council of Trent ... I thought the essence of her offense to consist in the honour which she paid to the Blessed Virgin and the saints ... Then again, her zealous maintenance of the doctrine of the rule of celibacy which I recognized as Apostolic, and her faithful agree-

ment with Antiquity is so many other points were dear to me, was and towards her; But still my reason was not affected at all.[11]

Newman's *The Idea of a University*, published in 1873, was a compilation of his lectures on education written in the preceding two decades. Five years later, Trinity College, Oxford, elected Newman as its first honorary fellow. It was a year later, and at the urging of Bishop William Ullsthorne, that Newman was created a cardinal by Pope Leo XIII. After several years of increased weakness, Newman celebrated his final mass on Christmas day, 1889. He died at Edgbastion on the following August 11, 1890.

THE ANTI-CHRIST IN NEWMAN'S DAY

Prior to John Henry Newman's initial writings on the Anti-Christ, there were in England three different points of view about the matter. The first of these, what we will call the Demonic Theory, was held by thinkers who thought that the Anti-Christ was a representation of evil. British scholar R. S. Storr, a contemporary of Newman's is a good example of this view. Storr and others point out that both Paul and John of Patmos describe the Anti-Christ as having a distinctively concrete form. Thus, he believed the Anti-Christ to be a concrete, demonic being.

A second position on the Anti-Christ prior to Newman writing on the issue is the view that Anti-Christ is a person, but that person existed in the past. In this study, we have seen many thinkers who thought Antiochus IV, Nero, Diocletian, Simon Magnus, and many others identified as the Anti-Christ. This view does not appear fully to satisfy many of the biblical prophecies about the Anti-Christ. Additionally, writers who held this view seem not to be able to transcend the limits of their own experiences.

The third opinion on the Anti-Christ in Newman's day is the view that the Anti-Christ is to be identified with particular popes in the Roman Church, or with the system of the papacy in general. This was by far the most popular Anglican view on the Anti-Christ in John Henry Newman's time and place. As we have seen in a previous chapter, it was held by Huss, Wycliffe, Luther, Calvin, Zwingli, Melancthon, Theodore Beza, and almost all Protestant writers of the Continent in the sixteenth to eighteenth centuries. Even Sir Isaac Newton (1642–1727), following earlier Englishmen like Thomas More, held the papal Anti-Christ view.

The papal Anti-Christ view was also held by British theologians prior to the time of Newman. It was held by Thomas Cranmer, Hugh Latimer,

Nicholas Ridley, Walter Hooper, Luther, Tyndale, Joseph Philpot, William Jewell, William Bradford, and King James himself.[12] As we shall see in the next section of this chapter, John Henry Newman, prior to his conversion to Catholicism, was fond of this third theory of the Anti-Christ. Newman seems to have held the view from the letter to his Aunt Elizabeth written in 1816 discussed above, to the mid-1830s when he began to have doubts about the theory.

Biographer Charles Harrold writes about this period in Newman's life: "At this time also he read Thomas Newton's (1704–1782) *Dissertations on the Prophecies* (1754) and was convinced that the Pope was the Anti-Christ predicted by Daniel, St. Paul, and St. John. The effects of this book, he tells us, remained a 'stain upon my imagination' until 1843."[13] Harrold continues: "And now, though he was not yet sixteen a deep conviction took possession of him: it would be the will of God that he should lead a single life. His conversion—so quiet, so intellectual, so almost bookish—was now complete."[14]

NEWMAN'S EARLY VIEW ON ANTI-CHRIST

From the time Newman wrote this letter to his aunt in 1816, to well into the 1830s, he held a view similar to the papal Anti-Christ theory. He was ordained a priest in the Anglican Church in June of 1824. By Christmas time of the same year, Newman delivered a sermon on the pope as Anti-Christ at the Oxford town church of St. Clement's. No notice was given the sermon, Misner argues, because "people had taken for granted all their lives . . . that Rome was Anti-Christ."

By 1827, Newman had read John Keble's admonitions published in the *Christian Year* that it is best to look toward Rome with sorrow and not fear. Keble wrote, "Speak gently of our sister's fall." Newman's respect and admiration of Keble gave him cause to begin to reevaluate the papal Anti-Christ theory.

Because of these admonitions of Keble, Newman took no side on the bill for Catholic emancipation proposed in 1828–1829; but Newman's Anti-Catholic sentiments from the period can be seen in his correspondence with Hurrell Froude.

Around the same time, Godfrey Fausset, the Lady Margaret Professor of Divinity at Oxford, in a sermon entitled, "The Revival of Popery," also spoke eloquently in favor of the papal Anti-Christ theory. Misner points out that no one was surprised by Fausset's identification of the papacy with the Anti-Christ. Misner remarks: "It is instructive for the general state of the Anti-Christ myth at that time in university circles that Fausset's sermon surprised no one with its talk of the Roman Anti-Christ."[15]

It is likely that Newman heard Fausset's homily, or at the very least was in agreement with its content. Thus, the earliest view of John Henry Newman on the doctrine of the Anti-Christ, was essentially one in agreement with the papal Anti-Christ theory of the Reformers.

INFLUENCES ON NEWMAN'S EARLY VIEWS ON ANTI-CHRIST

The Bishop Newton to whom Cardinal Newman refers is to Thomas Newton (1704–1782).[16] In his *Dissertations on the Prophecies Which Have Remarkably Been Fulfilled*, which was first published in 1754, and then again in 1758, Newton advocates the Reformation theory of the papal Anti-Christ. Newton became Anglican bishop of Bristol in 1761, and he gave an entirely new caste to the idea of the Anti-Christ. In recasting the doctrine, Newton denied the historical, political affiliations of the Anti-Christ. Paul Misner, sums up Newton's view of the Anti-Christ: "Though he made extensive use of earlier interpreters of the prophecies who were haunted by thoughts of Rome and its popish hierarchy and its evil doings, he himself was not. The jaws of the beast, the fear that his peaceful life and that of his contemporaries, would soon be flung head long into a period of apocalyptic destruction presaging the end, the hope for the second coming."[17]

Misner adds, "It seems he was more concerned with the Deist threat than a Roman one."[18] Nevertheless, Newton identifies the "little horn" of the beast and the "Man of Sin" with the papacy in chapters 13 to 17 of Revelation. In the second volume, Newton discusses the prophecies of Paul and John's letters. He ends the second volume with a "Recapitulation of the Prophecies Relating to Popery." In this essay, Newton writes: "If the bishop of Rome had sat for his picture, a great resemblance and likeness could not have been drawn than that contained in the scriptural passages concerning Anti-Christ."[19]

McGinn describes the work of Thomas Newton and other British Enlightenment thinkers: "The majority of Enlightenment thinkers, of course, had little patience with Anti-Christ and apocalyptic calculations, which were mostly confined to commentators on the Apocalypse and popular prophets."[20]

McGinn goes on to suggest that Bishop Newton's comments on the Anti-Christ in his *Dissertations on the Prophecies* were more an exhaustive response to Deism than they were an exposition of the papal Anti-Christ theory.[21]

In addition to Bishop Newton, other English divines also had an influence on Cardinal Newman's early view of the Anti-Christ as the papacy. William Warburton (1698–1779),[22] bishop of Gloucester, and Richard Hurd, (1720–1808),[23] bishop of Worcester, both may have influenced Newman's early thoughts on the Anti-Christ. It was through Warburton, in his *Introduction to the Study of Prophecies*, published in 1772, and Hurd, the editor of Warburton's *Collected Works*, that Newman arrived at the conclusion in his youth that the papacy was the Anti-Christ.

Misner mentions the work of John Wesley who published a work containing a treatment of the Anti-Christ as pope in 1754 called *Explanatory Notes Upon the New Testament*. In the third volume of this work, Wesley repeats the papal Anti-Christ belief. Misner also mentions John Gill's *An Exposition of the Prophets*, published in 1758, as a possible source for Newman's early view on the Anti-Christ.[24] Commenting on these sources mentioned above, Misner concludes: "It was through this line that John Henry Newman came into contact with and accepted the Anti-Christ doctrine in his youth. This is the school he then questioned and finally repudiated along with many, but not all, of the new high churchmen of the Oxford Movement."[25]

By 1835, Newman preached four Advent sermons on the Anti-Christ, published as Tract 83 in 1838. James J. L. Ratton, in his book, *Anti-Christ: An Historical Review*, describes Newman's Advent Sermons on the Anti-Christ: "The Encyclopedist, however, quote Cardinal Newman's dissertation on the subject of Anti-Christ. The one is entitled, 'The Patristic Idea of Anti-Christ.' It considers successively his time, religion, city, and persecution. It formed the eighty-third number of the *Tracts of the Times*, and has been republished in the volume entitled *Discussions and Arguments on Various Subjects*."[26]

Ratton adds: "This article of Newman's, first published in his Anglican days, in 1838, he republished it in later years, so that he might have the opportunity of revising his work from a Catholic point of view."[27]

Newman tells us in the beginning of these sermons that

> I follow the ancient Fathers, not that thinking on such a subject they have the weight they possess in the instance of doctrine and ordinances... This I saw is the mode in which the Fathers speak as regards doctrine; but it is otherwise when they interpret prophecy. In this matter, there seems to have been no Catholic, no formal and distinct, or at least no authoritative tradition; so that when they interpret Scripture they are for the most part giving, and profess to be giving, either their own private opinions or vague, floating and merely general anticipations.[28]

After this, Newman goes on to summarize what he has to say about the "Time of Anti-Christ": "That the coming of Christ will be immediately preceded by a great, awful, and unparalleled outbreak of evil, called by Saint Paul an 'apostasy,' a falling away in the midst of which a certain terrible man of sin and child of perdition, or Anti-Christ, will appear."[29]

In these sermons, Newman makes the claim that Newton and the other Protestant commentators mentioned above, that the Anti-Christ prophecies have not yet been fulfilled. The Anti-Christ of the New Testament, Newman argues in these sermons, is not portrayed as a long line of wicked rulers, but as a single ruler who will arise shortly before the end of time, and the Second Coming of Christ. Newman says this in the first of the Advent sermons: "It has been more or less implied in the foregoing remarks, that Anti-Christ is one man, an individual, not a power or a kingdom. Such surely is the impression left on the mind by the Scripture notices concerning him, after taking fully into account the figurative character of the prophetic language, and such was the universal belief of the early Church."[30]

Newman again refers in the same Advent sermon to the idea that the Anti-Christ shall be one individual: "Further, that by Anti-Christ is meant some one person is made probable by the anticipations, which have already occurred in history, of its fulfillment in this way."[31]

Newman goes on in the first Advent sermon on the Anti-Christ to argue that some of these historical figures have been Antiochus IV Epiphanes and Julian, "who attempted to overthrow the Church by craft and introduce paganism back again."[32]

In the second of the Advent sermons, Newman reiterates many of the Church's early judgments about the Anti-Christ. Among these are the judgments that the Anti-Christ will pretend to be the Messiah; that the

Anti-Christ will "sit in the Temple of God;"[33] and that the Roman Empire is the wounded beast of Revelation.

Newman spends most of the space in the third Advent sermon discussing how the Roman Empire, and not the Roman Church, is related to the early Church's view of the Anti-Christ. He points out that many of the prophecies from Revelation about the End Times have yet to be fulfilled.

Newman also argues against the Papal Anti-Christ Theory in the fourth of the Advent sermons, in which he again reiterates many of the early Church's judgments about the Final Enemy. In the fourth Advent sermon, he points out that the early Church identified the Anti-Christ with the Roman Empire, and not the Roman Church. He also speaks of the Anti-Christ being identified with a "display of miracles, such as the magicians of Egyptian effected against Moses."[34]

In his essay, "The Patristical Idea of the Anti-Christ," Newman makes the argument that the Roman Church and the Papacy cannot be the Anti-Christ because Daniel's fourth kingdom, which is Rome, must be destroyed before the abomination of desolation will occur. Newman points out that the fall of Rome occurred centuries ago, but at the same time, he maintains that Rome still exists. As Ratton sums it up: "Cardinal Newman, in giving his countenance to the Anti-Christ theory, does so expressly on the understanding that the Roman Empire still exists."[35]

If the Roman Empire still exists, then it has not yet been destroyed. If it has not yet been destroyed, then the prophecy of Daniel has not yet been fulfilled. Thus, the Papacy cannot be the Anti-Christ.[36]

Ratton speaks of the end of these Advent Sermons: "This last idea is Newman's own. He was inclined to believe in Anti-Christ, notwithstanding the contradiction between the opposer of 'every existing worship, true or false,' and the 'patron of the Jews and restorer of their worship'; but his belief was conditioned by the assumption that the Roman Empire still exists."[37]

Later Newman will use this same argument for the exact opposite reason. That the Anti-Christ cannot be the Roman Church and specifically the Pope because the Roman Empire no longer exists.

At the end of these Advent sermons, Newman makes two conclusions: "To these observations I will add only two remarks: first, that it is quite certain that if such a persecution had been foretold, it has yet to come . . . Next, I observe that signs do occur from time to time, not to be able for us to fix the day, for that is hidden, but to show us it is coming."[38]

This new view of Newman's also had antecedents. Among those are the "Futurist" theory we have explored in the chapter on the Anti-Christ and the Reformation, as well as H. J. Rose's *British Magazine* that advanced the futurist view from 1835 on.[39] In the next section of this chapter, we shall explore these four sermons of Newman, preached in 1835 and published in 1838.

Later, in an essay entitled, "History of My Religious Opinions," Newman writes of his early view on the papal Anti-Christ: "I read Joseph Milner's Church History, and was nothing short of enamored with the long extracts from Saint Augustine, and the other Fathers which I found there. I read them as being the religion of the primitive Christians: but simultaneously with Milner, I read Newton on the Prophecies, and in consequence became most firmly convinced that the Pope was the Anti-Christ predicted by Daniel, St. Paul, and St. John."[40]

In another place in the same essay, Newman again describes his early view: "When I was young, as I have said already, and after I was grown up, I thought the Pope to be the Anti-Christ. At Christmas of 1824–25 I preached a sermon to that effect. In 1827, I accepted eagerly the stanza in the Christian Year, which many people thought too charitable, 'Speak gently of thy sister's fall.' From that time I knew Froude, I got less and less bitter on the subject."[41]

The Froude to whom Newman refers is Richard Hurrell Froude, one of the leaders of the Oxford movement. Froude (1803–1836) was an Anglican priest. He was the son of Archdeacon R. H. Froude, and the elder brother of James Anthony Froude, and a friend of John Keble and John Henry Newman, with whom he collaborated on the *Lyra Apostolica*, a collection of religious poems. After Froude's death, Newman and other friends edited Froude's *Remains*, a collection of Froude's papers. Newman and Froude were very close friends, but the friendship began to strain when Newman started on the road to give up the papal Anti-Christ theory.[42]

OTHER POSSIBLE SOURCES OF NEWMAN'S VIEW OF THE ANTI-CHRIST

In addition to the sources mentioned in the previous section of this chapter, several of Newman's contemporaries also wrote about the End Times and the coming of the Anti-Christ. Among these thinkers is Thomas

Mozley (1806–1893), who raised the issue of whether Napoleon or the pope is a better candidate for the Anti-Christ.[43] Mozley was a pupil of Newman's at Oxford, and converted to Roman Catholicism a few years before Newman.

Other contemporaries of Newman's who wrote extensively about the End Times were: Edward Irving (1792–1834);[44] Henry Drummond (1786–1860); and John Nelson Darby (1800–1882). All of these thinkers could be labeled millenarian thinkers. Irving published the most on these issues. His *For the Oracles of God* (1823), *For Judgment to Come* (1823), *Babylon and Infidelity Foredoomed* (1826), and his *Expositions of the Book of Revelation* (1831) all dealt extensively with the End Times, the coming of the messiah, and the appearance of the Anti-Christ.

John Nelson Darby completed a new translation of both Testaments. In the notes to his translations of Revelation and Thessalonians, he makes a number of references to the End Times and the Anti-Christ. Henry Drummond was the eldest son of the elder Henry Drummond. The son was educated at Oxford and became a member of parliament in 1810. In the end of his life, he took a keen interest in religious subjects, and published numerous books and pamphlets on such topics as the interpretation of prophecy.

Other contemporaries of Newman combined a firm anti-Catholicism with a denial that the prophecies connected to the Anti-Christ are related to the papacy. Among these thinkers were John Keble, Samuel Roffey Maitland, William Palmer, and T. H. Todd. Keble (1792–1866) was a member of the Oxford Movement and gave his name to Keble College, Oxford in 1870. About his *The Christian Year*, Gregory Goodwin says is "Keble's greatest contribution to the Oxford Movement and English literature." The text contains a number of observations on the end of the world and the coming of the Anti-Christ.

Samuel Roffey Maitland (1792–1866) was an English lawyer and biblical scholar. He also became the librarian to the Archbishop of Canterbury. Maitland discovered Ribera's commentary on the Apocalypse in the library, and began to support the Spaniard's idea of a future, one man Anti-Christ.

James H. Todd, professor of Hebrew at the University of Dublin, also assented to Maitland's futurist idea of the Anti-Christ. Indeed, Todd published a number of pamphlets and books on the subject. It is likely that

John Henry Newman was aware of all these men and their works on the End Times.[45]

INFLUENCES ON NEWMAN'S LATER VIEWS OF THE ANTI-CHRIST

As we have seen, by the mid-1830s Newman began to change his earlier view that the pope is the Anti-Christ. His change of mind about this issue was concomitant with a number of other thinkers, close to Newman, who influenced the Englishman on these issues. John Keble, a member of the Oxford Movement, seems to have discarded the papal Anti-Christ theory as early as 1824. Keble's biographer, Kenneth Ingram, suggests as much in his work, *John Keble*, published in London in 1933.[46]

Samuel Roffey Maitland (1792–1866), historian, librarian, and archivist, gave up the theory from 1826 on. Misner comments on these later influences on Newman's later view on the Anti-Christ: "Samuel Roffey Maitland and certain Irish high church scholars such as William Palmer (Fellow of Worcester College, Oxford), William Burgh, and James Henthorn Todd have no use for the theory."[47]

William Palmer, another prominent member of the Oxford Movement, spent much of his energy in fruitless endeavors to have the Anglican Church recognized as a branch of the Catholic Church. Like Newman, Palmer converted to Catholicism ten years later than his colleague in 1855. As a Catholic, Palmer wrote a commentary on the Book of Daniel, in which he argues strenuously against the papal Anti-Christ theory.

William de Burgh, a descendant of one of the largest land-owner families in Ireland, was born in 1816. Burgh was a staunch opponent of the papal Anti-Christ theory throughout the nineteenth century. T. H. Todd (1805–1869) was the librarian for Trinity College, Dublin in the middle of the nineteenth century, has been discussed in an earlier section of this chapter.

All these thinkers were important influences in Newman's decision to change his views on the Anti-Christ, and ultimately to convert to Catholicism by the mid-1830s, Newman had begun to discard the papal Anti-Christ theory, and that is reflected, as we have shown, in his Advent sermons written in 1835, and published in 1838.

OTHER NEWMAN ARGUMENTS ON THE ANTI-CHRIST

In addition to the materials mentioned above, Newman seems to make nine major objections to the Papal Anti-Christ theory. First, he suggests that if any part of the Church is Anti-Christian, then the whole Church is Anti-Christian, including the Church of England. In a second argument, Newman points out that the Papal Anti-Christ theory was gradually developed by three historical sources: the Albigenses, the Waldenses, and the Fraticelli, between the eleventh and sixteenth centuries. Newman asks "Are these the expositors from whom the Church of Christ are to rely?" His answer is no.

In a third argument, Newman maintains that the defenders of the Papal Anti-Christ theory have made several key blunders. They cite Saint Bernard as identifying the Beast of the Apocalypse with the Pope, when in the passage in question Bernard is speaking of the Anti-pope. The proponents of the Papal Anti-Christ theory also quote Joachim as believing the Pope and the Anti-Christ are one and the same, while Newman shows that Joachim believes the Anti-Christ will overthrow the Pope and usurp his See at the end of time. Newman also points out that the advocates of the Papal Anti-Christ theory appeal to Gregory the Great as saying that whoever is the universal bishop is the Anti-Christ; but Newman points out that Gregory is referring to the "forerunner of the Anti-Christ and not the Final Enemy himself."

In a fourth argument against the Papal-Anti-Christ, Newman suggests that Protestants were driven to the theory out of the necessity of opposing a popular answer to the popular and cogent arguments advanced by the Church of Rome for her Divine authority. In a fifth line of argument, Newman argues that Warburton, Bishop Newman, and Hurd, the advocates to the Papal-Anti-Christ theory, cannot be matched against the saints of the Church of Rome. Newman specifically mentions Saint Charles Borromeo, Saint Bernard, and Saint Francis de Sales as figures whose moral character far surpass that of his contemporaries who assert the Papal-Anti-Christ theory.

In a seventh argument, Newman says that if the Church is to suffer like Christ, and if Christ were called Beelzebub, the true Church must expect a similar reproach; thus, the Papal-Anti-Christ theory becomes an argument in favor of the Roman Church.

In an eighth argument, Newman says the gibe "If the Pope is not Anti-Christ, he has bad luck to be so like him," is really another argument in favor of the claims of the Pope; since the Anti-Christ stimulates Christ, and the Pope is an image of Christ, the Anti-Christ must have some similarity to the Pope, if the latter be the true Vicar of Christ.[48]

And finally, one other argument that John Henry Newman makes against the Papal Anti-Christ Theory is that he points out that Queen Victoria came to the throne in 1837, at which time she was 18 years old. Now if we multiply the 18 times 37, we get 666. Newman making light of the numerology that was employed in his time to establish the pope as the Anti-Christ, returns the favor by suggesting that the Queen is the Anti-Christ.[49]

NEWMAN'S LATER VIEW OF THE ANTI-CHRIST

The first of Newman's Advent homilies was titled, "The Times of Anti-Christ." He opens the sermon by pointing out that New Testament writers thought the End Times were at hand; but Newman also points out that Paul points out in Thessalonians that some things need to happen before the Man of Sin and the Son of Perdition are to be revealed. Newman points out that the Anti-Christ will only come "immediately" before Christ, so the Anti-Christ has not yet come.

In this first homily Newman also points out that the time of the Anti-Christ is to be three and a half years, which is an additional reason for believing the pope cannot be the Anti-Christ. Newman goes on to point out that the "great tribulation, such as was not since the beginning of the world to this time," has also not yet come to pass, nor have we seen as ruler who has preached to all the nations of the world.

Next Newman raises two objections to his view in this first homily. First, that Scripture says that many Anti-Christs are already at work; and second, that Scriptures suggests that some power is now withholding the Anti-Christ, so that he might later be revealed in his own time.

Newman responds to the first objection by pointing out that the Church has seen many false Christs in its history, and it is these to which Scripture refers. Newman identifies the "restraining force" as the Roman Empire, the Roman Church, which will stand until the coming of the Anti-Christ.

In this first homily Newman also maintains the Anti-Christ will be one man, an individual, not a power or a kingdom. Newman also sketches out his view of the scriptural characteristics of the Anti-Christ, including his deceitfulness, and that he will preach apostasy.

In the first Advent sermon on the Anti-Christ Newman tells us that he has perused the writings of a number of the Church Fathers on the Anti-Christ. For the most part, Newman suggests that these early writers say little about doctrine and far more about their particular interests in whom the Anti-Christ might be. Newman concludes about the Fathers: "Yet, though the Fathers do not convey to us the interpretation of prophecy with the same certainty as they convey doctrine, yet in proportion to their agreement, their personal weight, and the prevalence, or again the authoritative character of the opinions they are stating, they are to be read with deference; for to say the least, they are as likely to be right as commentators now."[50]

Newman continues: "In some respects more so, because the interpretation of prophecy has become in these times a matter of controversy and party. And passion and prejudice have so interfered with soundness of judgment, that it is difficult to say who is to be trusted to interpret it, or whether a private Christian may not be as good an expositor as those by whom the office has been assumed."[51]

In this first sermon, Newman raises the question of how best to interpret passages about prophecy in the biblical text, and seems to suggest that the common man may be as good an interpreter as the scholars are. Throughout his comments on the Anti-Christ, both in these Advent homilies and in his other works about the issue, Newman continuously returns to this question about interpretation, almost always returning to the view that the question of exegesis is certainly a subjective matter.

In the second advent sermon Newman suggests that St. Paul and Saint John speak of the same figure when they write about the Anti-Christ. He points out that both say that the spirit of the Anti-Christ already was at work in their own day, and he points out that both men suggest the Final Enemy will deny the Father and the Son, and will sit as a God in the Temple.

Newman goes on in the second advent sermon to use Daniel chapter eleven to extricate more attributes of the Anti-Christ. He suggests he will be "against the God of gods." Newman also speaks extensively about John

5:43, which he believes to be a "prophetic allusion to Anti-Christ, whom the Jews were to mistake for the Christ."⁵²

Newman's second Advent sermon on the Anti-Christ is called, "The Religion of Anti-Christ." He begins this sermon by quoting several Old and New Testament passages about the Anti-Christ, and he discusses the views of several early Church Fathers about these passages.

He begins the third sermon, "The City of Anti-Christ," with a discussion of "the Great Harlot," the enchantress who seduces the inhabitants of the earth. Newman identifies the city as Rome. About Rome's connection to the Anti-Christ, Newman tells us: "The connection of Rome with the reign and exploits and Anti-Christ, is so often brought before us in the controversies of this day, that it may be well, after what I have already had occasion to say on the subject of the last enemy of the Church, to consider now what Scripture has to say about Rome; which I shall attempt to do, as before, with the guidance of the early Fathers."⁵³

Newman goes on to enumerate a number of biblical prophecies about Rome that already have been fulfilled, as well as a number that have not been fulfilled. The prophecies that have not been fulfilled are further evidence that the papal Anti-Christ theory is false. Among those that have not been fulfilled is Daniel's prediction that a great empire of the world will be divided into ten. He also points out that it is difficult to say if the Roman Empire is gone.

Newman begins his fourth Advent sermon from 1835, "The Persecution of Anti-Christ," by quoting several texts that allude to the persecution of the Anti-Christ. Newman points to four ideas that follow from these texts. First, a persecution awaits the Church before the End Times; second, this persecution will be attended by the cessation of all religious worship; third, the desolation of abomination that takes place in a holy place will have to occur; and finally, the reign of Anti-Christ will be accompanied by miracles such as those by magicians in Egypt. Newman concedes that the abomination of desolation may have been the worshipping of Caesar in the temple at Jerusalem, but there is no evidence that all Judeo-Christian worship has ever been completely halted. Thus, by the writing and delivering of these four sermons in the fall of 1835, Newman has given up on the idea of the papal Anti-Christ.

Newman wrote one other essay on the idea of the papal Anti-Christ. It is called, "Todd's Discourse on the Prophecies Relating to Anti-Christ." It was written for an October, 1840 edition of the *British Critic*. In this essay, Newman lays out the work of J. H. Todd (1805–1869), who opposed the papal Anti-Christ theory, and argued in its place a version of the Futurist position.

Ian Ker, in his biography of Newman tells us this about this essay from the *British Critic*:

> The October number of the *British Critic* carried a review article by Newman on the Protestant idea of the Anti-Christ. He admitted that there was a strong temptation to call the Pope Anti-Christ because of the ease with which it disposes of the plausible and apparently cogent proofs with which Rome fights her battles. It was the Protestant counterpart to the dogma of the Pope's infallibility in the Roman system. But one would have to be almost an angel to "unchurch" the greatest part of Christendom, and to hold that the greatest multitude of Christian bishops are children of the devil was no light matter.[54]

Ker goes on to point out that Bishop Newton was the "main source" for the English Protestant position on the Anti-Christ, but this is followed by Ker, quoting Newman from the essay in the *British Critic*, commenting on Bishop Newton:

> But a man so idolatrous of comfort, so liquorish of preferment, whose most fervent aspiration apparently was that he might ride in a carriage and sleep on down, whose keenest sorrow that he could not get a second appointment without relinquishing the first, who cast a regretful look back upon his dinner while he was at supper, and anticipated is morning chocolate in his evening muffins, who will say that this is the man, no merely to unchurch, but to smite, to ban, to wither the whole of Christendom for many centuries, and the greater part of its even in his own day ...[55]

Ker continues:

> This superb sneer is followed closely by the sarcastic admission, "Who would not rather be found even with Whitefield and Wesley, than with ecclesiastics whose life is literary ease at best, whose highest flights attain but to Downing Street or the levee? And once again the satire of *Present Position on Catholics* is foreshadowed in this assault on the inherent inconsistency of Anti-Popery—"how men, thinking that the Beast of the Apocalypse, can endure the sight of any of his servants ... or can sit with them in the same Council or Parliament, or can do business with them, buy and sell,

trade and traffic, or can gaze upon the architecture of churches built by Anti-Christ.⁵⁶

This essay of Newman's on the Protestant Anti-Christ contains the most vitriolic of the Cardinal's opinions on the Papal Anti-Christ theory. He not only criticizes Bishop Newton, but he also levels his scalpel at all the English Anti-Papists.

In "The Protestant Idea of the Anti-Christ," Newman sketches out the views of James Todd, eighteenth-century British theologian who traced the Papal Anti-Christ identification from the Waldenses and Fratercelli, to modern Protestant theology.⁵⁷ Newman liberally quotes Dr. Todd, and argues vehemently against the view. Along the way, Newman makes several arguments in response to Todd. Most of those can be found in a later section of this chapter.

Newman sums up these four Advent Sermons on the Anti-Christ, when he wrote:

> The coming of Christ will be immediately preceded by a veritable and unparalleled outbreak of evil, called by Saint Paul an apostasy, a falling away, in the midst of which a certain terrible man, a child of perdition, the special, singular enemy of Christ, or, will appear; this will be when the revolutionists prevail, and the framework of society breaks to pieces; and that at present the spirit he will embody and represent is kept under the that be, but that on their dissolution, he will rise his own evil way, under his own rule, to the exclusion of the church.

In these sermons, many of the traditional elements of the Anti-Christ can be seen, including the notion that the Final Enemy will be outside the church, and he will come in a time of political and religious turmoil.⁵⁸

Charles Frederick Harrold describes Newman's attack on Bishop Thomas Newton in his "The Protestant Idea of the Anti-Christ": "Here we may note in passing, Newman attacks one of his favorites in his youth, Thomas Newton, whose *Dissertations on the Prophecies* has implanted in him the doctrine of the Pope as Anti-Christ. Nowhere in Newman's writings is there a more scathing and merciless portrait which is intended to show that only "a man so idolatrous of comfort, so liquorish of preferment," could have propounded such a doctrine."¹

---

1. Ibid, 80–81.

In lecture three, "The City of the Anti-Christ," Newman explores "the connexion of Rome with the reign and exploits of Anti-Christ." Newman points out that the Papal Anti-Christ theory is alive and well in his day. Using the New Testament prophecies regarding the Anti-Christ, Newman concedes that many of these already have been fulfilled in regard to Rome; but he also points out that many have not: "I say, the Roman Empire has yet to be divided into ten . . . In the first place, the Roman Empire did breakup as foretold. It divided into a number of separate kingdoms, such as our own, France, and the like; yet it is difficult to number ten accurately and exactly."[59]

Newman continues in this third lecture: "Next, though Rome has certainly been desolated in the most fearful and miserable way, yet it has not exactly suffered from ten parts of its former empire, but from barbarians who came down upon it from regions external to it. In the third place, it still exists as a city, whereas it was to be 'desolated, devoured, and burned with fire.'"[60]

Referring to a "gold cup in her hand full of abominations" from Revelation 17, Newman says it is an "expression which surely implies some seduction or delusion, which she was able to practice upon the world, and which, I say, has not been fulfilled."[61] Like the other three Advent lectures on the Anti-Christ, in this third one, Newman takes great pains to show that many of the biblical prophecies about the Anti-Christ are yet to be fulfilled, and that they will all eventually be fulfilled in the future, but not by the Roman Church.

The principal argument Todd and Newman make is whether Christ has appointed a representative body of Him on earth during his absence? Newman writes: "If He has, the Pope is not Anti-Christ—if He has not, every bishop in England, Bishop Newton, Bishop Warburton, Bishop Hurd, is Anti-Christ; every priest is Anti-Christ, Mr. McNeile, Dr. Jortin, and Dr. Fausset inclusive."[62]

Newman goes on to argue that Christ has appointed an established representative on earth in the person of Saint Peter and the institution of the Roman Church. It follows then, in Newman's view, that the pope cannot be both Christ's representative on earth and the Anti-Christ at the same time.

At the end of "Todd's Discourses," Newman makes some observations about why Protestant leaders are so suspicious of the Roman Church Fathers. He blames it on:

> The dread that the doctrine and system which these divines teach is denounced in prophecy as the element of Anti-Christ, and savours of the predicted apostasy. When pressed with arguments from Scripture or reason, they cannot perhaps answer them, but they see, as they consider, the end to which the Catholic system tends. They judge that the teaching recommended to them is of Anti-Christ, because it has before now resulted in Popery; and under the impression that Popery is Anti-Christ, they say to themselves that somewhere or other there must be a fallacy in the reasoning, for that the fruit is the proof of the tree.[63]

In 1840 Newman was looking out for arguments to bolster his earlier view in the four Advent sermons. At the same time, Newman was also staunchly against the Roman notion of the infallibility of the pope; but Newman also suggests one other new argument in his essay on Todd's *Discourses*. The prophecies that heretofore have been used by the Protestants to prove that the pope is the Anti-Christ, Newman maintains, could also be used to show that the Anglican Church is the Anti-Christ. Newman's conclusion is put very simply: "Now, let a candid Protestant decide: is he prepared to match Warburton, Newton, or Hurd against the saints of degenerate Rome?"[64]

Newman asks if this candid Protestant is prepared to sit in judgment on such thinkers as Charles Borromeo and Blaise Pascal "with nothing better than Newton for saint, doctor, bishop, and confessor?"[65]

In the fall of 1845, Newman entered the Catholic Church. He immediately resigned his position at Oriel; he could not have held it as a Catholic. Newman had reached the mid-point of his ninety-year life, thus he spent the second half of his life as a Roman Catholic. He was ordained in May of 1847. By the writing of Newman's *Apologia Pro Vita Sua* in 1864, the papal Anti-Christ theory had died a natural death. The only mention of the concept in his autobiography is in reference to the earlier struggles of the 1830s and 1840s.

Newman's theological reputation and stature grew steadily from then on. In most of his writings after his conversion, Newman defended the doctrines of the Catholic Church, including the veneration of Mary and the infallibility of the pope. He gained an international reputation as a powerful defender of the faith. His writings of all kinds were widely praised, by Catholics and Protestants alike.

On May 12, 1879, at the age of 79, Newman received the award that crowned his life's achievement. Pope Leo XIII made him a cardinal. All of England celebrated the honor, for Newman, more than any other individual, had turned around England's view of Catholics. No more would they be called intellectually inferior or morally depraved, just because they were Catholics.

Cardinal Newman died on August 11, 1890, but his reputation and stature continues to grow. His ideas so much anticipated those of the twentieth century that Newman is often called "The Father of Vatican II." On January 22, 1991, Pope John Paul II signed a decree recognizing Newman's "heroic virtues," declaring him "venerable," the first step on the path to sainthood.

NEWMAN ON THE ANTI-CHRIST IN HIS SERMONS, LETTERS, AND OTHER ESSAYS

In addition to these major works John Henry Newman wrote on the Anti-Christ, he also makes several references to the Final Enemy his letters and sermons. In a letter to his friend Tom Mozley, Newman calls Dr. Hampden, the writer of the *Elucidations*, "that stolid, dull, and kindly man who was the future model for Trollop's Bishop Proudie, a forerunner of the Anti-Christ." Newman refers here to a character, Bishop Proudie, in Anthony Trollop's novels. Although the Bishop is stolid and kind, he is also at times devious, leading Newman to believe the bishop may be a forerunning of the Anti-Christ.[66]

In a sermon from Newman's collection, "Lectures on the Present Position of Catholics in England," delivered on August 11, 1851, Newman refers to the Anglican treatment of the Roman Church, when he writes:

> It was then a thought of genius, and, as I think, preternatural genius, to pitch upon the expedient which had been against the Church from Christ's age to our own; to call her in the first century Beelzebub, so in the sixteenth, Anti-Christ; it was a bold, politic, and successful move. It startled men who heard; and whereas Anti-Christ, by the very notion of his character, will counterfeit Christ, he will therefore be, so far, necessarily like Him; and if Anti-Christ is like Christ, then Christ, I suppose must be like Anti-Christ; thus there was, even at first starting a felicitous plausibility about the very charge, which went far toward securing belief, while it commanded attention.[67]

Newman seems to be suggesting here that if the Anti-Christ, according to some thinkers in the Protestant Reformation, is to be a parody of Christ, then the opposite must also hold: that Christ is a parody of the Anti-Christ.

In another sermon entitled "Contest Between Faith and Sight," Newman makes a number of observations about First John, verse 4. He says this about the verse:

> The dangers to which Christians are exposed from the influence of the visible course of things, or the world as it is called in Scripture, is a principal subject of St. John's General Epistle. He seems to speak of the world as some false prophet, promising what it cannot fulfill, and gaining credit by its confident tone. Viewing it as resisting Christianity, he calls it the "spirit of Anti-Christ," the parent of numerous progeny of evil, false spirits like itself, the teachers of all lying doctrines, by which the multitudes of men are held captive.[68]

This sermon was preached on May 27, 1832, three years before his four Advent Sermons, and while Newman still held to the Papal Anti-Chris Theory. Speaking about this early period, Newman writes: "When I was young, as I have said already, and after I was grown up, I thought the Pope to be the Anti-Christ. I considered, after Protestant authorities, that Saint Gregory I about A.C. 600 was the first Pope that was the Anti-Christ . . . The Church of Rome was bound up with the cause of Anti-Christ by the Council of Trent."[69]

Newman wrote these words long after he had given up the Papal Anti-Christ Theory and had become a member, and a priest, of the Roman Church. Later in life, when he wrote about this early period in his academic life, he often treats himself as a seasoned theologian coming to the beliefs of a fledgling believer, one who will see much maturity and development to come.

In an essay on the fourth century in his *The Development of Christian Doctrine*, Cardinal Newman discusses various names that early church heretics had for each other. Newman points out that the Donatists called the Roman Church in the fourth century "traitors, sinners, and the servants of Anti-Christ."[70] Newman adds that the Luciferians calls the Church a "brothel," "the Devil's harlot," and the "Synagogue of Satan."[71] All of these names are employed later by the Church in reference to Anti-Christ or his followers.

One other place where Cardinal Newman mentions the Anti-Christ in his other works comes in relation to a discussion of "The Theology of the Seven Epistles," by Saint Ignatius. Newman says in his *Historical Sketches* that "The whole system of Catholic doctrine may be discovered, at least in outline, not to say in parts, filled up, in the course of his seven epistles."[72]

NEWMAN'S FINAL COMMENTS ON THE ANTI-CHRIST

In the final writings of John Henry Newman, the only mentions of the Anti-Christ come in his spiritual autobiography, *Apologia Pro Vita Sua*, published in 1864. In the *Apologia*, Newman describes his earlier view on the Anti-Christ, inspired by Bishop Newton and Richard Hurrell Froude. Newman also points out in a second entry on the Anti-Christ in the *Apologia* that in the mid-1830s, he "began to form theories on the subject, which tended to obliterate it [the papal Anti-Christ theory]."[73] Newman continues: "Yet, by 1838, I had got no further than to consider Anti-Christ as not the Church of Rome, but the spirit of the old pagan city, the fourth monster of Daniel, which was still alive, and which had corrupted the Church which was planted there."[74]

The only other references to the Anti-Christ in Newman's *Apologia* are a reference to his 1824–25 Christmas homily on the papal Anti-Christ; and a reference to Newman using some arguments of Bernard Gilpin, where he says "the Protestants were not able to give firm and solid reasons"[75] for believing the papal Anti-Christ theory. Newman points out that Hurrell Froude attacked Newman for doing this. Newman adds: "I felt that my language had a vulgar and rhetorical look about it. I believed, and really measured, my words when I used them; but I knew that I had a temptation, on the other hand to say against Rome as much as I could, in order to protect myself against the charge of Popery."[76]

Most of the comments that Newman makes about the Anti-Christ in his later works, come in several references in his *Apologia*. In these four references, Newman rehearses his early and later views of the Anti-Christ, as well as how he came to change his mind about the subject. Newman, from the publication of his four Advent sermons in 1838, until his death in 1890, was a cleric staunchly against the idea that the Pope is the Anti-Christ. By 1838, Newman's ideas had changed about the matter, and his changed view did not waver for the rest of his life.[77]

THE ANTI-CHRIST IN NEWMAN'S OTHER WRITINGS

Most of what we have said so far in this chapter is born out in Newman's other writings, particularly his letters and essays. Before his conversion, we can see his belief in the Papal Anti-Christ theory and then gradually, we can see his position begin to change, until finally, he argues positively against the view.

In one letter when he was still committed to the Papal Anti-Christ Theory, Newman suggests that the real impetus for the theory was the Council of Trent.[78] But a few years later, when he had begun to change his mind about the matter, Newman, he wrote, "If the Bishop of Rome be Anti-Christ, then we owe our conversion to Anti-Christ, and our orders are devil's orders."[79] Newman makes a similar claim in one of his letters while still an Anglican, when he wrote, "If Rome is the Anti-Christ, so is England."[80] In another letter while an Anglican, Newman wrote, "We do not behave as though we really believed the Pope to be Anti-Christ and Rome Babylon."[81] Newman makes a similar remark in his *Essays*, when he says, "Rome must not monopolize the title of Anti-Christ. We Anglicans should claim to share them."[82]

By the time Newman had converted, Newman refers in one of his letters to the "palmary argument of the Reformers, without which they never could have made head, was that Rome is Anti-Christ."[83] In another of his letters after his conversation Newman alludes to the theory that the Anti-Christ was among the Turks, something we saw earlier in the Christian tradition among the Reformers.[84]

In another letter after his conversation Newman makes an argument against the Papal Anti-Christ Theory, and argues instead that the Anti-Christ is "the spirit of the old pagan city, still alive and corrupting the Church there."[85]

In an essay called "The Role of False Witness," published in the Newman reader, Cardinal Newman again writes about his rejection of the Papal Anti-Christ Theory. About the Reformers Newman writes: "So was it at the time of the Reformation, the multitude would never have been converted by exact reasoning and by facts which could not be proved; so its holders were clever enough to call the Pope Anti-Christ, and let that startling accusation sink into men's minds. Nothing else would have succeeded; and they pursue the same tactics now."[86]

The Anti-Christ and John Henry Newman

In another of Newman's letters and essays he also reflects his various views on the Anti-Christ Legend, from his Anglican days, in the transition from Anglican to Catholic, and after his conversion. It is enough now to say this material reflects his differing attitudes toward the Anti-Christ over time.[87]

In his *Discourses Addressed to Mixed Congregations,* Newman makes a number of references to the Anti-Christ, including a discussion of the fore-runners of the Anti-Christ (pp. 57–59); the Anti-Christ's Religion (pp. 64–68); a discussion of why the Anti-Christ has not yet come (pp. 48–51); a summary of the prophetic statements concerning him (p. 74); four characteristics of his coming (pp. 98–99); some parallels that Newman saw between the Anti-Christ and the French Revolution (pp. 69–70); and he speculates on the meaning of the number 666 (p. 73). In his *Essays*, Newman suggests that the Papal Anti-Christ theory was started by the Albigenses, the Waldenses, and the Fraticelli, (pp. 117–21). He also says that the term "Anti-Christ" was used too freely by the early Church (pp. 12–15); and that the prophecies about the Anti-Christ are only to be interpreted by the few (p. 129).

In the *Virgin Mary*, Newman discusses whether the language about Anti-Christ is figurative or literal (pp. 221–22); and he speculates in the same work why the Pope is taken for the Anti-Christ. In *On Consulting the Faithful in Matters of Doctrine*, Newman tells us: "The Anti-Christ must look like Christ, otherwise he would not be counterfeit; but if Anti-Christ is like Christ, then Christ must be like the Anti-Christ."[88]

John Henry Newman also preached on the idea of the Anti-Christ in a number of his homilies, including a sermon called, "Contest Between Faith and Sight," published in his *Sermons*. In this homily on I John 4, Newman writes:

> The danger to which Christians are exposed from the influences of the visible course of things, or the world (as it is called in Scripture), is a principal subject of Saint John's General Epistle. He seems to speak of the world as some false prophet, promising what it cannot fulfill, and gaining credit by its confident tone. Viewing it as resisting Christianity, he calls it the "Spirit of Anti-Christ," the parent of a numerous progeny of evil, false spirits like itself, the teachers of all lying doctrine, by which the multitude of men are held captive.[89]

Newman makes similar remarks in a number of his other sermons, including sermons 10 and 11.[90] These two sermons are also about I John, and Newman makes the same claim that there is one origin to all false doctrine, Satan and the Anti-Christ.

ANTI-CHRIST AND THE DANGER OF CORRUPTING REVELATION

In many places in Newman's corpus he suggests that the word Anti-Christ is another name for the danger of corrupting revelation. Newman describes this danger exactly and gives it a personal name, "the work of Anti-Christ."[91] Gunter Biemer describes this tendency in Newman: "This 'malignant principle' has already been at work since the time of the apostles, planning and working for the great apostasy, the destruction of the Church and her doctrine."[92]

In the Advent Sermons, Newman suggests that every opponent of the Church in the course of history is a precursor of the real, primordial adversary. Newman says "Just as every event in this world is a type of those that follow, history proceeding forward as a circle every enlarging."[93] Newman says that until the hour of Anti-Christ, the efforts to make the power of evil triumph continues with ever-growing force. The longer that time goes on, the more intense will be the activity of the corrupted force, and thus the greater danger to true doctrine.[94] Newman says the Church always lives in the midst of corruption because it lives in the world.[95]

Cardinal Newman develops these ideas in an essay called, "The Development of Religious Error." This essay grew out of a controversy with Dr. Fairbairn, who had accused Newman of skepticism. Newman tells us that religious error lives outside the Church, even though it constantly makes assaults on its members. Newman says it "disturbs the laws of development." The results of these disturbances are perversions and corruptions of traditional Christian doctrine. This is the way the religion of the world, the religion of Anti-Christ, came to be.[96]

Thus Newman suggests that constant efforts must be made to distinguish the true Christian doctrine ever more clearly and sharply from the false. The closer the Second Coming of Christ draws near, the more intense will be the conflict, and it will reach its climax with the arrival of the Anti-Christ. By then, in Newman's view, the clear contours of genuine doctrine will be fully developed.

The tradition of error is doomed to destruction from the very beginning, since, in Newman's words, "corruption is the break-up of life, preparatory to its termination."[97]

JOHN HENRY NEWMAN'S INFLUENCE

Newman's influence in the history of the Church cannot be exaggerated. He was influential in his own time in a number of areas, including the conversion of Gerard Manley Hopkins, and many others, to the Roman Church. Newman was also influential in Hopkins' joining of the Jesuits. Newman wrote this congratulatory letter to Hopkins: "I think it is the very thing for you. You are quite out, in thinking that when I offered you a 'home' here, I dreamed of you having a vocation for us. This I clearly saw you had *not*, from the moment you came to us. Don't call the 'Jesuit discipline hard,' it will bring you to heaven. The Benedictine's would not have suited you.[98]

Although Newman never called himself a mystic, he showed that his spiritual judgment is apprehended by direct intuition. In this sense, Newman was quite influential in the writings of several twentieth-century Catholic mystics, Hopkins among them.

Newman's influence within the Anglican church was also immense, even within the more strictly Protestant denominations. In these contexts, much of his permanent influence is in regard to the importance of dogma. In regard to his teachings about the church Newman was far less followed. Some have argued that this is principally due to his inadequacies in knowing Christian history. For two or three decades, Newman was the indisputable leader of the Oxford Movement, as well as a whole host of Anglicans who converted to Roman Catholicism.

The natural tendency of Newman's mind is often (and correctly) spoken of as skeptical. Indeed, many twentieth century writers who thought of themselves as skeptics considered Newman to have been one of their progenitors. Newman disagreed with many in his time about the nature of the authentic church. His *Tract 85* is almost solely devoted to answering that question.

Newman was an intense man. He had a magnetic personality, easily attracting thinkers like himself. He thought of his own work as ordained by God. As a poet, he had inspiration and genuine power. R. H. Hutton describes some of his early poetry as "unequaled for grandeur of outline, purity of taste and radiance of total effect."

The longest and last of Newman's great poems, "The Dream of Gerontius," is recognized by some critics as the greatest depictions of the life beyond the grave since Dante. His prose style, particularly in his Catholic days, was imitated by many. It was attractive to many, even those who often did not agree with him.

Newman also tells us in his *Arians of the Fourth Century* that "there is something true and divinely revealed in every religion. Thus, it might be argued that Cardinal Newman was also a forerunner to the history of religions approach, as well as the comparative study of religion.

CONCLUSIONS

Our primary interests in this chapter have been in exploring the views of John Henry Newman on the Anti-Christ. As we have seen in this chapter, Newman's earliest views on the matter were consonant with the Protestant Papal Anti-Christ theory we have described in an earlier chapter. From the age of 15 on, there is evidence that these were Newman's earliest views on the matter. They are expressed in his letters, as well as a sermon he gave at Christmas time 1824–1825. The chief source for Cardinal Newman's early view on the Anti-Christ was Bishop Thomas Newton's *Dissertations on the Prophecies*.

By the mid-1830s, Newman's views on the Anti-Christ began to change. By the publication of his four Advent Sermons on the Anti-Christ, Newman's perspectives on the matter were permanently altered. This new view is best expressed in the four Advent Sermons, as well as in Newman's essay on the work on T. H. Todd on the Anti-Christ.

In these works, Newman gives a number of arguments for rejecting the Papal Anti-Christ identification. Many of these arguments come from a close analysis of early Church Fathers on the issue, or from subsequent thinkers who influenced Newman on the Anti-Christ issue later in life.

Among these influences who help to change Newman's mind on the Anti-Christ were John Keble, William Palmer, William de Burgh, and Samuel Roffey Maitland. The real period of the transformation in Newman's views on the Anti-Christ, as we have shown, is the period from 1835 to 1838. Before that time, all evidence points to the papal Anti-Christ theory. After that time, all evidence indicates that Cardinal Newman no longer held that view.

In the tenth and final chapter of this study, we will analyze and discuss perspectives on the Christian doctrine of the Anti-Christ in the contemporary period. As we shall see, views about the Anti-Christ have been more widely disparate in the late twentieth century to the present than in any previous ages.

NOTES

1. Most of the insights in this chapter come from an essay written by Paul Misner, "Newman and the Tradition Concerning the Papal Anti-Christ," *Church History* 42 (1973) 377–95. The edition of Newman's *Apologia Pro Vita Sua* used in this chapter is that published by Longmans Green in 1947. This edition is edited and contains a preface by Charles Frederick Harrold. For secondary sources I have consulted the following: Margaret Grennan, *The Heart of Newman's Apologia* (New York: Longmans Green, 1934); J. D. Folghera, *Newman's Apologetics* (London: Herder, 1928); and Walter E. Houghton, *The Art of Newman's Apologia* (New Haven: Yale University Press, 1945). Other secondary sources I have consulted include: Gerald Magill, "The Consolation of Rhetoric: John Henry Newman and the Realism of Personalist Thought," *Theological Studies* 56 (1995) 786ff.; Edward Oakes, "Newman's Liberal Problem," *First Things: A Monthly Journal of Religion and Public Life* 43 (April 2003) 43–51; on Newman's theology, see Americo Lapati, *John Henry Newman*, Twayne's English Authors Series 140; Stephen Fields, "Personal Catholicism: The Theological Epistemologies of John Henry Newman and Michael Polanyi," *Theological Studies* 62 (2001) 660–63; and Gerald Magill, "The White Stone: The Spiritual Theology of John Henry Newman," *Theological Studies* 55 (1994) 589. I have also consulted many of the entries on *John Henry Newman: Bibliographical Supplements to British Book News on Writers and Their Work*, edited by J. M. Cameron (London: Longmans Green, 1963). Cardinal Newman's *Letters and Correspondence* was edited by his niece, Anne Mozley. (New York: Longmans Green, 1903). Newman entrusted the letters and memoranda dealing with his Catholic years, 1845–1890, to Reverend W. Neville, his literary executor. Works by R. W. Church, J. B. Mozley, and Wilfrid Ward, *The Life of John Henry, Cardinal Newman Based on His Private Journals and Correspondence*, 2 vols. (London: Longmans, Green, 1912) should also be consulted, as well as the appreciation of E. A. Abbott, *The Anglican Career of John Henry Newman*, 2 vols. (London: Macmillan, 1892). I have also extensively consulted Frank M. Turner, *John Henry Newman: The Challenge to Evangelical Religion* (New Haven: Yale University Press, 2002) in the construction of this chapter.

2. For more on the Plymouth Brethren, see Roy Coad, *A History of the Brethren Movement* (London Regent College Publishing, 2001); and Natan Dylan Smith, *Roots, Renewal, and Brethren* (London: Hope, 1996).

3. Newman was so impressed with the idea of the via media that he began a journal in that name, inviting many of sympathetic theologians of the day to contribute, including Pusey and Froude. Newman also made several of his own contributions to the journal, which was published by Longmans, Green between 1830 and 1841.

4. For more on the Oxford Movement, see Kenneth Leech and Rowan Williams, *Essays Catholic and Radical* (London: Bowerdean, 1983) and Edward R. Norman, *Church and Society in England 1770–1970: An Historical Study* (Oxford: Clarendon, 1976).

5. Dean Church, *Letters* (London: Macmillan, 1894) 134.

6. The edition of Newman's *Apologia pro Vita Sua* I have used in preparing this chapter is that of Ian Ker (London: Penguin Classics, 1995).

7. Newman, "Manuscript Number 100." Archives and Manuscript Department, Pitts Theology Library, Emory University.

8. Newman, *Apologia*, 6. For Newman's life, I have consulted the following: Ward, *The Life of John Henry, Cardinal Newman*; Edward Sillem, *The Philosophical Notebook of John Henry Newman* (New York: Humanities, 1969–1970); Stephen Dessain, *John Henry Newman on Faith and Certainty* (Oxford: Clarendon, 1976); and Ian Kerr, *The Genius of John Henry Newman* (Oxford: Clarendon, 1989).

9. Ibid.

10. Newman, *Apologia*, 6–7.

11. Newman, *Apologia Pro Vita Sua: Being a History of My Religious Opinions* (London: Kessinger, 2004) chap. 2.

12. One other British scholar who held the Papal Anti-Christ view is James A. Wylie (1808–1890). Wylie was educated at Marischal College, Aberdeen and the University of Saint Andrews. He was ordained in the Presbyterian Church in 1831. In Wylie's "The Papacy is the Anti-Christ," published in Edinburgh in 1888, he begins this essay this way:

In the life of Christ we behold the converse of what the Anti-Christ must be; and in the prophecy of the Anti-Christ we are shown the converse of what Christ must be, and was. And when we place the Papacy between the two, and compare it with each, we find, on the one hand, that it is the perfect converse of Christ as seen in His life; and, on the other hand, that it is a perfect image of the Anti-Christ, as shown in the prophecy of him. We conclude, therefore, that if Jesus of Nazareth be the Christ, the Roman Papacy is the Anti-Christ.

(James A. Wylie, preface of "The Papacy is the Anti-Christ," [Edinburgh: Moray Place, 1888]).

13. Charles Frederick Harrold, *John Henry Newman: An Expository and Critical Study of His Mind, Thought, and Art* (London: Longmans Green, 1941) 4.
14. Ibid.
15. Misner, "Newman and the Tradition Concerning the Papal Anti-Christ," 379. John Gill (1697–1771) was one of the founders of the Baptist Church in England. He was a self-taught Hebrew scholar, and the author of many books and pamphlets about theological matters. His most famous work remains his two-volume *A Body of Doctrinal Divinity*, published in 1769.
16. Thomas Newton (1704–1782) was an English cleric, biblical scholar, and author. He was a fellow of Trinity College, Cambridge, and for a short time (1761–1762), Newton was the bishop of Bristol. In addition to his *Dissertations on the Prophecies*, completed in 1754, Newton also constructed an annotated edition of "Paradise Lost," including a biography of Milton in 1749.
17. Ibid., 391.
18. Ibid.
19. Ibid, 386.
20. Bernard McGinn, *The Anti-Christ* (San Francisco: HarperCollins, 1994) 238.
21. Ibid.
22. William Warburton (1698–1779) was an English cleric and churchman. From 1759 on Warburton was Bishop of Gloucester. For a time in the 1750s, he was also chaplain to the King.
23. Richard Hurd (1720–1808), Anglican divine and writer was made Arch-Deacon of Worcester in 1767, and in 1783, he became bishop of the same Diocese. In 1772, Hurd edited and published the works of William Warburton. Hurd's own works appeared in a collected edition in eight volumes in 1811.
24. John Gill, *An Exposition of the Prophets* (London, 1758).
25. Ibid., 384–85.
26. James J. L. Ratton, *Anti-Christ: An Historical Review*. (London: Burns and Oates, 1897) 2.
27. Ibid.
28. Quoted in Ratton's *Anti-Christ*, 2.
29. Ibid, 2–3.
30. Newman, *Discussions and Arguments on Various Subjects*, 198.
31. Ibid.
32. Ibid.
33. Ibid., 202.

34. Ibid., 206.
35. James J. L. Ratton, *Anti-Christ: An Historical Review* (London: Burns & Oates, 1897) 148.
36. Ibid., 153.
37. James Ratton, *Anti-Christ*, 4.
38. Ibid., 207.
39. Misner, "Newman and the Tradition Concerning the Papal Anti-Christ," 389.
40. Newman, *Apologia*, 6.
41. Ibid., 48.
42. For more on the *Lyra Apostolica*, see the work by that name published in London by Methuen in 1901. This work includes poems by J. W. Bowden, R. H. Froude, John Keble, R. I. Wilberforce, I. Williams, and John Henry Newman. Also see Alexander Whyte, *Newman: An Appreciation in Two Lectures*, also published by Longmans Green, in 1902.
43. Thomas Mozley, *Letters From Rome*, 2 vols. (London: Longmans Green, 1891) 72.
44. For more on Edward Irving, see Gordon Strachan, *The Pentecostal Theology of Edward Irving* (London, 1973); Arnold Dallimore, *The Life of Edward Irving* (Edinburgh: The Banner of Truth, 1983); and Timothy Stunt, *From Awakening to Secession* (Edinburgh: T. & T. Clark, 2000).
45. Misner, "Newman and the Tradition Concerning the Papal Anti-Christ," 378–84.
46. Kenneth Ingram, *John Keble* (London, 1933) 66.
47. Misner, "Newman and the Tradition Concerning the Papal Anti-Christ," 389.
48. All eight of these arguments are in an article on Newman by A. J. Maas published in the *Catholic Encyclopedia* (New York: Appleton, 1907) vol. 1.
49. Charles Frederick Harrold, *John Henry Newman* (London: Longmans Green, 1945) 198.
50. Ibid., 94.
51. Ibid.
52. Ibid., 64.
53. Newman, *Discussions and Arguments on Various Subjects* (South Bend: Notre Dame University Press, 2004) 64.
54. Ian Ker, *John Henry Newman: A Biography* (Oxford: Clarendon, 1988) 184.
55. Ibid., 185.
56. Ibid.
57. Charles Frederick Harrold, *John Henry Newman* (London: Longmans Green, 1945).

58. Ibid.
59. Ibid.
60. Ibid., 81.
61. Ibid. Several other passages of Newman's on the Anti-Christ can also be found in *Newman the Theologian: A Reader* (Notre Dame: University of Notre Dame Press, 1990).
62. Ibid., 91.
63. Misner, "Newman and the Tradition Concerning the Papal Anti-Christ," 391.
64. Newman, "The Protestant Idea of Anti-Christ," in *Newman Reader*, edited by Francis Connolly (New York: Image, 1964) 171.
65. Ibid., 170.
66. T. Gornall, ed., *The Letters and Diaries of John Henry Newman*, vol. 5 (Oxford: Clarendon, 1981) 91.
67. Newman, *Lectures on the Present Position of Catholics in England*, Lecture six. August 11, 1851.
68. Newman, *Oxford University Sermons*. Sermon number seven, 120.
69. Newman, *History of My Religious Opinions from 1833 to 1839*, chap. 2.
70. Newman, *An Essay on the Development of Christian Doctrine* (London: Longmans, Green, 1897) 254.
71. Ibid.
72. Quoted in Rattan's *Anti-Christ*, 115.
73. Newman, *Apologia*, 6.
74. Ibid., 110.
75. Ibid., 50.
76. Ibid.
77. For more on Newman's *Apologia*, see the edition edited by Daniel O'Connell (Chicago: Loyola University Press, 1930). This edition also has a forward by British critic, Hilaire Belloc. I have also consulted the Penguin Classics edition, published in 1995; and the Kessinger edition, published in London in 2004. A good treatment of the *Apologia* is Rodney Stenning Edgecombe, *Two Poets of the Oxford Movement* (Madison, NJ: Farleigh Dickinson University Press, 1996).
78. Newman, *The Virgin Mary* (London: McAdam Cage, 2006) 206.
79. Ibid., 219.
80. Newman, *Two Essays on Miracles* (Eugene: Wipf & Stock, 1998) 114–15.
81. Ibid., 146–47.
82. Newman, *Essays*, 151–52.
83. Ibid., 218.

84. Newman, *Letters and Diaries of John Henry Newman* (Oxford: Oxford University Press, 1981) 195.
85. Newman, *Essays*, 146.
86. Newman, *Apologia*, 121.
87. Joseph Rickby, *An Index to the Works of John Henry Newman* (London: Longmans, Green, 1918). Rickby has 34 entries for "Anti-Christ." Many of those are in his *Essays*, in his *Discourses Addressed to Mixed Congregation* (London: Gracewing, 2002), or in the *Apologia*.
88. Newman, *In Consulting the Faithful in Matters of Doctrine*, edited by John Coulson (New York: Rowman & Littlefield, 1985) 141–44.
89. Francis Connolly, *Newman Reader* (New York: Image, 1964) 120.
90. Ibid., 134.
91. Newman, *Advent Sermons on Anti-Christ* in *Tracts for the Times*, Tract 83, vol. 5, 1–54.
92. Gunter Biemer, *Newman on Tradition* (New York: Herder & Herder, 1961) 135.
93. Advent Sermons, 4.
94. Newman, *The Development of Religious Error*, in Wilfred Ward, *The Life of John Henry, Cardinal Newman*, 2 vols. (London: Longmans, Green, 1912) vol. 1.
95. Ibid.
96. Ibid.
97. Ibid.
98. Quoted in Ian Ker's *John Henry Newman: A Biography* (Oxford: Clarendon, 1988) 624.

10

The Anti-Christ in Contemporary Life

This plan will be put into operation by the figure of the Anti-Christ after the preordained thousand years are over, the term allotted by astrology to the reign of Christ.

—C. G. Jung, *Answer to Job*

Immediately we turn to the textual descriptions of the Anti-Christ, we are faced with an enormous gap between the verbal imagery and the visual actualization.

—Rosemary Muir Wright, *Art and Anti-Christ in Medieval Europe*

Is he alive and here today? Probably. Because when he appears during the Tribulation period he will be a full-grown counterfeit of Christ. Of course, he'll be Jewish. Of course, he'll pretend to be Christ. And if in fact the Lord is coming soon, and he will be an adult at the presentation of himself, he must be alive somewhere today.

—Jerry Falwell, speech given at a conference, on evangelism in Kingsport, Tennessee, October, 1999

INTRODUCTION

IN THIS CHAPTER, WE shall explore six different ways in which the Christian conception of the Anti-Christ has been described in life in the twentieth and twenty-first centuries. The first of these categories we shall call "People Identified with the Anti-Christ." In the contemporary period, there have been more than a dozen people in the twentieth and twenty-first centuries who regularly have been identified as the Anti-Christ. We shall begin this chapter by exploring those identifications.

In a second section of this chapter, "Anti-Christ in Literature," we shall discuss a number of short stories and novels in which the Anti-Christ figure is prominently displayed. In a third section of the chapter, we analyze and discuss a number of modern films in which the Anti-Christ is featured.

In the fourth section of this chapter, we shall review contemporary scholarly works on the Anti-Christ, from the late nineteenth century to the present. In the concluding section of this chapter, we shall explore the manifestations of the Anti-Christ figure in contemporary culture. Chief among these manifestations, as we shall see, are a number of writers, many of the millennial thinkers, who have written about the End Times, and the coming of the Anti-Christ.

PEOPLE IDENTIFIED WITH THE ANTI-CHRIST

In the last seventy years, a number of people have been identified with the Anti-Christ. These thinkers can be divided into three basic types. The first type is people identified with political power. Like Antiochus Epiphanius IV, Nero, Peter the Great, and Napoleon before them, Adolf Hitler, Benito Mussolini, Josef Stalin, Vladimir Putin, and Mikhail Gorbachev, all have been identified as the Anti-Christ. The chief reasons for these identifications are that they all possess, or did, enormous political power, and they all have been called manifestations of pure evil.

Francisco Franco (1892–1975), dictator of Spain from October 1939 to his death in December 1975, has also been called the Anti-Christ, in the same way that Hitler and Mussolini were identified that way. This judgment mostly grew out of the fact that Franco was a ruthless leader, as exemplified by the fact that he had thousands of Spaniards shot during the Civil War, and the few years following it.

A second category of people identified with the Anti-Christ are individuals who are extremely wealthy. Chief among the nominees in this category have been Bill Gates, Warren Buffett, and Michael Dell. Other rich folks who have been identified with the Anti-Christ are Microsoft billionaire, Steven Ballmer, oil baron railroad magnate, Phillip Anschultz, Microsoft billionaire Paul Gardner Allen, Donald Trump, and Hungarian born billionaire George Soros. These individuals are identified with the Anti-Christ, one suspects, because of their ability to control peoples' lives, and because they wield tremendous power in the contemporary world.

The Anti-Christ in Contemporary Life

Other people designated as the Anti-Christ in this category are Meg Whitman, the CEO of eBay and Eric Schmidt, the mastermind behind Google. Whitman has been nominated because of the belief that the Anti-Christ will control all buying and selling in the world, something that eBay, some critics say, already is doing. Eric Schmidt has been nominated for similar reasons, in that Google is taking over the world, one product at a time.

A third category of contemporary people identified with the Anti-Christ are famous people who may be famous for their money, their power, or because they are in show business. Individuals in this category are Henry Kissinger, David Hasselhoff, religious leader Pat Robertson, and Charles, the Prince of Wales.

A number of post-Tribulation Christians in Texas have adopted the idea that Prince Charles is the Anti-Christ. The prophecy of Daniel 9:27, these critics argue, refers to the Oslo Peace Accords, when the Anti-Christ made peace with Israel, or so the theory goes. Writer Tim Cohen and others are firm believers that the Prince of Wales is the Anti-Christ.[1]

The final category of people nominated as the Anti-Christ includes various other political leaders who are often identified with the demonic as well. Chief examples in this category are Sadaam Hussein, Osama bin Ladin, Anwar Sadat, Ronald Reagan, and George W. Bush. Hussein and bin Ladin are nominated because of the view of much of the west that they are demonic. Bush is mentioned because much of the Islamic world sees the American leader as the Djaal, the Islamic version of the Anti-Christ. Anwar Sadat was nominated as the Anti-Christ in 1981 by Mary Stewart Relfe, the founder of the 666 System. In her 1981 book, *When Your Money Fails*, Relfe uses Revelation 13 to argue that the Anti-Christ will mark his followers, and those without the mark will be forbidden to buy and sell consumer goods. Relfe suggests that the 666 System will have a 666 bar code imprinted on the foreheads of all of Anti-Christ's followers. Relfe advises Christians to pay off their debts, get rid of their credit cards, and convert their assets to gold and silver.[2]

This literalist approach of Relfe's and other evangelical Christians concerning the End Times and coming of the Anti-Christ are described by Bernard McGinn as "nothing more than a cardboard figure" of the Anti-Christ tradition.[3] McGinn says that it is ironic that since most of these fundamentalists who believe the rapture will come before the Anti-Christ persecutions begin that the final Enemy is so banal a persecutor.[4]

Some have attributed the number 666 to Ronald Reagan, the 40th President of the United States. On the grounds that his given name, middle name (Wilson), and surname each have six letters, thus 6–6–6 or 666.

Some thinkers who hold the Reagan-Anti-Christ view point out that James Brady, one of the President's heads, was shot in the head and miraculously recovered. This may be a parallel to Revelation 13:3.

Pope Benedict XVI selected retired Bologna Bishop, Cardinal Giacomo Biffi to preach the annual Lenten retreat to the Pope and top members of the Vatican. Although Cardinal Biffi is known for his orthodoxy, he is also well known for his contemporary preaching on the Anti-Christ. Indeed, the *Times* of London reported in 2004 that Cardinal Biffi describes the Anti-Christ as "walking among us."

Two other items that ought to be mentioned in this category is the claim by Jean Dixon that the Anti-Christ was born somewhere in the Middle East on February 5, 1962. Dixon claims that this individual may be a descendent of ancient Egyptian Pharaoh Iknaton, or Queen Nefertiti. Bernard McGinn describes and discusses this claim of Dixon's in his *Anti-Christ*.[5] McGinn points out that Dixon identifies the year 1999 as the time that Anti-Christ will reveal himself and his new religion.[6]

The other item is the claim made by several of his contemporaries that John Whitesides Parsons was the Anti-Christ. Jack Parsons was the founder of the experimental rocket research group at Cal Tech. Werner von Braun called Parsons "the true father of the American Space Program" because of the latter's contribution to solid rocket fuel.

Other individuals nominated for the Anti-Christ in contemporary life include: actress Lindsay Lohan, Britney Spears, Scottish song writer Sandi Thom, financier Jeffry Chodorow, and Bill Clinton. Ms. Spears has been nominated because of her recent behavior during rehab in March of 2007, when staff reported that she screamed "I am the Anti-Christ!" to frightened staff members. She is reported to have made this cry after having scrawled the number 666 across her forehead.

Paul of Tarsus has been theorized by some Islamic thinkers, as well as British philosopher and political theorist, Jeremy Bentham to fulfill the role of the Anti-Christ. Like Thomas Jefferson and others of Bentham's day, he believed that Saint Paul was responsible for a corrupted view of the doctrines of Jesus of Nazareth.

Contemporary Scottish song-writer and performer, Sandi Thom, has been nominated by some contemporary British thinkers, principally because of the content of a number of her songs, including, "I Wish I Was a Punk Rocker."

Mr. Chodorow, the owner of a chain of restaurants, has been nominated as the Anti-Christ by David Chang. Mr. Chang suggests that Mr. Chodorow has a world plan for domination. Chodorow also declared war on the *New York Times* food critic, Frank Bruni in a full page ad in the *Times* on February 21, 2007. This has led some thinkers to see this as further evidence that Mr. Chodorow is the Final Enemy.

Mr. Clinton has been suggested as the Anti-Christ by several contemporary, conservative, religious thinkers. They point out that the former president's position on homosexuality and the legalizing of stem cell research are reasons enough for believing the identification. Those who nominate Mr. Clinton also point to his inviting Ozzie Osbourne, the former front man of the group Black Sabbath, to the White House. Osbourne's tendency toward the demonic is further evidence that Bill Clinton is the Anti-Christ.

A number of contemporary thinkers also point to Harry Potter, with his abilities in magic, as the Final Enemy, and if not Harry, then his creator, Scottish writer, J. K. Rowling. One other contemporary theory about the Anti-Christ is that he and his army will be aliens, capable of overtaking the world and forcing everyone to worship them.

McGinn points out that considerable logic lay behind the identification of Noah Hutchins of the Southwest Radio Church of Pope Paul II as the Anti-Christ. Mr. Hutchins made this announcement in April of 1984, especially after the Pope's miraculous recovery from being shot. The Pope's wound, however, was not to the head, as suggested in Revelation 13:3: "One of the heads seemed to have received a death blow, but its mortal wound had been healed. In amazement, the whole earth followed the beast."[7]

Televangelist Pat Robertson, in the year 1980, announced that the Anti-Christ was alive, and was about twenty-seven years old at the time. Constance Cumbey in her book, *A Planned Deception*, suggested that Robertson's interest in the Middle East and his preaching and teaching styles may be indications that Mr. Robertson is the Final Enemy.[8]

Other contemporary thinkers have suggested that Tim LaHaye, conservative, evangelical, minister, author, and speaker is the Anti-Christ. LaHaye's 2006 book, *The Rapture*, contains what LaHaye calls the "666 connection." In 2002, LaHaye opened a new student center, which he calls the School of Prophecy. These and many other facts have led some thinkers to proclaim that Tim LaHaye is the Final Enemy.

Benjamin Crème, a follower of Madame Blavatsky, nineteenth century founder of the Theosophical Society, and her heir to the throne, suggests in his biography that Blavatsky told him that the "World Teacher," who will go by the name Maitreya, a synonym for the Christ, will rule the earth at the end of time. Crème wrote in 1959 that he would appear in twenty years. Later he claimed that Maitreya was living in suburban London. Since that time, Crème has prepared the world for the Maitreya's reappearance. Crème has also suggested that a major television network has agreed to interview the Maitreya at a time of the prophet's choosing.

A similar view was held by Alice Bailey in her book, *The Reappearance of the Christ*,[9] as well as in Crème's *The Reappearance of the Christ and the Master of Wisdom*.[10]

Jordan Ballor of the Action Institute for the Study of Religion and Liberty suggests that Superman is an archetypal Anti-Christ figure. Ballor's book, *Anti-Christ Superman: The Superhero and the Suffering Servant*, shows Superman as a Christ-figure, a well as an Anti-Christ figure. In discussing Nietzsche's idea of the *Ubermensch*, Ballor tells us: "Nietzsche's Superman is a being who embodies the will to power, for "Life itself to my mind the instinct for growth, for durability, for the accumulation of forces, for power: where the will to power is lacking, there is decline. Faster than a speeding bullet, more powerful than a locomotive, able to leap tall buildings in a single bound." The comic book figure of Superman is the embodiment of invincibility and power."[11]

Jose Luis de Jesus Miranda, a minister with a large Latin American following, claims simultaneously that he is God and the Anti-Christ. Miranda also claims that the Bible has been mistranslated, and it actually says that the Anti-Christ is Jesus Christ's replacement on earth. Miranda also maintains that sin and Satan do not exist, and that heaven is to be found here on earth. Miranda also has 666 tattoos on multiple places on his body.

The Rev. P. Huchede completes his *History of Anti-Christ* by referring to what he calls "a recent anonymous author of the precursors of Anti-Christ."[12] Huchede says this person has made an "ingenious calculation" in which the 1,290 days/years of abomination in Daniel 9:27 refer to the life of Mohammed. In the year 622 Mohammed fled from Mecca. If we add 1,290 years to that, we arrive at the belief that the persecution of Anti-

The Anti-Christ in Contemporary Life

Christ "will commence in AD 1953, and end in 1957, as it is to last during three years and six months."[13] Huchede points out that "other commentators say the Anti-Christ will be born in the year 1855. "This is the opinion of the pious Holzhouzer."[14] The Rev. Huchede ends his book by saying, "We must confess that there is nothing more problematical than these computations."[15]

Most recently, Democratic Presidential aspirant, Barack Obama has been identified as the Anti-Christ in a variety of internet sites. Most of this material, like many other candidates for the Final Enemy, base their argument on the numerology of the candidate's name, which they argue, adds up to 666. One of the problems with this kind of calculation is that one can make any name add up to 666. It is not truer of Barack Obama than any other name.

A number of Protestant thinkers at the end of the twentieth century tried to revive the Papal Anti-Christ theory. Chief among these thinkers is Ian Paisley, contemporary Irish Presbyterian.

Ian Paisley, through his European Institute of Protestant Studies, has reprinted the classic book of Dr. J. A. Wylie, entitled, *The Pope is the Anti-Christ*. In the literature that accompanies the book, Paisley quotes Wylie:

> The same line of proof which establishes that Christ is the promised Messiah, conversely applied, establishes that the Roman system is the predicted Apostasy. In the life of Christ we behold the CONVERSE of what Anti-Christ must be; and in the prophecy of the Anti-Christ we are shown the CONVERSE of what Christ must be and was. And when we place the Papacy between the two, and compare it with each, we find on the one hand, that it is the perfect CONVERSE of Christ, as seen in his life; and on the other hand, that it is the perfect image of the Anti-Christ, as shown in the prophecy of him. We conclude, therefore, that if Jesus of Nazareth be the Christ, the Roman Papacy is the Anti-Christ.[16]

One final individual who has been identified with the Anti-Christ in contemporary culture is Sam Walton, Wal-Mart founder and entrepreneur. A number of on-line writers have turned Walton's name into 666 numerology. Other evidence include the fact that Wal-Mart was incorporated on October 31st, Halloween, and that if you rearrange the letters of Walton's name you get, "Low Satan, rule me mo."

The Legend of the Anti-Christ

ANTI-CHRIST IN LITERATURE

Seventeenth-century Christian writer and preacher John Bunyan (1628–1688), wrote an extensive essay on the Anti-Christ. It was not published until 1692, four years after Bunyan's death. Bunyan's essay, "Of Anti-Christ and His Ruin," begins with a preface: "Anti-Christ has agitated the Christian world from the earliest ages; and his craft has been to mislead the thoughtless by fixing upon the humble followers of the Lamb his own opprobrious proper name. The mass of professed Christians, whose creed and mode of worship have been provided by human laws, has ever been opposed to the sincere disciplines of Christ."[17]

Bunyan gives a fairly traditional account of Second Thessalonians in which Bunyan says that in II Thessalonians 2:8, "The Great God has decreed the downfall and ruin, 'that wicked—whom the Lord shall consume with his mouth.'"[18] Bunyan tells us about the Anti-Christ that "All who are found partakers in his community, must be consumed with an everlasting destruction."[19] Bunyan also warns us that "The dread enemy may yet come in a different shape that he has hitherto assumed."[20] He adds: "When mankind, by the spread of knowledge, shall throw off the absurdities and disgraceful trammels of hypocrisy, fanaticism, and tyranny, which has so long oppressed them; they may be experiencing a vast overflow of infidelity, and perverted reason assume the place of Anti-Christ."[21]

For the most part, Bunyan holds a traditional view of the Anti-Christ, but he also warns that our understanding of the figure may not be as thorough as we may believe about what will happen in the end of time.

Since the late nineteenth century, a number of fiction writers have used the Christian Anti-Christ in short stories and novels. These works come predominantly from Russia, England, and America. One of the earliest of these modern pieces of fiction is Vladimir Solovyev's "A Short Story of the Anti-Christ," published shortly before his death around 1900. Solovyev (1853–1900) taught philosophy at the University of Moscow until he withdrew from his post due to academic politics. He wrote philosophical texts, as well as fiction.

Solovyev's *Tale of the Anti-Christ* was originally published in 1900. There is a modern English edition published by Holmes Publications Group in London in 1989. In the tale, Solovyev suggests that the Anti-Christ will arise when he announces his reign of a kind of United States of Europe, called the NWO. In the story, Solovyev tells a history of dealing with the Anti-Christ. "The Serbs were the first in the 14th century to face Anti-Christ, when the Turks invaded their lands. However, after five centuries of slavery, they survived, but Satan has been waiting to crush them."[22]

In another of Solovyev's works, *War, Progress, and the End of History*, the Russian philosopher predicts a war with the Japanese, where Japan wins the war and conquers much of the world. The Japanese are eventually driven back by the Europeans. Solovyev predicts the arising of a brilliant writer and thinker who will unite the world, and decree everlasting peace. This leader, an Anti-Christ-like figure, summons the major religious leaders of the world, promising them anything if they would only bow down to his sovereignty. Solovyev suggests the Jews will accept him as Messiah, until they learn that he is not a Jew. Then will begin a final battle to the north of Israel, as well as an eruption of volcanoes from the bottom of the Dead Sea. Solovyev says of the leader, "The approaching end of the world strikes me as some obvious but quite subtle scent—just as a traveler nearing the sea, smells the sea breeze before he sees the sea."[23]

Andrey Bely (1880–1934), in his 1916 novel, *Petersburg*, has a central figure who is no other than Peter the Great. In the novel, he comes in the figure of the great Bronze Horseman, a statue that dominates the city. In chapter six entitled "The Guest," the central figure, Dudkin, has been reading the Book of Revelation. Immediately following this scene, the Anti-Christ meets up with the Devil, where the latter pours his spirit into the former.[24] *Petersburg* is a tale of conspiracy and betrayal set in the days of the 1905 revolution. Yevgeny Zamyatin, Russian critic, said that Bely's relationship to the Russian language is like James Joyce's *Ulysses*' relationship to English.[25]

Bely is often called the most talented novelist of the "second generation," the writers who emerged from the Symbolist Movement at the turn of the century. The period is often called the "Silver Age." Its participants emphasize spiritual and mystical elements in their art. When Bely was young, he frequented the salon of M. S. Solovyov, where he was introduced to the apocalyptic philosophy of Vladimir Solovyov, who regarded poetic Symbols as "windows of eternity."

Polish writer Czeslaw Milosz sees Solovyev's "Tale of the Anti-Christ," as a piece of science fiction in the sense that "that which is predicted is told as something that already has occurred."[26] Milosz seems to imply that the best way to interpret the Solovyev story is with Frederick Nietzsche's view of the myth of the eternal return.

Some scholars have suggested an Anti-Christ theme to be found in Anton Chekov's "The Black Monk." The tale was written and published in 1894, and has recently been adapted to a play by David Rabe.[27] The play was first performed at the Yale Repertory Theatre in May of 2003. The play featured Sam Waterston as the principal character, Pesotsky, who has a number of Anti-Christ characteristics.

Some critics have pointed out the similarities between the Anti-Christ and Fyodor Dostoyevski's character the Grand Inquisitor from *The Brothers Karamazov*. Dostoyevski also writes of the imminence in the coming of the Anti-Christ in his *Diary of a Writer*, completed in the mid-1870s.[28]

In an unpublished paper on the Anti-Christ in Russian literature, Michael A. Pesenson suggests a number of Dostoyevsky's other works display characteristics of the Final Enemy. Pesenson tells us this about the Christ-like Prince Myshkin in the Dostoyevsky novel, *The Idiot*:

> In a state of pre-epileptic frenzy the prince proclaims, "Catholicism is the same as an unchristian faith…that's in the first place; secondly, Roman Catholicism is even worse than atheism…Atheism only preaches nullity, but Catholicism goes further; it preaches a distorted Christ, a Christ it has calumnied and defamed, a counter-Christ. It preaches the Anti-Christ, I swear it does, I assure it does."[29]

Pesenson goes on to identify the character of Nikolai Stavrogin in Dostoyevsky's *The Demons* as the novelist's "most explicitly Anti-Christ like character."[30] Indeed, in his *Diary of a Writer*, Dostoyevsky makes it clear that he thought the end of the world and the coming of the Anti-Christ was near when he wrote, "The Anti-Christ is coming to us. He is coming. And the end of the world is near—nearer than they think."[31]

Dmitri Merezhkovsky (1865–1941) wrote a trilogy of novels about Peter the Great and his son Alexis. In these books, *Julian the Apostate* (1894), *Leonardo da Vinci* (1896), and *The Anti-Christ: Peter and Alexis* (1902), Merezhkovsky renews the earlier Russian claim that Peter the Great was the Anti-Christ. Merezhkovsky's later books, *Emperor Paul* (1908), *Alexander I of Russia* (1911), and *The Decembrists* (1918), expand the writer's theory of history. He also wrote *Christ and Anti-Christ*

(1895–1905) and *The Kingdom of Anti-Christ* (1922), where the writer again identified the Tsar with the Anti-Christ.[32]

Among modern English writers who wrote of the Anti-Christ are three of note: Robert Hugh Benson (1871–1914), Charles Williams (1886–1945), and C. S. Lewis (1898–1963). Benson was the son of Edward White Benson, Archbishop of Canterbury. After being educated in the classics and theology at Trinity College, Cambridge, he was ordained a priest in the Anglican Church by his father in 1895. Eventually, after the death of his father, he was ordained a priest in the Roman Church in 1904. Benson is important for our purposes because his science fiction, *Lord of the World*, published in 1907, has the Anti-Christ as one of its central characters, a man named Julian Felsenburgh.[33]

The Benson novel suggests that the real enemy of Christ is what today is called secular humanism. McGinn says of the novel, "Despite its fictional form, Benson's pictures of the Anti-Christ can be judged the most serious Catholic presentation of the Final Enemy in the twentieth century."[34] McGinn continues: "The English monsignor obviously felt Anti-Christ was a growing threat to the world, and that only the strictest of divisions between Rome and the modern humanistic world could preserve the faith. He would not have welcomed the Second Vatican Council."[35]

Charles Williams, in his novel, *All Hollows Eve*, written and published in 1945, also contains a character that looks remarkably like Simon Magnus, the Roman magician identified with the Anti-Christ. Williams uses the parody of Christ by making his Anti-Christ's descent into Hell look remarkably like the ascension of Jesus.[36]

Williams writes:

> An opaque cloud gathered. It had been so when the other Jew ascended; such a cloud had risen from the opening of the new dimension into which he had physically passed, and the eyes of the disciples had not pierced it. But that Jew had gone up into the law and according to the law. Now the law was filling the breach in the law ... The shapes began to advance and it also. The Clerk stood rigid, at his feet the body of his mistress; across the floor those other clerks came.[37]

Like many writers before him, Charles Williams chose to tell the story of the Anti-Christ by using the device of parody, including being born of a harlot, as well as having a crucifixion and a resurrection.

The Legend of the Anti-Christ

Clive Staple Lewis, in his *Chronicles of Narnia* series, also introduces an Anti-Christ figure in the final volume, *The Last Battle*, published in 1956. In this book, Lewis brings the *Chronicles of Narnia* to an end.[38] It deals with the end of the world in Narnia and sums up the series by linking the experiences of the human children of Narnia with their lives in this world. *The Last Battle* contains an Anti-Christ figure, a character named Shift the Ape. Shift spreads heresy, and eventually sells Narnia into slavery. Another character, Puzzle the Donkey, works for Shift, and parallels very closely the New Testament idea that the Anti-Christ will be a false prophet.[39]

When a lion skin appears in a stream, Shift seizes the opportunity of making Puzzle look like the great lion, Aslan. Puzzle, who is eager to please Shift, occasionally questions Shift's judgments; however, Shift manages to talk Puzzle into following his plan. Shift finds success as the animals spread the news to the king that Aslan is in Narnia again. Little heed is given to those, for example the centaurs, who warn against the false Aslan. Shift does not let anyone speak to Aslan, or Puzzle dressed in a lion skin. Instead, Shift says that he will relay Aslan's messages and commands to the talking beasts of Narnia.

Shift says that "Tash is only another name for Aslan" when the beasts wonder what Tash, the god representing the opposite qualities of Aslan, has with their loving god, Aslan.[40] Puzzle eventually escapes from Shift and confesses to the king what he has done, which earns him forgiveness in the end from the real Aslan. When Puzzle leaves the ape, Shift tells his followers how the donkey fooled them. However, he continues talking about Aslan and Tash together so that Tash is finally called upon, arrives, and kills a number of beings, including the Anti-Christ figure Shift. The idea that the Anti-Christ will come before Satan is paralleled here when Shift prepares the way for Tash to arrive.

Bruce Marshall's 1931 novel, *Father Malachy's Miracle* about the nature and validity of the miraculous has a scene in which the Anti-Christ is mentioned. The protagonist of the book, Father Malachy, a Roman Catholic priest, is contemplating the Divine presence behind the tabernacle door. Marshall tells us: "For behind the tabernacle door he knew, behind that faded violet curtain which he couldn't see, Jesus Christ lay cradled, as He had promised, in Bread until time should once more pass back to timelessness and Himself to rout Anti-Christ, riding upon a cloud in great glory."[41]

In addition to the stories and novels mentioned above, several contemporary scholars have completed works on literature and the End Times. Of these works, those by Frank Kermode and David Bethea are the most important. Kermode's *The Sense of Ending: Studies in the Theory of Fiction* is the British literary critic's take on apocalyptic literature.[42] It was originally published in 1967 and revised in 2003. Kermode's central claim is that great literature imposes a consciously false conception of time. Kermode writes: "The clock's 'tick-tock' I take to be a model of what we call a plot, an organization that humanizes time by giving it a form; and the interval between 'tock' and 'tick' represents purely successive, disorganized time of the sort we need to humanize."[43]

Kermode argues that time in its pure form is disorganized and that all fiction is an attempt to disorganize by imposing on it structures with a beginning and end. We have been led to believe that plots, whether historical or literary, are ways of humanizing time; and this is particularly true about narratives about the end of the world.

David Bethea's *The Shape of the Apocalypse in Modern Russian Fiction* was published by Princeton University Press in 1989.[44] Bethea argues that modern Russian fiction has a new apocalyptic genre in which the reader is made privy to some secret knowledge revealed in the Apocalypse. Bethea includes all the Russian writers we have mentioned above as part of this genre.[45]

Harry Black's *Satan's Masterpiece: The Anti-Christ* was a 1944 book that included a number of songs that Mr. Black apparently believes will be sung by the Final Enemy. Other works on apocalyptic fiction include books by M. N. Abrams, John R. May, W. Warren Wagar, Robert Heinlein, and Douglas Robinson. These books are mostly about the place of the book of Revelation in modern literature. May and Robinson deal with American literature, Abrams and Wagar with apocalyptic literature in general.

In Robert Heinlein's novel, *The Number of the Beast*, the main characters of the novel reinterpret the number 666 to be 6^{6^6}, or 10, 314, 424, 798, 490, 535, 546, 171, 949, 056, which is also the number of possible universes in the book.[46]

Writer Aaron Hanson has suggested that John Gardner's Grendel is an Anti-Christ figure. Hanson says:

> Grendel is Gardner's Nietzschean Anti-Christ. He roams the fens striking terror, at will, into the minds of all. The monster is invincible (before Beowulf's arrival). Grendel repeatedly destroys the meadhall and devours its occupants. He proves the king helpless, the warriors humiliated, the priests worthless. The community's confidence and continuity is in tatters. Grendel is the annihilator, but not the nihilists. Rather, men are the nothingists: the pitiful. The fen monster is the Nietzschean teacher of reality: the will to power.[47]

Perhaps the most popular literary treatment of the Anti-Christ theme is the Left Behind Series written by Tim LaHayne and Jerry B. Jenkins. The series has twelve books in all. Many of them feature an Anti-Christ figure whose name is Nicolae Carpathia. Carpathia is the leader of a world government known as the Global Community. He is secretly the Anti-Christ, and one day will marshal the forces of the Global Community against the followers of Jesus Christ.

In literature and music: the Sex Pistol song, "Anarchy in the UK," sung by Johnny Rotten sings, "I am an Anti-Christ." Pepito, son of Senor Diablo from the Jhonen Vasquez comic *Squee*, is an Anti-Christ literary figure.

Three other works of contemporary music with Anti-Christ themes are Marilyn Mason's *Birth of the Anti-Christ* and the German rock group *Das Ich's Anti-Christ*. Manson's CD was originally released in 2002 and contains songs with apocalyptic titles. Das Ich's CD was released in Germany in 2001, and then in the United States by Metropolis Records. Songs on *Anti-Christ* include: "The Garden of Eden," and "Sodom and Gomorra." Finally, *Anti-Christ* is the second full-length album by a Norwegian black metal band named Gorgoroth. The album was released in 1996 and then re-mastered in 2005. Among the songs on this album are several with eschatological names, including "A Rank Smell of Christian Blood," "Possessed (By Satan)" and "Heavens Fall."

Contemporary Canadian heavy metal band, Conqueror has a number of songs with apocalyptic themes, including "The Curse," "Blood hammer," and "Hammer of Anti-Christ." One reviewer describes the album as "Raw and fast blasting aggression, covers the area in black metal between Blasphemy and Destroyer 666."

The character Randall Flagg, a fictional figure in a number of Stephen King's novels, is sometimes associated with the Anti-Christ. Like the Anti-Christ of early Christian history, Flagg is an accomplished magician and sorcerer. He also has a number of supernatural abilities, including necromancy, prophecy, and influence on people's behavior. Randall Flagg first appears in King's 1978 book, *The Stand*. He also has significant roles in *The Eyes of the Dragon* (1987) and *The Dark Tower* (1982).

James Blish (1921–1975) was an American science-fiction writer who spent much of his adult life in England. His character Agares in his 1959 novel, *The Day After Judgment* is another modern Anti-Christ figure in English literature. And Neil Gaiman and Terry Prachett's novel, *Good Omens* is another British novel, first published in 1990. Clive Barker, English born American critic, has said of this novel, "The Apocalypse has never been funnier."

Voltaire, in his novel *Candide*, published in the middle of the eighteenth century, mentions the Anti-Christ. The reference comes when Candide's girl friend, Cunegonde and the hero, Candide, meet up with an orator, who had been lecturing a crowd on the subject of charity. The orator says to the couple, "Do you believe that the Pope is the Anti-Christ?"[48] "I have never heard anyone say so," replied Candide, "but whether he is or he isn't, I want some food."[49]

Voltaire seems to be commenting on the widely held belief among Protestants in late eighteenth century Europe in the Papal Anti-Christ theory, including the Huguenots, French citizens who held the view.

Terry Pratchett and Neil Gaimon's book, *Good Omens*, contains an Anti-Christ figure, a small boy named Adam.[50]

Gerard Bodson in his book, *Cracking the Apocalypse Code* suggests that the defeat of the armies of the Anti-Christ refers to the defeat of Germany in World War I, and its subsequent recovery during the Nazi era. In this view, Adolf Hitler is the Final Enemy, and the Nazis become Gog and Magog.

Finally, Matthew Moses' *Anti-Christ: A Satirical End of Days* is a contemporary novel in which God is a vegetable in a wheel char, Jesus is the fascist CEO of a Corporate Church, while a Cold War is going on between Heaven and Hell in America. The protagonist, Matthew Ford is an Everyman struggling through college attempting to find his place in things.[51]

Ford travels to Heaven, is tempted by Hell, gets into a feud with Jesus, and then meets the moronic leader of the free world. Along the way, he creates a self-help movement that divides the inhabitants of the world, leading to a final zombie charge on Mount Megiddo in the last conflict, Armageddon.

ANTI-CHRIST AND FILM

The second half of the twentieth century to the present has also seen an influx of films with the Christian Anti-Christ as a major theme. The *Seventh Seal* (Swedish: *Det sjunde inseglet*) is a 1957 film directed by Ingmar Bergman, starring Max von Sydow who plays a Medieval knight traveling across a plague-ridden landscape. In its most famous, scene, the knight plays chess with Death, the man's life hanging in the balance.

The title of the *Seventh Seal* comes from its references to the Apocalypse, chapter 8:1, which begins, "And when he had opened the seventh seal, there was silence in heaven for the space of half an hour." This phrase is used at the beginning, and again at the end, of the film. Bergman developed the film from his play, "Painting on Wood."

Rosemary's Baby, a 1968 film based on a 1967 novel by Ira Levin, was directed by Roman Polanski, and features Mia Farrow, John Cassavetes, Ruth Gordon, and Sidney Blackmer. Farrow and Cassavetes are a newly married couple, and Gordon and Blackmer are their shifty and mysterious neighbors. Rosemary, the Farrow character, becomes convinced that her neighbors plan to use her yet to be born baby in a Satanic ritual. The film implies that Rosemary's baby was conceived by the Devil himself, and that the offspring, whose mark is 666, will be the Anti-Christ. These satanic themes are reinforced in the film by the use of the color red. Rosemary uses a red pen to mark her calendar; when entertaining the neighbors, they offer them red wine; various characters have red clothing and handkerchiefs.[52]

The *Omen* is a 1976 film directed by Richard Donner and starring Gregory Peck and Lee Remick. The film tells the story of a boy, Damien Thorn, who was switched at birth with the wealthy child of an American diplomat. Damien's father, played by Peck, is unaware that the boy is actually the offspring of Satan and destined to be the Anti-Christ.[53]

The *Omen* came at the tail end of a series of demonic child films such as *Rosemary's Baby*, *I Don't Want to Live*, *To the Devil a Daughter*, and *The Exorcist*. The *Omen* also had two sequels, *Damien* (1978) and *The Final Conflict* (1981).[54] *Damien* stars William Holden as Richard Thorn, Lee Grant as his wife, and Jonathan Scott-Taylor as Damien. Damien, the

Anti-Christ, is now 13, and comes to an understanding of who he is in this film. Damien is guided by an unholy disciple of Satan, while dark mystical forces eliminate all those who suspect the boy's identity.

The Final Conflict, the sequel to the *Omen* is directed by Graham Baker, and features Sam Neill as Damien Thorn. Damien is now an adult who plots to eliminate his future divine opponent, while a cabal of monks plot to stop him.

Fear No Evil is a 1981 film directed and written by Frank LaLoggia. The film stars Fred Armstrong, Stefan Arngrim, and Frank Birney who plays a priest. The plot involves a high school student that turns out to be the Anti-Christ, the son of Lucifer. He does battle with two arch angels who lead the forces of God at the end of time.

Thirty years after the appearance of the *Omen*, contemporary Australian director, John Moore, recently has done a re-make of the film. Live Schreiber plays the Gregory Peck role, and Julia Stiles is in the Lee Remick role. Seamus Davey-Fitzpatrick plays the role of Damien Thorn.

A Film About a Small Anti-Christ is a Russian film made in 2006, and also directed by John Moore. On June 6, 1966 (6/6/66) a Devil offspring is born in Rome according to predictions in Revelation. Eventually, the child turns out to be the Anti-Christ.[55]

In addition to these omen films, a number of other films about the Anti-Christ have appeared in the thirty years since the *Omen*. Among these are a 1974 film, *El Anti-Cristo*, directed by Alberto de Martino, and starring Carla Gravina, Mel Ferrer, and Arthur Kennedy. The film opens with a bizarre Catholic ritual where the Blessed Mother imparts incredible healing powers to several characters, including Ippolita, played by Carla Gravina.[56]

Ippolita is there because she wishes to be cured of her lameness, but when things don't work out as she planned, she witnesses the ghastly suicide of a heretic who plunges to his death denouncing Christ. Ippolita is paralyzed from the waist down. When placed under hypnosis to discover the cause of her paralysis, bizarre visions of satanic rites begin to plague Ippolita. She begins to remember that in a former life she was a witch and was burned at the stake. Eventually, Ippolita begins to walk again, but she turns into a murderous seductress who could become the host for the Devil himself. The film features an unsuccessful attempt at exorcism by a wise, Italian monk. This film was originally released in the United States under the title *The Tempter*.

The Legend of the Anti-Christ

Apocalypse Now is a 1979 American film, directed by Francis Ford Coppola and starring Martin Sheen, Marlon Brando, Dennis Hopper, and Robert Duvall. It tells the story of an Army captain Benjamin L. Williard (Sheen), who is sent into the Cambodian jungle to assassinate Special Forces Colonel Walter E. Kurtz (Brando). The film is based on elements from Joseph Conrad's novel, *Heart of Darkness*. It was also heavily influenced by Werner Herzog's 1972 film, *Aguirre: The Wrath of God*.

Bram Stoker's *Dracula* is a 1992 horror film produced and directed by Francis Ford Coppola. It is based on a novel by Bram Stoker, and stars Gary Oldman, Keanu Reeves, Anthony Hopkins, and Winona Ryder. The beginning of the film tells how Vlad III, the Impaler, has defeated an "overwhelming Turkish force invading his homeland in 1462."

The film has a number of Anti-Christ elements, including a scene where Vlad renounces God in a chapel, where he lies wounded, his face contorted to that of a demon. Count Dracula's dragon crest or sigal, called the "Order of the Dragon," uses a dragon as the family crest. Stoker's *Dracula* won a number of Academy Awards.

More recently, the *Omega Code* is a 1999 film, directed by Robert Marcarelli, and starring Caspar Van Dien, Michael York, and Catherine Oxenburg. The plot suggests the existence of a secret code that can only be discovered in some scrolls of the Torah. Whoever possesses this code is in control of our world. Michael York plays the part of Stone Alexander, the Chairman of the European Union. Alexander becomes power-crazed, and eventually is declared Chancellor of the United States. York's character is very much an Anti-Christ figure, and Van Dien plays Dr. Gillen Lane, a world famous motivational speaker with degrees in religion and mythology from Cambridge. The Dr. Lane figure has uncanny similarities to the false prophets of the Apocalypse.[57]

Megiddo: Omega Code II is a sequel to *Omega Code*. It was produced in 2001 and directed by Brian Trenchard-Smith. Michael York stars in the sequel as well, along with Chad Michael Murry, and Diane Venora. In the plot of this film, Stone Alexander murders his father so he can use the old man's media empire and his immense wealth to gain control of the Earth. The only thing standing in the way of this Anti-Christ figure is his brother, who is also president of the United States.[58]

Lost Souls is a 2000 film starring Winona Ryder, Ben Chaplin, and John Hurt. It is directed by Janusz Kaminski. In the film, Maya Larkin (the Ryder character) helps the authorities to catch a man named Birdson

(John Diehl) who claims to know the name of the man who will be the son of Satan and who will begin a reign of evil over the entire world. Larkin discovers that the name of the man in question is Peter Kelson (Ben Chaplin), an author of true crime books who has no religious faith. Maya and Peter must work together to reverse the plan of Lucifer. John Hurt plays the role of an exorcizing priest, and Victor Slezak plays a second priest.

Contemporary German film direction, Uwe Boll, has been identified by some contemporary critics as the Anti-Christ. Some have likened Darth Vader in the Star Wars movies as having Anti-Christ characteristics and powers. Other contemporary films that have been mentioned in relation to the Anti-Christ are: "Outbreak," a 1999 film starring Dustin Hoffman, Rene Russo, Morgan Freeman, and Kevin Spacey. The film centers on an outbreak of a fictional Ebola-like virus called Motaba.

The 1999 film, the *Mummy* has a number of features that bring to mind the Anti-Christ idea. It is set in Egypt, where an ancient Egyptian prince is resurrected as a supernatural human being, who is a false prophet who tries to convert religious leaders to his cause.

The *End of Days* is another 1999 film. Satan appears in New York City at the end of the millennium, December 31, 1999, searching for a bride. One of Satan's wishes in this film is to create a son, who will be the Anti-Christ. *Little Nicky* is a 2000 film directed by Steven Brill. It stars Adam Sandler, who plays the part of the son of Satan, who is sent to earth, where his nasty brothers already are causing trouble. Some of the plot of *Little Nicky* recalls the beasts of Revelation, as well as the Anti-Christ and false prophet of chapter 13 of the Apocalypse.

Another contemporary film that uses the Anti-Christ legend is Taylor Hackford's *The Devil's Advocate*, which stars Al Pacino, Keanu Reeves, and Charlize Theron. Lawyer Kevin Lomax has never lost a case. He now defends a Mr. Gettys on a child molestation charge. During the trial, he discovers that his client is guilty. Ultimately, Lomas wins the case, after harshly questioning the alleged victim.

At a celebration for winning the case, Kevin is approached by a representative from the firm of Milton, Chadwick, and Waters, a New York city firm. They want him to join their firm. Eventually, it becomes clear that one partner, John Milton, is really Satan, and also Kevin's father. After these realizations, Milton tells Kevin that he wants him to conceive a son with his half-sister. That child, Kevin learns, is to become the Anti-Christ. In the end of the film, Kevin commits suicide, ending his father's plan.

The Spanish satiric comedy, *The Day of the Beast*, a 1995 film, the Anti-Christ was to be born in Madrid on Christmas day, 1995. The film was directed by D. Alex de la Iglesia, and stars Alex Angulo, Armando de Razza, and Satiago Segura. Alex Angulo plays a priest who takes up in Madrid's underbelly.

An interesting Internet conspiracy theory about the Anti-Christ has been spawned as the result of a renewed interest in the Mary Magdalene-Jesus Christ relationship. The conspiracy seems to tie together the blood of Jesus, the Holy Grail, and the Da Vinci Code. The theory, which is also advocated in the film by the same name, suggests that a future Arthurian-like Messianic figure from Christ's bloodline will rise up, not as a new Christ, but as an Anti-Christ.

In addition to these feature films, Orson Willes has narrated a video version of Hal Lindsay's *The Late Great Planet Earth*. In the video, which includes interviews with Lindsay, he speaks about bible prophecies and the coming of the Anti-Christ. This 90 minute video also includes interviews with contemporary scientists like Aurelio Peccei and Paul Ehrlich, as well as actors who play biblical roles like Jeremiah, John the Apostle, and the Whore of Babylon.[59]

Other contemporary videos and DVDs on the End Times and the coming of the Anti-Christ have been produced by Aurora Productions in Escondido, California. This series of video clips entitled, *Armageddon Video Clips* was produced in the 19990s, and features image of plagues, famine, earthquakes, as well as a number of images of the Anti-Christ.

"A Woman Rides the Beast," is a video about the Whore of Babylon and her place in the Anti-Christ's future empire. It is also produced by Aurora Productions.[60] Charles E. Blair's "The March of Prophecy," is a "fast paced expedition through time of 6,000 years of biblical prophecy."[61] Ken Peters' "I Saw the Tribulation," is a three hour video about the more than 10,000 prophecies that Peters has had about the End Times.[62] Bill Gallatin's "Countdown to Eternity," is a "provocative look at the signs of the times" related to the End Times and the coming of the Anti-Christ;[63] and Eternal Productions' "Messages From Heaven," is an 80 minutes video that uses movies and television programs such as the X-Files, Star Wars, and City of Angels to illuminate biblical prophecies about the end of the world and the coming of the Anti-Christ.[64]

Finally, Russ Doughton Films in 2000 produced a *Prophecy Survival Guide* that consists of a 123 page book with "37 questions, 81 answers, 66 Scriptural quotations, and numerous illustrations" about biblical prophecy. This *Prophecy Survival Guide* also features a 90 minute video with answers by four renowned scholars and 44 film clips on biblical prophecy.[65]

For the most part, these videos related to the End Times and the coming of the Anti-Christ are produced by evangelical Christian organizations. What they all have in common, for the most part, is a belief that contemporary world events signal the arrival of the End Times and the coming of the Anti-Christ.

These videos are often associated with a number of contemporary theological treatments of the End Times and the coming of the Anti-Christ. One fine example is a collection of essays published by RBC Ministries in 2004. This book has four essays, including one called "What Can We Know About the Anti-Christ?" by Herb Vander Lugt. Vander Lugt's analyses concentrates on the significance of the number 666. Indeed, he says, "We have organized our study around three sixes."[66] Vander Lugt continues:

(1) Six things we know about him.
(2) Six things we don't know.
(3) Six things we should do.[67]

Vander Lugt goes on to confirm that what we do know of the Anti-Christ is "His Times." What we don't know is the "exact date." And what we should do is "be ready."[68] Vander Lugt goes on to make a number of speculative claims about what various passages in Daniel, Paul, and the Johannine letters mean; but he does little more than reiterate various aspects of the Christian Anti-Christ Legend: that he shall be a great deceiver; that he shall be a political figure, etc. Like most contemporary materials on the End Times, particularly those written or published by evangelical Christians, the essay by Vander Lugt lacks scholarly perspective and provides little that is new beyond new Apocalyptic visions.

A number of television shows have also had Anti-Christ characters. Damien from *South Park* is the son of an obvious parody of the Omen movies. Lucy, the Daughter of the Devil on Cartoon Network's Adult Swim animated series; and the Sinner Aion from the anime series Chrono Crusade claims to be Christ, while acting like an Anti-Christ figure. The character of Christina in the *Point Pleasant Series* is a female Anti-Christ figure.

The Legend of the Anti-Christ

One final media element in the contemporary discussions of the Anti-Christ is the attempt by 72 year old atheist, Charles Merrill, who after being turned down for using the moniker "Offensive" as his internet identification, then chose "Charles 666," followed by simply, "the Anti-Christ."

After using the Anti-Christ identification for some time, readers of the Hendersonville, Florida's *Times-News* complained about the username and the newspaper suspended Merrill's account. Merrill, who is a long-time supporter of the Freedoms From Religion Foundation, charges that the *New York Times*, which owns the *Times-News*, has violated his First Amendment rights by suspending his account.

Finally, in October of 1999, Jerry Falwell, Chancellor of Liberty University, gave a speech to 100 people in Kingsport, Tennessee suggesting that the Anti-Christ is alive and well today. In the same speech, Falwell says the Anti-Christ will be a male Jew who will pretend to be Christ, when he is not. It is clear from Falwell's remarks that he was alluding to several ideas to be found in the history of the Anti-Christ Legend, including the notions that the Anti-Christ will be a Jew.

In addition to making this claim that the Anti-Christ is alive and well, Mr. Falwell, in an interview on CBS television's *Sixty Minutes*, in October of 2002, the Virginia minister also called the prophet Mohammed a "terrorist." This judgment of Falwell's is part of a long history of seeing Mohammed, and Islam in general, as the Anti-Christ, going all the way back to Christian responses to the Moslem invasion of North Africa and the Iberian Peninsula in the seventh and eighth centuries.

Bernad McGinn speaks of Edgar Whisenant, "a retired NASA engineer, who published his brief work, *On Borrowed Time*, in 1988."[69] Whisenant suggests 88 reasons for believing that the rapture would take place on Rosh Hashanah between September 11 and 13, 1988. Needless to say, Whisenant's prediction did not appear to materialize on those dates.

A number of contemporary thinkers have attempted to identify the seven year peace treaty in Daniel 9:24–27 with various treaties and pacts in the modern world. The signing of the historic peace agreement between the State of Israel and the PLO at the White House on September 13, 1993, is one example of this phenomenon.

The Anti-Christ in Contemporary Life

ANTI-CHRIST AND MODERN PSYCHOLOGY

Carl Gustave Jung (1875–1961) was one of the great psychologists of the twentieth century. He is important for our purposes because of his work, *Aion: Researches into the Phenomenology of the Self*, a book that contains a discussion of Jung's view of the place of the Anti-Christ in western history. In order to understand Jung's view on the Anti-Christ, we must first describe a number of concepts in his basic psychological theory. Chief among these ideas are his notion of the Collective Unconscious, as well as his idea of the Shadow Self.[70]

Jung believed that in addition to one's conscious life, and an individual's unconscious life, there also exists what he calls the Collective Unconscious. This realm of reality is a collection of images, symbols, and archetypes that are common to all human beings. This subjective realm of the collective unconscious can only be plumbed through the soul in art, mythology, dreams, religion, and mythology. Jung devoted much of his life to discover these themes that exist across time and place, and in every individual.

Among these archetypes is what Jung calls the Shadow Self. He defines the shadow self as "the diametrical opposite of the conscious self, the ego." It represents everything that the conscious person does not wish to acknowledge within themselves. Someone who is kind, for example, has a shadow self that is harsh or unkind. Someone who is convinced he or she is ugly, had a shadow self that is handsome and beautiful. Jung suggests that the shadow self in dreams is often represented by dark figures of the same gender as the dreamer, such as gangsters, prostitutes, or demonic beings.

Jung considers the Anti-Christ as one of these shadowy figures in the Collective Unconscious. In the *Aion*, he traces the Anti-Christ archetype both in ancient Jewish sources and the New Testament, and in astrology. Jung writes, "We are justified in speaking of a Christian aeon which will find its end with a Second Coming. This expectation coincides with the astrological conception of the Platonic month of Pisces, corresponding to 2,000 years of Christian development."

Jung continues: "The Anti-Christ idea is revived in our time because of the dechristinization of our world, the Luciferian development of science and technology, the fruitful material and moral destruction left behind by the Second World War, which suggests 'the eschatological events foretold in the New Testament.'"[71]

In another essay, Jung wrote that if an archetype image "is not recognized consciously, then it appears from behind in its wrathful form as the dark son of chaos, the evil doer, the Anti-Christ. In referring to John of Patmos' claim that the reign of Anti-Christ will begin after a thousand years, Jung wrote: "Already the atom bomb hangs over us like a sword of Damocles. Could anyone deny that John foresaw at least some of the dangers which threaten our world? Not nature, but the genius of mankind has knotted the hangman's noose with which it can execute itself at any moment."[72]

Jung traces the Anti-Christ archetype all the way back to Babylonian myths about order controlling chaos and Persian dualism, the same places we began this study. The Anti-Christ legend has developed as a perverse imitation or parody of Christ.

In his *Answer to Job*, Jung again brings up the subject of the Anti-Christ. He asks:

> Why this wearisome forbearance toward Satan? Why this stubborn projection of evil on man, whom he has made so weak? Why not pull evil up by the roots? Where did God's darkness go—that darkness by which Satan always manages to escape his well-earned punishment? This may well be the meaning of the belief in the coming of the Anti-Christ. The expectation of the Anti-Christ is a far-reaching revelation... Despite his fall and exile, the devil is still the prince of this world... God still hesitates to use force against Satan. Presumably, he still does not know how much his own dark side favors the evil angel.[73]

Jung seems to suggest that not only do human beings have a shadow self related to the archetype of the Anti-Christ, God has one as well. For Jung, expressions of this archetype are natural occurrences, something that lies in the deepest regions of the human psyche.

Jung believes that the archetype of abysmal evil, the Anti-Christ was most evident in the Nazis. Since that time, it has revealed itself in modern life, both in our unconscious minds, as well as the development of weapons in warfare. Jung believes that we must regain our optimism, only if we are realistic about the human capacity for evil.

Robert Spira's *Six, Six, Six: The Anti-Christ Speaks* is a discussion of the Gospel of Matthew and its apocalyptic visions of chapter 24, using modern psychology.[74]

ANTI-CHRIST IN CATASTROPHIC MILLENNIALISM

Catastrophic Millennialism, also called premillennialism, is a view that the end of the world that is predominant both in Evangelical Protestantism, as well as a variety of other Christian movements. Unlike progressive millennialism or post-millennialism, catastrophic is a pessimistic world view. It assumes that things will go from bad to worse until Jesus ushers in the End Times.

Two centers for the belief in catastrophic millennialism are the Dallas Theological Seminary and the Chicago-based Moody Bible Institute. Modern catastrophic millennialism is heavily influenced by the theory of dispensationalism, the father of which was English scholar, John Nelson Darby (1800–1882).

Dispensationalism argues that God uses "dispensations" in directing world history. Starting with the reference of seventy weeks in Daniel 9:25 dispensationalists hold that this refers to the time of the Jews. This is to be followed by a series of other ages, ending with what they call the Rapture and the Tribulation.

The Tribulation will last for seven years. It will begin with the signing of a treaty between a powerful Gentile leader and the State of Israel. This Western leader will pose as a great ruler, but, in reality, shall be the Anti-Christ himself, a man empowered with unique abilities by Satan.

In the Left Behind Series, the Anti-Christ is a man named Nicolae Carpathia, a Romanian politician who suddenly emerges on the world political stage and takes over the United Nations, transforming it into a one-world government called the Global Community.[75]

Dispensationalists argue that the first three and a half years of the Tribulation is the period in which the Anti-Christ will keep his covenant with the State of Israel. In the final three and a half years of the Tribulation the Anti-Christ will go on to betray Israel. In the second half of the Tribulation, the Anti-Christ will enter the Temple in Jerusalem, where he will forbid any further Levitical sacrifices. He will then establish an idol to himself in the Temple. He will persuade many that he has died, but he will be resurrected from the dead by Satan, ushering in the Final

Days—where only those bearing the mark of the Beast (666) will be allowed to buy and sell.

What to make of this movement is not entirely clear. Bernard McGinn sums up the modern sensibilities to believe these proclamations when he writes: "It may no longer be possible for most of us to believe in the legendary figure of a coming individual who will sum up all human evil at the end of time. But at the end of this millennium [written in the mid-1990s], we can still reflect on deception both within and without each of us."[76]

ANTI-CHRIST IN MODERN SCHOLARSHIP

One final way in which the Anti-Christ idea has entered modern life is in the many scholarly works in the last 120 years on the Final Enemy. In this penultimate section of this chapter, we shall examine some of that scholarly work.

The earliest of modern treatments of the Anti-Christ in English literature is the work of British scholar, Samuel Roffey Maitland (1792–1866). Maitland's *An Attempt to Elucidate the Prophecies Concerning Anti-Christ* was published in London in 1830.[77] Maitland waged a vituperative crusade in the nineteenth century against the work of John Foxe, the editor of *Acts and Monuments*. Maitland's *Prophecies* was a response to nineteenth century Protestant millennial movements. Andrew Penny has produced a modern description of the relationship between Foxe and Maitland in his *John Foxe, Evangelicalism and the Oxford Movement: Dialogues Across the Centuries*.[78]

The earliest treatments of the Anti-Christ in the period from the late nineteenth century to the present were done at the close of the nineteenth century. Wilhelm Bousset's *Anti-Christ Legend* translated from the German by A. H. Keane in 1896 was a classic study of the idea of the Anti-Christ. Bousset mostly describes the biblical materials, as well as the history of the Anti-Christ in the history of Christianity.[79]

A second early study on the Anti-Christ was R. H. Charles' commentary on *Revelation*, in which the British scholar makes a number of observations about the Anti-Christ. Richard Henry Charles was educated at Queen's College, Belfast and Trinity College, Dublin. His *Apocalypse of Saint John* was published in two volumes in 1920. Charles also completed a commentary on the book of Daniel in 1929, where he also makes a number of observations about the Anti-Christ.[80]

A third late nineteenth-century scholar who wrote about the Anti-Christ was German, Hermann Gunkel (1862–1932). Gunkel in his *Schöpfung und Chaos* was one of the first scholars to point out the similarities of ancient Near East texts' relationship to the ordering of chaos in the biblical tradition.[81] Gunkel shares this view with Bousset. They claim that the Babylonian Tiamat, queen of the abyss and darkness, aided by the powers of her domain, rebel against the higher gods, only to be defeated by Marduk. This view eventually gave rise to the early Christian idea of the Anti-Christ, a figure with superhuman powers who sets himself up as equal to God.

A fourth early work on the Anti-Christ in modern biblical scholarship is Wilhelm Bornemann's commentary on Thessalonians, published in 1894. Bornemann was important because he gave a sustained argument in favor of Pauline authorship of Second Thessalonians. He also made a number of observations about the nature of the Anti-Christ in his commentary on the same biblical work.[82]

A final nineteenth-century contribution to the scholarship of the history of the Anti-Christ is Rev. P. Huchede's *History of Anti-Christ*, originally published in New York in 1884. Huchede provides a readable, yet authoritative outline of the Catholic history of the doctrine of the Anti-Christ, using scripture, the early church fathers, and the history of the Catholic tradition. Marianland recently has published a modern edition of the book.[83]

In more recent scholarship, Bernard McGinn's *The Anti-Christ: Two Thousand Years of Human Fascination with Evil*, published in 1994 is an excellent study of the history of the Anti-Christ image in Christianity.[84] It remains the most complete study to date. McGinn's book contains ten chapters on the history of the Anti-Christ, including an essay on "Anti-Christ: Our Contemporary." McGinn's volume also contains a number of iconographic images of the Anti-Christ.

The best contemporary study of the iconography of the Anti-Christ is Rosemary Muir Wright's *Art and Anti-Christ in Medieval Europe*, published by the Manchester University Press in 1995.[85] Wright begins with the Beatus manuscripts mentioned in chapter seven, and continues on to illuminated manuscripts to the fourteenth and fifteenth centuries.

Wright's work is very scholarly, and the volume includes 65 images of the Anti-Christ.

The fullest treatment of the Anti-Christ in the Middle Ages is the work of Richard Kenneth Emmerson. Emmerson, in his *Anti-Christ in the Middle Ages: A Study of Medieval Apocalypticism, Art, and Literature*, explores the history of how the idea of the Christian Anti-Christ moved from biblical materials to Medieval apocalyptic theology, art, and literature.[86] Emmerson's volume also contains a number of iconographic images of the Anti-Christ, and includes sections on German Doomsday books, English literary treatments of the Anti-Christ, and Dante. Like McGinn, Emmerson has also written a number of essays in various journals on the idea of the Anti-Christ.[87]

Other contemporary scholarly treatments of the Anti-Christ are works by Christopher Hill, Robert Fuller, and L. J. L. Peerbolte. Hill's *Anti-Christ in Seventeenth Century England* examines the idea of the Anti-Christ, mostly in a number of radical Protestant sects. Hill points out that these groups tended to identify the Anti-Christ with their enemies, particularly Catholics and Anglicans.

Robert C. Fuller's *Naming the Anti-Christ: The History of an American Obsession* is a study, published in 1995 by Oxford University Press.[88] It is a scholarly work, in which the author maintains that Americans are particularly prone to demonizing its enemies from the days of the Puritans to the present era. Peerbolte's *The Antecedents of Anti-Christ: A Traditional-Historical Study of the Earliest Christian Views on Eschatological Opponents* is a 1996 study published by Brill in Leiden.[89] Peerbolte's thesis is that changes in attitudes and perspectives on the Anti-Christ change along with differing perspectives on the parousia. Fuller also does a fine review of evaluating early and contemporary literature on the Anti-Christ.

Two other contemporary studies of the Anti-Christ worth mentioning are those by G. W. Lorein and Greg Jenks. Lorien's *The Anti-Christ Theme in the Intertestamental Period* was published by T. and T. Clark in 2003.[90] Lorien does a very thorough review of the literature on Anti-Christ from Bousset and Gunkel to the present. Lorien also explores the early connections of images of the Anti-Christ to early Jewish sources, and suggest there are three basic sources for the early Christian views of the Anti-Christ. Lorien also supplies a definition for the Anti-Christ: "A man will appear at the end of time, wholly filled with Satan. He will be an arch-deceiver, and a murderous and unjust tyrant, and a false god, turning himself and others away from existing religions."⁹¹ The major flaw with Lorien's work is that little that he says is new, and he tends to find more allusions to the Anti-Christ than are actually appropriate.

Greg Jenks is an Australian priest whose *The Origins and Early Development of the Anti-Christ Myth* was published by Walter de Gruuter in 1990.⁹² Jenks covers much of the ground also dealt with by Lorien, Emmerson, McGinn and others, including chapters on "The Origins of the Anti-Christ myth, the Anti-Christ Myth in the 3rd century," "the Anti-Christ Myth in Scripture," "Sketches of the Anti-Christ," "the Activities of the Anti-Christ," and "the Antecedents of the Anti-Christ"; but again, there is very little in Jenk's work that is original.

Most recently are three other studies on the Anti-Christ, two in America and one in Germany. Steve Wohlberg's *End Times Delusions: The Rapture, the Anti-Christ, Israel and the End of the World*, published by Treasure House in 2003,⁹³ is another volume that attempts to tie the coming of the Anti-Christ to contemporary world events. Ingvild Richardsen-Friedrich's *Anti-Christ Polemik* is a scholarly study of the history of the Anti-Christ from the Reformation to the present.⁹⁴ The work was published by Peter Lang in 2004. Richardsen-Friedrich does a very good job of discussing the papal Anti-Christ in Germany in the 16th and 17th centuries, but there is very little that is original about her work beyond that point.

Kevin L. Hughes' *Constructing Anti-Christ,* the other American volume, deals with many of the early Medieval sources dealt with by McGinn.⁹⁵ Hughes argues that the western doctrine of the Anti-Christ and the Last Days are entwined with the development of Medieval New Testament exegesis. Hughes suggests that Second Thessalonians is the most important locus for doctrinal speculation about the Anti-Christ and the End Times.

Hughes carefully examines commentaries on II Thessalonians from the fourth to the twelfth century, and finds that they serve as an "architecture" for the development of the doctrine of the Anti-Christ as it is portrayed in later Medieval art and literature. Hughes maintains that the distillations from this period became the most foundational elements of later orthodox Christian views of the Anti-Christ.

Paul Boyer's *When Time Shall Be No More: Prophecy Belief in Modern American Culture*, published by Belknap Press in 1994 is a clear and comprehensive review of modern American millennial movements. It is the best contemporary discussion of the varieties of Anti-Christ belief in America.[96]

Most recently, Robert E. Lerner's "Constructing Anti-Christ: Paul, Biblical Commentary, and the Development of the Doctrine in the Early Middle Ages," is an article published in *Church History* (2006). Lerner develops the idea of the Anti-Christ from Christianity's beginnings to the early Middle Ages. Much of the material in this book can be found in an earlier article by Lerner, written for *Speculum*.[97]

Finally Geert W. Lorien in his article, "The Anti-Christ Theme in the Intertestamental Period," published in the *Journal of Hebrew Scripture*, develops the Anti-Christ theme in the Old Testament, the New Testament, and in the literature between the testaments. Lorien argues, among other things that the Man of Sin and the Man of Lawlessness are different figures than in the traditional doctrine New Testament view of the Anti-Christ. He also argues that there is no need to appeal to Babylonian and Persian mythology for discussing the origins of the Anti-Christ figure. In his view, the Old Testament has all the elements for the birth of the doctrine.[98]

ANTI-CHRIST AND MODERN THEOLOGY

In the twentieth and twenty-first centuries a number of Christian theologians have written about the Anti-Christ. Chief among these is Rudolf Bultmann's *History and Eschatology*, a series of lectures given as the Gifford Lectures in Scotland in 1955. Bultmann understands the Anti-Christ as a key element in the first century Christians' world view. He argues that this world view must be "demythologized," so that what remains is the central teaching of the Final Enemy.[99]

Father John O'Connor, in a two-hour video entitled "The Reign of Anti-Christ," shows how we will recognize the Anti-Christ through Biblical texts and current events. He also suggests the Anti-Christ is alive and well and acting in the world today.[100]

Villanova theologian, Keven L. Hughes, in a number of articles, as well as in his recent book, *Constructing Anti-Christ*, suggests that the idea of the Anti-Christ is best understood by looking carefully at the history of the exegesis of II Thessalonians. Hughes says that the understanding "provides the architecture for the developing doctrine of the Anti-Christ."[101]

A movement known as the Tribulation Survival Teaching does not accept the idea that Christian believers are going to be raptured before the Anti-Christ is to be revealed and before what they call the "Great Tribulation" begins. They teach their followers that they should accumulate arms and food stuffs necessary to survive the period of tribulation that is to come.[102]

Frank Peretti, in his 1999 novel, *The Visitation*, points out the similarity of Biblical descriptions of the Anti-Christ and the charismatic charm of many of the contemporary world's political leaders. Peretti weaves a story of deceit, deception, cunning, and misinformation indulged in by modern political thinkers that look surprisingly like the traditional Anti-Christ.[103] Paul Ricoeur cautions against reading "signs of the times" as indications that the end of the world is at hand. McGinn describes Ricoeur's view, when he writes: "A more effective option seeks to find in the symbolic worldview of apocalyptic eschatology not just a mythology to be discarded, but a symbolism to be pondered, as Paul Ricoeur has suggested. Such a strategy can also allow a greater role to the external history of the Church as contrasted with the internal historicity of each believer, though not necessarily for a literal reading..."[104]

Of major contemporary Catholic theologians, Karl Rahner (1904–1984), was probably the most influential in writing about eschatological issues. Rahner was a Jesuit, born in Germany and died in Austria. His theology was a great influence on the Second Vatican Council. Rahner's *Grundkurs des Galubens*,[105] "The Foundations of Christian Faith," is the most systematic and developed of his theological works.

Morenna Ludlow, in his *Universal Salvation: Eschatology in the Thought of Gregory of Nyssa and Karl Rahner*,[106] published in 2000, sums up Rahner's picture of eschatology:

> Rahner's suggestions for the basic content of eschatological assertions are given in Appendix B. They can be summarized as follows: time and history will end, and will end with the gracious victory of God. The period after the incarnation, death, and resurrection of Christ and before the parousia, will be characterized by conflict between Christ and the world (Anti-Christ). The end will be a consummation which can be expressed in many different ways: for example, God's judgment, at the resurrection of the flesh and the transfiguration of the world, as the beatific vision in the kingdom of God, or as hell.[107]

Rahner had a fairly conventional view of the Anti-Christ that emphasizes the tempting and deceptive aspects of the figure, as well as the natural emphasis of human beings to do evil.

At a Good Friday Liturgy in 2002, the Preacher of the Papal Household, Father Raniero Cantalamessa, a follower of Rahner's said that other religions are not merely tolerated by God—but positively willed by Him as an expression of the inexhaustible richness of his grace and His will for everyone to be saved."[108] Cantalamessa used 1 John 1:22 to argue that Islam, Judaism, Hinduism, Buddhism, and any religion that rejects Christ, according to Scripture, "is an Anti-Christ religion."[109] Cantalamessa also used 1 Timothy 4:1 that false creeds are "doctrines of the Devils."

It goes without saying that this view is not only tolerated by God but willed by Him raises a number of moral questions about Father Cantalamessa's view of God, as well as who is worthy of salvation. Plus it also raises a reexamination of Rahner's point of view on the End Times, a view in print that says nothing of the damnation of all who are not Roman Catholic.

CONCLUSIONS

In this chapter, we have explored a number of ways in which the idea of the Anti-Christ can be seen in contemporary life and culture. More specifically, we began the chapter by exploring the number of people in the contemporary world who regularly have been identified with the Anti-Christ. Many of these individuals, as we have seen, are political figures, but not all of them have been.

We continued this chapter with an exploration of a number of literary works in the contemporary world with the Anti-Christ character or theme as a central concern. As we have seen for the most part, these works of fiction are either Russian or British, two places in contemporary life where the Anti-Christ legend is alive and well.

In a third section of this chapter, we have explored the many modern films that have the Anti-Christ figure or theme as a central part of the narrative. Most of the films we have examined are American, though, as we have seen, there are some European movies on the Anti-Christ idea.

In a fourth section of this chapter, we have examined the ideas of Swiss psychologist C. G. Jung on the Anti-Christ. Jung sees the Anti-

Christ as a permanent part of the history of the human psyche, and the divine psyche as well.

At the close of this chapter, we have explored and discussed major nineteenth, twentieth, and twenty-first century scholarship on the idea and history of the Anti-Christ. The earliest modern scholarships on the issue were works by Bousset, Gunkel, and R. H. Charles. More modern scholarship we have explored includes the excellent work by McGinn, Emmerson, and Rosemary Muir Wright.

More than anything else, what we have seen in this chapter is that the idea of the Anti-Christ is alive and well in contemporary life and culture. As in many ages before our own, we have identified the coming of the Anti-Christ with contemporary events. We have made books and films about Anti-Christ in unprecedented numbers. And, perhaps most importantly, we have kept the idea of the Anti-Christ as a manifestation of contemporary life.

The idea of the Anti-Christ is alive and well in contemporary literature, film, psychology, theology, and scholarship; but perhaps the most important manifestation of talk about the Anti-Christ in contemporary life are the many discussion and groups related to millennial thought and apocalyptic visions in the contemporary world. Indeed, there are more people in the contemporary world believing in apocalyptic visions and the coming of the Anti-Christ than ever before; and it is likely to remain that way for a very long time.

NOTES

1. Tim Cohen, *The Anti-Christ and a Cup of Tea* (London: Prophecy House, 1999).
2. Bernard McGinn, *Anti-Christ: Two Thousand Years of Human Fascination with Evil* (San Francisco: HarperCollins, 1994) 261.
3. Ibid.
4. Ibid.
5. Ibid., 260.
6. Ibid.
7. Revelation 13:3 (RSV).
8. McGinn, *The Anti-Christ*, 260.
9. Alice Bailey, *The Reappearance of the Christ* (New York: Lucis, 1978).

10. Benjamin Crème, *The Reappearance of the Christ and the Master of Wisdom* (Tara Center, 1980).
11. Jordan Ballor, "Anti-Christ Superman: The Superhero and the Suffering Servant," in *Action Commentary* (Grand Rapids, June 28, 2006) 5.
12. Rev. P. Huchede, *History of Anti-Christ* (New York, 1884) 128.
13. Ibid., 129.
14. Ibid.
15. Ibid.
16. J. A. Wylie, *The Pope is the Anti-Christ* (Dublin: European Institute of Protestant Studies, 1999) with a précis by Ian K. Paisley, M.P., M.E.P.
17. John Bunyan, *Of Anti-Christ and His Ruin* (London: Meadow, 2007) 8.
18. Ibid.
19. Ibid., 9.
20. Ibid.
21. Ibid., 10.
22. Vladimir Solovyev, *Tale of the Anti-Christ* (London: Holmes, 1989) 7.
23. Vladimir Solovyev, *War, Progress, and the End of History* (London: Holmes, 1990).
24. Oleg A. Maslenikov, *Andrei Bely and the Russian Symbolists* (Berkeley: University of California Press, 1952) 134.
25. Ibid., 18.
26. Czeslaw Milosz, quoted in McGinn, *Anti-Christ*, 266.
27. Anton Chekov, *The Black Monk* (London: Kessinger, 2004).
28. Fyodor Dostoyevski, *The Brothers Karamazov* (New York: Penguin Classics, 1993).
29. Michael A. Pesenson, "Changing Perceptions of the Anti-Christ in Russian Literature and Culture from the Middle Ages to the Silver Age" (unpublished manuscript).
30. Ibid., 26–27.
31. Ibid., 28.
32. Dmitri Merezhkovsky, *The romance of Leonardo Da Vinci* (New York: Signet, 1964); also see *The Birth of the Gods* (London: Dent, 1926).
33. Robert Hugh Benson, *Lord of the World* (London: Kessinger, 2004).
34. Bernard McGinn, *The Anti-Christ*, 269.
35. Ibid., 270.
36. Ibid., 213.
37. Quoted in McGinn's *Anti-Christ*, 271.

38. C. S. Lewis, *The Last Battle* (New York: Macmillan, 1956).
39. Ibid.
40. Ibid, 31.
41. Bruce Marshall, *Father Malachy's Miracle* (New York: Pocket Books, 1931) 123.
42. Frank Kermode, *The Sense of Ending: Studies in the Theory of Fiction* (Oxford: University of Oxford Press, 2000).
43. Ibid, 173.
44. David Bethea, *The Shape of the Apocalypse in Modern Russian Fiction* (Princeton: Princeton University Press, 1989).
45. Ibid, 99.
46. Robert Heinlein, *The Number of the Beast* (New York: Ballantine, 1989).
47. Aaron Hanson, "Thus Spake Grendel: The Niezschean Anti-Christ of the Fens," unpublished paper (College Park, 1997).
48. Voltaire, *Candide* (New York: Penguin Classics, 1947) 27.
49. Ibid.
50. Terry Pratchett and Neil Gaimon, *Good Omens* (New York: Torch-books, 2006).
51. Matthew Moses, *Anti-Christ: A Satirical End of Days* (London: Book-Locker, 2007).
52. "Rosemary's Baby" (1968), directed by Roman Polanski.
53. "The Omen" (1976), directed by Richard Donner.
54. "The Exorcist," (1973), directed by William Friedkin; "Damien" (1978), directed by Don Taylor; "To the Devil a Daughter" (1976), directed by Peter Sykes; "The Final Conflict" (1981), directed by Graham Baker.
55. "A Film About a Small Anti-Christ" (2006), directed by John Moore.
56. "El Anti-Christ" (1974), directed by Alberto de Martino.
57. "Omega Code" (1999), directed by Robert Marcarelli.
58. "Megiddo: Omega Code II" (2001), directed by Brian Trenchard-Smith.
59. "The Late Great Planet Earth" (1979), directed by Robert Amram.
60. "Armageddon Video Clips" (1998), directed by Michael Bay.
61. "The March of Prophecy" (2000), directed by Charles Blair.
62. "I Saw the Tribulation" (2000), directed by Ken Petyers.
63. "Countdown to Eternity" (1997), directed by Bill Gallatin.
64. "Messages From Heaven" (2000), Eternal Productions.
65. Russ Doughton, "Prophecy: A Survival Guide" (2000).

66. Herb Vander Lugt, "What Can We Know About the Anti-Christ?" in *Understanding the End Times* (Grand Rapids: RBC Ministries, 2004) 47.
67. Ibid., 47–53.
68. Ibid., 50.
69. McGinn, *The Anti-Christ*, 259.
70. Carl Gustav Jung, *Aion: Researches into the Phenomenology of the Self* (Princeton: Princeton University Press, 1979).
71. Ibid.
72. Ibid.
73. C. G. Jung, *Answer to Job* (London: Brunner-Routledge, 2002) 77.
74. Robert Spira, *Six, Six, Six: The Anti-Christ Speaks* (Los Angeles: Quartz Press, 1997).
75. Tim F. LaHaye, *Left Behind: A Novel of the Earth's Last Days* (Carol Stream, IN: Tyndale, 1996.
76. McGinn, *Anti-Christ*, 280.
77. Samuel Roffey Maitland, *An Attempt to Elucidate the Prophecies Concerning Anti-Christ* (London: Rivington, 1830).
78. Andrew Penny, *John Foxe, Evangelism, and the Oxford Movement: Dialogues Across the Centuries* (London: Mellen, 2002); also see, *John Foxe at Home and Abroad* (London: Ashgate, 2004).
79. Wilhelm Bousset, *The Anti-Christ Legend: A Chapter in Christian and Jewish Folklore with a Prologue on the Babylonian Dragon Myth* trans. A. H. Keane (London: Hutchinson, 1896).
80. R. H. Charles, *Apocalypse of St. John*, 2 vols. (Dublin, 1920).
81. Hermann Gunkel, *Schöpfung und Chaos* (Göttingen: Vandenhoeck & Ruprecht, 1895).
82. Wilhelm Bornemann, *Commentar zu den Thessalonicher-Briefe* (Göttingen: Vandenhoeck & Ruprecht, 1894) 348–83 and 400–537.
83. Huchede, *The History of Anti-Christ* (League City, TX: Marianland, 1986).
84. Bernard McGinn, *Anti-Christ*.
85. Rosemary Muir Wright, *Art and Anti-Christ in Medieval Europe* (Manchester: Manchester University Press, 1995).
86. Kenneth Emmerson, *Anti-Christ in the Middle Ages: A Study of Medieval Apocalypticism, Art, and Literature* (Manchester: Manchester University Press, 1981).
87. Kenneth Emmerson, "Anti-Christ, Simon Magnus, and Dante's 'Inferno, XIX,'" *Traditio* 36 (1980) 373–98); Emmerson and McGinn, *The Apocalypse in the Middle Ages* (Ithaca: Cornell University Press, 1992).

88. Robert C. Fuller, *Naming the Anti-Christ: The History of an American Obsession* (Oxford: Oxford University Press, 1995).
89. L. J. Lietaert Peerbolte, *The Antecedents of Anti-Christ: A Traditional-Historical Study of the Earliest Christian Views on Eschatological Opponents* (Leiden: Brill, 1996).
90. G. W. Lorien, *The Anti-Christ Theme in the Intertestamental Period* (Edinburgh: T. & T. Clark, 2003).
91. Ibid, 7.
92. Greg Jenks, *The Origins and Early Development of the Anti-Christ Myth* (Berlin: de Gruyter, 1990).
93. Steve Wohlberg, *End Times Delusion: The Rapture, the Anti-Christ, Israel and the End of the World* (Franschhoek, South Africa: Treasure House, 2003).
94. Ingvild Richardsen-Friedrich, *Anti-Christ Polemik* (Berlin: Lang, 2004).
95. Kevin L. Hughes, *Constructing Anti-Christ: Paul, Biblical Commentary, and the Development of Doctrine in the Early Middle Ages* (Washington, DC: Catholic University of America Press, 2005).
96. Paul Boyer, *When Time Shall Be No More: Prophecy in Modern American Cutlure* (Cambridge: Belknap, 1994).
97. Robert Lerner, *Contructing Anti-Christ: Paul, Biblical Commetnary, and the Development of the Idea in the Early Middle Ages* (Sacramento: Gale, 2006). Robert Lerner, "Anti-Christs and Anti-Christs in Joachim of Fiore," *Speculum* 60 (1985) 553–70.
98. Geert W. Lorien, *The Anti-Christ Theme in the Intertestamental Period*, Journal for the Study of the Pseuepigrapha Supplement Series 44 (New York: T. & T. Clark, 2003).
99. Rudolf Bultmann, *History and Eschatology* (New York: Harper Torch-books, 1962).
100. John O'Connor, "The Reign of Anti-Christ," (Marianland Videos, 1998).
101. Kevin L. Hughes, "A Theology of Anti-Christ: Peter Lombard's Commentary in 2 Thessalonians in its Medieval Exegetical Context," in *Proceedings of the American Society of Church History* (Theological Resaerch Exchange Network, 1997); "Augustine and Anti-Christ: Strategies of Synthesis in Early Medieval Exegesis," *Augustinian Studies* 30 (1999) 221–33; "Visionary Exegesis: Visions, Text, and Interpretation in Hildegard's *Scivias*," *American Benedictine Review* 50 (1999) 311–26; *Constructing Anti-Christ* (Washington, DC: Catholic University Press of America).
102. Mary Stewart Relfe, *When Your Money Fails* (Montgomery, AL: Ministries Press, 1981).
103. Frank Peretti, *Visitation* (Nashville: World, 1999).

104. McGinn, *The Anti-Christ*, 277.
105. Karl Rahner, *The Foundations of Christian Faith* (London: Darton, Longman & Todd, 1978).
106. Morenna Ludlow, *Universal Salvation: Eschatology in the Thought of Gregory of Nyssa and Karl Rahner* (Oxford: Oxford University Press, 2000).
107. Ibid., 145.
108. These quotes from Father Cantalamessa's sermon are taken from a *Catholic News Service* report from April 2, 2002.
109. Ibid.

Afterword

Why So Much Emphasis on the Anti-Christ and Demonic in the Contemporary World?

> There is no doubt that healthy-mindedness is inadequate as a philosophical doctrine, because the evil facts which it positively refuses to account for, are a genuine portion of reality; an they may after all be the best key to life's significance, and possibly the only openers of our eyes to the deepest levels of truth.
>
> —William James, *Varieties of Religious Experience*

> If a way to the better there be, it lies in taking a full look at the worst.
>
> —Thomas Hardy, *Letters*

> Dread of the impure and rites of purification are in the background of all our feelings and all our behavior relating to fault.
>
> —Paul Ricoeur, *The Symbolism of Evil*

ONE FINAL QUESTION WE might raise in this study of the Anti-Christ is why there is so much discussion, so much emphasis on the Anti-Christ today, in ways that have not been popular since the twelfth to fourteenth centuries? Our age is one where evil and the demonic are discussed in unprecedented ways. Two World Wars, hundreds of smaller, and using the word Holocaust as a proper noun, have made our age a different one. And with this material have also come a variety of millennial movements with questions about the End Times, the demonic, and the Anti-Christ at their core.

One way to begin to answer this question about why now is to point out that in the last century we have begun to understand human nature in unprecedented ways. The works of psychologists like Freud and Jung, as well as ethologists like Lionel Tiger, Robin Fox, and Konrad Leonz, have given us a better picture in the last 100 years of what might be called a science of man.

Sociologist Ernest Becker tells us this of what he thinks of basic human nature: "That man is first and foremost an animal moving about a planet shining in the sun. Whatever else he is built on this. The argument of these people [the ethologists] is that we shall never understand man if we do not begin with his animal nature."[1]

Becker goes on to point out a basic agreement concerning human nature that is shared by Freud, Jung, and Otto Rank: that at the heart of human nature are enormous capacities to do the moral good, as well as to do overwhelming acts of evil. If Ernest Becker were alive today [he died in 1975] he surely would maintain that the renewed interest in the Anti-Christ principally comes from our developing capacity to understand human nature.

This idea that evil desires lies at the heart of human nature has been maintained by a variety of thinkers before the modern period. Perhaps the oldest theory to hold this view is the ancient Hebraic belief that all human beings are born with two *yetzerim*, (inclinations or imaginations), one to do good (the *yetzer tov*), and the other to do evil (the *yetzer ha-ra*). This theory of the two yetzers can be seen in a number of passages in the Hebrew Bible.

This view that an inclination to evil is part of human nature is also expressed in Freud's ideas of thanatos and eros—that we are born with tendencies to both good and evil, and in Jung's idea of the shadow self discussed in chapter ten of this work. Even earlier, Immanuel Kant seems to hold this same view. Susan Neiman, in her book, *Evil in Modern Thought*, discusses Kant's position on human nature. Neiman writes: "Kant introduced a counterpart to miracle: certain forms of disaster. Nature gives us the beautiful but also the sublime, and the latter is shot through with violence. In an instant of lightning, or a volcano's explosion, we experience something close to beauty—but for the realization that the world is not made for us after all."[2]

Neiman goes on to point out that what is true of nature, in Kant's view, is also true of human nature: we have enormous capacity to produce both good and evil. One way to point out an answer to why so much interest in the Anti-Christ now, in this present time, is to say that our age is better at dipping the ladle into our dark, human capacities, and bring them to the surface, than any age before.

It may be the case that in this age we are better, because of the violent world in which we live, at stroking the strings of basic human nature, than any age since the High Middle Ages. Indeed every sage of great natural and human suffering, renews the human capacity to understand or make meaning of evil. First century Christians had to make sense of the Roman Empire—something they saw as evil. In response, they built catacombs, among other things.

Ancient Judaism had to made sense of the destruction of the Temple in 70 CE. In Jesus' day, the Zealots responded to Roman domination by resorting to violent means. In the mid-eighteenth century, the Lisbon earthquake of 1755 served a role not unlike that played by the Holocaust in our own day. The Allied powers responded to Hitler in violent ways, as do the insurgents in the current wars in Afghanistan and Iraq. Ernest Becker would argue that all this history is evidence for our natural human capacity to make evil.

The image of the Anti-Christ in western history has always been an image of deception, pretending to be something other than what one really is. Deceiving and lying, an intention to deceive, are further evidence of our human abilities.

Bernard McGinn points out that many of the negative predictions about the end of the world in contemporary times are really forms of secularized apocalyptic rhetoric. McGinn goes on to suggest that "The persistence of apocalypticism in the secular vein rests, in large part, on one of the fundamental characteristics of humanity: the necessity of living in expectations."[3]

McGinn concludes:

> We are defined by our hopes and therefore also by hope's opposite, fear of future evil. The great world religions have dealt with human hopes and fears in a number of ways, sometimes arguing that they are mere illusions, other times linking them to recurring cosmic cycles of various kinds, or as in the case of the apocalyptic mentality born among Jews of the Second Temple period, incorporating present hope and fear into a view of universal history finally vindicated in a cataclysmic divine judgment.[4]

Bernard McGinn argues, then, that human's capacity to think about the coming of evil in the future is another element of human nature that goes into the mix in understanding contemporary thinkers on the End Times. Given what we know of human history, our age seems peculiarly able to forecast evil that is to come in the future. That capacity would seem to make it all the more difficult to develop a theory of history that will incorporate evil and suffering in the grand scheme of things.

In the final chapter of his *Anti-Christ*, McGinn warns that it would be a mistake to suggest that "contemporary forms of deception and their relation to the Anti-Christ legend is a purely extrinsic way as an evil that is only outside us." McGinn writes:

> Evil is both within and without. If we are all part of a culture in which forms of deceit, both over and covert, in many ways, we can admit that the most dangerous form of deceit is self-deceit, our ability to convince ourselves that we are doing what is best and for the best reasons, even when this is not the case—and somehow, however obscurely, we *know* it not to be the case. This is just another way of putting Augustine's ancient message: "There you have your Anti-Christ—everyone that denies Christ by his works."[5]

Another major contribution to why the increase in discussions of the Anti-Christ in the contemporary world is the increase in technological sophistication in the modern period. Countless new inventions and discoveries in the twentieth century have allowed us to change the environment of disease, warfare, politics, and religion, so that in an increasingly violent world, we might also see an increase in discussions related to the End Times and the Anti-Christ.

Discoveries in the areas of medical technology, the technological sciences in general, as well as the development of advance weapons in the twentieth and twenty-first centuries, have provided many new venues for showing the human capacity to do evil, in ways that were not possible just a generation or two ago.

It may no longer be the case that ideas about the Anti-Christ are commonly held in most of western culture. But four things about human beings that will continue for a long time to come are our intrinsic ability to do evil and produce suffering; our ability to understand the possibility of evil to come in the future; our ability to continue to develop new technologies; and finally, our innate ability to deceive. In his *Varieties of Religious Experience*, William James calls the ability of humans to produce mass evil and suffering the "worm at the core of all our pretensions to happiness."[6]

Why So Much Emphasis on the Anti-Christ

In our age, discussions about the Anti-Christ may well have increased in our time because of our increased understanding of human nature, as well. Freud, James, Ernest Becker, and other have pointed out that human beings have an innate capacity to bring evil and destruction—a capacity, they argue, that is different than the abilities of any other species. Perhaps the best way to explain the increased interests in the demonic and the Anti-Christ in our time is to say that we are better at expressing this innate ability far better than any age before us.

More than 1,500 years ago, Saint Augustine spoke of his innate capacity better than anyone before or since. He believed it is related to what we now call *peccatum originale*, or "original sin." Augustine knew better than most the capacity of the human race. And he believed that at its core *homo sapiens* have the capacity for, and often do, the most horrific acts. Is there any wonder why we talk so much about it today?

NOTES

1. Ernest Becker, *Escape from Evil* (New York: Free Press, 1975) 4.
2. Susan Neiman, *Evil in Modern Thought* (Princeton: Princeton Univer-sity Press, 2002) 88.
3. Bernard McGinn, *Anti-Christ* (Chicago: University of Chicago Press, 1994) 277.
4. Ibid., 279.
5. Ibid., 279–80.
6. William James, *Varieties of Religious Experience*.

www.ingramcontent.com/pod-product-compliance
Lightning Source LLC
Chambersburg PA
CBHW071238300426
44116CB00008B/1092